GW00992517

Idolatry of Blood

Religion for a
Post-Modern World

FRÉDÉRIC ZÜRCHER

Order this book online at www.trafford.com
or email orders@trafford.com

Most Trafford titles are also available at major online book retailers.

© Copyright 2015 Frédéric Zürcher.
All rights reserved. No part of this publication may be reproduced, stored in a retrieval
system, or transmitted, in any form or by any means, electronic, mechanical, photocopying,
recording, or otherwise, without the written prior permission of the author.

Scripture quotations marked NIV are taken from the *Holy Bible, New International
Version*®. *NIV*®. Copyright © 1973, 1978, 1984 by International Bible Society.
Used by permission of Zondervan. All rights reserved. [Biblica]

Print information available on the last page.

ISBN: 978-1-4907-5380-5 (sc)
ISBN: 978-1-4907-5382-9 (hc)
ISBN: 978-1-4907-5381-2 (e)

Library of Congress Control Number: 2015900630

Because of the dynamic nature of the Internet, any web addresses or links contained in
this book may have changed since publication and may no longer be valid. The views
expressed in this work are solely those of the author and do not necessarily reflect the
views of the publisher, and the publisher hereby disclaims any responsibility for them.

Any people depicted in stock imagery provided by Thinkstock are models,
and such images are being used for illustrative purposes only.
Certain stock imagery © Thinkstock.

Trafford rev. 02/12/2015

 www.trafford.com

North America & international
toll-free: 1 888 232 4444 (USA & Canada)
fax: 812 355 4082

A False Hope Is About To Produce
A Worldwide Tragedy

Frédéric Zürcher

DEDICATED TO

This book is dedicated to the millions of thinkers and authors who have contributed comments, insight, views, and countless hours of research, trying to determine whether or not divine agencies or supernatural powers exist in the universe. Regardless of their conclusions, they are all beneficial, even if sometimes they might be misguided. They have all contributed insight and stimulated reasoning while broadening the pool of human knowledge. The passing of time and continued growth of knowledge will either sanction or refute previous conclusions. Humanity's quest for truth cannot advance without trials and errors. At some point in his life, Thomas Edison knew thousands of ways to make a light bulb or a battery that did not work. In the end, even the impractical knowledge he gained contributed invaluable information—he knew what did not work. Today's thinkers are essentially divided into three camps in their assessment of supernatural intelligent life and forces of the universe. One group believes, or wants to believe, in the "only true God" of Scripture, though a multitude of variants characterize their beliefs. Others believe that intelligent supernatural forces are ever-present throughout the universe and nature. A third group rejects all inferences to intelligent supernatural forces and energies in the universe. If there is a fourth group, they are probably open to all three without taking position for any particular view. For those who do not believe in supernatural forces, matter and life in the universe are the products of accidental circumstances. While they view life as an observable, undeniable cosmic reality, far from them the idea that it was created with a purpose or loving devotion. Regardless of one's views, seekers of truth should all be applauded for their contributions to the pool of human knowledge. This author is only throwing one more stone in this murky pond while nurturing the hope that humans have not yet given up on trying to understand why we are here, how it all began, and where we are going.

ACKNOWLEDGMENTS

Countless people deserve recognition as well as my heartfelt gratitude for their views and contributions to knowledge related to the origin and purpose of life. Many have expressed their thoughts with a great deal of courage and unconcern for their reputation, sometimes despite threats of maltreatment. It is abundantly clear that without such brave contributors this book would not have been written. It is not possible to thank them all because many of them belong to the stage of past history while others are still with us. There is growing sensitivity in the media, with special interest groups and people in high places bent on disavowing even the most remote possibility that intelligent supernatural forces might indeed be present in the universe. It is my hope that the rather sensitive nature of nonconventional suggestions made in this book will not offend anyone. May the readers be inspired to rethink some of the most fundamental issues of life and death regardless of which side of the fence they choose to stand. The main purpose of this book is to show that there is a logical and viable solution to the problem of evil and that the solution can be credited to God alone. Left to their own views, humans would have never recognized or implemented such a rational solution. Perhaps logic alone will suffice to persuade that there is indeed a God, and perhaps we would do well to listen to Him more attentively. The message He has tried to convey through the ages should be reconsidered through the prism of sound logic rather than through misguided human traditions and interpretations responsible for contributing confusion cast in totally distorted views of God and the divine.

CONTENTS

CHAPTER 1

Is There a Solution to the Problems of Our Human Condition?

Although some would argue that it is pointless to raise the question, it is increasingly clear that despite the exponential growth of knowledge on this planet no current ideology offers a tangible approach to the problem of evil. Despite some progress, the growing problems of our dysfunctional human family are becoming increasingly more alarming. While our so-called political correctness and many political and religious entities sermonize the world with messages of tolerance, it appears that xenophobia, bigotry, and radical religious dogmatism are on the rise. Our societies are suffering increasingly from the ill effects of widening gaps of irreconcilable differences liable to threaten the very existence of our human race. While on the surface progress appears to chug along in terms of human and civil rights, these improvements are mainly judicial in nature. Laws derived from such systems are more likely to hide the realities of growing resentments than to heal people's hearts and the pain and suffering our world is enduring. Indeed, much remains to be done, but are laws and stiffer enforcement really the key to the solution? Are we forgetting something far more important while we expect our democratically elected power-figureheads to save the situation by strengthening our legislative systems? If jurisdiction is not the answer to the human condition, where do we find it?

It is becoming quite clear that the jurisdictive progress made on the level of our courts does not necessarily translate into progress on the level of people's hearts and relationships. Laws have their place, but they are utterly powerless to change a human heart. At best they can impose behaviors capable of making people more law abiding while increasing the very resentments laws are designed to correct. In terms of practical ethics, confusion reigns. Neither laws nor science have come to the rescue. If anything, as scientific knowledge grows, ethical guidelines are increasingly blurred. Sciences bring confusion by opening new ethical dilemmas and loopholes than solutions. Several factors are responsible for tearing apart our social fabric. But sadly, despite the amazing achievements of our modern world, societies appear increasingly more powerless in the face of growing numbers of potentially lethal precipices. On several fronts, all it would take is a small hiccup in the cogwheels of our administrative machineries to throw us all right back to the Stone Age. A more serious belch could spell instant oblivion of the human race.

With their lances and hatchets our ancestors could only destroy one another one at a time. Back then, only cataclysmic events such as floods, earthquakes, tsunamis, epidemics, and rare encounters with meteors could devastate or destroy large numbers of people in a single event. While such occurrences have traditionally been attributed to God, today things are different. The evils of humanity have already destroyed more lives than all the so-called acts of God combined since the dawn of civilization. Human evil could soon be blamed for bringing worldwide chaos and the obliteration of entire segments of society. All it would take is the mismanagement of financial, social, political, ecological, or religious endeavors, and these have become so common that we no longer pay attention to them. The availability of weapons of mass destruction capable of annihilating life on our planet several times over is no longer in question. It is a reality since the aftermaths of World War II—an alarming reality barely a half a century old. We have not yet had the time or the will to process the consequences of such devastation. For those who consider life an accident of nature it would be just another cosmic event of which the gravity would be just as negligible as the purpose for which life became a reality. But for those who believe in God, or for those who would believe in His existence, would such an outcome be conceivable? Could God have created life without a clear purpose?

Scripture warns of an abomination that will cause desolation

Scripture makes mention of an "abomination" that will bring the very kind of "desolation" we are talking about. How could the Holy Script have predicted such a development at a time when swords and spears were still the most dangerous weapons available? Neither science nor modern ethics provide hope to escape the growing malaise that could bring worldwide desolation. Sixteenth-century French humanist François Rabelais recognized the potential danger before the industrial revolution when he said: "Science without conscience is but ruin of the soul." Interestingly, when searching for a culprit for this sad state of affairs we find increasing numbers of scholars and politicians prone to blame religion, and truth be told, they are not wrong. Does that mean that religions should be abolished? Not if we are willing to recognize the problems of religion with the will to correct them. One does not have to know a great deal about religions to recognize that while they have all done some good in the world, they have often provided false solutions and false hope while utterly failing humankind—indeed, we have all witnessed at least some of their destructive propensities. Let us avoid the temptation of singling out any one of them. As we shall see, from assessing the messages they proclaim on the basis of sound logic, it becomes apparent to conclude that to some degree at least, that they are all guilty.

Does this rather harsh conclusion imply that religion is not the answer to the problem of evil and that we should throw out the baby with the bathwater, as many suggest we should do?

Perhaps all religions should reconsider what they teach

It appears quite clear that religions as we know them today have not yet provided humankind with valid answers despite the fact that they all claim to be the ultimate answer—that fact alone could well be their biggest weakness. If they are persuaded that they have the answer why should they bother to look further for better answers? At the very least they should all be striving to lead people away from evil, but do they? Modern Christianity is more likely to be tolerant toward evil than to condemn it. In fact, tolerance is touted as the new spirituality. It has become the most important sign that a person has been converted. But isn't utter tolerance an open door to increased evil? Could lawlessness create even bigger problems than the legal system we just labeled powerless to change hearts?

The main problem of religions is that they fail to offer rational approaches to alleviate the growth of evil and violence in our world. If there were a religion that could accomplish the feat of improving the human heart by empowering it to drive away evil on purely logical grounds, such a religion would likely gain recognition and widespread approval. A religion offering reasonable solutions with tenets founded on pure logic would also be recognized as perfectly acceptable even in a highly scientific world where logic is recognized as the principal driver of progress. Such a religion could become the temple of true knowledge of which the tenets would be recognized as built on the solid rock of logic rather than on the shifting sands of mystical adulations and superstitions (see Lk. 6:46–49). Some five or six centuries ago the Reformation reacted against incoherent traditions and superstitions, but the work was never completed.

The main hypothesis considered in this book is the possibility that the religions of our world have all failed humanity, and this, only because they have all fallen short of proclaiming God's perfectly logical message revealed as the prescription to eradicate evil. Instead, by and large, religions fall to the temptation of accepting irrational mystical solutions created by humans on the altars of superstition.

Jesus made a phenomenal prediction

Jesus made a claim that even Christianity has failed to consider seriously. He said that God will someday make known to humanity all the truth they need to bring about true and lasting freedom (Jn. 8:32). Since true freedom cannot be attained without unity of belief and purpose in an atmosphere of perfect mutual trust, it must be concluded that truth capable of bringing about such unity continues to elude even the most influential religious figures of our world. Indeed, true freedom will remain unachievable as long as evil continues to inhabit the human heart, because true freedom is not possible in the presence of evil. Yet instead of reforming the human heart, civil and religious institutions insist on reforming human behavior through increasingly more complex systems of regulation and enforcement.

To be effective, the truth Jesus was speaking of must have the power to chip away at the problem of evil ingrained in all our hearts. Will such a religion ever be suggested, and if it is, will it ever gain recognition and acceptance? The only way it could is for such a religion to be founded on sound logic, not the subjective insights and intuitions suggested by various forms of superstitious mysticism the religions of our world advocate.

If humans are indeed the product of an intelligent Creator who made them truly free, it goes without saying that He also had to make them perfectly and unconditionally altruistic, or they could not have enjoyed true and absolute freedom. The freedom that was theirs before the fall will be again be the freedom enjoyed by those who recognize and accept the mind-set God gave Adam and Eve at Creation. No freedom can survive the least presence of egocentricity because the least level of egocentricity make a person unreliable and potentially deceitful. And it must be said, the least lack of mutual trust in a society destroys freedom for all.

While today a large contingent of philosophers denies the possibility that true freedom is possible, we must admit that if they are right there is no God. On the other hand, if a god made this statement to humanity through Jesus, he is a liar—a possibility Scripture denies. Thus we are compelled to ask, what happened? Why have we lost our freedom to the point that even philosophers deny its potential existence? If God created humans free, and they lost their freedom because evil reared its ugly head, at some point in time humans must have deviated from the perfectly altruistic mind-set they were given at Creation. To do so they must have *willfully* chosen to accept an evil mind-set, that is to say: they accepted to adopt a self-centered and indiscriminately self-serving way of life, even when serving others. With such a mentality they became immediately undependable, untrustworthy, dishonest, deceitful, and disloyal—in other words, they became utterly treacherous.

If we accept the idea that humanity was not originally created evil, we must also accept the possibility that they were created perfect and free. Thus they must have chosen *on their own free will* to follow a path that God warned them not to take, as Scripture clearly affirms they have done. If we can believe Scripture, humans were not created with a pagan mind-set[1], they developed the pagan mind-set on their own. Deviations from God's ways took place on several occasions. As we shall see, it took place in the Garden of Eden, immediately afterword with Cain, and

---

[1] The word "pagan" is not viewed as a specific religion in the context of this book. It is viewed as all ideologies and religions attempting to control human behavior through rewards and punishments. The pagan mind-set leaves humans entirely at the mercies of governments and religious faiths eager to reward or punish on the basis of humanly prescribed perceptions of good and evil viewed as proper and improper behavior. Pagan religions are all rooted on deviations of God's instructions given through His prophets, and later through the ministry of Jesus.

again after Noah, after Abraham, after Moses, and again after Jesus. At the risk of agreeing, in part at least, with Christopher Hitchens who authored *God is Not Great*,[2] or Karl Marx who called religion the opiate of the masses, it is unfortunately true that all the religions of our world are still poisoned with the venom of pagan mindedness. Scripture warns against this damaging mentality from cover to cover. We shall attempt to analyze what the pagan mind-set is and why humanity can be so negatively impacted by its destructive influence on religious philosophy. Scripture affirms that it is a mentality that has the potential to ruin the world to the point of oblivion. We shall see that pagan mentality could well be the "abomination that brings desolation" to the world as predicted by both the prophet Daniel and later by Jesus (Dan. 9:27; 11:31; 12:11; Mt. 24:15; Mk. 13:14).

This book attempts to demonstrate, not only the fact that pagan views and attitudes are omnipresent in both the religious and secular realities of our world, but also that Scripture can be read through pagan paradigms that lead away from the truth that would set us free. A non-pagan path of interpretation will also be suggested to help correct at least some of the false and destructive interpretations of the past. Because they are founded on pagan perceptions of God and pagan perceptions of His message, errors of interpretations have led to false solutions to the human dilemma. These false interpretations have led to false conclusions with regards to the way human behavior should be altered. These false interpretations have molded the human mind to such a point of confusion that they are likely responsible for all the major problems humanity is facing today.

"The truth that will set you free" (Jn. 8:32) Jesus talked about is also called salvation, because it is truth that heals the disease called evil. This truth is at the heart of "the kingdom of God," because it is a realm of life fully dependent on perfect mutual trust founded on true love that procures real and lasting freedom. Indeed, according to Scripture the world has not always been entirely pagan. Humans became essentially self-absorbed and egocentric because God's message containing the solution to evil was repeatedly overlooked or corrupted with religious concepts of human invention. Those concepts have also influenced

---

[2]   Christopher Hitchens, *God is Not Great: How Religion Poisons Everything*. Hachette Book Group USA, New York, NY. 10169, 2007.

negatively people's attitudes and ways of life to the core. These pagan concepts have brought various levels of corruption to all our political, commercial, judicial, and religious systems. With pagan mind-sets humanity is bound to remain entirely reliant on ever more complicated legal systems and ever more costly freedom-denying forensics to satisfy the demands of our so-called courts of justice.

As we shall see, blaming or punishing the guilty is never the way justice is served in God's realm. But unfortunately, human standards of justice have been falsely attributed to God. His justice is valid only if it has the power to transform the human heart. To be valid it has to offer people both the opportunity and the means to become just or righteous, something no earthly judicial system can accomplish. Considering that Judeo-Christian Scripture claims to offer the solution to the problem of evil, could it be that the message from God upon which it is founded continues to be misread and misunderstood to this day? Could the concept of *Sola Scriptura* be valid only if its message is understood correctly? Could it be that its message has remained hidden behind the Veil of superstition that separates the Holy Place from the Most Holy Place of His Sanctuary? All this will be explained as we progress, but we must ask: Has humanity been so misguided that we have all failed to recognize the exact nature and timeless value of the message God has been trying to communicate for millennia? Unfortunately, the answer appears to be yes.

The solution to the human condition cannot be mystical in nature

One point upon which we should all be able to agree, considering the scientific age in which we live, is that the solution to the problem of evil, if there is one, cannot be founded on mystical grounds.[3] Mystical approaches to the improvement of the human condition have failed humankind miserably since the dawn of civilization. Let us not repeat the mistakes of the past with expectations of different results— Einstein called such a practice "the epitome of insanity." Time has come for modern humanity to bury once for all any mystical approaches to problem-solving, even in matters of religion as regards attempts to resolve the problem of evil. Indeed, the mysticism of yester-millennia has not only proven ineffectual, it should also be recognized as wholly harmful and destructive. It has only served to confuse the playing field of theology to such a degree that humanity has never been more confused. Such confusion is clearly responsible for leading the human family ever closer to calamities of biblical proportion.

---

[3]   This statement does not imply that religion should reject all mystical manifestations. However, God offers a solution to evil that should not require the use of mystical lenses to be discoverable. If God must first be proven to exist before accepting His solution to the problem of evil, humans will never be in a position to accept the solution. My contention in this book is that it is the solution God offers that will end up proving His existence. If God's solution can be recognized as founded on pure logic it will stand on its own merits, and humans would soon discover that they could never have arrived at such a solution on their own. God would have to be recognized as the originator of this universal truth. Thus, regardless of one's conclusions about the existence of God, His perfectly logical approach to the problem of evil should stand the test of pure logic forevermore. Explaining the incarnation of Jesus, His miracles, or the infinite lifespan of God are indeed mystical realities, but they should be irrelevant to the solution of which the validity must rest on purely logical grounds. God used mystical means to bring the solution to the attention of humans, but not to prove it. The miracles are the signature of God on His message to humanity. Since humans are wired to understand truth on logical grounds, they will not fail to recognize its fail-safe value when corruption has been removed. As long as truth is said to rest on irrational concepts perceived as "faith," it will never be possible to distinguish truth from error in matters of religion, nor could such irrational concepts be applicable to life.

If God offers a solution in Scripture or elsewhere, it cannot be founded on incomprehensible or incoherent concepts, such as they are taught and proclaimed by the religions of our world. Churchgoers have been led to believe incomprehensible jibber-jabber viewed as essential elements of faith by which they can be saved. If God is the Creator of life and matter, it follows reason that He is also the Creator of sound logic. Thus, if a message He has given fails to meet the most basic test of logic it should be rejected on the grounds that it could not possibly come from the God who created logic. If God is not logical, He cannot be the Creator. Everything He said regarding the solution to the human problem should therefore be verifiable on the strength of sound logic, recognizing that even the source that contains His universal message of truth known as the Bible is in fact imperfect for reasons the mystics will always refuse to consider.

It is true that proving the existence of a Creator God will never be possible on the grounds of empirical evidence. How could the Infinite One be measured empirically? It is an oxymoron. Finite humans would lack both the wording and the methods of measurement. God cannot be proven any more than the source of energy assumed to have produced the Big Bang. Unfortunately, thus far at least, any effort to approach Scripture on the solid bedrock of logic has been overridden, and even scorned, especially, it must be said, by church leaders and experts in matters of theology and Scripture. No wonder Jesus reprimanded the religious leaders of His time. He considered them more responsible for the problems of the world than the political leaders. Let us remember that the religious leaders Jesus was addressing were the only ones on planet Earth who had been given the privilege of access to the words of prophets who spoke and wrote on God's behalf. No other religious group of His time could make that claim.

Attempts made to approach the study of Scripture on purely rational foundations have been systematically rejected and disallowed on the grounds that God being infinite is beyond human understanding. Does that mean however, that God is beyond sound logic and that He would allow communications with prophets in terms that the intelligent beings He created cannot understand? But this question begs another: Could it be that the perpetrators of this view fear that if God's message were to be recognized as being perfectly logical and simple to understand, the message of truth would render obsolete all human creators, manufacturers, and merchants of religious faiths?

Indeed, if a practical and simple solution to the problem of evil became readily understandable on the grounds of pure logic, everyone could recognize it as truth, and everyone would become a priest of sorts. As we shall see in the following pages, God never considered the priesthood to be His representatives for the purpose of defining truth, judging people and actions, or officiating cleansing and payments for sins. Indeed, their duty has always been to communicate to the people God's way to overcome evil. With a religion entirely founded on sound logic our traditional religious leaders commonly called pastors, priests, rabbis, or gurus would all become obsolete and looked upon as megaliths of religious bygones. And what's more, there would be only one God and one religion for all people.

Surprisingly perhaps, Old Testament (OT) Scripture makes it clear that God wanted and even planned the obsolescence of all religious leaders. In Israel their understanding of the priesthood had been influenced during the centuries of captivity spent in pagan Egypt. In fact, even the New Testament (NT) confirms the concept. It clearly states that God never gave up the idea of creating a kingdom of which all citizens were to become true kings and priests of the kingdom of God. More importantly perhaps, the Holy Book makes it clear that God will ultimately accomplish His purpose, though it also predicts that not everyone will accept to participate.

The "truth" of which Jesus and Scripture are all about is a description of the way by which God plans to eradicate evil. In the OT, God's message in this regard was stated in the conditional tense. He told the Israelites coming out of Egypt: "If indeed you listen to my voice . . . you will be for me a holy nation made up of kings and priests" (Ex. 19:6).[4]

---

[4] This is a paraphrased translation by the author from the Greek Septuagint (LXX). This Old Testament was translated into Greek from existing ancient Hebrew manuscripts about two centuries or more before Christ. Most of our current Bibles are translated from Masoretic Hebrew texts that became the authoritative Hebrew Bible between the seventh and tenth century CE. In this book CE designates the "Common Era," the timeline of history since the birth of Jesus previously called AD the period of history since Christ. Now however, BCE designates the historical period of time before Christ or Before the Common Era previously known as BC.

Here God was calling all Israelites, young and old, male and female, to become active priests and kings in the Promised Land. It is interesting to note that despite the failure of the Israelites to fulfill this specific request of their God, centuries later the Apostle Peter of the NT indicates that God never gave up the concept. Writing to a group of faithful followers of Jesus, Peter stated in a letter: "But you are a chosen people, a royal priesthood, a holy nation, a people belonging to God . . . who called you out of darkness into his wonderful light" (1 Pet. 2:9 NIV[5]). This text could have been translated to say: "But you are the ones chosen to be the kings and priests of the holy nation . . ."

Following the advent of Jesus the Apostles rekindled God's design to create on earth a people who understand what God meant by this seemingly impossible and utopian way of life from a human perspective. All followers of Jesus were called to become kings and priests on this earth, but this work is not yet fulfilled—one might even wonder if it has begun in a religious world where ordination is practiced without biblical foundation and often disallowed for women. In fact, the practice of ordination is a pagan concept. Only the lack of logic applied to religion can be blamed for the delay in the fulfillment of God's purpose to have a people made up of priests and kings. An attempt is made in this book to explore why God's desire to have a holy nation on earth has failed to become reality to this day, and why it is needed before His return. Now that logic has finally become a widespread commodity in our Post Modern world, it is through the lenses of logic that Scripture will be explored to determine how God's holy nation will eventually come about. This will probably happen sooner than later because everything on this planet appears to indicate that the resolution of major problems is eluding us. From the perspective of Scripture, it is a sign of the end.

About two millennia have passed since a small group of people began to form what was to become a vast kingdom of priests before the end. The "royal priesthood" should be expected to grow exponentially during the closing days of world's history; such a development will not happen without fierce opposition, great hostility, and even bloody persecutions in

---

5   Unless otherwise indicated, all quotes from the Bible in this book are from the NIV. *The Holy Bible, New International Version*, copyright 1973, 1978, 1984 by International Bible Society. Used by permission of Zondervan Publishing House.

the name of faith in God. Here is what Jesus said: "They will put you out of the synagogue; in fact, the time is coming when anyone who kills you will think they are offering a service to God" (Jn. 16:2). Here the word synagogue probably implies both establishments called synagogues and the sum total of all those who study Scripture. Just as Jesus was killed in the name of preserving a religious institution, His true followers of the last days will suffer similar fates. At the beginning of His ministry, Jesus went so far as to say: "Blessed are you when people insult you, persecute you and falsely say all kinds of evil against you *because of me*" (Mt. 5:11, emphasis mine). Jesus was talking about reactions to His perfectly logical message of truth brought to the attention of the world on God's behalf. The Apostle John makes that point very clear in his Revelation of Jesus Christ where end-time world conditions are described in symbolic language. What that book clearly conveys is that ultimately God will triumph in His endeavor, though at the moment things may look rather bleak. A special light will shine to guide sincere followers of Jesus and students of Scripture just before the desolation of the end.

It is probably safe to say that today no religious entity is actively proclaiming God's intent to establish a group of people entirely made up of priests, gurus, or ministers on planet Earth. No established church community trains its believers to become priests, kings, or queens in their own right on the merits of the message Jesus came to proclaim. On the contrary, religious establishments claiming to represent Jesus are more inclined to welcome the administrative and religious stratification of their leaders. They consider that God establishes spiritual leadership, when in fact God wants all believers to become leaders fully able to proclaim the love of God and how it is acquired. There is a strong inclination among religions to maintain a ruling religious class of leaders regardless of the dark destiny this may bring. They have failed to understand God's resolve to ordain with His truth every man, woman, and child to the pure simplicity and beauty of His own priesthood—a priesthood of which He is the Alpha and Omega (see Rev. 21:6). Far from the religious leaders of this world is the idea of making their prestigious jobs obsolete by teaching all their church members how they can become true priests by following the message of Jesus, the ultimate High Priest (Heb. 9:11).

Even the OT predicted that someday God's resolve would become reality and that this reality would come sometime before His final return to earth. The prophet Jeremiah predicted it long ago when he wrote: "No longer will a man teach his neighbor, or a man his brother, saying, 'know the LORD,' *because they will all know me,* from the least of them to the greatest" (Jer. 31:34, emphasis mine).

Many feel that no solution is needed, all is well on planet Earth

Today many are those who appear quite satisfied that things are going well on planet Earth. They remain persuaded that the theory of evolution is gently chugging along its blissful course. They go so far as to write such books as that of Harvard Professor, evolutionary psychologist, Steven Pinker, titled *The Better Angels of Our Nature: Why Violence Has Declined.*[6] Here the author uses statistics to imply that the world is becoming increasingly more safe and secure. Was Benjamin Disraeli exaggerating when he said: "There are three types of lies— lies, damn lies, and statistics?" Perhaps, but it is fact that politicians are all busy trying to impress their constituents with statistics that may not reflect legitimate truth. They talk about eradicating poverty in a world where they portray themselves as actively involved in the abolishment of malnourishment and homelessness. With still over 15 percent of people living at or below the poverty level in USA, reality shows that we may have actually gone in the wrong direction despite unprecedented levels of help offered to the poor. The same could be said about violence in the world. Progress is going in the wrong direction.

The question that begs an answer is this: Is society really less violent today than it was? If society is less violent is it because people are less violent at heart, or because forensics and other methods of dissuasion are improved? And if we are less violent, can we really trust statistics? City leaders gleefully assert that crime rates are in decline, but is that a sure sign that people are more caring of their neighbors than in the past? On the other hand, scientists and health professionals tout an expansion of longevity. Assuming that all these improvements were factual, a reality check of current events would quickly reveal that life and the pursuit of happiness are privileges hanging by a very thin thread. God alone knows how long the thread will continue to hold the weight of expanding

---

6   Steven Pinker, Viking Penguin, 2011.

human depravity propelled by growing disregard for others regardless of statistics claiming otherwise.

Can Scripture really be trusted?

Even theologians and religious leaders have sometimes been known to ridicule Scripture. It is true that some stories appear difficult to accept at face value. The Flood of Noah is a good example. Yet there is circumstantial evidence corroborating that such a flood could have happened, so why dispute the possibility? The timing calculated by most Christians is probably wrong because it was done using the biblical Chronology suggested by the Masoretic text from which most current Bibles are translated. Such calculations place the Flood at about 2400 BCE, which is not possible for a number of reasons. Calculations made on the basis of the much older Septuagint commonly used at the time of Jesus, push back the Flood of Noah to at least 4000 BCE or before, making it far more plausible. We also know that the world's population jumped from about two hundred million at the beginning of the Common Era to about six billion only two thousand years later. With this in mind, in consideration of the theory of evolution claiming that modern humans have walked the planet for the past 200,000 years, how can it be explained that the world is not hugely overpopulated? Sure, some theories exist, but are they plausible?

Let us play devil's advocate for a moment and assume that there were only two people on the planet 200,000 years ago, when evolutionists claim the human race, as we know it, began. Assuming that they doubled in numbers only every thousand years, a rate of growth far inferior to the slowest estimated growth of the past 2,000 years, the world would have reached the equivalent of our current world population within 32,000 years. In other words, with an impossibly slow rate the current level of the world population would have been reached 168,000 years ago. While arguments are used to explain the incredibly slow rate of population growth, they are all based on assumptions often incompatible with evolutionary theories. Whose account should we believe?

It is also important to note that if there were no mountains or deep trenches in the oceans and the surface of the land were flattened, the entire earth would be covered by a mile and a half of water. At the very least, this fact lends credence to the possibility that a worldwide flood could well have taken place.[7] Interestingly enough, God told Moses that before the creation of the world its surface was already entirely covered with water (see Gen. 1:2). How could Moses have known 3,500 years ago that if it were more flat the world contains enough water to easily submerge its entire surface?

While other elements of circumstantial evidence could be pointed out, one merits special attention because it involves the religions of our world. If modern humans evolved with racial and cultural differentiations taking place over the past 200,000 years, is it not bizarre, and even absurd, to think that they have all developed similar rituals involving bloody sacrificial offerings to the gods, essentially at the same time? The rituals were all very similar in nature and purpose; they all involved cleansing of the soul and appeasement of the gods. Is it conceivable that people evolving over such a long period of time could all have developed more or less at the same time the idea that somehow they could benefit from the clemency of divinities by offering them a bounty of blood sacrifices? The idea is absurd from an evolutionary perspective, because if people were the product of natural selection they would not have all been suddenly inclined to develop such nearly identical irrational religious concepts. Nor is it conceivable that they would have come to believe clear around the planet that it might be possible to appease deities by offering them bloody offerings.

Indeed, the fact that all races and cultures of people have piously practiced these religious peace offerings in one form or another rather recently, can be attributed to the account of Noah. As he came out of the Ark he offered a number of animal sacrifices for the sole purpose of requesting God's favors, not for the purpose of changing the state of human hearts (see Gen. 8). This account of Scripture is a clear indication that pagan concepts were alive and well long before the Flood of Noah. It could even be suggested that pagan concepts were responsible for the violence Scripture affirms to have been prevalent before the Flood (Gen. 6:5). The fact that all continents have practiced such offerings to the gods could well offer circumstantial evidence that Noah did exist, that he is

---

7   This calculation is not difficult to make on the basis of the fact that the surface of the earth is nearly 70 percent ocean of which the average depth is 12,450 feet. The remaining 30 percent of land mass represents an average elevation of about 2,250 feet.

the father of all humans on the planet today, and that he did offer such sacrifices upon coming out of the Ark.

As we shall see, these particular types of sacrifices were *not* made in response to a request from God. Noah chose on his own volition to offer gifts to God while imploring Him not to allow the repeat of such a destructive event. This explains why about 2,000 years after Noah, Abraham was still offering sacrifices with the idea that he should somehow appease God.[8] The same holds true for his descendants, all the inhabitants of the world. Clearly, from wherever they migrated following the Great Flood, they took with them this irrational bloody custom that must have flourished abundantly during antediluvian times. A religious custom God had never requested and never approved.

The commonality of religious practices centered on blood sacrifices is likely to have provided the substance that led to huge religious schisms over time. While the practices were similar, the variety of interpretations over their nature and purpose as well as the gods they were to appease caused divisions and disagreements—each thinking that they had the true form of worship the gods would recognize. Schisms related to the interpretation of religious sacrifices continue to cause religious rifts to this day. These rifts translate into significant cultural rifts. Even the Christian community is divided over the huge variety of interpretations related to the torture Jesus suffered on the Cross. Seeing the "sacrifice" in a different light brings divisions.

It is most commonly believed that Jesus was a sacrifice offered to appease God the Father—a view we will challenge. The post-Flood civilizations not only offered sacrifices to different gods but they attributed incoherent religious symbolic meanings to these sacrificial practices. Religious sacrificial systems have done more to reduce the value of life than to honor and appreciate its importance. Those found to be in disagreement with traditional interpretations and purpose of the sacrifices were instantly labeled as infidels, thus guilty of defamation for failure to worship adequately the official divinities. Such acts were considered sacrilegious and punishable by torture or capital punishment. Tolerance toward others faiths was considered treason while killing infidels who held different views was considered highly honorable.

---

[8]   See Appendix A showing graphs based on Masoretic and Septuagint Chronology since the Flood of Noah.

It must be noted that even Abraham was so steeped in the practice of sacrificial offerings that he jumped to improper conclusions regarding the sacrifice of his own son. In keeping with traditional notions of propitiatory sacrifices he was prepared to slaughter his son to please and appease God. Are we to deduce from these accounts that God wanted sacrificial blood? The purpose of this book is to offer a vastly different outlook on this extremely sensitive theological issue. Idolatry of blood continues to be the object of worships worldwide. Unfortunately, Christian beliefs related to this issue are far from resolved. We must come to realize that Scripture vehemently condemns such practices, yet we falsely view Scripture as teaching that they were the will, desire, and even the pleasure of God.

It is true that depending on how Scripture is read and translated it sometimes appears to promote both the importance and the futility of sacrificial offerings. Should we deduce that Scripture contradicts itself in this regard? Here again, confusion reigns because corruption has degraded the integrity of the message from God on several fronts. The statements of Scripture have been manipulated by faulty translations and interpretations. Most of Scripture is an account of what people did, whether or not God approved of their deeds and practices.

This is just a summary of some of the questions this book explores in greater depth. May the reader enjoy the journey with an open heart regardless of views and conclusions reached by this author.

Bon voyage!

CHAPTER 2

The Problem of Evil

It should come as no surprise to Christians that growing numbers of concerned thinkers, scientists, philosophers, and political leaders are increasingly more vocal in calling to secularize society. On the cover of a recent book titled *The End of Faith* by Sam Harris, the well-known professor of law at Harvard University, author of *America on Trial,* Alan Dershowitz provides the following assessment of the book: "Harris's tour de force demonstrates how faith—blind, deaf, dumb, and unreasoned—threatens our very existence." In his assessment of the same book, Peter Singer, author of *The President of Good and Evil: The Ethics of George W. Bush,* echoes a similar sentiment: "At last," he writes, "we have a book that focuses on the common thread that links Islamic terrorism with the irrationality of all religious faith. *The End of Faith* will challenge not only Muslims, but Hindus, Jews, and Christians as well." Peter Singer does not hesitate to label all faiths as irrational.

In his book, Harris examines some of the most blatant problems religions have brought to the societies of our world. His main complaint is the arbitrary manipulative role of faith, which he asserts is often reprehensible and responsible for driving people to violence in the names of irrational belief systems. He provides numerous accounts of disgraceful acts perpetrated directly or indirectly on the strength of religious beliefs in the name of faith, or worse yet, in the name of God. Unfortunately, while Harris is all too correct in his observations, he fails to recognize that no religion on our planet is truly representative of the religion Jesus advocated against all odds.

For reasons we shall examine, no Christian religion can be clearly identified as promoting the message of unconditional love and mercy toward all people, as Jesus proclaimed it. This book is an attempt to show how the religion of Christ should have been understood and where Christianity appears to have gone astray. Rectifying a two-thousand-years-old trajectory gone awry may not be easy, and at times, the facts related to the departure from the message of Jesus may well be alarming to the reader.

If the world could accept the message of Jesus as He meant it, the results would be spectacular. The displays of unconditional love would be demonstrated everywhere. Neither a sense of duty to do what is right nor a strict dedication to irrational faiths or belief systems and their rules can produce such love. Pure altruism would be the product of a heart so genuinely transformed by a message perfectly coherent and logical. It would change people on the strength of the rationale conveyed by the divine message alone. That rationale is so perfect that it could only come from God, because it is a concept totally foreign to the mentality of naturally born humans. God's message is so persuasive that it becomes the person's faith on the strength of its indisputable logic recognized as undeniably correct. By dutifully accepting to obey rules of conduct, or by submitting to doctrines or dogmas devoid of rationale, a person is made to conform to external impositions—such approaches to behavioral control can only shrink and ultimately destroy personal freedom. This is never the way God operates because it would be an infringement on personal choices, thus a restriction of freedom. True love cannot survive in a freedom-restricted environment. And when imposed, love ceases to be love; thus such love could never be from God because it would not be love emanating from a loving heart. Imposing love on anyone is taking it away.

"Give me liberty, or give me death!" said Patrick Henry, governor of Virginia in 1775. Indeed, God created humans to be free in the absolute sense of the word, but such freedom has to emanate from a clear understanding of love and freedom. Anything short of absolute freedom is tyranny. In fact, God Himself does not want His created beings to be subjected to rules requiring law enforcement and verdicts. God has created a system founded on a message so logical that when accepted, the logic of the message itself empowers people's hearts to be changed. His message has to sink in sufficiently to become a personal persuasion from which it becomes increasingly more difficult to deviate. This is in fact how love is made to grow in the human heart—through persuasion founded on indisputable logic.

When a persuasion is incorrect or lacks logic it also lacks the power to influence a person's mind and actions. Why should anyone believe something that does not appear to be rational? With the so-called faith system the influence of the system on a person's actions is limited to the gullibility of the subject, not the strength of the message. A false faith, which amounts to an incorrect message, has the power to manipulate attitudes and behaviors, not the power to persuade. On the other hand, a true belief system or faith persuades the subject to do the right thing on the strength of its logic. A logical belief system to which a subject can subscribe totally and willfully out of persuasion becomes a guiding light for life. Such guidance is bound to keep the bearer of the message in tune with God and His unique way of life. With such a reliable mental guide a person grows increasingly free, because the correctness of the belief system becomes the rudder of that person's life. Though aways free to sin, a person far prefers to act upon the dictates of love.

When a belief system fails to be rational it cannot be from God who is the Creator of logic. Scripture calls the mind-set created on the strength of God's perfect logic, the "faith" all humans are invited to recognize, appreciate, and make their own. With such a guiding force a person is motivated to think and act from an intrinsic force of action perfectly acceptable to God and all other love-promoting intelligent life in the universe. These are the loving individuals who make up the kingdom of God. With this definition of faith it can be deduced that righteousness is indeed by faith, because it is the product of a powerful rational persuasion that comes from God. The person does what is right on the basis of a universally recognized and perfectly rational belief system that comes from God.

Through ages past, the religions of our world have been unremittingly cast in molds of traditions responsible for misguiding both religious and secular belief systems. To a large extent, this includes Judaism and Christianity despite the fact that they have the books of prophets who spoke on God's behalf. While all religions have undergone alterations in form and fashion associated primarily with cultures and times, in substance, the pagan molds from which they are cast have never been broken. These traditions are so firmly anchored that they have impacted the core mentality of all populations and all cultures regardless of religious affiliation or total lack thereof.

Additionally, these traditions have greatly contributed to a flawed diagnosis of the human condition. They have successfully concealed the only therapy capable of reducing evil in our egocentric violent world. Needless to say, these traditions have also provided both the background and the groundwork for a faulty perception of the "only true God" (Jn. 17:3). In turn, a faulty perception of God has led to a faulty understanding of His message, thus voiding its power to transform humanity. With the correct understanding of God's message the world would not only be more peaceful, but it would also be far more productive and prosperous. Poverty cannot exist in the absence of egocentrism. To misunderstand God is to misunderstand life along with all the privileges His kind of life can bring to the world. "Give," said the Lord, "and it shall be given to you" (Lk. 6:38). Indeed, if we all understood the importance of giving, as Jesus understood the meaning of this word, we would all benefit from the overwhelming generosity of others. All gifts would emanate from a sincere dedication of people to the welfare and well-being of others. We would all share the bounties that come from sharing the blessings of prosperity and affluence true love alone can bestow. What are we waiting for to recognize the obvious? Is it not time to apply the divine principles of true love in our collective lives?

Distorted perceptions of God and of His message are largely responsible for leading the world astray and, ultimately, to desolation and chaos. It is because we are misguided about God that humanity remains blindfolded as it advances ever closer to the inevitable precipices of self-annihilation. All distortions of God and His message have pagan origins. But pagan thinking did not originate with godless people, as commonly thought. A careful study of the sacred texts shows that the most damaging distortions of God and His message can be traced back to the first two generations of humans living on the planet. Indeed, pagan thinking of which the foundational principles comprise all ungodlike belief systems of life, politics, and religions are currently clashing ever more violently everywhere. While these faulty beliefs are deplored throughout Judeo-Christian Scripture, they continue to influence all secular and religious governances of our world. The faulty attitudes of our first parents toward God and His message have affected negatively the entire population of the world.

Any concept, ideology, or way of life that does not come from God is pagan by definition. Let us review some of the most glaring pagan views and attitudes introduced to the world during the lifetime of the first two generations of humans who ever lived according to Scripture. A review of the beliefs that led to their actions shows that they have impacted negatively the mentality of the entire human race:

The generation of Adam and Eve

Scripture calls the first generation of humans that of Adam and Eve. A study of their mental attitudes and actions reveals that they were responsible for at least three highly damaging attitudes toward their Maker and His modus operandi for the universe. Those attitudes have impacted all societies of the world negatively ever since:

1. When in trouble, they failed to seek the help of their Maker

Following their ingestion of a fruit from a tree God warned them not to approach (Gen. 3:3); Adam and Eve immediately recognized that they were in trouble. Unfortunately for them and their offspring, they failed to accept responsibility for the real cause of their problem. Then they compounded the detrimental impact of their thinking by failing to seek the help of their Maker. He alone could have provided them with the necessary support and guidance to resolve the problem before things got worse. But they chose to rationalize the problem by attributing their flawed behavior to the mere ingestion of a fruit. They chose to ignore their failure to think correctly in a spirit of love as the real problem. This was in fact the knot of the problem; incorrect thinking was entertained in their minds before choosing to drift toward the Tree of Knowledge of Good and Evil. The product of thoughts lacking love caused them to take the fruit. Thus it was a flawed thinking process that led them to their sinful acts.

What Adam and Eve knew with perfect clarity of mind was that something ominous had suddenly changed, but they remained unwilling to admit that the problem resulted from their failure to think correctly. Then, instead of looking for God's way to cure the mind-related problem they tried to avoid its symptoms, doing something wrong and unloving. Instead of seeking help from the only One who knew the formula for the cure, they attempted to resolve the problem on their own through methods of their own invention. Pagan thinking is always human attempts to resolve problems on their own. As a result, their nakedness of body became an issue, not their nakedness of mind and spirit that led to the act. A study of the circumstances surrounding the issue of nakedness shows that it was unrelated to their ingestion of the fruit itself; instead, it was directly related to the faulty attitude of their minds and hearts that led them to partake of the fruit. The problem was not the fruit; it was the faulty mind-set that led them to the fruit. It was the faulty mind-set of Adam and Eve that brought evil to humanity, not the ingestion of a fruit. Indeed, Adam and Eve had chosen to adopt a spirit, or mind-set that was in opposition to the mind-set, or Spirit of God. Thus the spirit they adopted was unholy. They had willfully compromised the Holy Spirit God had created and uploaded in their minds at Creation. Having adopted a mind-set that was not from the God in whose image they were created, they introduced an idolatrous pagan mind-set to their newly created innocent world. Innocence has suffered ever since.

Indeed, self-gratification led by egocentricity was created in the minds of Adam and Eve because their spirit lacked sufficient regard for the welfare and well-being of others. True love had been allowed to depart. A pagan, or unholy spirit, had contaminated their hearts before any external influence intervened. Left unchecked, the least deficiency of concern for others produces immediate mutual distrust, competition, and an irreversible growth of pride in all its ugly forms. All this led them and their descendants toward a growing tendency to focus on self and family, which ultimately led to the creation of clans, tribes, nationalities, racial differentiation through inbreeding, and a huge diversities of cultures and religions created by humans, not God.

The moment a person becomes self-serving, that person can no longer be trusted because at any moment that person could choose to take advantage of a given situation. It is the lack of mutual trust propelled by intensified human pride that has taken humanity down the slippery slopes to mutual annihilation. Indeed, Adam and Eve's pride disallowed the required humility to seek help from their Maker who alone would have offered them a viable solution. Without God's help to overcome the problem, mutual annihilation became wholly predictable and unavoidable. A person prone to self-gratification and self-aggrandizement cannot be trusted; it is that simple. They did not seek to become "like God" (Gen. 3:5) once again. Though the solution God could have offered them would have brought salvation, or healing, they could not find sufficient inner strength to seek His help and save their inflated pride at the same time. There is indeed no room for both God and pride in a human heart.

Adam and Eve must have known down deep in their hearts that their Creator had the solution to all problems, but instead of resting their security in God they rested their comfort in their newly found pride. Indeed, proud Adam would have appeared weak before Eve for his inability to rise to the occasion, and Eve would have appeared disloyal if she had sought the help of their Maker. Instead of seeking the solution from the only source of truth available in the universe, Adam and Eve chose to follow the self-comforting advice the devil had just suggested. The newly found sense of self-comfort led them to hide from God with whom they were now in competition for lordship, and to cover their bodies with fig leaves (Gen. 3:7). In doing so they made manifest their intents to dismiss any help their Creator could provide, though knowing that He would have offered it freely, and without causing them the least loss of self-worth or freedom. His advice would have protected and enhanced both their self-worth and their freedom for the rest of eternity. Had His perfectly logical advice been sought and heeded, it would have eradicated the evil attitudes that were just beginning to burgeon in their hearts and minds (see Gen. 3:8).

Religions today are still affected negatively by this mind-set

By some standards, taking the fruit could be considered a minor offence. But it is the departure from right thinking that was responsible for producing the act that as soon as consummated destroyed trust for all forms of life on the planet. That was the moment when it became evident for the entire universe to see that mutual trust no longer existed on planet Earth. The departure from correct thinking triggered the destruction of mutual trust that could only lead down the path of mutual destruction. Humanity has not yet reached the point of no return, but unfortunately we are marching on at great speed, and it can all be blamed on wrong thinking. Can this march of madness be halted, or is it too late?

Unfortunately, seeking the advice of "the only true God" (Jn. 17:3) is all too rare. It appears that individuals and the religions of our world are persuaded, as were Adam and Eve, that they already have the key to the solution. They even think that the solutions they have are based on Scripture. The problem is that some choose deliberately to ignore God's advice altogether while others interpret His nature and message through pagan concepts. Yet they all call their belief systems, the truth. All religions claim to have it. In this regard religions are far more arrogant than atheists, because at least atheism does not claim to have the last word on anything. Because the religions of our world have developed their own version of God's truth, they praise God while praying for His bountiful mercies and blessings. Their rituals have become essentially useless because they are meaningless. Meaningless repetitive praises continue to represent the bulk of modern worships in all religions, monotheist and polytheist alike.

2. Wrong thinking leads inevitably to wrongdoing

Adam and Eve also failed to recognize that it was their willful departure from right thinking that led them to misconduct. Instead of feeling guilty for their faulty thinking they felt guilty for their actions. Ultimately, it is not their actions that led humanity down the path of self-destruction; it was their faulty thinking that has been perpetuated ever since. Their faulty thinking was the result of an intentional shift of paradigm. They willfully replaced the brain mapping God had created in them with a flawed version. Taking the fruit only confirmed that they were already confused. They had already rationalized God's immutable rule of life founded on perfect love. Interestingly, the Tree was called the Tree of Knowledge of Good and Evil. When they found themselves standing by its side, the Tree should have been for them a glaring signpost telling them that they were in the process of mixing good and evil in their minds. It is this mixture that produced an inebriating cocktail of confusion. So lethal was the cocktail that God alone could have provided the antidote needed to neutralize the potion, and He still offers it freely to all people. By mixing "good," which is caring for others first, with "evil," which is a focus on the "me first" principle of life, the confusion of mind sent humanity into a tailspin that would remain forever irreparable without help from God.

Since they had been created perfect, the shift that occurred in Adam and Eve's minds was willful, thus their own fault. Having been created with a brain clearly polarized on thinking in terms of serving the welfare and well-being of others even when compelled to serve self, Adam and Eve failed to recognize the real nature of their culpability. They should have felt guilt for willfully accepting that their judgment was flawed because it was led by intentional illogical thinking designed to rationalize truth. All this rationalization was concocted to preserve their self-image otherwise called pride.

The problem Adam and Eve faced was that they only accepted to take responsibility for their acts of taking the fruit, not for accepting a thought process lacking the most basic ingredients of sound logic. As a result their minds became focused on actions alone, as though their mind-set, or faith, had been left unscathed. The foundations for self-righteousness also called righteousness by works were laid, and they have been solidly anchored in the human mind ever since. By focusing on their actions they turned everyone's attention away from their flawed rationale. They preferred to be blamed for a minor misdemeanor than to recognize a major flaw of discernment. Their approach to the problem of evil by abandoning God's pure logic could only aggravate the problem. Indeed, it caused them to become increasingly more focused on serving self at the expense of others. This lamentable mentality was vulgarized when "acting correctly" became the requirement to serve God in order to benefit from His blessings and salvation.

The mental departure from serving others to the new mental focus on self, produced the instantaneous destruction of mutual trust. In fact, this mind-shift necessitated self-reliance because all people had to be considered with the suspicion that they might also be self-serving. This human condition could only heighten both pride and distrust. Indeed, how can a person focused on serving self be trusted? At any junction of life that person could suddenly choose to serve his or her own interests at the expense of others. This modus operandi became the law of both humans and the jungle. It replaced the most fundamental principle of eternal life upon which God's realm was initially created. In scientific terms, it is called "the survival of the fittest."

Seduced by a way of life for which serving self had suddenly become the primary focus, Adam and Eve were led to believe that God was angry with them, not because they failed to think rationally, but because they took a fruit that belonged to Him. Their departure from God's principle of life was suddenly substituted by the idea that disobedience to a law of conduct was the problem, not their willful departure from a universal and immutable principle of life.

Indeed, the mind-set of unconditional altruism had suddenly been substituted by a sense of duty to perform, and performance had to be measurable on the scale of one's willingness to submit to the rules and will of higher authorities. It was no longer thinking rationally that was important; it was: Where do I rank in submitting to rules. The higher the rank, the greater the responsibilities offered by higher authorities, and the greater the rewards. The need to climb the ladder of social status gave rise to competition and a perpetual need for self-aggrandizement. What better way is there to feed pride? The focus was placed on what should be "done" to please others in order to gain recognition, not on what and how a person "ought to think" (faith) to be in harmony with God's perfectly logical principle of life.

Not only was a legal forensic system of behavioral control and government instituted, but a caste system was also needed to manage society. All this opened the door to various forms of competition and rivalry along with all the ills such a system of life could bring. Because of their newly developed legal outlook, misbehavior had to be sanctioned with appropriate punishment. Thus, like the devil, they began to perceive sin, not as a departure from right thinking, but as disobedience for which God was left with no choice other than to punish the offender. They viewed disobedience as a societal problem that required punishment. Instead they should have realized that all the consequences referred to as "curses" following the sin in Eden were in fact the natural consequences of departing from the only persuasion of heart that could have maintained life eternally. The "others first" paradigm of life had given way to the "me first" mind-set responsible for destroying mutual trust and freedom on the planet.

Religions today are still affected negatively by this mind-set

It could be said that in the image of Adam and Eve the religions of our world have been focused on curing the symptoms of the disease, not the disease itself. They all claim to deal with the problem of misconduct one way or another, rather than recognize God's cure for the disease. We live in a world where we want to control the actions of people rather than correcting the faulty rationale we all inherit at birth in an environment of distrust and self-protection. The problem is not in the DNA of the flesh we inherit; it is the egocentric thought process of self-protection. This state of mind we receive at birth needs to be reversed at all cost. Scripture claims the change possible and calls it the new birth. God's contribution is not mystical in this regard; that would be an imposition. With such an imposition freedom and logic could no longer be the standards by which truth can be recognized. God does not invade human freedom by using heavenly agents to produce a change of mind. Because "God is love" (1 Jn. 4:8), He would never use supernatural forces to impose a belief system or a code of conduct on anyone. The so-called action of the Holy Spirit is not what most Christians believe, as we shall see in a later chapter. God's contribution to the solution is offered as a purely logical approach to correct the problem of evil. If recognized and accepted, the path leads to God's truth that sets sinners free. Only an absolute truth can set us free. Jesus is "the way, the truth and the life" (Jn. 14:6). Indeed, He offers freely the way to the truth that gives life, and He paid the price of the Cross to bring it to our attention.

Adam and Eve's unwillingness to recognize guilt for faulty thought patterns was made manifest when they started to blame others for their deeds. Their unquenchable need to be right out of pride suddenly became untamable. Because Eve offered Adam the fruit he accused the woman God had created for him, declaring her responsible for leading him to the Tree. He was unwilling to recognize that his own mind-set had rejected sound logic. No self-admitted expression of wrong thinking appears in his dialogue with God, only a mere recognition of minor misconduct. Likewise, Eve's accusations implied that the Creator Himself was at fault for allowing the serpent to occupy a place in the Tree of Knowledge of Good and Evil (Gen. 3:12–13). Here again, the serpent may have encouraged the faulty mind-set, but the wrong thinking founded on self-gratification that led her to the Tree was her own irrational thinking for which the serpent cannot be blamed.

The text implies that both Adam and Eve agreed to portray God as the thoughtless One. Why did He bother to forbid the ingestion of a mere fruit in a paradise of plenty? They failed to recognize that their mental attitude was the problem. It was neither God's fault nor the devil's; it was the orientation of their desires to serve self without consideration of consequences that would affect all life on earth. Considering that they were blaming God for their actions, was it still possible for Adam and Eve to continue to trust Him fully? Or to trust one another? Or anyone else for that matter? Of course not! Even God had become their archenemy, un-admittedly perhaps, but this explains why they attempted to hide from Him and operate on the strength of their own rationale rather than God's.

Humanity has not changed since the days of Adam and Eve. In many houses of worship the nature of the theology presented portrays God, unwittingly perhaps, as autocratic, egomaniacal, and the commander in chief of the universe who gives orders while failing the most basic levels of common sense and compassion. Indeed, if listed, the religious beliefs of this world could produce a long list of strange acts and decisions falsely attributed to God. For now, let us just consider one: He is not only presented as having decided to kill all of humankind because Adam and Eve failed to obey, but He is also presented as having vowed to persecute forever or kill once for all those who fail to love Him upon His final Return. No wonder atheists refuse to believe in the God of Christians. Is it surprising that intelligent thinkers labor actively to strip religion out of public life?

The main concerns of most worshipers are with the actions God may choose to take for or against them. They worship Him to enjoy His blessings and to beg for grace in the face of punishment they falsely believe they deserve for their misconduct. They pray to avoid punishment while on earth, and salvation from eternal punishment after death. Christianity is far too concerned with how God deals with inadequate behavior and not nearly concerned enough with the cause of their inadequate behavior for which God offers the solution. But the change cannot take place without the correct knowledge and understanding of the only true God and His message that saves. God has gone out of His way to demonstrate that it is possible for a sinner to undergo a change of heart.

The majority of Christians simply assume without support from Scripture that God must act alone to displace evil in the universe. It is clear that left on its own, humanity would have never understood the principle of life that saves. This is why God had to communicate repeatedly through the ages the message of truth that saves, and finally once again for all times, at the price of the Cross. Jesus made it clear when He said: "Anyone who does not take his cross and follow me is not worthy of me" (Mt. 10:38). Does that sound like sinners have nothing to contribute to the fight against evil? What is the cross of which sinners are to accept the burden? Obedience? No, it is learning to think as Jesus did, and as God does, and as did Adam and Eve before they chose to depart from God's ways. The following statement would make this perfectly clear if it were translated correctly. From the NIV we read: "Whoever finds his life will lose it, and whoever loses his life for my sake will find it" (Mt. 10:39). The verb translated "finds" is the Greek *heuriskos*. Thus the text should have been translated to say: "Whoever strives to save his or her own life will lose it, and whoever does not, will find it." Indeed, focusing on serving others at the price of one's own life is the message of the Cross, as it should be the life and message of all those who claim the desire to follow Jesus. With this in mind, righteousness by faith should be understood as doing right by a strong belief (faith). And that belief is that we should love others, and even our enemies at any cost to us (Mt. 5:44).

3. Adam and Eve failed to side with God

No wonder Jesus advocated choosing God even over one's own family (Mt. 12:47–50). For Adam and Eve to choose one another over God was idolatrous thinking and behavior. Salvation is not a matter of choosing one person versus another; it is a matter of choosing the mind-set of God as communicated and demonstrated when Jesus revealed it in words and actions. Redemption is about regaining what was lost in Eden because it is the restoration of the image of God we lost when Adam and Eve sinned. The biggest loss was not the loss of life itself because of the "me first" mentality that destroyed trust; it was the loss of God's "others first" unconditional mind-set. Redemption is about healing the disease of evil in us by reestablishing the image of God's character in the human brain and heart.

As a matter of principle a person should never be rejected, not even an enemy, just as Jesus proclaimed (Mt. 5:44) and demonstrated all the way to the Cross (Lk. 23:34). Adam should have never felt that he was in a position to choose between Eve and God. Since he had the mind of Christ in him from Creation, he could have chosen to retain God's mind-set without having to reject Eve as a person. Rejecting the way a person thinks does not have to be a rejection of the person. An enemy is clearly a person who disagrees with us, but Jesus made it clear that we should love enemies just the same. Adam could have accepted God's mind-set without rejecting Eve as a person. This would have prompted him to be compassionate toward her as a person without accepting to share with her the self-serving mind-set she had just acquired. The problem was that Adam had already acquired the same mind-set as Eve. Thus intellectually he was in agreement with her, as they were both into self-gratification, including the way they valued their relationship with one another. That was idolatry.

What is wrong with idolatry? The problem is not just the worship aspect, or bowing before something or someone other than God; far more importantly, it is the endorsement of a modus operandi contrary to that of God. It implies rejecting the only way a free, intelligent individual can live eternally. Idolatry is always self-serving, even when all external manifestations may appear to be altruistic or motivated by one or another form of spirituality. Whatever is given to others or religiously practiced is exercised with expectation of benefits, thus it is neither true altruistic giving, nor godliness.

The problem is that even the word "worship" has been ascribed a pagan meaning. To worship God in truth is not a matter of praising Him or bowing before Him in prayers of thanksgiving and supplications. Nor should it be exercises in futility involving physical expressions of elation before the Almighty along with mindless executions of meaningless rituals. Anything said or done in worship that fails to motivate a change of heart that harmonizes with God's is not constructive worship that leads to salvation—therefore it is futile. Such worships are all about doing and very little about learning how and why a sinner must learn to think correctly. A church is both a school and a hospital, not a bar where people go to adulate and forget their troubles away.

To worship God means seeking to know Him for who He is, in truth, and to recognize that His character and modus operandi should also be that of the worshiper. Far too much emphasis is placed on what we like to call "having a relationship with God." Again, this is like the bar where people seek to forget their troubles by drinking and connecting frivolously with like people and calling it a relationship. Far too little emphasis is placed on knowing God in truth, His true nature, and the importance of recognizing His mind-set as entirely altruistic. All intelligent beings of the universe created in His image were created with His mind-set, but many failed to maintain His faith. It is for this reason that the universe is in a state of chaos, just as was planet Earth before God created human life (see Gen. 1:2). True worship is about relearning and reestablishing God's universal eternal truth from Him who is the source of truth that makes possible eternal life in true peace and freedom. It is precisely for this reason that the Almighty sent Jesus to bring it to our attention once again, but this time, He did it once for all (see Heb. 9:26).

Frédéric Zürcher

The idolatry of which Adam and Eve were guilty is precisely in the fact that though having a direct relationship with God and knowing Him in person as none of us have, they deliberately discarded the knowledge uploaded in their brains at Creation. They chose to supplant in their minds a flawed image of their Creator now perceived as One who punishes mistakes, not One who heals His wounded children. Worse yet, the flaws have morphed to the point of depicting God as a sort of monster that needs blood and death to be appeased. This is idolatry of the worst possible kind because it paints a picture of God that looks like the devil's. Knowing the future, God knew what He was talking about when He said to the Israelites: "You shall have no other gods before me. You shall not make for yourself an idol in the form of anything in heaven above or on the earth beneath or in the waters below. You shall not bow down to them or worship them; for I am the Lord your God, and am a jealous God . . ." (Ex. 20:3–5). This commandment includes all physical images that could be made and worshiped along with all false mental images of God humans produce in their sick, rationalizing minds. Only the true reality of God should ever be considered, contemplated, and mentally assimilated, because it is the only image capable of healing the sin disease. An image that makes God look like a monster willing to think illogically or lacking love is the purest form of idolatry. It is the image the devil wants humans to keep in mind and worship. What a tragedy!

By bonding with one another, Adam and Eve removed themselves from the only source of truth that could make eternal life possible for them and their descendants. They became one another's personal possession as well as one another's gods. Though created to be one another's helpmates united in the purpose of perpetrating God's modus operandi in a groaning universe (Rom. 8:22), they abandoned the cosmic mission for which they were created to help God reestablish peace and order in a universe in chaos. Indeed, as far as Hubble's Telescope can reach, there is evidence of chaos, the kind of chaos God talks about when He came to this planet to create humans.

Indeed, the devil was already in the universe and may have been there for a very long time. Adam and Eve must have been aware of this fact or they would not have been instructed not to approach the Tree of Confusion. Having both departed from God's way of life, Adam and Eve bonded to one another for the sake of survival that could only bring death, not for the sake of eternal life in a new eternal

32

universe yet to be re-created. Their association with one another was no longer founded on mutual service and gift of self to the other, but on the selfish and egocentric motivations to use one another to fulfill their personal ambitions and purposes. A long-held tradition of humans is founded on conventional wisdom that says, "If you give me I give you." It is a mentality that has ruined the world because it has destroyed unconditional benevolence and depicted the only true God as having the same mentality—perfect idolatry that God despises.

We must remember that God's original universe could not have been the universe as we see it today through Hubble's Telescope or as Adam and Eve could see it when they were created. Even scientists agree that planet Earth is a rare if not unique exception in a universe of chaos. Why is there so much chaos throughout the visible space of the universe? If God is perfect as Scripture describes Him, He must have created a perfect universe where supernovas do not explode, meteorites and meteors do not threaten life, and tectonic plates remain stable and unbroken. Yet before Creation, God declared our planet a place of chaos (Gen. 1:2). If the universe is not perfectly safe, it is clearly not because God created it unsafe as we see it; it is because the very powerful intelligent beings He created and for whom the entire universe was their "Garden of Eden," chose to depart from the way of life God had offered them—we call them angels. Like humans since the departure from Eden, their struggle to survive has become destructive and violent. God does not change (Heb. 1:10–12; 13:8; Is. 40:8), therefore God's universe, His Kingdom, was originally conceived on the principle of unconditional concern for the welfare and well-being of others before self. This is the kind of universe God wants to reestablish. Jesus Himself made that clear, when speaking of the universe He said: "Until heaven and earth disappear, not the smallest letter, not the least stroke of a pen, will by any means disappear from the Law until everything is accomplished" (Mt. 5:18). We shall discuss later what yet remains to be accomplished.

Possessions are things we hoard. When Adam and Eve chose to become one another's possessions they reduced the value of life to the value of things we hoard. The fundamental principle of love that engenders respect was lost. It is not a principle of the kingdom of heaven, because perfect love produces unhindered mutual respect and benevolence toward others. With true love in the heart, respect is spontaneously natural, not dutiful, nor imposed or sanctioned by laws of civility. With a system established on possessions was also born the notion of fences, walls, and borders, all of which are erected to divide rather than to unite the human family God created to be one in spirit and mentality, though infinite in individuality, that is, in the way each one of us chooses to express unconditional love.

Religions today are still affected negatively by this mind-set

Christian churches today have fallen into a similar pattern of idolatry. Instead of relying on God for answers, they rely on hierarchical, administrative, religious, and secular systems that only serve to perpetuate traditions responsible for mistaken views of God and salvation. They rely on human authorities such as priests, pastors, or gurus to tell them what to do or what not to do, but not so much to tell them the way they should think to be in harmony with the only true God of the universe. Many are those who adhere to a religion or theology because they admire a spiritual leader and his or her views. "If it is good enough for them," they say, "it is good enough for me." The problem with such an attitude is that they are often told what to do and how to live, but not how to think in a way that honors God and the reason for which He created each one of us.

A woman at the well of Jacob said to Jesus (Jn. 4:20), "Our fathers worshiped on this mountain, but you Jews claim that we must worship in Jerusalem." A study of the answer Jesus gave her shows that it is neither where we worship nor what we do to worship God that is important. He told her that we must worship God in the spirit of truth (see Jn. 4:24)—which is the spirit of welfare and well-being of others before our own, always and unconditionally. To worship God means seeking every avenue there is to know Him for who He is "in truth," and recognize in His modus operandi the only way for us to live eternally. We can no longer afford to intellectually and spiritually walk north and south at the same time. When split about where to draw the line between "me first" and "others first" we are intellectually trying to walk in two opposite directions at the same time.

This is the mistake Adam and Eve made, and ironically, this was also the mistake the Children of Israel made at the beginning of their journey out of Egypt. They were quick to tell Moses: "We will *do* everything the LORD has said" (Ex. 19:8, emphasis added). They wanted God to tell them what to do. Instead, they should have listened to Him that they might learn from Him how to think rationally about religion. Doing what we are told to do does not change the way we think. In fact, doing what we are told places the burden and responsibility of thinking rationally on others. It is for this reason that humans fail all too often to think in terms of what is best for the well-being of the entire universe, not just for their personal and private lives. It is interesting that as much as humans claim to love freedom they tend to have a preference for submitting to the authority of others. This mentality can only lead to loss of freedom. Instead, we should all learn from God how to think rationally in order to enjoy true and perfect freedom.

The Role of the Devil

As did Eve in the Garden, religious organizations are far too eager to blame the devil for all the ills of the world. When the story of what happened in Eden is read with an open mind, it is clear that the devil was not directly responsible for changing the mind-sets of Adam and Eve. He merely contributed to reinforce the "me first" mentality that was burgeoning in their minds. Insidiously he managed to steer them in the wrong direction by nurturing their ego and sense of self-reliance.

1. A mindless question unrelated to the real problem

The devil is credited for having deceived Eve, even in the NT. Paul said that he was "afraid that just as Eve was deceived by the serpent's cunning, your minds may somehow be led astray from your sincere and pure devotion to Christ" (2 Cor. 11:3). Notice Paul's concern for the "minds" of his converts. He was afraid that their minds might be tainted by corrupted messages, just as was the mind of Eve with the serpent. The first thing the devil did was to ask Eve a rather mindless question: Did God really say that you should not eat from some Tree in the Garden (Gen. 3:1)? The question to which they all knew the answer was merely rhetorical. It was intended to get Eve thinking about the irrationality of God for imposing such a ridiculous prohibition. In reality God was not trying to prevent Adam and Eve from going to the Tree or to eat of its fruit, He was offering them a tangible signpost to guard them from yielding to wrong thinking. By His grace God had given them a last chance to recognize a glaring sign that they were on the wrong path. Straying toward that Tree was an indication that they were departing from their intrinsic built-in devotion to unconditional altruism. It was a sign that their departure from the way of life was about to reach the point of no return. Unfortunately, even if they recognized the signpost they clearly failed to heed its message. This was made evident when the serpent began to talk.

Had Adam and Eve remained faithful to their built-in principle of life founded on unconditional dedication to the welfare and well-being of others, they would have never erred near the Tree in the first place. Having full access to the food and beauty of all the other trees of the Garden, the only reason for going near that Tree was to gratify a personal egocentric pleasure—no other reason. As we have mentioned, the least level of egocentrism opens the door to distrust, and this is the problem that would bring death on a planet where unconditional trust had to be maintained to enjoy eternal life in peace, safety, prosperity, and perfect freedom.

In His grace God has also given us signs to behold, that we might know when we depart from His way of life. Each of the Ten Commandments is such a sign. They are not intended to enforce or forbid actions; they are intended to help us learn how to think correctly. When we approach one of those signposts we should ask ourselves why we are about to do this or that and how could such an action be hurtful to others and why am I thinking about doing this? Is it to serve my selfish desires or is it about the welfare and well-being of others?

Religions today are still affected negatively by this mind-set

The theology of Christian churches is often concerned with mindless questions that detract from the real problem and the questions we should ask God about His plan of salvation—not the devil's. Why did Jesus come to this world? We immediately think that it was to forgive the sinful acts of humans, but think again, it was to help sinful humans to think differently, or rationally, that they might overcome sin or anything that could be hurtful to others. Only a new birth of the mind and heart can produce such a change in our thought patterns, and only if exposed to the light that comes from the Word of God. "There is only one way to heaven," said Jesus: "I am the way and the truth and the life. No one comes to the Father except through me" (Jn. 14:6). Indeed, as John puts it in the first chapter of his Gospel, Jesus is the Logos, that is, the Word of God we might also call the visible expression of God. In fact, He is the last Word of God. His life has everything to do with a change of mind that changes the heart, not a focus on forgiveness of sins that can only turn our thoughts toward self. All the churches and religions of this world talk about love, but how many of them say that the key to become loving is to change the egocentric mind-set of our birth by adopting the other-centric mind-set of Jesus? They are more likely to say that Jesus came to die to forgive sin, than to provide us with the truth that changes hearts that we might overcome the evil in us that produces sin.

2. "You will not surely die"

Once near the Tree, the serpent assured Eve that eating the fruit would not cause death (Gen. 3:4). Unfortunately, the devil was absolutely right. Yes, it is not because Adam and Eve ate the fruit that they died of old age nearly a thousand years later, it was because they had cultivated an egocentric mind-set. This acquired mind-set gave rise to self-protection and survival at any cost to other form of life, which destroyed trust and life. With such a mind-set it is logically impossible to expect life to go on eternally. All the natural impulses of God's created perfect nature was to offer services to other life. But unfortunately, God's formula was reversed. An egocentric mind-set produces inevitable death, which is all that God was trying to warn His children about. God was not telling Adam and Eve, "If you disobey I will surely punish you with death." He said: "If you adopt egocentricity as a way of life, death will become inevitable. And the fact that you have gone down that road will be made manifest if you ever eat fruit from that Tree." The law of the jungle has fully demonstrated that all forms of life on our planet have adopted Adam and Eve's egocentric way of life that leads to inevitable death—all that, not because they ate a fruit, but because trust was destroyed for all forms of life on the planet. The law of survival became the rule that kills.

It appears that all religions of our world have come to the conclusions that acts of disobedience have brought death by punishment. In reality, the way we think is the root cause of all pain and suffering in our world. By considering the act rather than the mind-set as being the culprit, all efforts to control society are focused on changing the way people act, as opposed to how they think. This error in dealing with evil has not only perpetrated wrongful acts, but also a totally false theology of salvation. Since falsehood has many facets, we have thousands of religions; all of them focused on providing people with the assurance of supernatural clemency and pardon without addressing the root cause of the problem or its solution.

Religions today are still affected negatively by this mind-set

Yet another pagan understanding was derived from the devil's allegations. Though God made it clear that Adam and Eve would die if they allowed their thinking to go down the wrong path, most religious organizations of our world teach that people cross over to another form of life after death. Thus, as the devil promised, no one really dies; their spirit goes on living in another realm. By thinking that there is no real death people are led to treat rather carelessly the statements of Scripture regarding sin, salvation, eternal life, and eternal death.

3. "Your eyes will be opened, and you will be like God"

Perhaps the most devastating pagan concept introduced by the devil was his last piece of advice to Adam and Eve. Indeed, the first suggestion of superstition was insidiously introduced in the minds of Adam and Eve. The serpent said: "God knows that when you eat of it your eyes will be opened, and you will be like God, knowing good and evil" (Gen. 3:5). Like magic, eating the fruit would accomplish something totally unrelated to the action and would bring amazing enlightenment and powers. It is like rubbing a ball of crystal to be enlightened; there is no relationship between the crystal and the potential for enlightenment.

The serpent offered the fruit as a miraculous potion that would serve people already in perfect health in a Garden where nothing was missing to bring them happiness. The devil offered the potion as if being created in the image of God was not good enough. Somehow this potion would improve on the perfection God had created in them because it would provide them with better vision and greater powers they did not need. What the serpent suggested was poison for the mind. Again, a mindless action was associated to unrelated expectations, which is what superstitions are all about. The concept is common to all the religions of our world today. If you do this or that, if you pray this way or that way, if you eat the wafer and drink the wine turned to blood, you have nothing to fear. Clearly, the devil's suggestion to eat a fruit could not suddenly produce supernatural effects. Shattering trust as the rule of life had immediate devastating effects, but not eating a fruit from a Garden God created.

Religions today are still affected negatively by this mind-set

This is superstition at its best! The devil was injecting in the brains of our first parents the notion that it was perfectly normal to expect unrealistic advantages from doing something unrelated to the expectation. Such superstitions are as pervasive in Christianity as they are in pagan religions. We have all heard preachers say that the blood of Jesus was a payment for sins. The problem is that no amount of blood unto death can pay for sins. Paying to obtain a favor is bribery or prostitution for which both parties are guilty of wrongdoing; it is never a solution. Yet the idea of the Cross as payment for sins is fundamental to Christianity despite the fact that Scripture does not sustain the concept.

Let us not be mistaken about that; however, it is clear that Jesus came and that His purpose for coming was entirely related to sin. He went all the way to His death to address the problem of evil that causes sin. However, believing that He came to die in order to pay for sins is not only accusing God of bribery, it is also idolatrous and superstitious. How can doing anything absolve sin? The Cross is a message (1 Cor. 1:18) not an action called a payment. If the Cross were a "paid in full" bill of sale, it would be a fact, not a message. The word "Gospel" comes from the Greek word *euangelion* that means Good Message, not good fact. The proclamation of a good fact would be an announcement, but the proclamation of a good message conveys useful information. Why did Jesus call sinners to seek His truth and the knowledge of God if the mere belief in a fact at the Cross were sufficient "faith" to gain salvation?

Preachers should say that Jesus came to deal with the problem of evil by teaching and showing how to overcome the problem all the way to His death. Indeed, His death provides the clincher in God's plan of salvation. Jesus paid the ultimate price of His life. There is no question about that, but not to pay for sins; it was to provide humanity with the message of truth that gives life in its fullness for eternity. Had Jesus failed to go all the way to His death, His message would have been incomplete. The most important element of the truth He came to share with the world would have been missing. He was teaching us what love is, how to love, and how much to love. That last element would have been missing, though it was the most significant piece of information He gave us. Love does not discriminate; even the enemy who places the innocent on a Cross deserves to be loved. Accepting the tyranny and abuses from unloving people is a demonstration of what love is. But how much we should love is clarified once for all: True love is manifested unconditionally all the way to the last drop of blood and the last breath of life. What a message!

The formula for salvation Jesus provided is entirely about learning how to think correctly that we might have a chance to act correctly. It is having "the mind of Christ" (1 Cor. 2:16) also called "the faith of Jesus" (Gal. 3:22 KJV). It must be noted that the Greek should definitely be translated "the faith of Jesus," as in the King James Version, not "the faith *in* Jesus," as most modern translations render the text. It is indeed the belief system *of* Jesus that sinners must acquire if they are sincere about overcoming evil. No other faith or belief system can accomplish the purpose of overcoming evil.

The Generation of Cain

The second generation was that of Cain and Abel. While Abel understood that the slaughtering ritual was intended to sear in the mind the importance of undergoing a change of heart and mind capable of changing behavior, Cain contributed two additional faulty views of God and His message. As were the faulty attitudes of Adam and Eve exacerbated by the devil, the faulty and destructive attitudes of Cain were also passed on to future generations. They have impacted negatively all the religions and mentalities of our world. Cain's contributions to the distortion of God and of His message include the following:

1. He would rather pay a penalty than to accept a change of heart

When Cain decided to build an altar he was clearly demonstrating his willingness to recognize some level of misconduct before God and fellow humans—building an altar was a public deed and the slaughter ritual involved a confession. For some reason human pride makes it easier to acknowledge misconduct than faulty thinking. With such an attitude there was total failure on Cain's part to recognize that unconditional love, which is an attitude of mind and heart, is the only absolute moral guide of life. Instead of seeking love Cain chose to build an altar on which he placed produce grown at the sweat of his face. This was an attempt on his part to appease those who were offended by his misconduct while refusing to let go of his pride. Recognizing publicly that something might be wrong with his mind and heart was too hard for his pride to consider. He viewed his sin as a minor error of conduct, not a lack of love in his heart.

There is no reason to believe that God intended the sacrificial ritual to be a confession of misconduct, but it is quite clear that He wanted it to be a confession of flawed mind and heart. Flawed conduct is quite obvious and more readily accepted as a problem. We all make mistakes. Flawed thought patterns are always the problem so why not deal with the root-cause of the problem rather than its symptoms? What good does it do to correct conduct considering that flawed thinking was responsible for conduct needing to be changed? God knows that better than anyone else, because He created us. Thus the ritual was intended to help sinners renew their dedication to God's everlasting principle of life, which is all about the way we think, our faith. The ritual was not instituted to obtain forgiveness by somehow paying a price for mistakes of the past. Nor was it intended to provide the assurance that those mistakes would someday be paid for by someone else, a few thousand years down the road.

It would have been pointless for Cain to build an altar if he did not recognize that something was wrong in his life. The problem once again is that he focused on his actions rather than on his thinking. Most humans are willing to recognize at least some of their misdeeds, but how they choose to deal with the problem makes all the difference between God's way of handling the problem of evil and the way the false religions of our world attempt to deal with sin.

Trying to change the way we act is never the solution because it is never possible to change the way we act without first changing the cause of the misconduct—a flawed heart. Trying hard *to behave* in more acceptable ways implies concern over what others think of us, not so much what we are in the depth of our hearts regardless of what others think. Thinking differently is the only way to change behavior, but such a change has to involve becoming more like God who loves unconditionally, or nothing has changed.

It is clear that Cain was seeking some kind of resolution and acceptance, or his attempt to practice the ritual would have been futile. We may ask however, was it the acceptance of God Cain was seeking, or was it the acceptance of his fellow humans? If it were to be accepted of humans it might have been an effort to safeguard his reputation and pride. Instead of listening to God's way of dealing with evil Cain attempted to satisfy the scales of human systems of justice: he was willing to pay the price of a penalty for his misconduct. In his attempt to gain acceptance Cain failed to contemplate God's provision to change a sinner's attitudes. In fact, a payment for offences committed resolves nothing. Only a change of heart recognized to be a requirement to avoid perpetuating evil is a viable solution; thus it is the only salvation because it changes hearts, not because it expunges sin.

Heeding God's message of truth would have made all the difference in Cain's life as well as in the lives of countless others. For every sinner who repents by accepting a change of heart, countless others benefit from the change. Listening to God's suggested approach to the problem with an open heart would have made it possible for Cain to undergo the required change of heart. Payments or penalties for misdeeds are merely a human invention designed to appease both the victims' anger and the sinners' guilt without having to undergo a change of heart (see Gen. 4:3–5). God's approach to the problem would have cost Cain nothing, and the change of heart would have motivated a change of behavior for the rest of his life here on earth and for eternity. Indeed, salvation should be understood as God's way to heal the sin disease, not an act to pardon or acquit offenders. The cure is free (see Eph. 2:8–9). It is a matter of accepting God's cure, because all the other ways are bound to fail—they are all idolatrous beliefs and practices that solve nothing.

It is interesting to consider how we deal with behavioral problems today. All the courts of our world have adopted Cain's system of satisfying the so-called balance of justice. The system applies a penalty to wrongdoers in proportion with the seriousness of the infraction made to codes of conduct. With this system, deeds are punished while faulty mind-sets are left unaffected. As a result humans all over the globe focus on avoiding misdeeds, not the faulty mind-sets that causes them. Payments or penalties are mistakenly believed to reset the balance of justice, but such punishments accomplish little or nothing. How can the balance of justice be reset for a murderer? Even the ultimate penalty falls far short of restoring justice.

It is never possible to reset the balance of justice by punishing or making someone pay a penalty; no price paid could ever bring a murderer's victim back to life. Yet all the courts of our world have adopted Cain's method of dealing with the problems of evil. Such methods of dealing with evil are merely attempts to dissuade people from *doing* something wrong by avoiding punishment but accomplish little or nothing to change the hearts of wrongdoers. Such legal measures only provide a Band-Aid approach to evil—it hides the problem but has no power to heal. It may hide the faulty thinking but fails entirely to treat the way a person thinks. In fact, humans have become so accustomed to dealing with evil by enforcing laws and attributing penalties that they have come to believe God operates and deals with humans in a similar fashion. They perceive God as eager to punish misconduct and requiring "fair" penalties to reset the balance of justice. The problem is that such methods to deal with evil do not come from God. In fact, Scripture is clear to show that God never wanted such a method to deal with evil, as our study will show.

Religions today are still affected negatively by this mind-set

The religious establishments of our world all believe that payments of one kind or another are necessary to restore the balance of justice. Some religions, including segments of Christianity, make sure sinners are obligated to pay up through sacrifices, payment in money, or other deeds. The rest of Christianity is persuaded that humans are too sinful to pay the infinite price God requires for their sins. Without support from Scripture they conclude that Christ came primarily to make the payment on their behalf on the Cross, and they call believing this travesty, righteousness by faith. We shall see that in God's Book salvation has nothing to do with penalties or payments of any kind. In fact, laws and penalties can only be counterproductive.

The grace of God is indeed infinite; it requires no payment to save anyone, not even a payment on the Cross. The Cross was indeed a huge price for Jesus to pay, but it was not to pay for the sins of the world; it was to provide increased clarity for sinners, that they might overcome sin, not excuse it. Did Jesus die for our sins (Rom. 4:25)? Indeed He did, but again, it was not to pay for them. It was to show the way to overcome sin, which is through the sinner's willingness to undergo a change of heart. The change is not instantaneous; the process of overcoming evil is as progressive as the growth of a tree, but in God's eyes the overcomer is as perfect as a tree at every stage of its development and as long as it continues to grow. Otherwise, like a tree, failing to grow leads to death.

2. A judicial system cannot improve a person's character

When Cain realized that God was serious about refusing to accept his offer to pay a price with an offering of propitiation (peace offering) to settle his offences, he began to fear for his life (Gen. 4:13–14). Indeed, Cain recognized that evil must be discouraged in a world where there is lack of trust and where evil reigns, but the method he chose was unacceptable to God only because it could not logically achieve the intended purpose. Payments for misdeeds accomplish nothing, and God knew it. How could God approve a method to overcome evil that does not work? In fact, Cain proved almost immediately to the universe that his approach was futile; he killed his brother. Since Cain was unwilling to consider God's prescription to overcome evil, he was left with no choice other than to establish a judicial system of his own invention whereby he intended to prove that paying for offences works, but thousands of years later humanity continues to demonstrate that it does not work.

God's fail-safe way to overcome the problem of evil by recognizing one's need to undergo a change of heart was discarded by Cain and all his followers. If Cain's approach to resolving the problem of evil had been acceptable to God, he, *as a person,* would have been approved by God. Cain would not have been rejected because God's formula would have produced the change of behavior possible only through a change of heart. No threat of punishment, penalty, payment, jail sentence, or capital punishment can change a person's heart.

Translations of the question God asked Cain generally read as follows: "If you do what is right, will you not be accepted?" (Gen. 4:7). We must note a subtle problem with this translation. The word translated with the verb "to do" is in fact the Hebrew verb *yatâb,* or "to be." Thus God would have said: "If you *are* what is right, will you not be accepted?" For a person *to be* what is right implies that the person is thinking correctly, logically. Indeed, a person who fails to think rationally can only fail to act accordingly. Thinking in logical terms is an absolute condition to achieve success. If the goal is to overcome evil, only a perfectly logical approach based on immutable truth should be considered. It is a condition for being right in order to do what is right. The purpose of the slaughter ritual (not an offering) was entirely intended to help a sinner recognize the need for a change of heart, not a payment for wrongdoing, nor a ritual to look forward to the day when Jesus would pay the required price. Salvation never comes at a price; it comes as the result of a changed heart. Since Cain was never instructed to practice a ritual involving a payment, God made it clear to him that sin is not what a person *does* or fails to *do*, it is about what a person fails *to be* because of his or her unwillingness to recognize the need for a change of heart, not a change of action. A change of action that is not the product of a changed heart is hypocritical in nature. Once corrupted and perceived as an offering, the slaughter ritual could no longer accomplish the purpose for which God intended. What's more, because the corruption of the ritual involved a departure from basic logic it could never accomplish God's intended purpose. The vital message from God was destroyed and the symbolism involved could no longer convey vital truth that saves by healing the sin diseases.

It is also important to notice that it was not the object placed on the altar of the ritual God disapproved; it was Cain himself. The disapproval of Cain was not a rejection of Cain; as the context of the story clearly indicates, it was a disapproval of his corrupted state of mind that could no longer keep him on God's side. God rejected Cain's mind-set, not Cain. God said to him, "If you *are* what is right, will *you*, as a person willing to think rationally, not be accepted?" It was the state of Cain's heart that was unacceptable to God, not Cain. His corrupted state of mind and heart could not possibly overcome evil.

Cain was not interested in God's advice. Pride had already taken residence in his heart to such a point that it became impossible for him, as a person, to accept God's advice. He knew better than God, or so he thought, on the strength of his flawless pride (Gen. 4:13–14), but not on the strength of his flawless logic. It is quite apparent from this account that Cain established the foundations of a judicial system that placed the blame entirely on people's actions, not on their state of mind or heart. His system of social control we now call government was based on the rule of law with its enforcement and penalties. It is the system that became the standard of social control in the city he built (Gen. 4:17).

Circumstantial evidence attests to this fact considering that all the cities of our world have adopted his system of rules and enforcement through penalties. In fact, the motivation to build cities was a response to the need to circumvent the absence of mutual trust through jurisprudence. Failure to trust humans and wild animals forced people to agglomerate in protected cities. Within their walls rigorous systems of laws enforced by punishment had to be established to deal with lawbreakers.

The cities and nations of our world represent the full spectrum of religions and systems of government. Yet without exception, they all maintain order on Cain's assumption that laws have the power to legislate behavior through enforcement and penalties. The word "justice" in the vocabulary of all human languages bears a meaning totally different from God's meaning. Humans look at justice as getting even with wrongdoers. Lady Justice is portrayed as a blindfolded woman holding a scale and a sword. The pictogram represents impartial and fair assessment of wrongdoing and the appropriation of fair punishment. God's justice would have to be represented by a pictogram showing the transformation of wrongdoers whose hearts have become just or righteous, thanks to a powerful persuasion.

This is because we are all born with the propensity to serve self, but let us remember that the propensity to serve self is not a sin unless it is nurtured without concern for the welfare and well-being of others. Only the truth from God has the persuasive power to help us change. A person born with the instinct of survival can only change that pervasive instinct to become altruistic by learning from God how to think differently. The natural instinct has to be overruled by a disposition of mind willing to recognize the only truth that is capable of making eternal life possible. The natural birth instinct of survival must yield to the unnatural instinct of caring for others first and foremost at any cost to self. That message of Jesus is the central message of the Cross. He went all the way to His death to make sure we got the message in its absolute fullness.

Laws sometimes keep people in line, but they lack the power to change the human heart. Some people follow laws to preserve their reputation as good citizens; others do it out of fear of getting caught and punished. Indeed, a person can be a "good" law-abiding citizen without necessarily having a good heart. Since only the acceptance of God's message of life can accomplish a real change of a person, God alone can be credited for the change. If accepted, His message persuades the sinner to accept what Scripture calls a "born again" experience that gives new direction to life. So incredible is the change that it might as well be called a miracle because without God both the idea and the method by which a human heart is changed would elude us. Neither could have germinated in a fallen human mind; therefore, we are entirely dependent on God for our salvation.

The history of our world bears proof of the fact that humans could not have elaborated the persuasive message or the methodology required to make a change of heart possible. The future of our world will continue to bear that out. For a long time humans have been aware that survival favors the fittest. It is assumed that it is the way of our world as it is the way of nature and that it has always been that way. But it is falsely assumed that no other system has ever maintained social order in the universe. The Apostle Paul sees it otherwise: "No eye has seen, no ear has heard, no mind has conceived what God has prepared for those who love him" (1 Cor. 2:9; Is. 64:4). This text should probably be translated to say: "No human mind has ever conceived what God has prepared for those *who love as He does.*" What God is preparing for us is to reestablish the way the universe used to operate before sin broke down trust in the cosmos. The original system was and will again be entirely founded on loving others with God's kind of unconditional love. This can be accomplished only by seeking His kind of heart on the strength of the only methodology available to restore sinners back to His image. The methodology will be discussed later but this is what salvation is all about: The restoration of God's character in the hearts of sinners. Only a religion founded on God's everlasting message of truth can change the minds and hearts of sinners to make possible the enjoyment of a universe where everyone loves as He does.

Religions today are still affected negatively by the mind-set of survival

The churches and religions of this world all teach love. Even the most pagan religions encourage more loving attitudes. But what kind of love do they encourage? Is it the kind that emanates from a changed heart, or is it love as it is imposed on people by the standards of their religion or culture? Indeed, standards of what love is or should be can vary widely. For some, love means killing others to impose a religious ideology. Many are willing to accept such standards of misguided love because it provides them prestige, recognition, and higher social status in their environment. God offers us not only a clear definition of what true love is and how to love, but He has also provided the process that brings it into the human heart against all odds. Religions do not underline the process, and they often fail to define the word "love" as does God.

Nothing Has Changed in Our Old World

An assessment of the above human failures to conform to God's thinking can only confirm that not much has changed in our religious and secular world, at least, not in terms of improving human character. Both our religious and secular ideologies are flawed because they are all more concerned with people's actions than the flawed thinking responsible for their misdeeds. We reward good behavior and achievements with ovations, medals, and other honors, and we snub, rebuff, and punish undesirable behavior. The former builds pride that should be shunned, the latter gets even by punishing, but neither improves the human condition. To add insult to injury, the laws of the land and most religious organizations accept the idea that rendering evil for evil is perfectly acceptable. They totally ignore several statements of Jesus, who said among others: "Do not resist an evil person. If someone strikes you on the right cheek, turn to him the other also" (Mt. 5:39).

Paul echoes the Master saying: "Do not repay anyone evil for evil" (Rom. 12:17). Life in the world as we know it is all about what we do and accomplish, not so much about what and how we think. An evaluation of modern Christianity on the basis of the teachings of Jesus and the Apostles would find all denominations guilty of pagan practices and beliefs. With the exception of a few forward theologians and thinkers who have expressed concerns about some of these attitudes, mainstream religions do not recognize them as problematic and even endorse most of them. This may well be a strong statement but the development that follows should shed some light. In fact, it is sad to note that Christian religions have essentially found ways to integrate very damaging pagan outlooks in their theology of salvation.

Scripture makes it very clear that God cannot condone these views because they fail to cure the root cause of evil. Interestingly, despite the fact that a vast segment of Christianity claims to no longer be under the law but under grace, as Paul affirms (Rom. 6:14–15), they are all in favor of having strong legal systems. They all endorse the application of forensics principles of fairness and justice. Somehow, they have managed to rationalize that they are not under the law but that God is under the law and that He made Jesus pay the penalty for sins. On the other hand, though many Christians claim to be free from laws in their religious life, they remain entirely dependent on the rule of law to control human behavior in their daily lives—as are all Jews, Muslims, pagans, and unbelievers. In fact, the legal systems of monotheist religions are often treated with greater veneration because they are viewed as divinely appointed.

Christianity tries to have it both ways. By creating a separation between their secular and religious lives they apply the rule of law in their secular life while claiming freedom from observing divine laws in their religious lives. There is a strange contradiction however; while they claim to be under no legal system from God, they apply to God the very forensic rationale of their secular legal systems. This should be called profane, not secular. They teach that in His dealings with evil, God is quick to establish justice by way of punishment, discipline, and even killing the unworthy if necessary. The well-known series titled *Left Behind* by Tim Lahaye paints a grim picture of God in this regard. When God eventually decides to end evil, He causes unspeakable chaos on planet Earth when He recalls His own to heaven. The scenario is not biblical, nor does it represent God or His character in a loving light. Evil will ultimately cause the chaos at the end of time, not God.

We have all heard the rants of some church leaders who accuse the lifestyles of some as causing God's anger punishing the world with cataclysmic events. They go so far as to say that on the day of His Judgment God will kill the wicked in a lake of fire, or that He will roast them in everlasting torment. Is there a way to make God look worse or more violent and cruel? Though they represent only about one-third of the world's population the Christianized nations have created more laws and penal codes than the rest of the world combined.

Human Flesh Traditionally Blamed for the Problem of Evil

A terrible misconception has occurred regarding the problem of evil. Much of it is still blamed on the material nature of human flesh. It is also for this reason that many Christian theologians claim that the flesh of Jesus was unlike that of humans. They postulate that if His flesh was identical that of humans He would have sinned like the rest of us. They argue that because He was born without the intervention of a human father His flesh was of a different nature. This assumption denies clear statements of Scripture while at the same time it implies that Jesus had an unfair advantage in overcoming evil. If this were true, the purpose of His mission could not have been to show humanity that evil can be overcome. If His death was the capital punishment humans deserve to appease the Father, there is no reason to believe that He came to show the way to overcome sin, He came merely to pay the price the Father required. With this view the death of Jesus is believed to pardon the shortcomings caused by human flesh and to acquit sinners.

Such an approach to religion conveys the notion that overcoming evil is of secondary importance in God's plan of salvation. It is an approach whereby salvation is viewed as a mere commercial transaction in which God wants a perfect human to die for the sake of legal fairness as a price paid for the sins of the world. No human father would require such payment, especially not a payment made at the expense of an innocent life that must be mutilated to acquit the guilty. On the other hand, the idea of overcoming evil is treated as impossible to accomplish in this life because we are made of material flesh. In this way God is presented as the One who takes responsibility both for the problem of evil and for its resolution through a payment of acquittal.

When it is assumed that God accomplished His purpose by sending His Son to pay for the sins of the world, false readings or false translations of key texts are generally offered as evidence. Such is the case of a passage in John's first letter where he writes: "He is the atoning sacrifice for our sins, and not only for ours but also for the sins for the whole world" (1 Jn. 2:2). With such a reading modern Christianity portrays God as taking full responsibility for the problem of evil while refusing the participation of sinners for its resolution. In their minds the participation of humans would be righteousness by works, not by faith. However, considering that free beings have strayed voluntarily from God's modus operandi, how can they return freely to a correct approach to the sin problem without the full participation of their free will? God's least interference with human free will would be a restriction of freedom, a privilege He has granted intelligent beings unconditionally for eternity.

While it is true that humans are powerless to resolve the problem of evil on their own, it is also true that it cannot be done without their participation. On the other hand, human participation should not be expected to be achievable on the level of their actions but on the level of rational thinking. Doing right on the basis of love resulting from rational thinking is righteousness by faith. However, doing right on the basis of correcting actions lacking love is righteousness by works. Thinking like God is impossible without a clear understanding of truth related to eternal life. When a sinner begins to think like God he or she is beginning to develop the faith that saves. Any other faith is powerless to accomplish the purpose. When human flesh is considered responsible for misdeeds, the need to acquire the ability to think like God on the basis of a correct understanding of His message becomes pointless. Thus His message can be dismissed on the grounds that we cannot help our condition. With this view we are and will remain as "filthy rags" (Is. 64:6) as long as we live, and there is nothing we can do about it, except wait for our death or the apocalyptic day of the return of Jesus.

Naively, and perhaps because of traditions, God is blamed for having made human flesh out of raw materials found in the dust of the earth (Gen. 2:7). It has been assumed for millennia that matter is unfit to produce a perfect being because such a being would have to be partially materialistic in his or her makeup, and thus powerless to ever become entirely spiritual. This thinking is related to a long-held philosophical debate called dualism. It involves a perceived struggle between mind and matter. It is for this reason that for centuries, official Christianity has considered human beings as victims chained to a material world by their malevolent material bodies. Thus it was taught that humans should be eager to shed their physical makeup by accepting to die at war in defense of the Lord's church. Death was believed to release their spirits eager to escape the bondages of their material bodies. This destructive mentality has produced the worst filth, diseases, as well as the shortest lifespans ever known to humanity. This period of history is sometimes referred to as the Dark Ages. Additionally, it is a philosophy that has opened the door to the revolting Crusades of a so-called Christianity having lost sight of Christ. This, because they perceived humans as hopelessly tainted by their material nature and their dependence on materialism to survive.

With this mentality the Creator is further blamed for the problem of evil because He has created a system of life whereby the materialistic sinful natures and tendencies of parents are passed on to their children. This implies yet another flaw in the way God conceived human life. Is it surprising that Christians tend to believe that Jesus took on the guilt of the world because, as a divinity who created humans He had to accept responsibility for the flawed material beings He created. It is as though He had to pay for the recall; but the concept is not Scriptural.

All this incorrect theology leads quite naturally to the idea that God considers himself fully responsible for the presence of evil in the world and for having failed to equip humans with the necessary resources to escape evil. As a result, a dominant view of Christians considers that faith is a matter of believing that Jesus came to die for the sole purpose of paying the price God demanded for sins. The concept does not only fall short of basic logic, but it is also painfully unfair. It lacks logic because how can dying to pay for anything resolve anything? A five-year-old understands that killing is a problem, not a solution. The concept is also unfair because God is presented as forgiving and accepting only those who are aware of the fact that Jesus came to pay for sins—all others appear to be out of luck, so to speak. Logic tells us that if humans are powerless in the face of evil they should all be treated with equal respect and they should all be offered salvation. Should anyone be lost just because they are not Christians and because they have failed to recognize that their sins were paid for on a Cross?

To explain the fact that Jesus did not sin, most Christians argue that Jesus came in pure flesh, possibly that of Adam before sin. But they conveniently forget that Adam's immaculate flesh failed to protect him from evil and sin, and the same could be said about Eve, considering that they were both the product of God's hand and that no human genetic factors were yet involved in their life.

Without admitting it very openly, two millennia after Christ, Christians are still implying by their theology that God is responsible for the sinful condition of our world. With such a theology they are repeating the accusations Adam and Eve made against God in the Garden. Having fallen into the trap of finger-pointing, a large segment of Christianity assumes that sinners should do nothing for their salvation. While it is true that they should "do" nothing to obtain salvation, it is also true that faith is about thinking correctly and that by changing the way sinners think they also change the way they act because they think correctly.

With a theology that rejects human participation in the plan of salvation the doors to logical and valid approaches to the problem of evil remain hopelessly padlocked. To support with Scripture the claim that sinners should do nothing for their salvation, Paul is quoted as writing: "All have sinned and fall short of the glory of God, and are justified freely by his grace through the redemption that came by Christ Jesus" (Rom. 3:23–24). But they should not forget that in verses 10–12 of that same chapter Paul had just quoted the Old Testament where it is said, "There is no one righteous, not even one; there is no one who understands, no one who seeks God. All have turned away, they have together become worthless: there is no one who does good, not even one" (see Ps. 14:1–4; 53:1–3; Eccl. 7:20). Indeed, the people of the Old Testament failed to listen to God's message of truth; thus it became impossible for them to grow in righteousness. They tried to keep the commandments without listening to the rationale God was suggesting that would help them keep the commandments out of love. They wanted to do what was right without thinking correctly. The faith element, which is the way a person thinks, was missing from the equation.

It is for this reason that Jesus came, so that humans would once again have the opportunity to hear, firsthand this time, the message of God's truth at the exception of which the growth of love that overcomes sin is impossible. Without the proper understanding of God's rational truth, righteousness, which is growth of love in the heart, remains forever out of reach. The Jews heard the message, but as Paul and the prophets declared, they failed to understand its rationale.

Here Paul is reminding his converts that the Israelites who preceded them failed to find righteousness only because they failed to listen to God's rationale; they only listened to the pronouncement of His laws. Keeping the Law should be the result of accepting God's rationale, not the means by which a person is saved. By working hard to keep the Law they could not be changed from within. Only the acceptance of God's message can help keep His Law. Paul reminds his flock that we are all born lacking the voice of God in our hearts, thus the new birth made manifest through baptism marks the point in a sinner's life when the message of God begins to be recognized and accepted. That is the Holy Spirit of God that begins to fill the hearts of sinners. Being Spirit filled means accepting the message of God that changes hearts by making them more holy.

Indeed, as Paul made it very clear, we are all born sinners, with the mentality of sinners; thus we have all fallen short of the glory of God. But Paul is quick to say that we are "made to become just," not "justified" as it is translated. Justification is not the acquittal of misdeeds as in human legal systems; it is becoming just thanks to a new rationale. This is where a serious problem of translation occurs in Scripture. The word translated "justified" is the Greek *dikaioō*. It should have been translated "rendered just," or "made to become just" through transformation, not justified, as in acquittal. The word "justified" meaning acquitted belongs to the human legal system, a system God disapproves just as He disapproved of Cain's attitude—a system God warned him not to consider precisely because it cannot change a sinner's heart. Transformation is possible only thanks to the grace of God, indeed! But He has always bestowed His grace upon us; such grace is the truth that saves. A truth He has communicated all along. Jesus came to teach the way for a sinner to become just. He did it knowing it would cost Him His life. God's plan to save the world was proactive, not a useless pronouncement of acquittal that would have accomplished nothing to resolve the problem of evil on this planet or anywhere else in the universe.

As already stated, righteousness is not the product of trying hard to do what is right; it is the product of correct thinking that would enable to a sinner to do what is right. As it turns out, humanity is still living under the law with its concerns on what people and God do from a legal point of view, rather than on the way we should all learn to think. As a result, all of humanity is still living entirely under the law rather than under God's grace. Grace is the message God delivered to humanity at great price. His message is the key to the problem of evil that far too few have been willing to hear and understand. As long as we continue to focus on what we do rather than how we think, we have no choice but to judge people's actions under a forensic microscope to ascertain an appropriate punishment. In the process, we accuse God of similar practice. Despite the fact that the legal systems have been operating since Cain, nothing is really getting better in terms of overcoming evil. As a race, humanity is drifting ever closer to self-annihilation because they are bound to laws powerless to change hearts. As long as there is failure to develop a new understanding of the way evil can be overcome, humanity will continue its journey toward the precipice of doom. It is the "abomination that brings desolation" (see Mt. 24:15). God has communicated the way to overcome. He did it through the messages of the prophets first and, more recently, through the message called the Good News Message Jesus brought to this world (see Heb. 1:1–2).

It is the message that counts, not the flesh

The purpose of God's message has always been to provide humanity with the wherewithal to change by turning progressively away from evil, but this is not possible unless the way we are brain-mapped to think instinctively from our natural birth is changed. Christ came to show us the way to replace and update the mind-set of our birth with a new one. This is how we are "born again" (Jn. 3:3). His message is the truth that gives life. Not only did He show the way, but He also lived it at the price of His life. But He also showed the universe, that with the right mind-set or faith, even death couldn't hold a person captive in a tomb. He was resurrected on the third day just as He predicted He would. A person who lives true love cannot be held captive in a grave. What a demonstration of new life!

We will discover that the mind-set of God was also the mind-set of Christ. It is the Holy Spirit of God. It is the way a person thinks that produces the change of heart. This new way of thinking is a "set apart," or "holy" way to think that leads sinners to overcome evil. It is a mind-set different from the mind-set of those of us who are not yet born again. The new mind-set is the exact opposite of the way humans think naturally from their natural birth. That is why it is so vital to be born again, as Jesus made it clear to Nicodemus.

As previously stated, by blaming the serpent for their misdeeds, Adam and Eve were actually blaming God. Likewise, by blaming the flesh we have inherited from our parents since Adam and Eve, Christians are likewise blaming God. They assume that we are all like "filthy rags" until God chooses to do something about it, and that does not happen until a sinner believes that Jesus died to pay for sins. In that respect Christians are no different from their atheist, evolutionist, and pagan friends. They all consider nature responsible for making humans into the flawed individuals they are. Even theistic evolutionists blame God in a way, because in their understanding of God's involvement in the evolutionary process they essentially admit that humans have not yet reached the ultimate goal. Thus it is not their fault that evil still reigns on this planet. Indeed, some blame God while others blame nature, but in the end the result is the same—none of us are willing to accept responsibility for the presence of evil in our world.

As long as humans consider that evil is not their fault, they will continue to lack the incentive to look for real and logical solutions to overcome evil. Interestingly, they all deny responsibility for the problem of evil and they all believe, optimistically perhaps, that in time the problem will be solved by whoever or whatever created humans as they are, with all their flaws. For evolutionists nature will eventually correct the flaws in the next millions of years. Meanwhile believers in God believe that He will somehow put an end to the problem of evil, whenever He decides to do so, and that it is none of our business to second-guess God. Pagans prefer to say that humans have not yet learned to cooperate with Mother Nature. Because they fail to cooperate with Her, She punishes those who fail to respect Her. As a result She holds back from them the keys to supernatural powers needed to eradicate evil. What a lame excuse! That power is only tendered to a select few believed to be enlightened; they are called mediums, psychics, or clairvoyants.

We probably all have the propensity to view ourselves as innocent victims of flawed inherited DNA, implying that we can't help being what we are. Atheists turn to the sciences for answers. But with the growth of science their approach to ethics is getting increasingly more complicated and confusing. Pagans turn to the good graces of the gods of nature whom they try to assist and coax, not realizing that nature itself is flawed, having already suffered the consequences of evil. Thus it should be recognized that nature is just as powerless to reflect the character of the Creator God as are people not yet born again.[9] All of Creation continues to suffer from the mutual distrust that reigns supreme throughout (see Rom. 8:22). All of nature has been forced to develop mechanisms of self-protection and survival scientists call "the natural selection." All ideologies and religions tend to pattern themselves on the assumption that God has created nature and its laws as we observe them today, but that is incorrect. As long as we fail to recognize that both nature and humanity have departed from the way God created them, the solution to the problem will continue to elude all of us. Faith, or our belief systems, should not be established on what we see, said the author of Hebrews,

---

[9]   This statement is true only if the concept of new birth is correctly understood, which is questionable in Christian environments. Accepting Christ is not accepting that He died to pay for sins; it is accepting His message of truth that sets sinners free. Additional details will be given later in this book.

but on a reality none of us have ever seen, but are intelligent enough to recognize as the only way perfect and eternal life is possible (see Heb. 11:1). Life on this planet as we know it has been harmed and damaged by the ever-presence of mutual distrust. As such, what we see reflects the exact opposite of God's way of life. It is indeed a way that "seems right to a man, but in the end it leads to death" (Prov. 14:12).

As already stated, the breakdown of absolute trust has ruined the entire environment, even the entire universe. Paul alluded to this fact when he wrote: "The whole universe *has been* groaning as in the pains of childbirth" (Rom. 8:22, emphasis added). Paul makes it clear that the problem affects not only the whole world in which we live, but also the entire universe. Unfortunately, with their fallen mind-sets fallen beings are more prone to share a denial of responsibility than to seek God's solution. To make matters worse, Christians recognize that they ought to "do what is right," but they remain totally confused as to how this should be done despite having God's clear message of truth that offers the only solution.

If we were to ask God directly, He would tell each one of us what He has already revealed in Scripture: Think right first, that is, with the correct faith which is the only valid belief system, and everything else will follow, including doing right; don't bother to try to do it any other way, because it won't work. Trying to do what is right places the focus of life on self, and the more the emphasis is placed on self, the more it becomes impossible to do what is right by placing others first, and the more we end up perpetuating evil.

Indeed, we must think what is right before we can do what is right. This is what Jesus meant when He said: "Seek first His [the Father's] kingdom, and His righteousness" (Mt. 6:33), and the rest will follow. I would translate the text a little differently: "Seek first His kingdom, and His righteousness will follow." Jesus also said: "The Spirit gives life" (Jn. 6:63). In other words, it is the way we think that gives life. He goes on to say: "The flesh counts for nothing." Again, He is saying: "Don't blame the flesh for your problems related to evil; the flesh has nothing to do with it." But Jesus does not stop there; He adds: "The words [*logos,* or message] I have spoken to you are spirit, and they are life." The spirit that comes from God, or the way He thinks is the only way to have and enjoy life eternally. Seeking God's absolute truth is all about seeking the message that God has promised would someday have the power to change people's hearts. With the acceptance of that message we become individuals on their way to be "born again" in the family of God to become one of His children.

Past and present errors of Christianity

Ever since the apostolic period there have been deep divisions in the ranks of those who call themselves Christians. Unfortunately, the most peaceful and closest to God often end up suffering abuses at the hand of those willing to be aggressive and take up arms. By doing so they actually demonstrate that they are not on the side of Jesus. Unfortunately, the aggressive camp has had the upper hand in defining Christianity at the expense of God's given truth. As a result Christian history is heavily stained with falsehood responsible for horrific bloodshed of which we have not yet seen the worst.

Since the sixteenth century, segments of Christianity with opposing views on salvation have been received with anger and the clatter of clashing armed forces. The rifts between factions have grown and multiplied ever since. Some were teaching that salvation was by accepting impositions, rituals, obedience, and submission to the church representing Christ. Others were teaching that salvation was by believing in Jesus Christ by faith as the Savior who made provision for salvation by paying for sins on a Cross. Unfortunately, all sides were probably wrong, but at least, they were searching. The problem is that they should have been searching in peace and mutual respect. God never imposes a way of life. That would be a violation of freedom. He never said or implied that the gift of His life given all the way to the Cross was a payment for sins. By now the divide between factions of Christianity has narrowed. All sides have taken small steps toward one another. Since in the view of this author all sides have been wrong, let us attempt for a moment to focus on the solution. Just a little more background is needed however.

It is important to realize that Christianity has come to view faith as an exercise in believing strongly certain doctrines or dogmas of a religious nature. Modalities and personal involvement vary from denomination to denomination, but parishioners are essentially told that their duty is to believe in Jesus their Savior and wait patiently for world events to unfold because God is beyond understanding and because there is nothing a Christian can do to be saved.

It is absolutely true that sinners can "do" nothing to earn salvation. However, it is abundantly clear that they should "think" differently by heeding what they read and learn from Word of God. It is not possible to think correctly without learning, and the only place where correct learning can be received is from God, no other source. It appears to this author that neither those who want righteousness by works nor those who claim it by faith are correct in their thinking. Indeed, salvation is not by *doing anything* or by *believing strongly something that fails to make logical sense*; it is a matter of *being transformed in mind and heart by the message from God*. The message becomes the faith of the follower of Jesus. If a faith fails to produce a change of heart that makes it more loving, that belief system is incorrect and cannot be from God. We are what we think. As Scripture proclaimed thirty-five centuries ago: "For as he thinketh in his heart, so is he" (Pr. 23:7 KJV). Indeed, as mentioned earlier, God said to Cain: "If you *are* what is right," how could you possibly do what is wrong? "Sin [or, wrong doing because love is lacking] is crouching at your door" (Gen. 4:7), said God. Salvation is entirely a matter of "right thinking" that if sincerely accepted leads to "right doing," which is all about becoming more loving. If a problem is stated incorrectly how can its solution be correct? Correct thinking is the only faith that has the power to touch and transform the heart of a sinner away from evil. Incorrect thinking has never made it possible for humans to achieve anything positive in life.

To improve behavior it is important to realize that God wants us to know Him in truth so intimately that we understand the focus of His thoughts. Notice that it is the "focus" of His thoughts that is important to us, not His infinite capacity to think. No matter how weak our capacity to think or how low our IQ, it is the focus of our thoughts that matter when considering righteousness. There are only two directions possible for the focus of a person's thoughts: The "me first" mentality, and the "others first." This is an oversimplification but it is a concept we are talking about. God's is entirely focused on others first, never considering His own advantage first, and such was also the life of Jesus. The moment there is the least bit of hesitation between the two, the human mind is thrown in a state of confusion. All relationships are affected, including our relationship with God. This state of confusion has existed ever since Adam and Eve chose to put self first. They consummated their egocentric attitude by eating the fruit from the "don't go there Tree," attesting that they were experiencing utter confusion regarding their relationship with God and their knowledge of God.

It is for this reason that Jesus said emphatically: "Eternal life is that they know Him, the only true God" (Jn. 17:3). Thinking or knowing that God will solve the problem of evil is indeed, knowing something about God. But failure to think correctly is failure to know Him in truth. The attitude of wanting no part to play in becoming more righteous is "faith" indeed, but it is not God's kind of faith, because it is a denial of God's unconditional "others first" altruistic mindset in whose image humans were created. When a person has a false understanding of God and His Word, no amount of faith can correct the problem, because it is a false faith. With a false understanding of the word "faith" and a false understanding of the word "righteousness" it is simply impossible for anyone to understand the true meaning of "righteousness by faith" (Gal. 5:5 KJV).

We are very fortunate in the English language that we have the word "righteousness." It applies to a person who does the right thing because that person thinks correctly. The problem is that we often fail to include the idea of thinking correctly as essential to do the right thing. Other languages are not so fortunate. In other languages the statement is translated "justification by faith," as the expression is sometimes translated in English. But this wording implies that the sinner is justified or pronounced righteous; it is an acquittal of sins by way of payment or punishment. Christians generally believe that an innocent victim dying on the Cross made the payment that *justified* them or *acquitted* them. This is pure superstition; by itself a death cannot change a person's heart, nor can it pay for sins committed by others.

What a payment cannot do, the *message* conveyed by the death of the Innocent One is so powerful that it has the power to change people's hearts. This is exactly what Paul was saying: "For the message of the cross is foolishness to those who are perishing, but to us who are being saved, it is the power of God" (1 Cor. 1:18). Indeed, it is the *message* of the Cross, the *message* conveyed by the death of Jesus that should be recognized as the real power of God, not the Cross itself, nor the death of Jesus. Only the *message* conveyed by this most important event in the history of the universe has the power to change people. Has anyone ever been acquitted by the death of someone else? If so, it was done by forensic error or by error of judge or jury, because it cannot be a fair judgment, thus it cannot be of God. Would the God of pure logic work out a way to heal from evil through a program lacking logic? Logic itself answers the question a five-year-old could figure out.

Of course it is important to trust God. But to do so one must understand Him "in Spirit and truth" (Jn. 4:23, 24). Free-willed individuals bear the responsibility to seek the truth of what God actually said, not a corrupted version of His words. It is important to seek in His message the elements of truth that motivate a change of heart, not an appeasement of the Father or a way to pacify the consciences of sinners. If the message fails to motivate change there has to be something wrong either with the message or with the comprehension of the message from God. Erroneous concepts of righteousness by faith have failed humanity for a very long time; it is time we consider its meaning with a different pair of eyes.

As already stated, "doing right" was not the problem in the first place—thinking right that leads to being the right kind of person that does what is right is the only method of overcoming evil available to free-willed individuals. Any other method would be an imposition that cannot come from God. Since all religious systems involve the intervention of outside forces upon sinners' hearts and minds, they cannot be from God. Either the church imposes its views and ways, or His Holy Spirit is falsely believed to impose on humans. The problem with either view is that external impositions deny freedom; therefore, they cannot be from God. The fact that God never imposes His ways on anyone should be our first clue. Only the devil is bold enough to impose his ways on anyone.[10] It is for this reason that a person's focus should not be on doing what is right; it should always be on learning from God, *how to think right*. But how is that accomplished? This book is an attempt to answer this most vital question.

A religion that comes from the "only true God" cannot dismiss the sinner's responsibility for the problem of evil. Doing so is contempt against God's plea to know Him in truth in order to be saved.

---

[10] Some would argue that the Holy Spirit directed men to do certain things, for example in the Acts of the Apostles. Indeed, correct thinking involving the idea of "others first" guided the actions of Jewish Apostles to bring the message of life to the Gentiles. All the first converts were Jews, but they did not keep the truth to themselves. Thus they were driven by the Spirit of God to share the blessings of the truth with others, because the knowledge of God that saves was inexistent.

By believing that God has already accomplished His purpose by sending His Son to the Cross, sinners are made to believe that somehow God wanted the death of Jesus to resolve the problem of evil. If such were the case, why are we still here 2,000 years later? And why are we still suffering so much from evil? Hasn't the problem been resolved and paid for long ago? Is God slow in delivering the goods for which a payment has been made at such a huge price?

Unfortunately, believing that a payment was made on the Cross to cover all sins has led sinners to foster the rather strange and irrational belief that salvation was made possible by way of a penal substitution. According to that theory the sins of humans were punished because God supposedly accepted their sins to be transferred onto the Person of Jesus before He died on the Cross, none of which is confirmed in Scripture. Jesus was killed in our place, they say. A common saying among Christians is that "He died the death we deserve that we might have the life He deserved." This view can only be a travesty. Not only because it lacks the support of sound logic, but also because it is not Scriptural. This theology makes matters worse by attributing this heinous act of murder to God the Father. Most translations of Isaiah 53 are correct to say: "Surely he took up our infirmities and carried our sorrows, yet *we considered* him stricken by God, smitten by him, and afflicted" (Is. 53:4, emphasis added). The text is clear to say that "we," the misguided people that we are, considered him stricken by God, when in fact God had nothing to do with His death; evil humans killed Him, not God.

Furthermore, it must be recognized that killing is an act powerless to resolve anything; it can only serve to perpetuate evil. It is at the price of blood and deaths that walls and borders of separation have been erected everywhere in this world. Even the administration of capital punishments on criminals has failed to resolve the problems for which they have been pronounced guilty. Calling the acceptance of this malicious concept, surrendering one's heart to Jesus, can only lead rational people away from God and from His Word because the beauty of His truth has been substituted with a vile concept of penal substitution. While modalities may vary from denomination to denomination, the basic message is relatively consistent throughout the Reformed movement and the rest of Christianity at large. To sum it up, it could be said that Christianity has grafted the sins of the world onto Jesus Christ, when instead they should have grafted onto the world the righteousness of Jesus's faith. Just as Isaiah 53:4 makes it clear, but humans got the message backward.

When it is taught that righteousness, which is all about overcoming evil, should be done by faith through the power of a mystical force called the Holy Spirit, a very important element is left out of the equation. We should remember that the least external imposition on a free-willed individual destroys the very free will that God has labored at great price to preserve for all intelligent beings of His creation. When Christians claim falsely that a sinner's attempt to change behavior amounts to salvation by works, they fail to realize that it is not one's behavior that should be submitted to God, it is one's thinking. God's perfect logic has been rejected and substituted with concepts analogous with superstitions. Again, the problem is not what we do; it is the wrong thinking that results from a faith founded on a false belief system. The "me first" thought pattern we all inherit from birth needs to give way to a different mind-set, one that comes from God. Jesus called the new way to think the "new birth" (1 Pet. 1:3) or being "born again" (Jn. 3:3 KJV) or "born from above" (Jn. 3:3). The new mind-set is the new birth of a person who begins to recognize that the mind-set we are born with can only lead to the extinction of life. Only a new mapping of the brain has the power to influence everything a person does for the better. Thus it is not an imposition of righteousness by works, it is righteousness that comes from thinking differently, or righteousness by way of a new faith, that *of* Jesus. The problem is that the new mind-set can be acquired only if God's truth is known and understood correctly. Not only we should know what this truth is, but we must also know how it is acquired. While this truth can be found throughout Scripture, it is our prerogative of free will to seek it and accept it on an individual basis.

In their theological discourses most Christians forget that God created intelligent life to be perfectly free; that is to say, entirely self-governing, without the least intervention of external forces or impositions of any kind. The person is entirely guided by his or her faith. Thus a person can become a king of sort, but only if he or she can live a life of love in the absence of all supervision. Correct thinking is the only force capable of motivating a correct action without the least imposition from an external force. God's truth becomes the motivational force that settles within the heart. It is a faith that directs a person's actions from within, not from without. Thus correct thinking that leads to correct behavior is never an imposition, it is the product of one's own desires of the heart; consequently it can never be a violation of a person's freedom.

It must be observed however that such a belief system is indeed from God. Without God humans would have never recognized the validity of the principle of life Scripture calls the Everlasting Gospel. The fact that God's truth activates a power within the human heart to act righteously does not imply that the resulting righteousness is not from God. On the contrary, God is not only the Creator, but He is also the Author of the truth that brings the power of righteous in a person's life. God has gone out of His way to communicate this transforming message since the first departure of humans from His truth in Eden. Adam and Eve failed to listen to God's perfect logic, and so has the rest of humanity ever since. It is time for us to change trends founded on belief systems foreign to God. False belief systems will ultimately bring the "abomination that brings desolation" (Dan. 9:27; 11:31; 12:11; Mt. 24:15; Mk. 13:14). The truth that comes from God is beautiful because it is never an overpowering force; it is a perfectly logical force of persuasion called "faith" that motivates ever-greater love. It is a transformative power that respects unconditionally everyone's individual freedom. How we acquire this love is the subject of the rest of this book.

CHAPTER 3

From a Failed Kingdom of Kings and Priests to Its Fulfillment

God told the Children of Israel in no uncertain terms that *if* they would *listen* to Him, the Promised Land they were about to enter would become a holy nation of which the citizens would be kings and priests (Ex. 19:6). God was telling them that if they would agree to "listen to me attentively" (Ex. 19:5 from LXX. Not "obey me fully" as in NIV), that is, to God's message of truth, it would transform their hearts and minds. With this message in mind they would become a peculiar people compared to all other nations. Every person living in the Land would become both a priest and a king. A startling statement indeed! One could wonder how every citizen of a country could become a king and a priest. Israel would have become a nation unlike any other in the world. In this atypical nation every person was intended to become entirely self-governing (kings) because they have become true representatives of God (priests) eager to live and teach His unique way of thinking that produces love. This perfect theocratic system of government, as God meant it to be, not as humans define it, was to be offered later to all people living on the globe.

The Pulpit Commentary agrees with this interpretation of the text. The beginning of the comment for verse 6 reads as follows: "Ye shall be unto me a kingdom of priests. Or 'a royalty of priests'—at once a royal and a priestly race—all of you at once both priests and kings. (So the LXX. render, βασίλειον ἱεράτευμα; the Targums of Onkelos and Jerusalem, "kings and priests;" that of Jonathan, "crowned kings and ministering priests.")." [11]

God's purpose is still to restore the ability of a people to govern themselves individually, that is to say, without the control or supervision of any external authority recognized, nominated or elected to dictate,

---

[11] The Pulpit Commentary, Electronic Database. Copyright © 2001, 2003, 2005, 2006, 2010 by BibleSoft, Inc.

control, or judge the actions of others. As Nietzsche said regarding the way of life Jesus was offering, it is utopia. For a person who fails to understand God it is indeed utopia. Yet when properly understood, not only does it make perfect sense, but the divine system of government can also be logically recognized as the only system that is capable of sustaining eternal life. In fact, Jesus had no spiritual leader to submit to. His relationship with the Father was not submissive; it was the full and unquestionable acceptance of living His paradigm of life, because it is the one and only paradigm that makes eternal and universal sense.

When true followers of Jesus will recognize and accept truth before the end of time, as Scripture predicts, no one in this group of people "set apart" (holy) will have to submit to a superior religious authority, not even to God's—they will have adopted His mind-set. Without a doubt, His paradigm of life will have taken residency in the hearts and minds of these last day citizens of heaven; thus God will indeed be living in them, and no longer among them. It is with this divine mentality that God initially hardwired the brains of our first parents in Eden. This is the paradigm of life they were to guard, protect, and cultivate in a Garden where a perfect ecosystem required no gardening as such, but they failed.

It is because all the required knowledge was already uploaded into the psyche of Adam and Eve that God could allow Himself to be absent from the scene. There was nothing more He could teach them; it was already all there at creation. God did not feel compelled to provide the newly created couple with constant uninterrupted guidance to make sure they would not stray. A careful reading of the text shows that God never ordered or commanded Adam and Eve to be or do anything other than what they wanted. His only recommendation was to help them avoid the only danger zone they might encounter. Going there would be highly detrimental to their welfare and well-being, as we have already explained.

Likewise, God's intended mission for Israel was to restore *in them* the mind-set God had programed in Adam and Eve before their fall. With it, Israel's system of government would have been totally different from that of other nations in the world. Imagine a system of life on the scale of the Promised Land where everyone is a priest who can be fully and unquestionably be trusted because they all have true love in their hearts and minds. Following their example, this divine system would have later been replicated by other nations, and perhaps on the scale of the world. It was the calling of Israel to demonstrate the superiority of God's real system of theocratic self-government through the replication of God's mind-set in each and every individual.

However, because humans are free they had to individually accept such a way of life, and this could be accomplished only through new birth of heart and mind. With such hearts all other nations would have been able to see and recognize firsthand that such a way of life comes from God. This way of life would have been the most powerful invitation to the nations of this world to follow after God's way. Such was God's original plan of salvation. The implementation of truth would have produced perfect freedom. God's plan was to disqualify evil and its "me first" mentality forevermore in the eyes of a world and universe already "groaning" (Rom. 8:2) from the pain and sufferings of evil. God cannot reestablish all things as they were before sin until His created beings demonstrate their willingness and acceptance to live His kind of life on the strength of His perfect logic.

Had the Children of Israel listened to the message from God rather than request from Him a long series of laws to follow so they would not have to think, the descendants of Jacob would have been transformed into a nation of highly productive and peaceful self-governed people. This would have been accomplished on the basis of such a high level of unconditional mutual love that perfect mutual trust would have produced unparalleled peace and prosperity with the added privilege of God's protection. Indeed, as we shall see, God never wanted them to fight wars, but here again, they failed (see Ex. 14:14). The prerequisites needed to ensure the success of this enterprise were entirely dependent on the correct formation of the priesthood. Their job was to communicate God's unique and fail-safe method to acquire true love. Their training was to be founded entirely on learning and teaching others how God's message involves a methodology to grow love in a human heart born deficient. Only God's message of truth could accomplish such a feat; no other system could. In this regard, the God of the Old Testament and Jesus of the New are by far the greatest philosophers of love this world has ever known, but the world is not listening. Since it is not possible to become a true priest without the correct knowledge of God and His message of truth, the required knowledge had to be pure and flawless. Not the least trace of human-conceived error about God or His message could be tolerated because the least corruption of His truth makes true love and eternal life impossible to achieve. But again, humans failed. The very priests, who were commissioned to share with the people the message given by God to the prophets, were largely responsible for corrupting its contents.

"This Gospel" is all about a kingdom that will succeed

According to the New Testament the knowledge of God's truth will someday be known and recognized globally. Not everyone will subscribe to the message, but it will be known globally. Jesus predicted this development two millennia ago when He said: "This gospel of the kingdom will be preached in the whole world as a testimony to all nations, and then the end will come" (Mt. 24:14). The end-time movement Jesus predicted will become reality only when the perfect unadulterated understanding of God's message will be made available just as Jesus brought it to the attention of the world 2,000 years ago. The unadulterated message will be understood in such logical terms that it will accomplish results so utopian that they will prove Nietzsche wrong. Indeed, Jesus did say, "With God all things are possible" (Mt. 19:26). When considering this text in its entire context we should perhaps read it to say: "But when God is known in Truth, all things are possible for those who listen to Him with open hearts." The future tense in Matthew 24:14 implies, as it does in the preceding verse, that this movement will occur shortly before the return of the Lord.

With God's system of government in place, true freedom would reign supreme because mutual trust could never be in doubt. This is not predicted to happen until after the return of the Lord. But with such a system there would be no pressure on anyone to compete for higher level of performance or prominent positions of authority. There would be no need for licenses, nominations, or elections to positions of power. In such a world everything in life would be about cooperation, collaboration, and coexistence in perfect peace born out of love and harmony with God. With a common message of life lived by all people, cultural differences would slowly vanish and a new culture born out of God's way of life would emerge. Everyone would be a priest because everyone's life would reflect the love of God.

The word "priest" should not be understood as it is today but as God intended the priesthood to be understood. Indeed, a priest was to be a person entirely dedicated on learning all there is to know about love and how it can be made to grow in a person's heart. Had they been faithful to their God-ordained calling they would have been recognized by the love that would have visibly been growing in their hearts. Their love would have never been in doubt, and their understanding of how love grows in a person's heart would have been communicated freely at no cost to the people. They were ordained to become the love experts of the world because true religion is all about love and nothing else. If such were the current burden on the hearts of today's priests and pastors, the word priest would take on the meaning God had always intended: a "true friend" of all people. This is how the Hebrew word *kohen* is sometimes translated in Aramaic Targumic translations of Hebrew texts.

It is only because God made humans intelligent that it is theoretically and logically possible for them to govern themselves individually in unrestricted freedom and perfect harmony. In such a perfect theocratic[12] system no one would ever think about inflicting harm or judgment on others for any reason. Thus it follows reason that God gave humans access to unconditional free will on the basis of the intelligence He gave them to govern themselves individually. Kings and priests would become obsolete. Such a group of people would truly form a community of sovereigns where no one is considered superior to anyone else in status or authority. It is to achieve this lofty goal that God gave humans the unconditional freedom to do whatever they want, because with love in the heart anything they would want would always be the right and loving thing to do. This also explains why many have abused their God-given freedom by taking part in some of the most evil deeds the world has ever witnessed. God is not responsible for these atrocities; the responsibility befalls free humans unwilling to listen to God. Sure God could have stopped them, but that would have been a violation of freedom, therefore a denial of love. Indeed, God could not go back on this greatest of all privileges given to intelligent beings. Taking away the least bit of their absolute freedom would be taking away from them both a portion of their intelligence and an equal portion of their free will. Taking away the least element of freedom also takes away an equal proportion of the people's privilege of love. The least imposition on anyone would limit both that person's freedom and that person's capacity to love.

---

12   In our context the word "theocratic" does not imply a religion with leaders given the authority to govern people on God's behalf, as it is traditionally understood, but as a system of government ordained by God according to which all people are self-governed on the basis of His message of universal truth that produces perfect love.

In a society where everything is regimented in all details there would be no room for love, and no need for it. Love would be dead, and this is where we are rapidly heading in societies where laws are perceived as humanity's only hope for peace and decency. This is in fact what the world demonstrated 2,000 years ago when the ruling classes chose to punish an innocent Person, just to make a political statement and maintain control over people. However, when He suffered this unjust fate Jesus showed the universe that under no circumstances should evil ever be opposed with the least level of evil. He who had access to all the power in the universe demonstrated that nothing is ever solved or improved by rendering evil for evil. Would the Father have felt differently? A rhetorical question indeed!

We must come to realize that if humans lacked the intelligence to be self-governing without exposing others to the least menace of injury or manipulation, they could never hope to be truly and completely free. Paradise would indeed be utopic, and the notion that there is a true and loving God of the universe would be a scam. As long as there is the least menace of any kind, paradise where peace founded on mutual trust that makes freedom possible could never exist. In God's kind of world no oppression or subjugation of any kind could ever arise.

Unlike humans, God created animals with intellectual limitations. To survive they were given powerful instincts. Because they are controlled by instincts their freedom is more limited. They are constantly subjected to compelling inner dictates they cannot override. Animals possess intelligence but not unrestricted freedom, thus their intelligence is also proportionately restricted. God could have created humans like them, but not if He wanted them to enjoy all the benefits of absolute freedom for which a superior level of intelligence is required to manage their unconditional autonomy. If they did not have absolute free will, thanks to a level of intelligence capable of managing absolute free will rationally, humans could never be truly or entirely free. Moreover, if God should take away from them the least portion of absolute freedom, they would never again be in a position to regain access to a level of rationale sufficient to return on their own to absolute freedom. This means that they could never again live in a supervision-free environment at the exception of which paradise founded on freedom capable of managing peace in perfect love, could not exist.

We are not saying that animals are not intelligent, but their intelligence is subjected to their instincts. In fact, their intelligence is rarely capable of overriding their instincts. When instincts are overruled it is almost always for reasons of survival of the species. They are sometimes led to mass suicide or *needless* destruction of other kinds of life; but these are most likely responses to their natural instincts. This dependency on instincts rather than pure rationale makes it impossible for animals to govern themselves individually and peacefully as equals.

As for humans, as soon as trust was broken because of their first self-centered action, an instinct of survival began to develop. That instinct tends to take precedence over the rationale upon which unconditional love and respect of others was initially founded. Interestingly, the attraction of humans to religion is, generally speaking, motivated by their instinct of survival. They want the supernatural forces of the universe to labor in their favor. When the instinct of survival becomes dominant another instinct develops: the need for leadership. When survival becomes an issue for a group of humans, they recognize instinctively that not everyone can take charge of the situation on his or her own. Leaders must either emerge or the group must choose them. The need for hierarchy is born out of the need for survival.

Animals have developed similar needs for leadership; we call them dominant males, queen bees, top dogs, or other names, though leadership and caste in the animal kingdom is far more complex than here suggested. But here again, the pecking orders animals have developed is not representative of God's kingdom or the way he has created them; it is simply a response to the world in which they live where mutual trust has been destroyed. In God's realm there was to be no dominancy whatsoever. True and absolute freedom can only find its fulfillment in the absence of dominant forces or authority. But for that to happen, freedom must be founded on such pure rationale that it has the power to persuade the importance of unconditional love along with a clear understanding of the consequences related to refusing love as a way of life.

"The Truth will Set You Free" (Jn. 8:32)

Jesus declared in no uncertain terms that it is the truth that will set His followers free from the bondages of evil. Would He have made such a utopian declaration if true freedom were unattainable? The statement is not conditional; He predicted that this would happen someday in the future. In fact, in a world where both truth and freedom are philosophically believed to be impossible, Jesus who predicts the advent of both in this statement is either expressing a divine reality that cannot be doubted, or He is a fraud. His statement implies that if humans were incapable of recognizing truth, freedom would elude them indefinitely. Since truth cannot be recognized in the absence of rational thinking, it is a mere deduction that true freedom will only be achievable on the grounds of solid rationale. Indeed, freedom cannot exist unless a person has life that includes sufficient power to modify one's environment at will. The life and capacity to modify we all have can be used constructively and destructively. If freedom is considered to be the privilege to transform matter indiscriminately, without concern of consequences or destructive outcome, then of course, freedom does not exist. A destructive use of life always translates into a restriction of freedom, thus a restriction of everyone's welfare and well-being. There is no room for destructive endeavors in the exercise of true self-determination, because such acts would only serve to destroy freedom.

If freedom is unquestionably recognized as the pursuit of making life better for others at any cost to self, as Jesus taught and lived the principle all the way to the Cross, then life for everyone who shares this principle is perpetually enhanced in peace. The full force of persuasion (or faith) can be achieved only when heard from the voice of unflawed logic, because reality can be perceived in truth no other way. The frequently quoted passage from the Gospel of John could have been paraphrased as follows: "When you will understand my teachings in truth because you will recognize them to be founded on solid logic, only then will you truly be my students, because God is the Father of logic. In fact, near the end of time you will finally get to know the truth that has the power to set you free" (Jn. 8:31–32, amplified and paraphrased by the author).

The secret of successful achievement is always dependent on intelligence enlightened by the discovery of truth founded on logic. How could a jetliner be made to fly if in the planning of its construction flaws of logic or the least disregard for scientific truth were overlooked? We all know the answer to that question. But the same could be said about religion, because true religion is the study of the immutable principles responsible for maintaining life, and enjoying it evermore abundantly. Jesus can be credited for that point when He said: "The thief cometh not, but for to steal, and to kill, and destroy: I am come that they might have life, and that they might have it [forever] more abundantly" (Jn. 10:10 KJV, brackets mine). Only one guiding light of truth makes living in true freedom possible: To live one's life for the sole purpose of enhancing the life of others unconditionally at any cost to self. With this principle of life everyone's life is enhanced because everyone shares the same persuasion or the same faith. Such was the faith of Jesus, and such should be our faith.

There are many false religious faiths, or persuasions that fail to deliver on their promises. Only truth founded on logic has the capacity to motivate the development of mutual trust that opens wide the door of true freedom—the kind of freedom God designed Adam and Eve to enjoy forevermore. When they partook of the Forbidden Fruit they made manifest the undeniable fact that distrust was now ruling every form of life on earth. Though someday many will understand the pitfalls of a system of life that destroys trust, many will continue to reject it. It is this refusal to rebuild trust among people and nations that will ultimately cause the utter devastation of the environment—it is the abomination that will cause desolation (see Mt. 25:15) the prophets and Jesus talked about. It is understandable that in such an environment of distrust philosophers say that freedom and truth cannot reign. They arrive at their conclusions through the observation of the current condition in our world and the universe in which distrust that produces evil cannot sustain true freedom because truth is elusive. In their evaluation of *visible* reality they disallow the *invisible* possibility that God did not create reality as we see it today; it became that way because of evil. Faith that comes from God is indeed "the evidence of things unseen" (Heb. 11:1 KJV).

As previously stated, in the midst of absolute confusion the grace of God was made manifest by the dedication of Jesus who did not hesitate to go all the way to the Cross to communicate once for all the eternal truth that makes overcoming evil possible. If He were not a loving God He would not have had to go to such lengths. He could have just allowed evil to reach its ultimate fate of self-annihilation and be done with the whole problem. But this would have done nothing to improve the universe; in fact, doing so would have labeled God as a tyrant lacking love to such a degree that no one could ever trust Him again. Thus, without perfect trust in one another and in God, eternal life could never again become reality. Either we accept the everlasting truth involving putting others first unconditionally, in which case we participate with God to the reestablishment of eternal life for all, or we deny it and remain participants in the self-fulfillment of inevitable doom. In fact, there is no middle road; in our lives we choose to contribute either to the cause of eternal life or to the cause of eternal death. The second coming of Jesus will occur when humans will be on the brink of causing total self-annihilation. Jesus made it very clear that "then, there will be great distress, unequaled from the beginning of the world until now—and never to be equaled again. If those days had not been cut short, no one would survive, but for the sake of the elect those days will be shortened" (Mt. 24:21–22).

Accepting God's grace is a very personal matter because it is the unconditional acceptance of His mind-set, the way He thinks. It is something no one else can do for us. It is of course the thinking Jesus manifested all the way to the Cross. The natural death we all end up suffering from sooner or later is as temporary for us as it was for Jesus. It is for this reason that Jesus called death a "sleep" (Jn. 11:11). When He will return as He promised He would (see Jn. 14:2, 3), those who at that time will demonstrate their willingness to dedicate their lives to the truth, as well as those who would have dedicated theirs to the truth if they had known the truth, will all be resurrected for eternal life after a period of sleep in their graves (Phil. 3:10–11). Since God knows the hearts He knows who are those who would have responded to His message of truth if they had known the principle of life. Jesus knew the heart of the thief on the cross next to Him just as God knows the heart of every single person on the face of this earth. Though the thief did not know all the truth that set people free, Jesus knew that if he had known this truth as God's people will in the last days, he would have accepted it and would have made it his own belief system of life for eternity.

There is hope. Scripture claims that an absolute level of freedom founded on perfect mutual trust will be made available once again to the human family—it is called salvation that restores the image of God in humans. The reward of paradise will come later. However, the concept involved needs to be understood and believed so strongly that those who believe in this principle of life will choose to apply it immediately while they still have life (see 2 Tim. 4:8). As long as humans continue to nurture religious beliefs dispossessed of pure logic they will never have the truth that sets them free. It is because humans were created perfectly free that God cannot, and will never impose on them His solution to the problem of evil. The best He can do to preserve individual freedom is to suggest the adoption of a new thought pattern by revealing, not what a sinner should do to stop sinning, but how he or she should think in order to overcome evil. This is the principle God was attempting to convey to Cain, but he refused to listen. In the end, Cain was left perfectly free to do as he pleased, and he chose not to accept the idea of thinking as God does. With all the power God possesses, He did not impose belief, action, or punishment on Cain. The suffering God predicted for Adam and Eve and their descendants was not a punishment; it was a consequence of living with a mind-set opposed to the logic of eternal life. Because Cain was created free, God could not impose on him to recognize or endorse the truth that saves.

It is the duty of intelligent free beings to listen attentively and logically to God's voice of wisdom, but it should be listened to for what He says, not what we want to hear with our confused minds. If what He says appears to lack the least element of logic, it is either because God is misquoted, or it is a counterfeit interpretation of His message. The moment God's message of Truth was corrupted it became logically meaningless. It is the meaninglessness of such errors that became the foundational shifting sand of all false religions.

Why Was the Old System of Salvation Made Obsolete?

The book of Hebrews in Scripture calls the formerly practiced system of salvation "obsolete" (Heb. 8:13 NIV)—a reference to Old Testament sacrificial rituals, though many consider it a reference to God's Law. Christians call the sacred writings of prophets before Christ, the Old Testament. This choice of words was made in part because the Greek word *palaioō* was translated "old" in the King James Version. In reality that word is Greek for "decay." It is true that when a fruit gets old, eventually it decays, but decay is always due to corruption. The word that should be used to translate *palaioō* is a matter of perception. What is clear is that something in the former system had gone awry. Should it be called the "Old Testament," or should it have been called the "Corrupted Testament"? As Jesus implied when He said: "I did not come to abolish the Law or the Prophets" (Mt. 5:17), it was not the message the Israelites received from God that He came to rectify; it was the corrupted misguided way the Israelites had come to understand the message that Jesus came to rectify. Indeed, a corrupted message cannot serve its intended purpose. The point I am trying to make is that the Old Testament did not become obsolete because God made a mistake when He communicated His messages through the prophets, but because humans had corrupted it to such a point that it could no longer communicate the truth that has the power to set sinners free.

The former covenant was mislabeled "old covenant." It only became obsolete because humans corrupted it to the point of rendering the saving truth unrecognizable and ineffectual. God's character and His approach to the restoration of love in the human heart were no longer logically perceptible in the interpretation of the prophets' messages because the priests had corrupted everything God said beyond recognition. Though the psalmist called the word of the Lord flawless (Ps. 18:30), and it may have been in his days, centuries later God's Word was declared decayed by the author of Hebrews. When we consider that God does not change, we are made to understand that Jesus came, not to bring a new message as He attested (Mt. 5:17), but to restate the formerly conveyed messages of truth in words and deeds because they had been falsified, misunderstood, or misinterpreted. We will discover that the corruption of God's Word did not happen only as it regards the Old Testament; it was repeated again early in the Christian era. As the years passed, the errors were compounded. Destructive pagan influences and interpretations originally distorted God's intended meaning in the OT, and the same concepts reappeared after Christ to corrupt His message just as He predicted (Mt. 24:11–24).

Traditional Holy Spirit theology fails to recognize that absolute freedom implies the absence of any external force of any kind to compel belief or behavior. Because the Holy Spirit is perceived as a Person of the Godhead, there is a chronic failure to recognize it to be the spirit of God, which is a persuasion founded on pure divine logic. Thinking like God is the only power available to overcome evil without freedom-destroying impositions made on sinners. The assumption that a third Person of the Godhead never mentioned in Scripture mystically enters a person's heart is misleading and destructive. The false idea that there is such a Person in the Godhead will be discussed later in this book. Scripture makes no claim to suggest that a supernatural power comes into us; it only makes the claim that thinking like God, or Jesus, is power that saves because it transforms the sinner from within. Only the forces of evil are willing to abuse the freedom of intelligent beings. Supernatural forces of evil are more than willing to impose and dominate while keeping humanity ignorant of the truth that comes from the only true God. Our forthcoming discussion on Trinity theology should shed at least some light on this sensitive subject.

When mutual trust was destroyed following the first sin, the instinct of survival became the default guiding force of all forms of life, not just human life. It is a highly destructive system against which Adam and Eve had been warned. All of nature had to adjust to the new reality of dealing with distrust. The only way this could be done was to dedicate all their resourcefulness to survival. Since the biological makeup of all life-forms involved the capacity to adapt to changes of environment, the breakdown of trust produced vast numbers physical and mental mutations—down to the cellular level the various forms of life were left with no alternative but to adapt. They were all impelled to survive at any cost, regardless of damages inflicted on other forms of life. Like humans, all of nature was subjected to a world where mutual trust was replaced with mutual suspicion and fear. Living organisms of all kinds had to adopt the default mode: survival as the only way to deal effectively with an environment of mutual distrust.

Since God created humans to be absolutely free to think and act as they wished regardless of consequences, if He ever chose to impose a solution it would have been a blatant violation of the freedom He gave and continues to preserve at great price. Furthermore, it would have been an insult to the intelligence He gave humans to enjoy the love that freedom makes possible thanks to mutual trust. Any imposition the Holy Spirit Person of the Godhead would impose on sinners would be tyranny. Such an incursion on God's part would have been irreversible, and freedom that makes true love possible would have been forever lost.

Because they fell to the temptation of serving self at the expense of others, humans have lost the mental mapping God had originally created in them. Since they lost willfully the mind-set from God humans can only return to it willfully. To recover the divine mind-set they must listen to God who has been trying to communicate how it is achieved ever since humans have chosen to depart from serving the needs of others before their own. In so doing they have also willfully abandoned true love as the only way to live eternally. In fact, as we shall see, the procedure required to reverse evil by receiving God's salvation, or healing, was already disclosed in detail before the creation of Adam and Eve.

The problem is that thus far humans have repeatedly scrambled the message designed to restore the original mind-set. The recipe or prescription to regain the original mental health has repeatedly been altered, modified, and corrupted by pagan influences. As a result the medicine now suggested by the religions of our world amounts to nothing more than quack medicine. Sometimes their prescriptions may sound good, but they do not work. What Scripture makes very clear is that humans possess sufficient intelligence and wisdom to understand God's key to the restoration of their original mind-set. What must be kept in mind however is that in order to be operative this key must be logically, and not mystically recognized as the only way to provide a lasting eternal solution. Once persuaded that it is the only viable solution, humans will also discover that they have in them the mental resources to embrace and absorb God's faith as the only motivating force capable of changing a sinner's modus operandi for eternity. God's solution is indeed the salvation He offers to all who are willing to sit like children at His feet to listen and learn from Him.

The Message of Jesus Was Also Corrupted

In modern Christianity the participation of one's implementation of God's plan of salvation (His prescription to heal the disease of evil in one's heart) has been entirely removed. It is as if a doctor (God) gave a prescription to a patient, a sinner, who either chooses to ignore it altogether (atheism) or to replace it with that of a quack doctor (religions of our world). To my regret, it appears that all systems of salvation proclaimed by Christian denominations today are faulty. Neither righteousness by works nor righteousness by faith, as they are currently defined, can provide a real solution. These views may have helped to keep some people in line or in the belief system, but they fall short of God's suggested procedure to overcome evil by changing the hearts and minds of sinners.

Righteousness by trying hard, or by works, has never worked

Those who believe in righteousness by works try to do something God might like, to avoid His punishment. They attempt to redeem themselves for their faults rather than to recognize that by showing them the way to the truth that saves, Jesus became their Redeemer. Their main thrust is to do what their church or religion tells them to do without bothering to think, because in their view God is beyond comprehension anyway. This is how all too many churches have manipulated their parishioners. They are told to believe "by faith," which means doing or believing without bothering to think rationally. Religious leaders and churches have taken full advantage of this manipulative practice by introducing dangerous mystical logic-defying components in the belief systems of their churches. Some of the most mindless involve mystical expectations through the use of holy water, the administration of self-mutilation, purchases of dispensations, wafers or wine believed to be transformed into the very flesh and blood of Jesus, and other unscriptural concepts. The problem with all mystical approaches to the problem of evil is that a person cannot be led to do what is right as long as that person fails to think correctly in the first place. Superstitions can only be responsible for holding back progress in all areas of life.

Rituals become superstitions when it is implied that such practices have in themselves the power to change anything, including one's thoughts and actions. These are mere presumptions unfounded on a clear message of truth that comes from God. Religions founded on righteousness by doing anything can only fail to show the way to thinking correctly. They make mere puppets out of their adherents. Learning to think correctly is the only way to change a person's behavior from within. All systems of righteousness by works involve impositions from external influences and authorities that can only be exploitive and oppressive. Such religious systems are responsible for destroying freedom, not enhancing it so that love may grow in the sinner's heart. Thus such religions cannot be founded on the truth that will set sinners free.

Current views of righteousness by faith are also misleading

The most popular views of righteousness by faith are likewise flawed. Though the world should be grateful to the Reformation for pointing religious thought in a direction that had been forgotten for twelve centuries or more, their conclusions are incomplete at best. When viewed through the lenses of logic a simple analysis of the general conclusions the Reformers reached suggests that an external mystical action has to come into play to control the behaviors of born-again Christians. That external power is called the Holy Spirit, or the third Person of the Godhead.

But as we indicated earlier, God would never use a supernatural force to impose on anyone because it would be an abuse of human freedom. This is not to say that the means to overcome evil are not entirely from God; on the contrary, all means to overcome evil are indeed from God, no matter what those means are.

All too many believe that unless a supernatural force is activated God is not involved, but nothing could be further from truth. It must be recognized that as long as the help from God is perceived as an external supernatural power able to dictate decisions and behavior, humans cannot be totally free. To be truly guided by intrinsic love, an intelligent individual must be unconditionally free to think and act as he or she desires in his or her own heart. Once dependent on external power to avoid evil, humanity would remain indefinitely dependent on external control of their actions. Thus it is only on the strength of indisputable logic that a voice from within can be activated to motivate against evil. The logic that makes the change possible is from God.

Countless events in history could illustrate the fact that humans are easily led to reject a concept only because the world around them has dismissed it as impossible, unrealistic, or utopic. Let us consider just one. Edward R. Murrow made a stunning statement shortly after the Wright brothers managed to fly a powered machine heavier than air in December 1903. Here is what he wrote: "The Wright brothers' first flight was not reported in a single newspaper because every rookie reporter knew what could and could not be done." This was indeed a time when the idea of flying such a heavy contraption could not be imagined possible by the public. Had the Wright brothers made the same assumption they would have never tried to fly; yet today no one disputes the fact that it can be done. The world was surprised, and the acceptance that it could be done came from an outside source. Today no one doubts that flying is possible. It has become an intrinsic belief of all people who have seen an airplane; it has now become an idea that no longer has to come from an outside source. Likewise, the idea that with a new paradigm of life it is possible to overcome evil does not negate the fact that God deserves all the credit for the paradigm, because humans would have never thought of it.

Why are humans so eager to be dependent on the action of a supernatural force to make them think or act in accordance with God's will? Did God fail to give them the rationale to learn from Him how it is done? The reason humans seek the dictates of supernatural forces is simple. It is for the same reason the Children of Israel requested God to give them a Law by which to live; they did not want to have to think how to distinguish right from wrong or good from evil. Let God decide, and let Him tell us what to do, which is righteousness by works. But those who believe that supernatural forces acting on God's behalf can make them behave are also avoiding the responsibility to think correctly. Both groups have found a way to avoid thinking, which amounts to avoiding faith. With either theological view, sinners lose both their freedom and their capacity to grow love in their hearts. God does not want to reduce sinners to the status of remote-controlled play toys; He wants them to learn rationally how to think correctly that they might act voluntarily in agreement with the only principle of life that maintains it forever.

Being declared right by faith brings up yet another problem. Whenever people would commit evil deeds the external supernatural forces coming from God would have to be blamed for failing them. It could be said that God has either forgotten to activate the remote controls, or worse yet, God must have wanted the evil deed to be committed. How practical, no matter what people do it is either God's will or a lack of faith. This is clearly a common belief of pagan religions. Since God is in control of everything, they assume that even the most destructive behaviors could not have taken place if God did not want them to happen. This line of reasoning would imply that all people are guided by God's will and powers; thus they are all reduced to objects in God's remote-controlled universe. Theologically speaking this view is known as predestination, but the concept is not from God.

This begs an important question. If there were really such an external force that God could use for the purpose of keeping people in line, why would God restrict or deny such a power to anyone? It could only be because He wants pain and suffering to be perpetuated. But again, what an ugly picture of God is painted with this theology! The fact is that such powers do exist in the universe, but let us be quick to say that God would never use them to manipulate one's thinking or actions, only the devil would stoop to such levels. Scripture calls this "devil possession," and it comes in a variety of forms. Though God has access to such powers, using it to remote control a person or a people would be abuse of freedom, thus God would never use such methods despite their availability. The Holy Spirit is not an external power: it is the Spirit of God that empowers from within, it is the way God thinks, and it is the mentality of God that must also be ours. It is a belief system that all His intelligent created beings should seek in order to become permanent citizens of His everlasting kingdom. Something is clearly wrong with the concept that humans cannot avoid evil on their own, but as previously said, they cannot avoid evil without receiving from God the only prescription God has provided to all people all the way to the Cross. Only then can they share with God the same mind and have in them "the mind of Christ" (1 Cor. 2:16) or the "faith *of* Jesus" (Rev. 14:12 KJV/RSV).

A closer look at traditional doctrines of righteousness by faith shows that contrary to Christians claims it is not the third Person of the Godhead people need, though it is indeed the Holy Spirit understood as the way God thinks. The more an external supernatural force is requested by a religious person, the more the devil is likely to respond to the request. The problem is not with the Holy Spirit; the problem is with a false understanding of the Holy Spirit as it is suggested to operate in the heart by Trinity theology.

The Bible clearly teaches that to overcome evil a person must have a Spirit that is Holy, that is a spirit or mind guided by God's Word, His message of truth. This spirit is needed to produce love that emanates from within a person. Such love is both the opposite and the antidote of evil (see 1 Jn. 4:18). Paul writing to the Romans said it best: "And hope does not disappoint us, because God has poured out his love into our hearts by the Holy Spirit, *whom* he has given us" (Rom. 5:5, emphasis mine). Contrary to most translators who personify the Holy Spirit by using the pronoun "whom" because of their Trinitarian biases, the Holy Spirit is not a Person of the Godhead who enters the heart. In fact, the RSV translates the same text using the pronoun "which," "through the Holy Spirit which has been given to us" (Rom. 5:5 RSV). Nowhere in Scripture is the Holy Spirit called a person other than the only true God. It is God's Spirit that was in Jesus; it is how He thinks permanently. It is His immutable mind-set. The human mind was created in the image of God's mind, but we have chosen to deviate from His way of thinking. The Holy Spirit is not a divine Person at work to change our thoughts and actions; it is a principle of truth so perfectly logical that the rationale involved has the power to change the way a person thinks and acts. It is worth repeating, God's message of truth is the only way a sinner's mind and heart can be changed and motivated to reject evil in order to do good without abusing the sinner's freedom.

Hard to believe perhaps, but even Jesus had to go through this process of change. The author of Hebrews makes the following statement: "Since the children have flesh and blood, he too shared in their humanity" (Heb. 2:14). A bit further he writes that to help Abraham's descendants "he had to be made like his brothers in every way, in order that He might *become* merciful and faithful . . ." (Heb. 2:17, emphasis added). The text does not say that He was merciful from birth but that He became that way, implying a learning process similar to that of any of His human brothers seeking salvation.

A messianic prophecy of the prophet Isaiah about His youth and development makes that point with clarity: "Therefore the Lord himself will give you a sign: The virgin will be with child and will give birth to a son, and will call him Emmanuel. He will eat curds and honey when [*or, until*] he knows enough to reject the wrong [*evil*] and choose the right" (Is. 7:14, 15 brackets mine). The high quality of the food here implied is probably a reference to the quality of the education Jesus received from the Father (see Is. 50). It is most likely because like all humans Jesus had to undergo the same change of heart that Jesus insisted on receiving the baptism of John the Baptist. The baptismal ritual does not bestow special powers on a sinner as commonly believed. Like a wedding it is a public demonstration of a new beginning that changes the status of a person. In this case the union is made with God by accepting His way of life founded on a totally new and opposite orientation of mind. The sinner has come to realize and affirm publicly that the "me first" orientation of the mind we all receive from birth must yield to a different and opposite mind-set if one wishes to live God's way. Jesus understood that principle like a student who was never rebellious and never turned His back on the teachings of the Word He received from the Father (see Is. 50:5). When the "others first" mind-set is lacking, eternal life remains unattainable, because such a person would continue to be unwilling to participate in God's divine way of life.

Jesus was born under the natural law of human birth (see Heb. 4:4) and like all humans he had to learn "obedience from what he suffered" (Heb. 5:8), or at the price of pain and suffering. Such knowledge does not come without pain and suffering. That is why it can be said that, "once made perfect he became the source of eternal salvation for all who obey him (Heb. 5:9). It must be observed that the words "obedience" in verse 8 and "obey" in verse 9 are translated from the Greek *hupakoe* and *hupakouo* respectively. Both these words could have been translated to say, "He applied what he had heard" from the Father to His life, rather than the idea of obeying orders from a higher authority. The two are very different. All too often translators of Scripture convey the notion of obedience when instead they should have conveyed the notion of applying to one's life the principle of eternal life out of an internal desire born out of a rational persuasion God has conveyed. Obedience implies a legalistic submission to rules or persons, and thus it would be righteousness by works, which is invalid in God's eyes because a person may obey without undergoing a change of heart.

If God had chosen to control the actions of sinners by way of a supernatural force rather than persuasion, which the omnipotent God could do if He so desired, He could instantly eliminate evil from the hearts of every person living on the planet. The problem is that such people would no longer have the freedom to sin, thus they would have also lost their God-given freedom to become loving on their own volition. They would have lost all access to true love, and life would be tyranny. If the Holy Spirit were a Person of the Godhead why would God choose to attribute it to sinners on condition? Why should it be a force that God avails only a select few to whom He is willing to grant it, and on condition that they believe in the blood He shed to pay for their sins? Since "God is no respecter of person" (Acts 10:34 KJV), would that not be "favoritism," as that same text is translated to imply in the NIV? Why should God be slow or selective about dispensing such radical power that would instantly eradicate evil?

Most Trinitarians fail to realize that even if a sinner requests the participation of a supernatural force from God so as to overcome evil, He would not grant it on the grounds that it would place that person on remote control. Such a state of dependency would imply that love cannot come from within, thus love would be dead. Would God play such a game with His created beings? He does not lacks access to such powers, but He would not make use of them knowing that such an action would destroy love as a principle of eternal life. It would be a destruction of the only way eternal life in true freedom can exist. This also means that eternal life could never exist in the universe. How could God participate in the destruction of love, which is a condition for intelligent beings to live eternally? Righteousness, which is the product of love, can only be imparted and imputed through a clear understanding of the knowledge of God, which implies "knowing the mind of the Lord" (1 Cor. 2:16). If we fail to understand that God is Himself all about the unconditional "others always first" principle carried all the way to the death on the Cross, we cannot have access to the Holy Spirit understood as God's mind.

Another fallacy of "righteousness by faith" theology is that Jesus is perceived as having lived the perfect life in place of the sinner and as having died a death of penal substitution instead of the sinner. This theology is called Vicarious Substitution, but Scripture does not offer any substance to support such a concept. On the contrary, Scripture teaches emphatically: "The soul who sins is the one who will die. The son will not share the guilt of the father, nor will the father share the guilt of the son" (Eze. 18:20). Is that rule for humans but not for God? No text in Scripture suggests that the righteousness of person can ever be assigned or transferred to anyone else, not even that of Jesus, or He would have been glad to tell us that He accomplished that purpose. Nor does Scripture imply anywhere that it is possible to transfer sins from one person to another, not even onto the Person of Jesus. The notions of substitution and transfers of sin are entirely of pagan origin; they have nothing in common with Scripture, but more on that later.

The same is true with the idea that a supernatural Person should be allowed to enter a person's hearts to dictate behavior; it is a concept not found anywhere in Scripture. Only the forces of evil are willing to dictate behavior, not the only true God who is entirely dedicated to preserving and defending freedom at any cost to Himself. Occult religions teach and practice spirit transfer, communications with spirits of dead people, reincarnation, as well as body and mind control, but Scripture speaks of such occurrences as demon possessions (Mt. 8:28; 1 Cor. 10:21).

Current teachings of righteousness by faith can be as Scripturally mindless and debilitating as righteousness by works, because they involve mindless understandings of God along with totally false and debilitating concepts of salvation of human fabrications. God did not punish the Innocent One called Jesus to save the guilty, and salvation is never by substitution or transfer of sin; it is by the correct knowledge of God and His everlasting truth that persuades sinners that unconditional love is the only way to conquer sin. Righteousness, which is love, comes from a message sinners can understand and accept. It is not to a Person of the deity that sinners must submit having accepted "by faith" that His death was a payment for sins. Christianity has come to assume without Scriptural evidence that the good works of Jesus are simply substituted to those lacking in the lives of sinners. But strangely enough, with their theology God only rewards with substituted righteousness those sinners who happen to believe the preposterous concept that Jesus died to pay for sins.

Sincere people have been indoctrinated with such religious views for centuries. God will not hold it against them anymore than He held responsible the Israelites for their belief in righteousness through obedience to laws. But at the end of time Scripture tells us that things will be different. Jesus has promised that the Spirit of truth would bring His followers into all truth (Jn. 16:13). God is patient, understanding, and merciful, but the day is coming when we will be confronted by a clear understanding of God's pure truth. It will unite God's people as never before. When that day will be upon us, difficult choices will have to be made. Those who have failed to believe until then will have no choice but to believe. And those who believe will be shocked to discover that what they believe is not acceptable as truth coming from God. His truth is simple to understand, but ridding our minds of the cobwebs of lies from traditions is not easy. The cobwebs of traditions include long-held pagan superstitions and beliefs in the actions of supernatural forces engaged in protecting and changing human hearts. Supernatural forces from God can touch our lives by bringing protection and guidance, but they cannot take possession of the mind or body of a created human being unless they are from the devil.

It is generally said that humans tend to take the path of least resistance. But it appears that Christianity has chosen the path of no resistance at all when they claim that Jesus did it in their place. This is choosing the false idea that humans should be remote-controlled from heaven, which is preposterous because it would destroy what God is all about, love. Jesus did not do it in their place any more than He did it to pay for their sins at the price of His innocent life, but He did it for sinners indeed. He did it to deal squarely and fairly with the sin problem, not by substitution, superstition, or payment, but by offering real solutions for a real salvation. He did it to show sinners the way to overcome the evil that produces sin, not to pull the wool over God's eyes with righteousness assumed to hide their sinful lives.

Paul makes an impressive statement regarding the end of time when God's truth will be known the world over: "Then we will no longer be infants, tossed back and forth by the waves, and blown here and there by every wind of teaching and by the cunning and craftiness of men in their deceitful scheming" (Eph. 4:14). Time has come for us to reach that level of Christlike maturity through a clearer understanding of God's Word of truth. But to reach that level of maturity, all the "cunning and craftiness of men in their deceitful scheming" must be discarded as rubbish. They have kept humanity from seeing the way to the truth that gives life for long millennia.

God's prediction of destruction does not abuse anyone's freedom

God never intended the life of free-willed intelligent people to follow either one of the two pathways to righteousness presented above. A mystical participation of pagan origin remains present on both sides, which probably means that neither is from God. In fact, if a religion failed to be mystical in some way, chances are that it would cease to be recognized as a religion. Yet God makes it clear in Scripture that no supernatural forces or incomprehensible concepts of salvation should be considered a part of God's real plan to save humanity from evil. If supernatural forces had to be involved, how would sinners know which ones to listen to? Healing must come from within; all that God can do is to provide the necessary information to accomplish the purpose. Christians call faith their unexplainable mystical expectations related to salvation. In this case the word faith implies that since both righteousness by works and by faith fail to be explained rationally, faith requires the acceptance of irrational concepts as God's solution. Considering that no current religious system operates on the strength of logic alone, it could be said that they all require pagan understandings of faith to be accepted. The word "faith" itself has been paganized; over time it has lost its God-intended meaning of a persuasion founded on pure logic. As such, it would have immense power to change hearts from within, and this would be true conversion.

Both the doctrines of righteousness by faith and by works are purported to make salvation attainable through mystical ritualistic practices given irrational meanings. Yet both are founded on information apparently drawn from Scripture. To obtain salvation with either, a sinner must either accept to *submit* to meaningless actions involving rituals and rules, which implies suppression of freedom, or by believing superstitiously that a sinless substitute has accepted to pay a *penalty* by dying *in the believers' place to cover their sins*. Strangely enough, this belief is founded on the legal notion that the death of the Lord satisfied the stringent requirements of a legalistic God who demands that justice be served—a non-Scriptural concept unacceptable on logical grounds. Even in human courts of law, an innocent person cannot be made to pay for the guilty. Why should it be considered acceptable for God to follow an unjust practice on irrational grounds? How can an irrational approach solve the biggest problem of humanity?

The idea that correct thinking is able to inspire correct behavior is occasionally found under the pens of philosophers and psychologists, and perhaps even that of a few theologians, but the concept is essentially absent from church pulpits. Sermons are about *doing* the right thing, by being kind, respecting others by accepting other people's views, along with tolerance for anything and everything. The problem is that all this talk places the focus of Christian life on *doing*, not on learning how to think correctly in order to do that which is right. Most Christians want to believe that God has Himself taken all the necessary steps to correct the problem, and in a way, He has, but not as they think He has. Torturing to death a sinless Person to pay for the sins of evildoers was never the way God intended to deal with the problem of evil. If He had, Scripture would have made that point transparently throughout, but it has not.

To prove the foregoing wrong many would quote Isaiah 53:10 and other texts from Scripture. The reason I know is because I have faced their frustration on several occasions. This particular text in Isaiah is translated to say: "Yet it was the Lord's will to crush him" (Is. 53:10). We must remember that when Scripture was translated in English and other modern languages, the dominant view of Christianity was that Jesus paid the price of His life to appease the Father in an act of propitiation, or expiation in some versions of Scripture. The problem is that the text was translated with an existing false paradigm. A more appropriate translation would read: "God reluctantly submitted to the idea to let him be crushed." Indeed God accepted to send the Son to planet Earth knowing He would be killed in the process of sharing God's eternal truth. It was not His will that Jesus should die in the process but it was His will that Jesus should give humanity a last chance to understand truth, knowing that they would kill Him. God did not send Him to die, but to teach and live the message of God humans needed to rectify their belief system without violating their freedom. Unfortunately He had to take the mission all the way to its ultimate end to make His point unmistakably clear, because if He had aborted the mission before dying, humans would have never known how far love for neighbors or enemies should go. Clearly, Jesus demonstrated that love is unconditional, even if it must be taken all the way to one's own shedding of blood and death.

To accomplish God's purpose to convey truth Jesus was persecuted all the way to the Cross. He brought to the world a message incompatible with the way humans live and think naturally, from birth. They could not accept such an extreme level of love. With the mentality of Jesus, wars and self-defense would have to be proscribed, because they are tolerable only if a person lacks love. It can be said that at the price of His life Jesus communicated the divine message of truth. The only way the message could be communicated without infringing on human freedom in the least, was to take it all the way to the point where love can be taken no further; it is the total gift of self, and it must be taken unto death if necessary.

Our study will show that *propitiatory* offerings to appease God rituals can do nothing to help sinners overcome evil, nor can they motivate wrongdoers to do good works. Out of thankfulness for God and His sacrifice some humans accept to pattern their lives after Christ out of compassion for what He did for sinners. This belief makes them kinder and more loving people who are likely to be more sensitive to the sufferings of others. Thanks to this view Christianity has not been totally useless or negative. While such a view has taken the Christian world to greater levels of sensitivity it has not prevented them from perpetrating some of the worst atrocities of war and intolerance toward others.

In our study we will also find that no penalty was ever imposed on Christ *by the Father* as payment for sins. Such concepts of salvation are simply false because they are authenticated neither by Scripture nor by sound logic. Jesus paid the penalty sinners pay for sin, He died as do all sinners because we all live in a world of sin. The difference is that He did not sin, but it was not the Father who made Him pay, it was His human brothers and sisters. In fact, Isaiah makes that point in the same chapter. "He was despised and rejected *by men*, a man of sorrows, and familiar with suffering. Like one from whom men hide their faces he was despised [by men, not God] and *we* esteemed him not. Surely He took up our infirmities and carried our sorrows, yet *we* considered him stricken by God, smitten by him, and afflicted" (Is. 53:3, 4, emphasis and brackets mine). We are the ones who considered Him stricken by God; this was not God's idea. The doctrinal belief that God wanted Him killed to pay the price for sin is a human invention. We must recognize that pagan-influenced faulty translations and erroneous interpretations of Scripture have sometimes led to false conclusions.

What appears quite clear is that Christianity has in theory adopted Christ as their Savior, but in reality they have riddled His message of salvation with pagan delusions going back to Adam and Eve. Let us not put the blame on any one church or religious group, all humans are guilty. Interpretations of Scripture have been laced throughout with ancient mythologies and false concepts suggested by the way nature and humans operate. Since Nature is also far from perfect, considering that it operates entirely on the need to survive through competition, it is unfit to provide a model to overcome evil. During the Medieval period the dominant Christian faith was misled to sell indulgences. This concept is as closely related to the story of Cain as can be found anywhere in Christianity. Indeed, no payment can be made to earn salvation. Later, dissatisfied with this unbiblical approach, another belief just as unbiblical began to spread: Since Jesus paid the penalty at the price of a righteous unmerited death, His righteousness supposedly qualifies to stand in place of sinners' own lack of love, which is their lack of righteousness. The false belief is that the perfect righteousness of Jesus can be attributed to a sinner and that by so doing the transfer of righteousness makes the sinner righteous. Where does such lack of common sense come from? Worse yet, it is a belief in a substitution of righteousness that supposedly clears sinners of their guilt because their guilt was passed on to Jesus who supposedly died on the Cross from the heavy weight of all the sinners' guilt! It was not the weight of their guilt that killed Jesus; it was the weight of the pain He bore in His heart because the very sinners He came to save were unwilling to listen to His message that makes eternal life possible by growing love in the heart. It was the guilt sinners were unwilling to resolve that killed Jesus, not the transfer of human guilt onto Jesus.

We should ask what exactly did Jesus pay for with His life by dying on a Cross? And who might have been the beneficiary of the payment? That question has been debated since the third century of our era. Until the latter part of the eleventh century CE, mainstream Christianity believed that the devil was the beneficiary of the payment made on the Cross. By then Anselm of Canterbury (1033–1109) realized that such a theology would imply that God negotiated with the devil to arrive at such an arrangement—and what a horrible arrangement that was. With this agreement the Son of God would have to first live a perfect human life before dying a cruel death on a Cross. Anselm reasoned that such a view destroys the Scriptural concept that God is omnipotent. Why should the Almighty have to negotiate with the devil and accept such a sinister bargain if He were omnipotent? There is no reason to believe that salvation was ever conditional on God's success to negotiate with the devil. Indeed, the devil was none other than one of God's created beings turned evil. This realization led Anselm to suggest that the payment was not made to the devil but to God the Father. A concept the bulk of Christianity continues to share to this day.

Unfortunately, Anselm's suggestion made God look even worse than did the previously held theology. He postulated that God was jilted by the human race for disrespecting Him by failing to obey His orders. On the basis of Romans 6:23 Anselm postulated that since God's rule of the universe is cast in stone, it requires any disobedience to be punished with the penalty of death. Thus, to save the honor of God all humans would have been killed because all sinned. However, he also postulated that since the death of sinful humans would not suffice to reset the scales of divine justice, the Son of God would have to save face for the Father by living a perfect life before dying a cruel death to pay for all their sins on a Cross. It is unclear where Anselm got this idea, because it is nowhere found in Scripture. Only a few mistranslated passages and a few false interpretations of Scripture make possible such convoluted conclusions.

Furthermore, with Anselm's view God is presumed merciless and legalistic to the hilt. As such He is the One who required all the bloodshed rituals of death in order to forgive sinners. Such a theology paints a picture of God as the worst murderers who believed it perfectly normal to kill His innocent Son. But that is not all. This invented theology makes of God a coconspirator with traitors the likes of Judas as well as the religious and secular leaders who plotted to have Jesus put to death. If this scenario were acceptable, Judas, the soldiers, and the leaders who killed Jesus as well as the people who wanted Barabbas released, would all have to be admired and appreciated for their willful collaboration with God (see Mt. 27:16–26). If they were acting on God's behalf to kill the Innocent One, there is every reason to think that they were dedicated servants of God who used them to achieve His purpose! But clearly this is not what Scripture teaches.

God supposedly wanted someone of infinite value to die because nothing of lesser value could possibly pay the debt of sin. A statement of the Apostle Paul may appear to support this view because he wrote: "The wages of sin is death" (Rom. 6:23). Thus it is assumed by proponents of the false theology that to pay for the sins of the world only God's Son could qualify and only if He was able to live a perfect life in order to offer a perfect sacrifice of blood and death that would finally satisfy the Father's anger.

The problem with this faulty reading of Paul's statement is that it is inspired by a faulty theology of God's wrath that fails to recognize Paul's own view of God's wrath. In his Epistle to the Romans Paul makes it clear that God's wrath has nothing in common with human anger. He summed up the wrath of God in the following verse: "Therefore God gave them over in the sinful desires of their hearts" (Rom. 1:24a). In other words, God's wrath is not anger eager to punish; it is His unfathomable dedication to the freedom of His created beings because no matter how damaging evil could become in the world He would not intervene to stop it. Indeed, it is evil that punishes humans, not God. From a human point of view such an attitude on God's part may appear as sheer madness, because as powerful as God is He refuses to interfere with the freedom He has given. He could have chosen to interfere with the will and actions of humans by reducing or destroying evil. But God's wrath allows evil to run its course for the safekeeping of love dependent on freedom as a system of operation for the universe. As we have said, God cannot interfere with freedom without destroying the very freedom that makes love possible.

Jesus did not die to pay for sins at all; something far more important and far more beautiful and desirable was taking place on the scene of cosmic history. The payment on the Cross was a dear price indeed, but it was never intended to be a payment made to the devil or to the Father. Nor can it be said that the Lord's death was God's requirement to cancel guilt and pardon sin. God is more than willing to pardon freely all sinners, just as Jesus rebuked Peter who wondered if forgiving seven times might be enough: "Jesus answered, 'I tell you, not seven times, but seventy-seven times'" (Mt. 18:22). In other words, humans should not bother to keep count. Should the merciful God be perceived less forgiving than Jesus suggested humans should be?

With these and other faulty theological doctrines and dogmas[13] a vast number of Christians spend their time in churches *doing and saying* what appears to make sense from a human perspective. They pray, sing, and go to church to make sure that God sees the strength of their faith and feelings of gratitude for Jesus who paid the price of the Cross for their sins. They believe that the expression of strong feelings of gratefulness toward their Savior makes them more deserving of His unmerited favors they call grace. These beliefs and practices are perceived as the sinners' expressions of faith that release them of guilt for sins committed. As a result Christians spend much of their time in churches praising God with gratitude for the bloody payment that was made on their behalf. All this church activity remains a focus on *doing* something for the Lord, thus it is still a form of righteousness by works regardless of the theology they choose to endorse. It is true that many Christians have been touched by the selfless act of Jesus. As a result, many are dedicated to *doing* good deeds in this world in a spirit of gratitude for what Jesus has done for them. Learning how to think like Jesus is rarely mentioned. It is undeniable that many Christians are kind to their neighbors and care for the sick and poor. Countless Christians have exhibited remarkable character and should be commended for their services to humankind. But could it not be said that every religion, even the most pagan and most secular, teach the importance of altruism? Indeed, even secular humanism is a philosophy that relies largely on the power of the human brain to resolve social problems through altruistic ethical means, thus it could be called a religion. Any ideology or field of study devoted to improve the human condition through altruism is a religion of sort; this would include most, if not all the political ideologies of this world. But why are humans so reluctant to try God's way as He brings it to our attention in Scripture?

God has a wonderful and simple plan to eradicate evil, and He will accomplish His purpose without destroying the freedom that makes love

---

13   A dogma is a religious belief for which there is no serious Scriptural foundation. A doctrine is a belief founded on information found or suggested by Scripture, whether the interpretation is correct or not.

possible. This also means that He will use love as His sole weapon to accomplish His purpose. This book is an attempt to reason with readers of all religious and philosophical backgrounds regardless of religious affiliation or lack thereof. Believing in fables has never resolved anything. Yet religions are essentially fables, except the one that comes from Jesus, but that one has yet to be recognized for what it is and proclaimed to the world. God has offered it freely throughout the history of humankind, but His people have not been listening.

To understand what has happened in the history of humanity, it must be recognized that for the most part pagan beliefs are distortions of God's message to humanity. Thus there is an undeniable link between pagan religions and modern Christianity. However, contrary to common beliefs Christianity is not the product of pagan religions. Scripture suggests that God instituted highly meaningful rituals long before the advent of Israelites, Judaism, or Christianity. God wanted to convey His message of truth to help sinners overcome evil, but instead His messages and related rituals were hijacked and distorted to produce what became the pagan religions of our world. The Children of Israel were later offered an opportunity to depart from pagan distortions and return to God's original message of truth once again, and for the purpose of setting sinners free, but they failed. The same can be said about Christianity. Thanks to the life of Jesus they were to return to God's original message to overcome evil, but once again they failed. Thus, to find truth all religious beliefs of Christianity should be reevaluated through the filter of sound logic. This is the only approach that will make possible the elimination of all irrational elements from religious tenets. Once accomplished, seekers of truth will be much closer to finding it than any currently existing religion.

This is in fact the advice Paul gave Titus. He was to encourage others by preaching "sound doctrines" (Titus 1:9). This implies that the doctrines he was called to share were to be acceptable on the grounds of logic. Religious views of which the logic is questionable should be rejected on the basis that they could not have originated from the only true God. While sound principles can be found in Scripture, they are often missed or dismissed only because a Veil of pagan falsehood responsible for blinding hearts and minds has permeated God's teachings.

Many are those who still search for the ultimate truth Scripture affirms will set free all intelligent beings willing to accept it and become a part of the everlasting kingdom. The approach suggested in this book is controversial because it does not fit the current trends or tenets of any existing religion. Let us not forget that millennia of religious traditions have furrowed deep grooves falsely assumed to be truth. Let us never insult anyone's courage to seek honestly the truth God has brought to light, even if mistakes are made in the process. As Winston Churchill said so eloquently: "Men occasionally stumble over the truth, but most of them pick themselves up and hurry off as if nothing ever happened."

God has given every intelligent being the wisdom and intelligence required to recognize truth or He would not encourage any of us to seek it (see Mt. 7:7). As our modern world has demonstrated multiple times, when a truth is recognized and accepted it has the power to change people and the way they live for the better. For example, truth about ecology has even changed the way we handle our trash. Truths about gravity, thermodynamics, propulsion, and aerodynamics have changed the way we transport goods and travel. Truth about the behaviors of electrons has changed the way we communicate. The same will happen with God's truth when finally it will be recognized and accepted by sincere people focused on seeking the "only true God" on the solid foundation of pure logical thinking.

This affirmation does not come from this author; Scripture stated the concept some 2,650 years ago under the pen of Jeremiah the Prophet of Judah: "The time is coming," declares the LORD, "when I will make a new covenant with the house of Israel and with the house of Judah. It will not be like the covenant I made with their forefathers when I took them by the hand to lead them out of Egypt, because they broke my covenant, though I was a husband to them" declares the LORD. "This is the covenant I will make with the house of Israel after that time" declares the LORD. "I will put my law *(way of life)* in their minds and write it on their hearts. I will be their God and they will be my people. No longer will a man teach his neighbor, or a man his brother, saying, 'know the LORD,' because they will all know me from the least of them to the greatest," declares the LORD. "For I will forgive their wickedness and will remember their sins no more" (Jer. 31:31–34, parenthesis mine).

Consider the above text from the quill of Jeremiah as saying: "For I will heal their problem of evil, thus I will no longer need to remember their sins" because they will be equipped with the knowledge of the LORD that will progressively enable them to overcome evil. The reason they will accept to undergo this amazing change of heart is simple. When the truth will be understood and proclaimed, at some point in time in the not-so-too-distant future, it will no longer be necessary to proclaim God's message. Everyone on the planet will have heard about it. It is a truth so simple that no high levels of intelligence will be required to understand it. Some will accept the message that has the power of logic to set sinners free, and they will recognize that it comes from God and that it is His way to produce the remission of the sin disease in the world. Empowered by the truth these people will become so focused on the welfare of others that they will probably be unaware of the progress they are making to overcome sin. Concern for their own salvation will no longer be on top of their brains because their own welfare will no longer be relevant in God's way of life. Changed by the truth they will be entirely focused on the welfare of others. The message from God is indeed the only medication powerful enough to bring about such a change of focus. The transformation from concern for self to concern for others will inevitably induce the remission of the sin disease.

When the day of truth will finally be upon us in this world, it will become so obvious that it is indeed truth that comes from God that pastors and priests will become an obsolete breed. In fact, it is to that end that they should all be laboring. God's purpose will have been accomplished. Indeed, "No longer will a man teach his neighbor, or a man his brother, saying, 'Know the LORD,' for they will all know me, from the least of them to the greatest, declares the LORD" (Jer. 31:34, also quoted in Heb. 8:11). According to this prophecy every person who accepts the truth will become a priest—that is to say, they will all be perfect friends to every person they encounter regardless of the divisions that separate the people of this world. They will all be self-governing kings who are at the same time perfect friends to all.

People who accept this divine calling will be guided by a power of persuasion so powerful that it will reside permanently in their hearts, and this, for all of eternity. As it was for Jesus, they will continue to be tempted while on this earth, but as God predicted through His prophets, Jesus, and His Apostles, His Law as a system of life will be indelibly engraved on their hearts and minds. Though the Ten Commandments themselves will not be engraved on their hearts, they will observe every one of them, not because they have to, but because they will want to live no other way. They will be compelled by the love that comes from God

(2 Cor. 5:14). A single word will need be engraved in their hearts to bring every one of them to live the Law of God, as did Jesus. That word is the word "love." They will have acquired it through the perfectly rational persuasion that comes from God's perfect logic. The message, as well as the transformation it produces will be recognized as God's doing. All that sinners will have to do is to accept the truth that will set them free. Altar calls to accept Jesus in one's heart will mean nothing less.

It is not enough to say: "I accept Jesus as my personal Savior." There is a process that must be recognized and followed for His faith to become our own. It does not happen by accident or by any magic; it happens by understanding. Once written on people's hearts this truth becomes an intrinsic belief system that guides a person's entire modus operandi in this life and forever. It is a persuasion that modifies sinners from within. It is able to change all actions and behaviors of believers. It is a truth that has become their permanent faith. Indeed, God places no external pressure on a free individual of His creation to think or behave any certain way. Thanks to God's communication of the truth at the price of the life of Jesus, one's persuasion in the "message of the cross" (1 Cor. 1:18) becomes one's modus operandi. Once accepted this message progressively restores the image of God in sinners, as they begin to mirror God's character in whose image they were originally created. This does not mean that humans become gods; it merely means that socially and ethically speaking they think like God. They become increasingly altruistic in all dealings and interactions with God and other people, as well as with their animals and physical environment.

This book is entirely dedicated to healing the most dreadful and most devastating disease of the heart—it is called evil. It is the indisputable destroyer of life and the earth. It is a disease we have all inherited because of the insecurities in which we are born. These insecurities are not God's fault; they are the fault of humans who thus far have refused or neglected to seek from God the cure He offers. The goodness of God is the exact opposite of evil; He is all about enhancing life and the earth for all His created beings, for "God is love" (1 Jn. 4:8, 16). Joining Him in His effort to restore His character in humanity has the potential to improve life for all, and ultimately, we will have the privilege to enjoy it more abundantly. Jesus made a powerful statement in this regard. Speaking of the devil and evil He said: "The thief comes only to steal and kill and destroy; I have come that they may have life, and have it to the full" (Jn. 10:10).

CHAPTER 4

Religion Should Have Been the Solution . . . But Something Went Wrong

Time is flying by on planet Earth. In terms of knowledge and human accomplishments the world is developing at an ever-increasing pace. However, in terms of religion, or to be more specific, in terms of the people's knowledge of "the only true God" (Jn. 17:3) and His "message" (Mt. 13:19) of peace and freedom, heavy clouds of confusion persist, and they appear more menacing every day. This fact should not be a reason for discouragement however. It should do the opposite in a way, because Jesus said: "Even so, when you see these things happening, you know that the kingdom of God is near" (Lk. 21:31).

If there is indeed a vital message that God has been trying to convey for millennia, should we not be interested in knowing what the message tells us? If we fail to know what Jesus told us, how we can choose to accept or reject it knowingly? How can we be free to make a choice if we don't know what the choices are? New denominations of Christianity spring out of the woodwork almost daily. Why is humanity still so confused about God and the one and only genuine brand of religion He offers? He claims to have the solution to the human problem of evil, but again, are we listening? Did we not have a visitor from heaven some 2,000 years ago? Did not God expect Him to clarify His message "once for all" (Heb. 7:27)? Did He not claim to be "the way, the truth, and the life" (Jn. 14:6)? No other person in the history of our world has had the audacity to make such a bold claim; should we not at least give His message equal opportunity to speak to our hearts?

Let us think about the claim Jesus made: What if He were everything He claimed to be? Should we not at least accept to study His philosophy of life on the merit of His message regardless of the miracles He performed? Should we not give it equal opportunity to be examined as we would the works of countless other philosophers, great or small? The message of Jesus has been assigned to the domain of religion; as such it has been dismissed from philosophy. The main reason His message is classified in the domain of religion is because it has been mystified through interpretations based on extra-biblical superstitions of pagan origin. Sure, Jesus performed miracles of a mystical nature, promised eternal life, and had access to extrasensory perceptions. But His message related to the way love grows in the heart should have been received independently of His miracles, prophecies, and other mystical manifestations. Amazing miracles were merely done to provide a signature of authorship to His message that could not come from someone other than the Creator. They were performed to bring the message to the attention of people who should have recognized it as coming from God. He alone could have empowered Jesus in such manner.

The message itself was never intended to be of a mystical nature. By suggesting a transcendental dimension to His message it was automatically aligned with all the mystical religions. By so doing an objective study of His message has been thwarted, which is exactly what churches have done. When properly studied the miracles were also intended to illustrate some of the teachings of the Master. But the miracles were only embellishments of His message. In God's approach to overcoming evil, none of the supernatural powers or blessings traditionally associated with pagan religions should have been incorporated; they should all have been dismissed as coming from the devil.

The greatest miracle God performed was to provide us with access to His message. The next greatest miracle is that people can receive the message He has communicated and be transformed by its pure logic despite the fact that it goes squarely against the grain of natural human instincts of survival. The message of Jesus should be contemplated on the strength of its practical substance only, even if in His life elements of a supernatural nature were present, but never used to serve Him personally. The moment a subjective element is introduced in the message from God its truth is inevitably clouded. Unfortunately, this is exactly what Christians have done in history. They have done exactly what Jesus predicted false teachers and prophets would do. In fact, Jesus never promised special blessings such as riches, better health, powers, fame, or special protection. On the contrary, His followers were warned that He had not "come to bring peace to the earth." Instead, He said: "I did not come to bring peace but a sword" (Mt. 10:34). He went so far as to predict that His message would turn a man against his father and a daughter against her mother. Indeed, the Jews expected a religious leader out of Him, and they got a philosopher who dedicated His life to teaching and living a concept of eternal life such as no philosopher before or after Him had ever begun to understand. His message had to be a philosophy able to touch people's hearts, because a mystical religious message such as pagans understood could not have accomplished the purpose. Persuasion, or faith, must come from perfect logic, or it lacks the power to produce the required conversion of heart.

Paul said it but his statement is often misunderstood. Speaking of the last days he expresses concern for those who fail to "escape from the trap of the devil" because they have failed to recognize the "knowledge of the truth," by "com[ing] to their senses" (2 Tim. 2:25, 26). The NIV translated the Greek *ananēphō*, "come to their senses." In reality this word would normally be translated as "becoming sober," as though people are inebriated to the point of not understanding something that makes logical sense. Immediately after writing these words to Timothy, Paul indicates that the problem will become crucial near the end of time for the world. "But mark this," he writes. "There will be terrible times in the last days. People will become lovers of themselves" (2 Tim. 3:1, 2a). Paul could not be more transparent. The problem is clearly one of "me first" mentality. He goes on to describe the problems this mentality brings out of people, "lovers of money, boastful, proud, abusive . . . without love, unforgiving . . . brutal . . . conceited," (2 Tim. 3:2, 3), and others. He ends this long list by saying: "having a form of godliness but denying its power. Have nothing to do with them" (2 Tim. 3:5). The last statement does not sound Christian-like. The translation is at fault. Paul is not saying to have nothing to do with them, but to have nothing to do with their teachings. The Greek word is *apotrepō* meaning deflect. It is impossible to deflect people, but it is certainly possible to deflect their mentality, their corrupted concepts of God and His message.

The Jews whose religion was paganized were expecting a supernatural intervention against the Romans and a new government established on laws God Himself would enforce. This could never happen, because it goes against the very message He was bringing at great price. Such an action would have imposed laws. And even if God had written them on the people's hearts at the people's request, such an action would have destroyed both freedom and love, thus it would have destroyed any hope of eternal life founded on love.

If Jesus were all that He claimed to be, why is Christianity still struggling with spiritual and religious confusion? Could it be because His message was received as a religion with a pagan perception of religion involving superstitions and supernatural interventions? Could it be that we have literally failed to study His message of truth as we would objectively approach the discourses of any great philosopher? Had humanity treated the message of Jesus as a philosophy instead of a religion, the world would be far more likely to recognize its priceless value.

Jesus was indeed either everything He claimed to be, and we shall attempt to validate His claim on purely logical grounds, or He was an imposter whose message is meaningless and utopic at best, as claim a number of philosophers, including famed German philosopher Friedrich Nietzsche who called His message pure utopia. If the teachings of Jesus were studied without expectations of supernatural expressions and blessings, as are those of world philosophers, the vital truth of His message would suddenly come to life and it would transform lives.

It appears that with the exponential growth of knowledge taking place on this planet over the last couple of centuries, if there were a true God He should become increasingly more perceptible and recognizable, not the other way around. Scientists and philosophers are leaving Christianity in droves because as scientific knowledge increases God is becoming increasingly more irrelevant to their search for knowledge. Yet if both Creation and logic are from God, all the knowledge gained is from Him, thus He should become increasingly more relevant. Unfortunately, Jesus has become a mere cultural and social convenience, if that. Voices from pulpits tell us we should have a relationship with Him because He is a friend. But increasingly, the relationship implied is to be developed supernaturally, on the basis of listening to His voice speaking to us and other dangerous superstitions. Such a relationship involves being filled with the Holy Spirit, but this spirit is viewed as the Third Person of the Divinity that supposedly speaks directly to the heart. It appears that the supernatural powers of the Holy Spirit are all that Christians seek. Surveys suggest that although Bibles are more readily available than ever before in history, Christians are less knowledgeable about its contents than they were just a half a century ago. Thus a sincere search for the knowledge of God from Scripture is becoming increasingly more irrelevant to modern versions of religion.

On the other hand, those people who still have the courage to believe in God and study their Bibles find themselves challenged by scientific atheism. To respond to their attacks they are all the more impelled to demonstrate to the world that Holy-Spirit-filled people have access to supernatural mystical forces. For them, health, wealth, and blessings are all the product of the Holy Spirit. They preach defiantly against the value of logic in religious matters because humans lack the capacity to understand God. But that is not what Scripture brings to our attention when it says that "No longer will a man teach his neighbor . . . saying 'know the LORD,' because they will all know me" (Her. 31:31). Though the demonstrative public miracles of modern religions can be disputed on the basis that some of them are staged, even if they were genuine they would be recognized as devoid of substance capable of making this world a better place to live. They essentially preach that the supernatural infusion of Holy Spirit is all that religion is about and all that sinners need to be saved. Their faiths and teachings are increasingly more akin to that of psychics, mediums, and animist healers. They need to include elements of supernatural power in their worships because they have dismissed logic as a means by which to seek God and express religious piety. This limits their ministry to providing the attendees with demonstrations of unexplainable supernatural forces for the sole purpose of proving that such forces exist in the universe, as indeed they do. But how are they to know for sure if those powers are from the only true God or from the prince of this earth Jesus identified as the devil? Indeed, the devil is the one whose philosophy of religion and life perpetuates evil that leads to death.

Because they lack the background needed to understand that pagan worships originated by distorting God's message, historians of religions consider that Judaism and Christianity as mere modernized extensions of pagan cults. In reality, as said earlier, pagan worships are distortions of God's originally ordained message of which the purpose was to help the first generations of humans to overcome the problem of evil. Unfortunately, because they have assimilated pagan views and practices, both Judaism and Christianity are now perceived as having pagan origins.

We must realize that according to Scripture the pre-Flood inhabitants of this world lived nearly one thousand years. Natural death from old age was not an issue for the first millennia. The only human deaths they could witness were the probably rare incidences of violence. Healthy individuals probably felt quite invulnerable, as do many younger people today. Thus, to sear into the minds of the first generations the fact that evil causes death, God appears to be the One who instituted a ritual designed to produce graphic images of death in their minds. But the ritual was intended to serve another divine purpose. Before the animal was slaughtered a confession of wrongdoing was to be made. Since wrongdoing is always the manifestation of failed love, the purpose of the confession was primarily a reminder that God's message of truth is the only way to bring back love in a sinner's heart. Since evil is always lack of love and lack of love is always due to excess pride, the animal represented not only the death sin causes, but also the sinner's willingness to kill his or her own prideful self.

Rejecting one's own egocentrism that leads to pride is the first step required to grow love in a sinner's heart. Knowing that sin produces death the sinner expresses thankfulness to God for His bountiful mercifulness always willing to give sinners another chance to grow love in their hearts no matter how far from love they have deviated. Since God protects our freedom, his mercy is bestowed on all sinners who sincerely desire a change of heart. It is only when a sinner no longer desires the change of heart that he or she has committed what Scripture calls the sin against the Holy Spirit. It is not God removing His mercy, it is the sinner's own rejection of the Holy Spirit, a rejection of the way God thinks with His "others first" unconditional mind-set. It is a willful departure from God's merciful spirit—God never takes away His Spirit; sinners remove themselves from it.

This is a question Jesus addressed. Speaking of the "blasphemy against the Spirit" He said that all sins are forgiven save one. Jesus goes so far as to say, "Anyone who speaks a word against the Son of Man *will be forgiven*, but anyone who speaks against the Holy Spirit *will not be forgiven*, either in this age or in the age to come" (Mt. 12:31, 32, emphasis mine). An aspect of this statement should beg an important question: If Jesus is a Person of the Godhead referred to as the Son of Man in this passage and the Holy Spirit is also a Person of the Godhead, why should they not both be treated equally? Trinity theology will be discussed later, but the point is that there is no Person of the Godhead called the Holy Spirit. We should also consider this passage in the light of our discussion at the end of the preceding chapter. The word "forgiveness" is an incorrect translation; the word "remission" of the sin problem would be more appropriate. Read with this understanding my amplified translation would read: "Those who rejects the Son of Man can recover because they have not yet rejected the way God thinks, but a person who rejects the way God thinks after knowing how He thinks in truth cannot recover from such a rejection, not in this life nor in a life after death in the age to come."

This text is all about the abandonment of God's "others first" attitude of mind and heart. When a person understands it and rejects it, that person has also rejected the purpose for which Jesus came to this world all the way to the Cross. If the Holy Spirit were indeed a Third Person of the Godhead, a refusal of forgiveness would be cruel and unfair on God's part. However, since the Holy Spirit is the acceptance of the way God thinks, rejecting the way He thinks in terms of "others first" is the sinner's own decision to separate himself or herself from the way God thinks. Thus this sin cannot be forgivable because it becomes insurmountable, not because God won't forgive, but because humans have rejected the principle of unconditional love that makes eternal life possible.

Only the lack of love in the heart is responsible for producing evil that leads to inevitable death. Thus the only solution to the problem of sin is greater love. But how is this done? God has given us the formula to accomplish this miracle of transformation all along. But more recently, Jesus came to show us the way to accomplish this transformation by going all the way to the Cross to give us a complete demonstration of the process as well as the result: unconditional love.

The reader might wish to know why this author is saying that the sacrificial system was not an offering made to God but a message intended to transform sinners' hearts? Since the Bible fails to make that point this author must be talking without proof from Scripture. It is true that the transformative purpose of the sacrificial system is not clearly established in OT Scripture. This is especially true when we consider the way humans have chosen to interpret Scripture on the basis of pagan traditions. On the other hand, we must also remember that the Bible also fails to say in clear terms that the sacrificial system was a way to present gifts to God to appease Him with bloody offerings. That interpretation is entirely derived from pagan thinking. How do we know then that the sacrificial system contained an educational message of transformation intended to make the heart of sinners more loving? Since this is bound to be a burning question in the reader's mind, let us answer in all simplicity:

1. **Neither God nor His message ever changes.** Numerous texts make that clear. "I the LORD do not change. So you, O descendants of Jacob, are not destroyed" (Mal. 3:6). God's word does not change either. "The Grass withers and the flowers fall, but the word of our God stands forever" (Is. 40:8). James in the New Testament confirms that the nature of God does not change and that His message stands forever. "Don't be deceived, my dear brothers, every good and perfect gift is from above, coming down from the Father of the heavenly lights, who does not change like shifting shadows. He chose to give us birth [new birth implied] through the word of truth, that we might be a kind of firstfruit of all he created" (Jas. 1:16–18 brackets mine).

2. **Since neither God nor His message ever changes, what makes us think that there is a difference between the message relative to the sacrificial rituals of the Old Testament and that of the baptismal and Last Supper rituals of the New?** The Bible does not tell us what the sacrificial ritual was intended to teach sinners, but it tells us the message the baptism ritual was supposed to convey to sinners. Since God does not change and since His message does not change either, we can safely assume that the meaning of the sacrificial ritual meant the same thing as the baptismal ritual instituted by John the Baptist and the Apostles. What does the NT tell us about the meaning of baptism? "We were therefore buried with Him through baptism into death in order that, just as Christ was raised from the dead through the glory of the Father, we too may live a new life" (Rom. 6:4). If baptism is a sign of new birth into a new life sinners are expected to accept, the new birth represents the death of the old egocentric prideful self, as Paul clarifies the concept two verses later when he says: "For we know that our old self was crucified with him so that the body of sin ["me first" pride] might be done away with" (Rom. 6:6 brackets mine).

3. **If God does not change, why has Christianity accepted the conclusion that baptism bears a different message than did the sacrificial rituals of the OT?** The answer to this question

can only be made with the help of logic. Clearly, the message of the New Testament is the final word on God's meaning of His message Jesus came to convey. Jesus kept repeating that He was talking on behalf of the Father. An example of that is given in the Gospel of John where Jesus is saying in His final prayer with His disciples: "For I gave them the words [*rhēma*, or outpouring of God's mind-set] you gave me and they accepted them" (Jn. 17:8a, brackets mine).

4. **The fact that the Israelites and the Jews after them interpreted the sacrificial ritual as a gift of propitiation made to God is sustained neither in OT Scripture nor the NT.** Influenced by pagan cults where propitiatory offerings were the primary substance of worships, the Children of Israel got confused over time. They assigned a pagan meaning to rituals God had given them to instruct them into the way of salvation. Such corruption of God's intended meanings became so deeply ingrained that they could no longer be rectified by sending more prophetic messages to correct a message corrupted beyond restoration. Messages intended to repair the false interpretations were given repeatedly through prophetic communications. Ultimately Jesus had to come in human flesh to make straight the path that was made crooked. This work began with John the Baptist: "He said, I am the voice of the one crying in the wilderness, Make straight the way of the Lord, as said the prophet Esaias" (Jn. 1:23, see Is. 40:3). It was because the theological message had been made crooked that it needed to be straightened out. It is for this reason that Jesus came to this world. Since the former symbols intended to bring salvation were corrupted, Jesus did not try to redefine their meanings, that would have been a waste of time and effort, but He introduced a new set of symbols with the same meaning, namely baptism and the Last Supper. Thus God introduced a totally new set of rituals with new symbols to replace the old ones that were made obsolete when humans corrupted them (see Heb. 8:13). The beauty of the new symbols is that they could not be interpreted as propitiatory gifts to appease God by paying for sins. They all represented one or another aspect of the gift of self dedicated to the renewal of one's heart by the power *of the message* of God reconveyed to humanity all the way to the Cross.

It is because the message of the slaughter rituals was lost that progress toward a change of heart could no longer take place. Jewish religion has become a set of dos and don'ts unrelated to the state of one's heart or correct thinking. Indeed, God's truth could no longer fulfill its God-given purpose to make sinners free. Jesus came to save the situation by renewing the message and by introducing new rituals involving new symbols. In fact, the New Testament should never have been called New; it should have been called the Renewed Testament.

Teachings involving animal slaughter, not offerings to pay

God is clearly the One who ordained the so-called sacrificial system, falsely called and mislabeled "sacrificial offerings." They were never intended to be sacrificial offerings, because, as we shall see, this is a pagan interpretation of God's originally instituted ritual—a ritual of which the purpose was to teach how to overcome sin, not a way to pay for them. Pagan sacrifices are gifts to the gods intended to secure their favors and pardon. God's ritual was the slaughter of an animal, not a gift to God of a dead animal. God's system was entirely educational and curative in purpose. These rituals were neither gifts to God nor a way to secure His forgiveness. They were intended as a way to overcome sin, thus a way for sinners to partake with God in the *remission* of the sin disease in the universe, not to forgive sin.

Even such words as "worship" and "meditation" as they are applied to religious practices have been assigned pagan meanings. Instead of a study of God's character and His amazing way of life that counteracts evil in the universe, worships have become cultural liturgies involving meaningless rituals seasoned with occasional good deeds for the self-centered purpose of securing God's blessings and protection. The only true meaning of worship should involve the study of the way God operates to help humans regain the perfect love our first parents lost in the Garden. That is in fact what salvation is all about. Few are the people who believe that there is a God whose message can be recognized and studied on purely rational grounds rather than on a mystical spiritual faith often empty of logic and common sense.

Like the word "worship," the words "spirit" and "spiritual" have also been assigned pagan meanings. God would never stoop so low as to employ supernatural means or forces to make anyone think or do anything. As previously said, such a disposition on God's part would be a violation of the very free will He labors to protect even at the price of His own life. Thus God has no other choice than to make available to the human family a perfectly rational message they can recognize as truth that changes hearts—nothing else. A genuine change of heart is vital, but it will never be imposed. If a message cannot be understood logically it is worthless because it will always fall short of being persuasive beyond doubt. A message of truth can only be accepted on the strength of its intellectual merits, not bizarre fairy tales founded on irrational mysterious superstitions that could never be recognized as logically persuasive. A close analysis of religions reveals that they are all founded on one or another form of superstitious beliefs lacking logic.

Seeking help from supernatural forces involving superstitious means is more than dangerous; it is a fatal mistake. It opens the door to external supernatural powers willing to abuse human freedom, as do the thieves and scammers of this world. The Apostle Paul called such powers the "spiritual forces of evil" (Eph. 6:12). Notice the use of the word "spiritual" here. Spiritual forces are not necessarily from God. If God and His message can indeed be perceived on perfectly logical grounds, neither the Creator God nor His message should ever be found to be at odds with logic or pure empirical science. Some have tried to affirm that the message of God might be coherent but not necessarily logical. To arrive at such conclusions one has to falsely assume that the logic of God is beyond human reach. This false assumption is unfortunately the argument that has opened the door for what most Christians call faith. They are concepts recognized to be beyond human comprehension that must be accepted by faith to be saved. While it is difficult to imagine that a coherent message could transcend pure logic, it is interesting to note that those who hold this view are also willing to hold to a theology of which most tenets fall far short of sound logic.

There are no less than 33,000 different Christian denominations in the world today.[14] Interestingly, the most superstitious Christian and non-Christian creeds are flourishing while the more traditional are

---

[14] David B. Barrett, George T. Kurian, Todd M. Johnson, *World Christian Encyclopedia: a comparative survey of churches and religions in the modern world*, 2nd ed. Oxford; New York: Oxford University Press, 2001.

in sharp decline. This trend implies one of two things: 1. Either the Christian religions are embracing pagan religious folklore that increases their attractiveness, or 2. Christianity has managed to misrepresent the message of Christ to such a point that only those denominations offering superstitious supernatural powers remain attractive. This would confirm the teachings of Christ who 2,000 years ago predicted this coming challenge. He said: "Many false prophets will appear and deceive many people" (Mt. 24:11). These false prophets can only be religious leaders teaching superstitious concepts with promises of gains, blessings and eternal life in the name of Jesus. This had been tried before, but Paul sharply rebuked using the name of Jesus by the magicians of his time (see Acts 19:13–20).

Unfortunately, there is reluctance in Christianity to challenge the teachings of false teachers through the use of sound logic. This is because they are themselves preachers of unsound logic. For some reason people have been taught that it is not acceptable to question a religious concept on the grounds that it lacks logic, because if a concept can be accepted without "faith," implying believed without proof, it no longer qualifies as faith; thus it is not a religion. Creeds must be offered as humanly irrational sacred concepts that God alone understands, especially when no rationale can be used to validate such beliefs. As a result, major tenets of Christian faiths are simply unacceptable to the purely logical minds of our time. In fact, some of the teachings are insulting to intelligent people in a world where education is producing increasing numbers of rational people. It is not surprising therefore, that many choose to reject Christian teachings on the basis of their meaninglessness, but that is not the way God intended His message to be received; God's message is perfectly logical.

The purpose of this book is to expose some of the most destructive teachings Christian churches have been promoting as truth. I also hope to show that alternative explanations founded on sound logic are far more plausible and attractive. Surprisingly, some of the most universally accepted Christian teachings are never revisited to make sure that they follow sound logic. Despite the fact that many of them are pagan in substance their validity is not questioned. It is amazing to notice that Christian denominations disagree on trivial teachings while they all endorse some of the most egregious elements of pagan superstitions lacking sound rationale. It is time to seriously consider the possibility that the message of Jesus was hijacked just as He predicted it would be. As a result, the Truth of His message remains hidden from sincere Christians who have learned to accept "by faith" some of the most meaningless interpretations proclaimed by some of most popular spiritual leaders of our time. On the other hand, countless would-be Christians are compelled to reject the tenets of Christianity on the grounds that they lack solid rationale. Because the most important and most common tenets lack the support of logic, God's intended message has become unrecognizable. This may have been done intentionally by leaders seeking to manipulate populations or mistakenly by well-intentioned but misguided students of Scripture. Let us just remember that a corrupted message makes it null and void.

This may explain why in the last millennium so little progress has been made in terms of world peace and social objectivity despite the overwhelming influence of Christianity in world affairs. All the more surprising is that despite radical dissimilarities between their messages Christian denominations all claim to have "the truth." How can each one be so different from the others while remaining confident that they alone have the ultimate truth? They all draw their information from the same source, which they all consider authoritative, yet they cannot agree. If unquestionable truth could be identified in Scripture, such truth would unite the "body of Christ" (1 Cor. 12:27), but the opposite is true. Were the angels of heaven mistaken when they announced the Lord's birth singing: "Glory to God in the highest, and on earth peace to men on whom his favor rests" (Lk. 2:14)? Were these just beautiful words of hope blowing in the winds of time? Perhaps these words should be considered valid, but only if humans are willing to study the message under the careful scrutiny of sound logic. Only then will the message become the remedy able to dispel evil because it is perfectly logical and within reach of human minds.

In this book a nontraditional approach to Jesus and His Message is suggested, but the attempt is founded on logic. This author hopes that the nontraditional approach will not annoy the readers.

We must first remember that in the two Temples of Jerusalem, as it was also in the Tabernacle, there was a Veil separating the Holy from the Most Holy place. This Veil was stained daily with blood from slaughtered animals until 70 CE when Roman forces led by Titus destroyed the city and its beautiful Temple. Symbolically speaking this Veil may well represent the false religions and traditions responsible for perpetuating senseless bloodshed in the world. Such bloodshed is entirely due to a false understanding of religion that separates humans from God, as does the Veil. As long as God's message will remain contaminated, the false message carried to the world will be directly responsible for the bloody paths of human history. It must be noted that Jesus held the religious leaders responsible for all the bloodshed (see Lk. 11:51, 52). Falsehoods represented by the Veil have hidden from view God's everlasting message of truth that should have induced the healing of people's hearts from evil that leads to uncontrollable bloodshed. If we are to believe the maxim of Jesus who said: "The truth shall set you free" (Jn. 8:32), the fact that true freedom continues to elude those who claim His name may well be an indication that the "truth" of which He was speaking continues to elude us.

Instead of proactively seeking answers to this dilemma on the grounds of pure logic, Christians continue to expect God to take these matters in His own hands miraculously, mystically, supernaturally, and superstitiously through pagan beliefs involving His blood to pay for sins. False theologies abound in this regard. Some await His return to resolve the problems of planet Earth, others expect a "secret rapture" leading to chaos for those not raptured, and yet others claim that His return will be a "spiritual" experience. The sad reality is that no denomination appears to believe that humans have a part to play in God's divine plan to heal the human heart from evil. Most Christians are simply waiting more or less passively for the miracle of transformation to take place perhaps before death or perhaps after, while holding to the false assumption that there is nothing God expects them to do to reduce evil in this world.

Since it is not possible to believe with any degree of assurance a concept that fails to be recognized as valid on rational grounds, it is no wonder that the freedom God's truth alone can convey continues to elude humanity. Truth related to God has not yet been seriously sought on the grounds of rational thinking. It is evident that Christian groups claiming to have the truth have not yet found the key to solving the problem of evil. In fact, because they fail to seek truth rationally they keep removing themselves from ever finding the truth Jesus claims will set free even the most rebellious and evil hearts. A careful study of rational atheists would probably show that they are often closer to God's truth than Christians who refuse to study God's message from a purely logical point of view.

We must consider a perspective of religion founded on the belief that Jesus came to communicate at the price of His life a message of truth that has repeatedly eluded humanity. But this approach requires rigorous logic in the evaluation of the message Jesus carried all the way to the Cross. It is not our sins that He carried to the Cross, it is the message that neutralizes evil. When considered on solid grounds, the message from God proves so persuasive that a person can be made to accept the message as a way of life even if there were no promise of eternal reward. If the acceptance of the message is indeed the only solution, why not accept to become intimately involved with the solution rather than to remain a part of the problem? Many are willing to die for much less worthy causes than the eradication of evil by replacing it with love.

This is not intended to be a scholarly treatise written with expectations of academic accolades. To do so would require a book to cover each chapter. As a product of the author's heart, this book is merely intended to spark the reader's attention to thinking about God and His everlasting message of truth in a different light. Perhaps we should say that this book is intended to encourage the reader to rethink and reconsider God, as well as the relevance of His message to a world in peril. It is not the purpose of this book to draw anyone away from churches, synagogues, mosques, or personal religious beliefs. On the contrary, if God is the God of humanity and the universe, His Truth belongs in all such places. This author remains persuaded that no human organization holds the key to God's Truth at this time while he also makes no claim to have it. The purpose of this discussion is to invite students of Scripture and thinkers of all creeds and beliefs to contribute to the search for truth that comes from the only true God.

If there is a God, and if He has indeed conveyed a message of eternal value, should we not all be willing to spread His message in all prominent places and include it in all human affairs? This should be our goal regardless of religious beliefs or lack thereof.

The problem is that as long as religions fails to be acceptable on rational grounds only the mystics will continue to be persuaded. The more reasonable the people the more unlikely they are to accept anything short of a rational common-sense approaches to God. As long as a religion fails to make sense, only a finite number of people can be expected to support its message. Too many people are prone to accept the religious machinations of those who promise well-being, health, wealth and salvation through supernatural means. Jesus was never dependent on such a message or such means to become perfect and to maintain the perfection of His character all the way to the Cross. Even those incredibly powerful final temptations failed to take hold of His mind and heart. Yet He had no help from above; He felt that the universe had forsaken Him. If logically minded people were to search for a rational religious message involving rational rituals they would never join a Christian group no matter how eloquent the message and how propitious the promises.

To put it simply, "the false gods" of yesteryear are mere pagan falsifications of the only true God and His message. Because God's message has been distorted it has become incongruous and illogical. Such messages presented to the world in the name of Jesus must be exposed as counterfeits worthy of the "false Christs" Jesus predicted. Unfortunately, because Christianity has suffered the contamination of pagan mindedness, as did Judaism and Israelites before them, it now conveys a false image of "the only true God" of the universe—thus it is an idolatrous view of God. Viewed through lenses of pagan traditions, Scripture cannot be the bearer of truth, but there is another way to read it, through the lenses of Jesus, but only provided His message is perceived and received through the lenses of pure logic.

Since Scripture claims that "the only true God" is the Creator of the universe, we should accept readily the idea that God is also the Author and Creator of sound logic that makes all progress possible. Thus God Himself must be perfectly logical in all His dealings and expectations of all the intelligent beings He has created. When supposedly intelligent beings infuse the least level of flawed logic in their belief systems they are simply not being intelligent and cannot be representatives of the Creator. If God is indeed an intelligent being, He cannot make use of flawed logic unless He intentionally wants to confuse intelligent people, but God "does not lie" (Titus 1:2). The devil is the one who confuses the world as much as he can; Jesus called him "the prince of this world" that "now stands condemned" (Jn. 16:11) because his lies are being exposed by sound logic. Thus, if Jesus is indeed the envoy of God, His message should be recognizable as Truth that can be validated on perfectly rational grounds, otherwise there would be no way to identify His message in a sea of falsehood. If for any reason the message of Jesus cannot be validated on the strength of sound logic, we should not be compelled to believe that the message is from the God of perfect logic. If the religion Jesus came to establish "once for all" (1 Pet. 3:18) lacks the least element of logic, such a message would have to be nothing short of a scam.

The reason there are so many religions today is precisely because they all take the liberty to consider the message of Jesus and the rest of Scripture without applying basic rules of logic to their study, they accept falsehood by faith. How could God's everlasting Truth[15] lack logic? If a religion fails the most basic tests of logic, how can such a religion qualify as contributing truth, much less the Truth that comes from God, the Master Logician of the universe? If any religion were indeed teaching the Truth of God's message, no one could logically argue against it, or prove it incorrect on logical grounds. In our modern world, a truth is a fact established on the solid bedrock of evidence founded on pure logic and repeatability or on empirical observations that cannot be denied. The validity of a truth must rest on the solid bedrock of indisputable logic, or the concept cannot be called a truth. All arguments raised to disagree with a truth must fail, but no religion has yet been able to meet such a level of indisputable validity. The mere fact that there are 33,000 different Christian denominations is proof enough that most people have disagreements with denominations not their own, and many disagree with doctrines and dogmas of their very own churches. Thus we are entitled to ask, where is the Truth that will set free people steeped in the tethers of mutual mass manipulation, control, and snowballing violence liable to annihilate the human race?

There is perhaps a bigger question scientists in particular are likely to raise. They will say: Is there really such a thing as absolute truth? This author is bold enough to believe that there is indeed at least one such Truth in the universe. It is the one God has shared with humans repeatedly through the ages. It is also the Truth Jesus had to come all the way to planet Earth to reiterate (Heb. 1:1–2) at the price of His life because it had been corrupted. Yet though He is "the exact representation" of God (Heb. 1:3), Jesus managed to bring the vital message without abusing anyone's free will in the least. He did it by coming to this world as a human.

---

[15] We now capitalize the word "truth" when speaking specifically of divine Truth. This is to differentiate God's absolute Truth from all other truths of the universe.

As Albert Einstein and other great minds have suggested and often demonstrated, even those truths believed to be universal are often quite relative. But let us remember that despite the relativity of time humans have made countless time-sensitive machines responsible for opening the gates of ever-greater scientific knowledge and accomplishments. Despite the relativity of matter, materials have been used and created to explore material realities in various regions of the universe. All this has been accomplished with remarkable accuracy of positioning and timing. The question we should be willing to consider is this: If despite the relativity of time and matter science can progress, why is humanity so bogged down with regards to understanding what is perhaps the only absolute Truth in the entire cosmos? Interestingly, Christian thinkers take advantage of scientific theories of relativity to back up their claim that God is indeed beyond human comprehension. This gives them license to maintain that various forms of blind faiths are acceptable and even necessary to maintain a relationship with the God of the universe.

Considering that God claims His Truth to be the only solution to all the problems of evil in the universe, should not such Truth become self-evident to all intelligent people exposed to it? Scripture calls this Truth the Gospel because it is indeed "good news." In fact, there is no greater or more important piece of information in the entire universe than the Gospel. In some places it is called "the everlasting covenant," because it is the only way everlasting life can be sustained. It is also called "the kingdom of God" because the entire universe will someday accept it as the only way to live forever. Scripture calls it a "kingdom," an archaic word perhaps, but it is a reference to a domain where life can be expected to last forever because God's Truth has been fully accepted by all subjects as the only way to live eternally. Indeed, that Truth has the power to eliminate all forms of evil, an *absolute* and *unconditional* requirement for peaceful life to be sustainable forever.

During His life on earth Jesus encouraged all people to diligently seek His kingdom of which His Truth is the centerfold. Not only does God reveal His unique Truth throughout Scripture, but when correctly understood His Truth becomes the absolute demonstration of His existence (Mt. 6:33). The reason is simple; without Him His Truth would have never been seen or perceived. All the failings of human history demonstrate this point beyond doubt and will continue to be demonstrated until the predicted end of this world's history. In mathematical terminology, God and His Truth are commutative principles. Proving either one proves the other. Since the Truth is far easier to prove because it is finite and logical, God is the infinite extension of His Truth. God's truth is indeed finite because it can only be taken as far as a person's own death. Beyond that point, a person can no longer live God's Truth. Thus, even though God is beyond understanding, His Truth is not. As Jesus said: "Salvation is that they know thee, the only true God" (Jn. 17:3 KJV[16]). Here and elsewhere, salvation should be understood as the solution, but only if those who believe His Truth are willing to live it all the way to their own death. The two words, salvation and solution are not only closely related etymologically, but they essentially mean the same thing. There is no real solution without salvation, and there is no real salvation without the solution, both imply salve, or the remedy that cures evil.

If the Truth that sets people free is not responsible for salvation with the implication that it offers a real solution to the most damaging of all problems by providing the remedy capable of solving the problem of evil, then what is salvation about? Is it just a cult? Is the word "salvation" just a word Christians use to talk about something no one can really understand logically? Is it just a false promise made to sinners by telling them that they can be saved or made free by simply believing that Jesus died to pay for sins? If so, how does such a belief really address the problem of evil in a tangible way? It excuses it, but does not solve it; therefore it is not salvation. What good is God's plan of salvation if it is conditional on the understanding that someone paid for sins by dying on a Cross while recognizing that the concept makes no logical sense whatsoever to the human mind? Why would God have bothered to send His Son to teach and live a Truth knowing that the message is beyond their capacity to understand? Worse yet, the claim is made that this Truth too complex to be understood is indispensible to the achievement of freedom and attainment of eternal life. If the Truth that sets sinners free remains beyond intellectual reach, the freedom that Jesus claims to result from Truth would likewise remain indefinitely unattainable, and the same would have to be true of salvation. Is God playing games with the minds of people He claims to love? What a morbid thought!

---

[16]   The text of the 1769 Authorized Version of the Bible, commonly known as the King James Version ("KJV"), is in the public domain.

On the contrary, because of His goodness and compassion God could not possibly be so heartless as to encourage humans to seek understanding related to Truth beyond their intellectual reach. Much less should salvation be attainable only through the acceptance of meaningless beliefs and rituals totally superstitious in nature. If rituals are indeed meaningless, eating the body of Christ or drinking His blood for Communion is nothing more than an insipid superstitious practice linked to an even more insipid belief about a God who wanted this blood to pay for sins. This statement is true whether or not the wine is understood symbolically as blood or literally as that of Jesus and whether or not the wafers actually turns into the human flesh of Jesus or remains a mere symbol of His life in the flesh.

Yet the concept that salvation is beyond human understanding is common in Christian religions. We hear pastors making such claims by quoting Scripture: "You must believe by faith," they say emphatically— whatever the word "faith" is understood to mean or imply. With such an approach to God and His message, the very incentives and motivations to seek Truth are destroyed. Just believe, they say, this is how you demonstrate your faith! Halas, believing anything other than a demonstrably understandable Truth is a total waste of time and effort, because it can only lead nowhere. It is like asking a GPS instrument to show a destination of which no one knows the address. Worse yet, it is like asking the GPS to lead nowhere and reaching a destination with the assurance that God Himself has led us there. Where is there room for human freedom if Truth can be that brazenly lacking of sound logic and how can such lack of logic be expected to accomplish anything positive to overcome evil?

Like God, a GPS instrument can get us to our destination only if we know where we want to go, and this is extremely important precisely because we were created free. In His grace, and out of concern for our freedom, God will never help us to reach a destination we are not seeking to reach. It is for us to know exactly where we want to go, and the address can be found only by diligently studying God and His message to humanity, but only if the study is made without preconceptions.

Contrary to common belief the destination is not eternal life. We can only say that eternal life is the ultimate reward for dedicating one's life to seeking and reaching the correct destination thanks to God's relentless revelations of His Way to the Truth that gives Life. Taking us to a place without our express consent or express understanding of where we are going would be abuse of freedom—today we would call that brainwashing, indoctrination, or even kidnaping with intent to torment. God did not give us freedom at Creation only to take it away at a later time—He gave it because without freedom love cannot be reality, and where love fails there is no eternal life; it is that simple.

God's Message of Truth Has Not Yet Been Identified

One thing is clear; the matter of God's Truth is far from elucidated in the world in which we live. We all believe and treat as valid the truths related to gravity, buoyancy, aerodynamics, time and seasons despite their theoretical relativity. Acceptance and conformity to these truths have made possible amazing technological advancements. Could the same thing happen in the realm of human relations if God's "Eternal Gospel" (Rev. 14:6)[17] of Truth capable of healing evil could be recognized as flawless and purely rational? Imagine the unifying impact of such a Truth if it were to be endorsed by the religions and people of our planet! Of course it would change the world for the better, but first this Truth would have to be clearly identified. If this were to happen there would be only two religious views left on our planet: God's, and all the religions of those who openly choose to oppose Him and His rationale.

We have now reached the heart of our subject. Since universally accepted truths related to gravity, kinetic energy, and aerodynamics have made Boeing 747s possible, couldn't God's Universal and Everlasting Truth make true freedom possible on this war-torn planet? Considering that absolute freedom cannot exist without absolute peace and that absolute peace cannot exist without absolute love, the Truth Jesus claimed capable of making sinners free must involve Truth that leads to genuine love. No other purpose can be considered.

Unfortunately, the differences of religions and ideologies are all developed and propagated for the purpose of exercising control and dominance in order to maintain unrivaled the prestige of clergy among people. It is for this reason that religious leaders want their views to

---

17   Unless otherwise stated, all quotes from Scripture in this book are from the NIV. *The Holy Bible, New International Version,* copyright 1973, 1978, 1984 by International Bible Society. Used by permission of Zondervan Publishing House.

become dominant and universally accepted. The problem is that with a flawed message they are only likely to intensify the problem of evil, not reduce it. Thus we can only look forward to more wars, more violence, more violations of human rights, more abuses of personal freedom, and more impositions coming from both political and religious persuasions, and God forbid, both combined into one single ideology to be imposed on people——unless it were the one that comes from God. With a human system in vigor the very freedom required to express true love would have to be chipped away bit by bit. The very religious organizations that were ordained by God to preserve freedom will have totally failed their mission to the world by taking it away. Only two options will remain possible when that time comes: 1. Remain a part of the problem or 2. Become a part of the solution through the plan of salvation and healing that God's Truth provides.

We cannot and should never blame our Christian predecessors for the problems of interpretations we face today. They did what they could with the heavily tainted knowledge and understanding of God and Scripture that was available to them. When the Reformers began their campaigns for Truth some five centuries ago, the world was not ready to understand all the subtleties of Scripture. Too much pagan baggage was burdening their search. The study of Scripture had been rigorously disallowed for centuries. Torture and death were the penalties for breaking the stringent rule, even for the clergy. But today, with unprecedented access to the written Word, we are much better equipped to recognize the message from God, even though many dark clouds of misinterpretation remain. They have tarnished Scripture almost indelibly—indeed, to the point that even the very elect would be deceived, if that were possible (see Mk. 13:22).

With their initial study of Scripture the Reformers failed to realize the extent of their duty to labor for the eradication of religious tyranny in all its forms. They were guilty of death sentences against such people as Servetus under John Calvin, wars of religion they led in the name of Jesus, and egregious racist comments. We could have done without the extremely harsh and downright un-Christlike statements of Martin Luther regarding the Jews. But these are all clear indications that despite their enlightenment the Reformers had not yet understood some of the most important teachings of God. The Reformers were all guilty of tyranny in one form or another, yet it is largely thanks to their contributions that democratic governments were eventually founded on principles that opened the way to greater consideration for human rights, freedom of worship, mutual respect, and even rules of war. It has been a long road, and we are not yet in view of the bright light at the end of the tunnel. Perhaps the time to reconsider all the questions regarding God and His message in the light of a logical approach has finally arrived. To do so, it is imperative to dismiss all the current mystical attributions of superstitious interpretations of the Gospel.

By and large, religion has always been about worshiping mystical or preternatural forces of the universe with the desire to sway the disposition of these forces in our favor. Even here, the "me first" attitude is present where it should be most absent. The main purpose of worship was to forestall divine punishment such as floods or earthquakes and to strengthen health, increase luck, and grow prosperity. As a result, humans have always felt indebted to these forces with feelings of guilt for their own shortcomings in the face of written or unwritten laws of life and nature. As did Cain who complained because God did not accept his generous gift in exchange for divine favors, with a similar pagan mind-set people are still led to believe that humans live at the whim of capricious gods—a clear reflection of Cain's attitude. This attitude leads them to think that it is their duty to work hard at the service of God or the gods, hoping that good deeds and kindness of behavior along with gifts and blood-offerings might secure them divine clemency.

While Protestantism has recognized some of the fallacies linked to rituals that fall far short of representing the message of Jesus, they failed to rid themselves of all pagan views, especially as they relate to the understanding of propitiatory offerings. While they preach that sinners cannot be saved by their good deeds or offerings, which is correct, they also claim that Jesus had to do it all in their place, by substitution—which cannot be correct only because it lacks the strength of persuasion through logic. Does that mean that God started out requiring good works along with blood offerings, and that He suddenly changed His mind to accept the idea that only One Person would have to produce the required good works and offer the perfect sacrifice to save all people? These questions will be revisited because sound logic is clearly lacking when considering such views.

Christianity claims that Jesus offered the ultimate offering of a perfect life filled with good works as a gift to God made on a Cross. And all this was supposedly done on behalf of all sinners that ever lived on this planet. There are countless problems with this view from the standpoint of logic. If salvation is not by works, as many Christians teach, why should God have required His Son to obtain salvation for sinners by His works, by His good deeds, and by offering His own tortured body and blood? One way or another, this approach to salvation in Protestant theology still amounts to salvation by works, but not their own—the works of Jesus. Strange thinking at the very least. To put it mildly, the entire outlook is false and pagan in nature. Though some passages of Scripture appear to imply such a view, it is only because the message has been corrupted. Works are works, no matter who does the works. If salvation is not by works, nobody's works should ever qualify to make up for the misdeeds of others. How could it be explained that giving medicine to a person who is not sick could heal a person who is about to die of a disease? The concept is flawed because it is entirely founded on pagan views held as "faith" despite the fact that they are founded on totally irrational thinking.

The more we study the religions of the world today the more we find that they all have something sinister in common: a pagan mind-set that has failed repeatedly to bring lasting peace and true freedom. If Truth is the key to freedom, as Jesus stated, the lack of freedom and peace are a clear demonstration that Truth, as God understands it, is not yet with us, and much less, in us. A new understanding of the message of Truth is yet a future event. Jesus predicted this development, and it is my hope that this book will at least contribute a little to the thinking required to understand the essence of the divine message.

Religions as we know them today have failed to bring practical answers. If Jesus and His message is the answer, there must be something about His message that has escaped us for the last 2,000 years. What is it? This book is but a small attempt to identify some of the missing pieces of the puzzle. Jesus Himself claimed that someday "the spirit of truth" would come to this world and would guide those who seek Him "into all truth" (Jn. 16:13). A superstitious outlook of this promise tends to discourage all attempts to understand this message given in the distant past. If external supernatural power has to be involved to fulfill this promise of God, the only thing we can do is to wait patiently for God to accomplish His purpose. But as we have said, this is terribly dangerous because another, claiming to be the Christ, would suddenly offer both power and new light.

But Scripture also claims that there will be a people at the end of time that will understand the message of Jesus as He meant it to be understood. In the book of Revelation John makes it clear that "no lies were found in their mouths" and that "they are blameless." (Rev. 14:5). This text is very interesting when considered from a nontraditional point of view. It does not say that God's representatives at the end of time will be people who cannot ever say a lie, but this is not what this text conveys. The Greek word *dolos* translated lies means decoy. We could say that in their message from God to the world there will be no decoy, no misrepresentation of the only true God in their message—in other words, no unTruth will be found on their tongues. The message they will proclaim will not be a decoy; it will be the absolute Truth. This implies that they have received all the Truth Jesus was talking about when He claimed that the spirit of truth would suddenly awaken the world. These people will clearly recognize and preach the Truth that will finally set sinners free.

To answer more directly the question stated in the title of this chapter, "Religion Should Be the Solution," the answer is a resounding yes! Religion should be the solution. But the solution is not recognizable in any religion currently known or practiced on our planet today. As Jesus predicted, false prophets would cloud the message He brought at great price some 2,000 years ago. Christianity is still suffering from idolatrous perceptions of the only true God. However, the spirit of Truth will bring about the final religion of Truth to the world. Scripture calls it the final "Remnant," both in the Old and the New Testament. Quoting Isaiah, Paul draws our attention to the last day seekers of truth: "Though the number of the Israelites be like the sand by the sea, only the remnant will be saved. For the Lord will carry out his sentence on earth with speed and finality" (Rom. 9:27, from Is. 10:22, 23). This final Remnant will be unlike any preceding Remnant of which there has always been a small number through the ages. This one will benefit fully from the spirit of Truth Jesus predicted would lead the people of God to the vital understanding needed to become truly free. Only His absolute truth can accomplish the purpose. This is the event that will ultimately free the entire universe from the grips of evil. This turn of event implies that a people will have gained understanding and accepted God's Truth as the modus operandi of their lives. This Truth will be so completely understood that nothing will be missing and no one will be able to contradict it rationally. No one will have to wonder if further truth will yet need to be discovered or understood. It will be all there for all people of the planet to see, recognize, and accept. It will be so clear that countless people will be willing to set aside all their previously held religious traditions to accept God's Truth with open arms and hearts.

When Jesus shall be fully exalted, Paul writes: "Every knee should bow" (Phil. 2:10). This means that even those people who refuse to accept the Truth as their way of life will recognize that God's message of Truth is indeed the only religion that makes sense and has the power to set sinners free.

Jesus quoted the beginning of Psalm 22 from the Cross as He was breathing His last saying: *"Eloi Eloi lama sabachthani."* Literally translated we have the following words: "My God, my God, why forsaken?" (Mark 15:34, from Ps. 22:1), This same Psalm concludes on a very interesting note: "All the ends of the earth will remember and turn to the LORD, and *all the families of the nations will bow down before him*, for dominion belongs to the LORD and he rules over the nations. All the rich of the earth will feast and worship; all who go down to the dust will kneel before him—[even] those who cannot keep themselves alive. Posterity will serve him; future generations will be told about the Lord. They will proclaim his righteousness to a people yet unborn—for he has done it" (Ps. 22:27–31 brackets mine). The allusion to those "yet unborn" is probably a reference to those "not yet born again" (Jn. 3:3, 7; 1 Pet. 2:23). As we shall see, the new birth takes on a totally new meaning when considered from a nontraditional, non-pagan perspective of God's message.

CHAPTER 5

Back to Basics

I t is impossible to discover truth if any fact related to the search is false or falsified. It is indeed impossible to resolve a problem as long as the root causes of the problem have not been identified. Thus, to resolve the problem of evil in our world, along with all the painful manifestations and consequences evil brings, we must first understand what evil is and why we have the problem in the first place. The simple and perhaps simplistic answer monotheistic religions offer is that sin is the problem. Yes, of course it is, but what exactly is sin?

The answer given is often simplistic when it is said that sin is misconduct, which amounts to saying that sin is a departure from accepted convention or law. In other words, sin amounts to doing something that is socially unacceptable. Indeed, a text in the First Epistle of John is often quoted to make this assertion: "Everyone who sins breaks the law; in fact, sin is lawlessness" (1 Jn. 3:4). But which law was the Apostle John talking about? Was it the Law of God referred to as the Ten Commandments, the Law of Moses that includes all 613 laws of the Pentateuch contained in the first five books of Old Testament Scripture? Or was John perhaps talking about yet another law?

Is there perhaps another word that could have been used instead of the word "law" in the translation of this text? Indeed, the Greek *anomia* could have been translated "unrighteousness," or "wickedness," as the opposite of righteousness. Neither of these terms necessarily implies breaking a written or unwritten code of law. In fact, it is possible to be a wicked person without breaking any law, but our world is so obsessed with legal systems to resolve social issues that the word "law" is the first word that comes to the mind of translators. Truth be told, in the Jewish economy of the time this word may well have been used to imply breaking a law. However, by the time the early Christians used the term, considering their message focused on love rather than on the law, they may well have understood that a person who is *anomia* is simply a person lacking in the area of love, or unloving, but not necessarily a person who disregards laws, though lack of love often leads to lawlessness. Thus the text could be translated to say: "Whoever continues to sin is a person who continues to lack love (or, who is unrighteous), for sin is indeed lack of love (or, unrighteousness)" (1 Jn. 3:4, my amplified translation).

One of the oldest known codes of law is that of Hammurabi. It dates back to 1750 BCE—about two centuries after Abraham began his journey to the Promised Land. This Code was probably written in the lifetime of his grandson Jacob or shortly thereafter. The rules of that code were merciless. In fact, mercy is usually considered to be counterproductive in a legal system. For example, §195 of the code reads: "If a son strikes his father, they shall cut off his fingers."[18] Humans have attempted for millennia to control social behavior through the use of stringent legal systems involving ruthless enforcement of penalties.

The law of which John was speaking was probably not a written or unwritten code of law; it was one's willful departure from an immutable principle of life that could just as well be called "the law of life," rather than a written or unwritten code of laws. So vital to life is the principle of life God has shared with humanity that failure to recognize and apply it to one's own life makes it rationally impossible to live eternally. Humans are so infatuated with their judicial systems involving courts of law where "justice" is debated and settled that they have become the only way to deal with misconduct.

Legal systems have become the faith of humanity regardless of religious involvement. Yet a closer look at the realities we witness every day demonstrates beyond doubt that our judicial systems do not resolve our social problems; they may even be counterproductive. It even appears that the more stringent a legal system the more disrespectful of the system people become. The only reason these systems are powerless to improve social order is that they lack the persuasive power to grow love in one's heart. In other words, our world has placed its faith in its legal systems despite the fact that its judgments and penalties have never accomplished the purpose for which they were designed. Einstein would probably say that it is insanity to perpetuate systems proven to be ineffective. No matter how deterring the consequences of breaking laws, penalties have failed to cure the real problem, which is lack of love. In fact, little or nothing is

---

18   Text taken from Harper's translation: http://en.wikisource.org/wiki/ The_Code_of_Hammurabi_(Harper_translation).

done in our court systems to motivate delinquents by showing them the importance of developing greater love and how to achieve that goal. Since such an approach would involve the method Jesus brought to the world it would be unacceptable on the grounds that it is a religion. Thus humanity is left with no alternative other than to perpetuate the insanity.

A loving and merciful approach to misconduct would be considered highly detrimental to the system. No formula to produce greater love is recognized or accepted in our world. The one Jesus and Scripture offers has been corrupted to the point of nonrecognition. Since attitudes can be neither taught nor imposed by force, humanity is left defenseless because the only way to change attitudes is through the power of reason on the solid grounds of logic. Once a philosophy of life is sincerely accepted as logically valid and constructive, the attitudes of a person can be expected to change, though only progressively.

The justice systems of our world have become so indispensible to its survival that they are universally believed to be the most effective means of adult behavioral control and modification, yet they accomplish neither. The judicial courts of the land have become the temples of its people, and strangely enough they have been inspired by pagan beliefs. They are not temples where mercy reigns; they are dens of distrust where mercy is intentionally avoided at all cost. Court buildings are made to look like temples where supreme authority reigns. They are the places where the judicial religions of people are implemented in an effort to guide, control, and regiment ever more rigidly the lives of its people. They are instruments of destruction because they destroy the most fundamental need of humans: freedom. Institutions theoretically designed to safeguard personal freedom are increasingly more responsible for destroying it. Globally and regardless of culture or religion people have come to place all their faith in laws of jurisprudence with the false assumption that they have the power to minimize evil. Though they may have a limited power to minimize evil behavior, they totally lack the power to reduce evil in the human heart. Despite the claim of countless Christians that they are no longer under the law they have totally failed to recognize that God considers all laws and all legal systems a hindrance to the development of love in a person's heart. In fact, forcing individuals to think or act in terms of submission to laws is a form of tyranny against which people are bound to rebel sooner or later, especially as new laws continue to be added to the codes. That rebellion may have already begun in our world.

Even a superficial reading of the book of Judges in Scripture points out that legal systems and their enforcements do not work. The behaviors of Israelites got worse over time, not better. After nearly four centuries of Judges ruling the Land from 1244 to 879 BCE, their legislative system proved counterproductive at best. This state of affairs in the Land brought them to want a king (see Judges 17:6). From the time of Joshua to the time of King Saul the Israelites promised God that they would live "by the Torah," meaning that they would willfully submit to its 613 rules. Judges traveled the land, adjudicating and giving advice regarding the way these rules should be kept. It was also their responsibility to decide whether or not the Israelites should go to war against their enemies. Considering that the Judges were often in disagreement it became evident that a monarchy would better serve the people's need for stability and security. As the legal system of Judaism became increasingly more ineffective they tried to resolve the problem by adding rules upon rule—many of these are included in the Talmud. The legal system became a substitute for the most fundamental principle of life every intelligent being should come to know, understand, and recognize as the only way to solve the problem of evil in our world and the universe.

While God's vital principle of life should be recognized as the *only* salvation available to the human race, it must also be recognized that it can never be forced upon anyone by any means. Rules, regulations, and the strictest of punishments are powerless to change people's hearts. The only way to change anything in the human heart can be achieved only by way of brainwashing or by way of providing sound compelling logic capable of persuading. Love can grow in a person's heart only if a new attitude born out of a new persuasion is formed in the depths of the heart. True love can develop only if it emanates from a personal intrinsic response founded on the solid ground of pure logic. Only then can it become a persuasion, or faith, that becomes a guiding light in life—no religion today provides a message sufficiently rational to produce such persuasion. Faith today is implied to mean, believe the irrational storyline of the church, not believe the pure logical rationale offered by a church.

The first thing a person must realize is that unconditional love is the only way a system of eternal life can be sustained. But lacking the objective rational intrinsic persuasion that it is the only way, meaningless alternatives are offered, such as believing that Jesus died to pay for sins. Faith, if it is correctly understood should not be defined as that of a person controlled by subjective beliefs more or less irrational, it should be the persuasion of a person who has thoughtfully and rationally recognized the imperative value of the principle of life, which is founded on true love. True love is never submission to pressures imposed by a religion or the expectations of socially acceptable behavior out of fear of penalties; it is the natural expression of a heart eager to contribute to the welfare and well-being of others before one's own. Legal systems do not work. They only get worse as they become increasingly more demanding over time. As the laws grow in number and complexity they slowly destroy the very freedom they are supposed to preserve. Indeed, the more laws are added to the books, the less freedom is left open for individual expression of love. Personal liberty cannot be preserved when personal responsibility is regulated by laws—thus laws destroy personal liberty. Laws become necessary only because of those individuals who refuse to take responsibility for their actions—as did Adam and Eve, as well as most, if not all, of their descendants.

Two choices are left for society to ponder. Stay the legal course bound to grow increasingly detrimental to liberty, thus to business and morality, or accept God's way that leaves no room for moral laws, because perfect love requires no such laws to govern society. Which law of morality can be broken when true unconditional love reigns? Thou shalt not kill? Of course not, how could a person choose to kill if perfect love truly reigns in the heart? Thou shalt not bear false witnesses, or destroy another person's reputation? Of course not, how could a person choose to destroy another's reputation with perfect love in the heart? How could anyone choose to recognize as supreme a god that fails to represent perfect love? Such a god would have to be a form of idolatry! But this is where the "cookie crumbles," so to speak. From the perception we get of God in the Old Testament, and from our simplistic interpretation of the New, it is clear that Christian religions of our world fail to produce in worshipers' minds the picture of a perfectly loving God. Jesus might be perceived as loving, but God the Father is not. Yet Jesus claims to be representative of the Father! "Anyone who has seen me," He said to Philip, "has seen the Father" (Jn. 14:9). The worshiper is left with the false notion that Jesus came to protect humanity from the wrath of the Father, when in reality He came to bring humans closer to the Father—as this is true atonement, the true coming at one with God.

The insane idea that Jesus came to protect sinners from the Father leaves the worshiper with a very confusing perception of God. We humans are expected to produce love of a higher quality than the love of the Father? Are we expected to love our enemies while the Father is not? How could that be? Heaven is described by many as a place where confusion reigns regarding love, considering that One member of the Godhead, Jesus, had to sacrifice himself to appease another, or should we say, the other Two. This is traditionally called propitiation, or expiation in Christianity. The concept is pagan and has nothing in common with the message of Jesus. The New Testament is clear to say: "I am not saying that I will ask the Father on your behalf. No, the Father himself loves you because you have loved me and have believed that I came from God" (Jn. 16:27).

All civilizations depend largely on their legislative systems to control individuals, communities, and even the entire world. The United Nations and the World Court in La Hague, Holland, are poised to impose evermore-stringent universal codes of law. Yet Scripture makes it clear that legal systems are powerless to improve people, much less the nations or our world. Legal systems can only turn people into worthless androids increasingly motivated to avoid the use of sound logic to live in freedom. With their legal systems humans are likely to remain indefinitely without seeking a sound solution to the problem of evil. It is a system that increases the number of government employees such as lawyers, judges, court clerks, police officers, jail and prison personnel as well as the military. But all that is just a smokescreen, it only gives the appearance of accomplishing a purpose such methods cannot achieve, but nothing more.

In reality legal systems only make things worse for all people in the long run. Human justice is primarily designed to administer appropriate punishment for noncompliance, that is, it is designed to render evil for evil. Yet Scripture clearly speaks against such a practice because rendering evil for evil accomplishes and resolves nothing. Jesus said: "Do not resist an evil person. If someone strikes you on the right cheek, turn to him the other also" (Mt. 5:39). Paul and Peter echoed the same principle when they encouraged the people never to repay anyone evil for evil (Rom. 12:17a; 1 Th. 5:15; 1 Pet. 3:9). Indeed, every time a law is implemented along with its penalties, a strand from the fabric of human freedom has to be pulled out—there may soon come a day when no strands will remain in the fabric, and freedom will be dead. With such a system the very freedom that makes altruistic love possible in society is under attack and will soon be destroyed. Why? Only because we have developed a blind faith in legislative systems just as we have developed blind faiths of religions for millennia. No blind faith can ever be expected to change things for the better; the only changes humanity can expect are for the worse, unless we could start preaching a new message containing a new philosophy of life. That would have to be a new religion.

The following assertion is perhaps the most depressing statement that could be made on this planet. The traditional efforts made to curb negative human behavior can be perceived either as brainwashing to persuade that legal systems are the best solution, or that worthless religious systems are the answer. Ironically, both are superstitious in nature because both the courts and religions provide expectations from actions or rituals that are in fact powerless to change anything for the better. Neither the judicial systems nor the current religions founded on incongruous expectations will ever be successful in making this world a more loving world. True education should never be indoctrination. The problem is that both the legal systems and the religious establishments are invested in indoctrination that amounts to brainwashing. Neither system is designed to teach young people to think for themselves. In such institutions teachers should be ashamed of the fact that their jobs are one or another form of indoctrination. If there is an institution of learning entirely devoted to developing social skills founded on thinking rather than responding to indoctrination, I would like to know where it is located. Institutions of learning are quick to imply that the study of sciences teaches a person to think, but unfortunately, this is true only in matters of empirical studies, not social expertise designed to grow the only solution in the hearts of students: true love. If the world was willing to get over its hang-ups, all systems of human control of the past should be open wide for serious review, including all political, judicial, and religious systems. In such a system the focus of education would be to grow unconditional love in the hearts of all people. What is currently taught is far more divisive than unifying. But how should this be done? The foregoing is an attempt to answer that question.

The Remedy Has to Wait for Jesus

In a phone conversation several years ago, the person on the other end of the line who was dear to me was touting the virtues of the leftist political agenda. Considering that this was a very intelligent student attending classes at UC Berkeley, I felt compelled to make the following remark: "It is not left or right political ideologies or the laws created to advance their political agendas that will ever save the world. Only the transformation of the human heart has the potential to accomplish such a feat. Unfortunately, more is done to teach and create laws envisioned to advance political ideologies than to educate people in the art and science of cultivating true love in their hearts." The student was rather shocked by the insane idea that life without politics would be possible if humans should suddenly choose to follow God's ways, rather than to perpetuate methods and systems that have failed for millennia. I tried to illustrate the idea with an allegory: "Envision a country with the absolute worst form of government imaginable, even pure anarchy. If the people of that nation were all good people with loving hearts, this country would be by far the most successful and most admired nation on planet Earth." I then asked a question: "What are we doing in our universities to improve the hearts of students rather than to indoctrinate them with political agendas and legal systems designed to enforce ideologies through law enforcement?" The answer was a deafening silence. The silence was not surprising, because any effort made in institutions of learning to improve people's hearts would be considered an attack on freedom despite the fact that current curriculums do just that; they destroy freedom. Ideologies driven by laws and regulations destroy the very freedom they seek to achieve. Thus love is slowly but surely placed on the back burner and will soon be entirely removed from the equation.

No solution to evil or salvation is attainable by enforcing laws, because laws can never improve the hearts of people; at best, they can only make them more law-abiding, which by definition, is a restriction of personal freedom. The legal systems of this world have become the idolatrous "faiths" of modern societies because they are mindlessly considered as the only fix-all solutions to the repression of social unrest, but they destroy the very love that would bring the solution.

This was in fact the problem of Cain who much preferred penalties than change of heart. The same was also true of the Children of Israel when they came out of Egypt. At that time Egypt was the most advanced civilization of our world, and they had the most advanced legal system on the planet. The country had been entirely controlled by religious and secular legal codes strictly enforced for the better part of two millennia before the Exodus. Like the Egyptians of that time the Children of Israel could not imagine that a better way to maintain social order might exist to improve society. Humanity had totally lost previous admonitions from God. Whipping and mutilating people or subjecting them to capital punishment for breaking laws was considered the only way to maintain order. The Children of Israel could not even consider the idea that listening to a message from God might bring them the only answer available in the universe.

Instead, they requested God to give them laws by which they would be controlled, not realizing that such control is an external imposition that destroys freedom and binds up a human heart. They left behind their servitude to Egypt only to accept the bondage of another form of slavery—laws. Out of pity for their lack of understanding and confidence, God gave them the laws they wanted. These varied considerably from those of Egypt, but they were still laws that could not change their hearts to make them more loving. That system is now called "Old Covenant," because laws cannot improve the human heart. By accepting such a system, the Children of Israel eventually discovered that laws were powerless to make them more loving, but they failed to recognize God's alternative. They discovered that laws can only do more harm than good but failed to realize that the means God offered them would eventually justify the end. Through the laws given them God was taking them just a small step closer to understand why and how negative the impact of laws can be. Jesus came to show them "the way to the truth that makes eternal life possible" (my amplified translation of John 14:6) without laws. Humans were to be delivered from the bondage of legal systems by way of a belief system that transforms people from within. Such a message can change even the most recalcitrant hearts but only if there is willingness to listen.

If the Rule of Law Is Not the Answer, What Is?

Ironically, the advanced civilizations of our world attempt to impose their ineffective legal system on the so-called developing nations where laws are scarce and poorly enforced. This is done in the name of Western progressivism with the idea that civility through the use of reason would soon improve the lives of superstitious civilizations. While reason is the key to progress, especially in the area of empirical sciences, reason applied to social ideologies regulated by the enforcement of legal systems has not improved society. It is not possible to regulate love or hatred because regulations destroy both. By contrast God teaches that the only way to change society for the better is by spreading a message founded on reason that has the power to change a human heart. In this message from God He also offers a specific procedure called the Truth that must be recognized and respected as the only solution. Scripture provides the infallible formula for those who are willing to listen to God, but once again, who is listening?

Humans have a history of interpreting God and His message rather than listening to Him for what He says. As a result, confusion reigns about God as it regards social organization capable of improving the human condition. The more humans try to bring about social change by way of legal systems, the more they will sink into the quicksand of counterproductive social controls that do nothing to improve hearts or society. The entire OT is the account of a struggle between God and what Israel wanted to hear Him say. God was trying to talk to their hearts while Israel tried to interpret what they heard God say in terms of governing laws. God wanted to make of Israel His people, but history shows that while they heard Him, they were unwilling to apply His message to the growth of love in the heart. Several of their prophets made that very clear. Speaking to the prophet Ezekiel about six centuries before Christ, God said to him: "But the house of Israel is not willing to listen to you because they are not willing to listen to me, for the whole house of Israel is hardened and obstinate" (Eze. 3:7). Why "hardened?" Because they were attempting to implement the will of God by way of legal systems, trying to promote obedience to laws, rather than through a rational message designed to change people's hearts.

Fortunately God is patient. It is still not too late for the descendants of Jacob or anyone else on this planet to listen to Him with the heart rather than through systems of government. It is only because the Children of Israel were unwilling to listen to God they were left with only one alternative to manage people, the rule of law. They became masters of legal systems; to this day, they are known as people who believe in the rule of law. But at the same time they also became worshipers of the legal systems of social controls, which is a form of idolatry. Instead of worshiping God whose message can transform people from within, they chose to apply themselves to the observation of laws that compelled them to accept rules of behavior with its external impositions on human action and behavior. Without realizing it perhaps, they accepted a form of slavery in the form of a legal system instead of opting for the true freedom God offers.

The big difference between a legal system and God's way is that laws make obedience compulsory. Life is all about obedience instead of being all about learning what true love is, how to love, and how much to love. God's approach to the problem is relatively simple; it merely involves a clear, open-minded understanding of His purely rational message. Once understood, God's message transforms people. Laws are always an imposition, but the immutable universal Truth requires to be recognized as indisputable on the grounds of logic, and then it becomes compelling on the merits of its perfect logic. It involves one's understanding that there is a way to live without the least imposition from external pressures, because with the Truth clearly understood, life becomes a matter of doing what the person really wants to do out of personal persuasion—this is true faith, and it brings true freedom. The eternal importance of God's approach to life must be clearly understood and accepted before it can become effective. Failure to accept makes a person rebellious against God. This is what the Bible means when speaking of a people whose heart is hardened. Because we are free, it is possible to reject God's way even with a perfect understanding of its perfect logic—just like people who might chose to ignore the laws of gravity while knowing that jumping would be suicidal. God's principle is so perfectly logical that it produces a persuasion so powerful that when accepted it motivates the free will to grow love for others, though never imposing love.

There is a huge difference between good behavior as a product of obedience and good behavior as a product of understanding and accepting God's perfectly rational and compelling principle of life. The legal system forces good behavior on citizens through rules and strict enforcement. It forces people into submission to acceptable behavior, or when applied to God, to use a common Christian vernacular, it is called righteousness by works. The reason God abhors righteousness by works is because it does not produce love by changing hearts.

When Isaiah said: "All of us have become like one who is unclean, and all our righteous acts are like filthy rags; we all shrivel up like a leaf, and like the wind our sins sweep us away" (Is. 64:6), he was talking about self-righteousness, not the righteousness that comes from the action of God's message of Truth on the heart. All of Israel had fallen for that hypocritical form of righteousness that fails to resolve the problem of evil. God's way motivates behavior from the inside, from deep within the heart. It provides wrongdoers with powerful reasons to change the way they think which causes them to do the right things. Behavior becomes the product of one's innermost persuasion, not the fear of painful consequences for breaking rules. A personal intrinsic force of persuasion is at work to motivate right doing. This persuasion is what Christians ought to call righteousness by faith. But for such faith to produce victory over evil, the nature and terms of this faith must be clearly and rationally understood. The Greek word *pistis* should be translated "persuasion," not "faith." Christian traditions of pagan origin apply a mystical understanding to that word. When righteousness by faith is understood on mystical grounds it is akin to superstition, thus pagan in nature. It led Christianity to the erroneous belief that Jesus was righteous in the sinner's place, by substitution—pure superstition because Jesus did not come to die a death of substitution. Such a view may stir emotions, but it fails to provide His clear procedure to change people's hearts.

God's only approach to righteousness is for free individuals to recognize His Truth and want it solidly anchored in their belief system. That divine faith has the power to make a person feel utterly foolish for behaving in opposition to its rational message. Doing right out of persuasion is doing right by faith because the word faith is understood as God understands the word— not a pagan interpretation of the word that implies believing something very strongly and blindly. It is a belief founded on a reality of life so absolute that no one can argue its validity or change its premise without deviating away from pure logic. As we said, no one, not even God can argue with His own pure logic, that is why He cannot change its requirements. It is simply the way it is, forever, and there is no benefit in ignoring or neglecting God's pure message as the foundation of Truth.

Instead of being ruled by constraining laws God wants all free individuals of the universe to be, or to become, knowledgeable about the only unchangeable reality of life that makes eternal life possible. When the value of this perfect system of government is clearly understood and fully accepted as one's modus operandi, the person wants nothing less than to live this system of life forevermore. It may not be easy or pleasant to live that message in a world of sin, but Jesus lived it all the way to the Cross. Guidance provided by the knowledge of any truth is far more valuable and far more freeing than guidance suggested by laws or superstitions, especially considering that they are dependent on demanding legal systems that remain powerless to improve character.

This topic has caused a great deal of ink to flow over time. Is God the God of a legal system of operation with its laws and enforcements for the universe, or is He a God of grace, as Scripture describes Him? Is He the Supreme Boss of a system founded on obedience to laws enforced by penalties and capital punishment, or is he the Author of a system that requires neither laws nor punishment when properly understood and accepted? Could there be anything other than grace in a system made to work without laws? Knowing the Author and message of such a system is ultimate grace. Knowing God, and His system of Universal Government, is the most incredible grace imaginable to finite mortals. It is the only knowledge that is capable of making eternal life possible.

It is precisely because God's system operates outside the legal systems that His system of life and government has to depend entirely on His infinite grace. Despite sin, God's grace is ensured by the His promises of resurrection from death—thus it is grace that transcends life and death. It is my contention that the general confusion about Scripture comes from the fact that humans have boxed God into a legal system of operation that does not exist in His Realm. As a result the word "grace" has been assigned a false meaning. Humans would say that grace is a matter of offering a pardon for breaking a law, while God would say that it is a system that works because neither laws nor punishments are valid ways to overcome evil; only a change of heart can accomplish the purpose. Not only is there no consensus among theologians on the subject of law and grace, as these words relate to salvation, but they also have a problem accepting the amazing concept that there is no legal system whatsoever in God's Realm because it is the invention of Lucifer who preexisted humans and became known as Satan. Why do we insist on applying to God a system He did not create and never wanted in the first place?

Is Sin Breaking Laws, Or Departure From the Principle of Life?

Though we have already covered the subject we must briefly go back to the story of the first sin in the Garden of Eden. There are elements of this story that we tend to consider only through our infatuation with legal systems because of our misguided faith in its ability to keep evil in check. With a legal system in mind we tend to look at the story of "sin" in the Garden of Eden as a break from God's command not to eat the fruit of a certain Tree. The general contention is that since the Law of God was broken when Adam and Eve ate the fruit, a punishment was legally *required* to maintain order. The problem with this line of reasoning is that it is a human perception of God's system of justice, not God's approach to resolve evil. Punishment is indeed the way humans would have handled the problem, though perhaps not for a fruit. When a law is broken the wrongdoer is made to pay a penalty to bring the scales of justice back in balance. Legal grace is perceived as the reduction of penalty or a pronouncement of acquittal. Human failure to recognize God's grace as something totally different and totally unrelated to the legal systems of this world has led Christianity down the wrong path.

Religious leaders of all religions have come to consider God through the lenses of human legal systems, which is an error. Sadly, a study of the problem reveals that the wrong understanding of God's attitude in Eden was reintroduced soon after the apostolic era of the Christian church. A perception of God through human legal systems gained momentum as time passed. Christ who said that He judges no one was perceived as the Great Judge of the universe with a human perception of justice. Yet John reported Jesus as saying: "You judge by human standards; I pass (that kind of) judgment on no one" (Jn. 8:15, parenthesis mine). The fact is that God wants nothing to do with human legal systems. The Apostles complained about false theories of salvation that were sprouting in various places during their lifetime (2 Cor. 11:13). Today, the legal systems of this world have reached a critical point because they are perceived as the only solution by both the secular and religious establishments. Humanity is about to demonstrate before the entire universe that legal systems are worthless and that they can only bring out the worst in human character. This in turn will also bring about the worst calamities the world has ever witnessed. Perhaps when this will become evident, some humans will realize that they should have listened to God much sooner.

A traditional legal reading of Genesis brings us to conclude that when our first parents took the Forbidden Fruit, God, the good Law Enforcer that He was, took matters in His own hands. Failure of strict obedience to His Law had to carry the price God had demanded, thus He had no choice but to enforce the law of Eden. And what a price it was, a death sentence! With a human perspective of justice God is falsely perceived as having punished Adam and Eve for misbehaving, going so far as to make a pronouncement of death penalty upon them for taking a mere fruit. Not only were they to pay the price for eating a fruit that was not theirs to take, but in His faithfulness to proper justice the sentence was also leveled on all their descendants for as long as time shall last. Isn't that the mark of a fair-minded, kind, and loving Father? But that was not enough of a punishment; humanity would have to pay a huge price for the stolen fruit because the death sentence would have been far too lenient. To produce food, men would have to pay the price of painful work that would produce heavy sweat all over their faces. Women would not be spared; their punishment was to suffer painful childbirth and subjugation to the male gender. Nothing about this view of God paints a picture of grace, much less that of a God of love, capable of infinite mercy. This is how distorted a picture of God we can paint through an evaluation of human acts viewed through the prism of forensic law.

This traditional view of the account clearly reflects an outlook on sin based on the way humans handle the problem of evil, not God's way. Because it is now seared into our natural instincts to use forensic methods whenever we have to deal with evil acts, we project our faulty mind-set on God who wants no part of such methods. A careful study of Scripture reveals that in reality these are the methods of the devil. Scripture insists on the fact that God is all about infinite grace, thus He should never be perceived as wanting retribution for sin. The fact that Christians and other religions have mistakenly applied a human legal stance to God has totally clouded the Truth of His system of salvation. God does not apply punishment to level the scales of justice; He knows that intelligent beings have sufficient intelligence to know better, but are they willing to give God's way a chance? Are they willing to deal with the problem of evil His way, rather than their way? Is the law of gravity a legal matter? Of course not! No one argues with this law of science. Neither the US Congress nor the International Court of Justice in The Hague has the power to repeal the law of gravity. Why? Because it is not a law; it is a universal fact. It is a principle of truth that cannot be argued with or circumvented without the application of other laws of science. Using other forces, gravity can be overcome to send objects beyond its reach, but it can never be obliterated or repealed. The same is true with God's principle of life called "the Truth," because it is a universal Truth; it defines the only way life can be preserved in everlasting peace.

What Really Happened in the Garden of Eden?

The first thing we must realize is that the instructions God gave regarding the fruit was not a law; it was a caution. God does not want laws to govern our behavior; He knows all too well that laws cannot achieve the purpose. He wants people's hearts and minds to take charge of their actions. Actions in tune with God's love are always acceptable to Him and to all intelligent, fair-minded individuals. The assumption that God pronounced a law in the Garden of Eden is only a deduction based on our jurisdictive outlook of the story. Nothing in the text tells us that the marginalization of the Tree or its fruit was a law. Nor does it attribute the deaths that followed as a punishment the Creator had wowed to administer personally by becoming an Executioner. What an insipid interpretation of a text that says nothing of the sort!

Indeed, the marginalization of both the Tree and its fruit was a caution. As we have seen, the death that followed was a consequence totally unrelated to the ingestion of the fruit. Going to the Tree was already an act of egocentricity liable to destroy trust. But when Adam and Eve went to the Tree, they demonstrated for the universe to see, as soon as the fruit was consumed, that neither of them was trustworthy. Before eating the fruit, going to the Tree was enough of an act to break trust, but the fact that trust was broken was not clearly established until they took the fruit and ate it. As soon as trust was visibly broken, death became inevitable for all forms of life. From one instant to the next all forms of life were suddenly plunged into the darkness of distrust and subjected to a new rule of life based on competition for survival. Such competition could only escalate the death toll and such a toll could only perpetuate death and all the forms of stress associated with competition and death were liable to cause wear and tear as well as all forms of strife, diseases, old age, and ultimate death.

The problem is that humanity is so programed to resolve all its behavioral problems through the authority of its jurisdictive systems that the story of the so-called Forbidden Fruit had to grow legislative legs, or the act could not have been interpreted as breaking a law. The same goes for the death that followed; without the jurisdictive interpretation, the death of Adam and Eve could never have been perceived as God's punishment for misbehaving. Worse yet, humans have become blind to the possibility that another method of improving human behavior might exist, let alone a system far more effective to improve behavior than enforcing useless laws.

It is without foundations from the text itself that the story of the first sin has been interpreted. It is generally read with the idea that the Creation Week account of Genesis was God's first ever act of Creation. With such a reading we fail to recognize that when humans were created and placed in the Garden, evil had already been present in the universe for an undetermined period of time. It is clear from the text that the universe already existed and the water and the solid mass on which it was standing was already present in that location. By the text's declaration it is clear that previous work of Creation had already taken place in the universe. Nothing tells us that the devil was created during the span of that first week of Creation any more than it tells us that the globe itself was created that week. It is because evil already existed in the universe that God had to caution Adam and Eve about its presence in the Garden and the universe. It would have been unfair on God's part not to caution Adam and Eve, just as it would have been unfair not to caution them about the consequences of self-centeredness that would lead them to the Tree. They also had to have been forewarned that accepting the evil of self-centeredness would cause them to entertain a mind-set that would lead to chaos and death. Death was not to be perceived as a punishment God would inflict on wrongdoers because of a broken law, but because the evil of self-centeredness causes death as well as other consequences.

Though God's grace has many facets, it resides primarily in one fact. For Him there is only one valid principle of life that free intelligent beings must know and endorse in the universe if they wish to avoid chaos and death. It is a principle that involves *always placing the best interests and well-being of others ahead of one's own, and doing so unconditionally.*[19] With this principle of life solidly anchored in one's heart and mind, everyone wins and everyone benefits equally from God's system of life under grace. Everyone gives; therefore, everyone receives. As Jesus said: "Give and it will be given to you" (Lk. 6:38), because everyone gives.

---

[19] This is not a matter of giving indiscriminately to others. That would not necessarily be in the best interests of others who would likely become dependent on givers for their survival without contributing, or doing so marginally. Such giving would not be beneficial to the receiver who would tend to become dependent and fail to participate adequately to the cycle of mutual giving.

In keeping with the principle of life, God Himself is entirely driven by the flawless logic of this principle of life and never departs from it. As Jesus made it clear, this principle involves loving everyone, including one's enemies. It involves wanting to live the divine definition of love more than wanting to protect one's own life. Thus God never hated the devil. Though He hated his way of life, because it leads to chaos and death, He had to be tolerant of the presence of evil in the universe. He knew that ultimately evil would prove itself powerless to maintain life, but flawless in its power to produce chaos and death. For this reason Paul could affirm: "The wages of sin is death" (Rom. 6:23). Indeed, the only thing that can be gained from evil is chaos and death. Sin is not just an act; it is the mind-set that leads to acts of destruction.

Since God loved the devil, though not his mind-set, He had to give the devil at least some limited representation in the Garden when He created the first couple. He even went so far as to allow the devil to occupy a central position in the Garden wherefrom he could exercise and proclaim his evil influence to anyone who would listen. His principle of life was no different than the principle of evil humanity has chosen to adopt: "Lookout for yourself first and foremost. Life is a right, not a privilege. Therefore, even if others should come to suffer or die as a result of your quest for self-preservation, there is nothing wrong with entertaining such an attitude." It is this attitude of self-preservation that ended up placing a totally innocent man named Jesus on a Cross. The self-preservation of human systems founded on laws was severely threatened by His message, thus He was made to suffer abuse, atrocities, ridicule, scorn, and torture unto death, though He had committed no wrong. Indeed, all the iniquities that our world is capable of perpetrating were laid upon Him without a shred of mercy (see Is. 53:6).

It is because there was danger associated with that central location in the Garden of Eden that this Tree was called the Tree of Knowledge of Good and Evil. It was not a place where our first parents were given a choice between obedience and disobedience to a law. It was a place where they were given a choice between maintaining the mind-set God had given them when they were created or compromise God's mode of life with a "me first at any cost to others" mind-set that leads inevitably to the death of all forms of life sharing the same environment.

The Genesis narrative is clear in this regard: "When the woman saw that the fruit of the tree was good for food and pleasing to the eye, and also desirable for gaining wisdom, she took some and ate it" (Gen. 3:6). Eve chose to please herself without sufficient regard to the consequences of breaking trust in her environment. She had to know that trust would be broken because God considered Eve with great satisfaction at the end of the sixth day of Creation when He "saw all that he had made, and it was very good" (Gen. 1:31). We must remember that if God made man and woman in His own image (Gen. 1:27), they were both in possession of the same "welfare of others first" mind-set that always characterizes God, considering that "God is love" (1 Jn. 4:8, 16). They had to know exactly what love is and that breaking trust would destroy love as well as life that love alone can sustain indefinitely.

The passage tells us that Eve began to place her own desires ahead of the welfare of others, an attitude that fails to reflect the nature of God that she was given at Creation. Somehow she replaced the perfect mind-set God had "uploaded" in her heart and brain with the opposite mind-set that enslaved her to a system of rules and punishment. She replaced the focus of esteeming others before self with esteeming self before others despite the fact that God had done all He could to protect her from the destructive mind-set. God protects everyone's unconditional freedom of thought and action, even if pain and suffering should be the outcome. Freedom that makes love possible cannot be protected at a lesser cost.

Eve's sin was not in the fact that she took and ate the so-called Forbidden Fruit; eating it was only the tangible manifestation of sin. The moment she separated herself from the mind-set of God to covet the fruit by responding to her desire to serve self, she was already rejecting the importance of *esteeming others before self* modus operandi God had created in her. She was replacing it with the "me first" mind-set that led her to take the fruit. All this began to happen on the prompting of her personal volition before encountering the devil. Because she had need of nothing in the Paradisiac Garden of plenty God had created, the only way she could consider taking the fruit was to discard voluntarily the mind-set God had uploaded in her psyche. The moment she turned her back on the mind-set God had created in her to entertain the idea of serving self, she had already sinned, though no one but God could know before the act. Eating the fruit is the act that betrayed her newly corrupted mind-set.

Indeed, God alone knows what is going on in a person's heart. The created beings of the universe are incapable of such knowledge, thus the act alone provides them with the clue that her mind was corrupted. In our forensic legal system we have to wait for a person to commit the intolerable act or prove that the act was manifestly in the planning stages before prosecution can be allowed to proceed. This is an interesting contrast with God's view of sin as expressed in His Tenth Commandment: "You shall not covet" (Ex. 20:17). For God the contemplation of an evil act is already sin because it is a self-serving mental disposition of mind that opens the door to acts perpetrated at the expense of others whether or not the act is ever concluded.

Unlike humans who need forensic evidence to prove ill intent, God does not need evidence provided by an act to know that sin is already brewing in a person's heart. If God were to punish sin, it would have been extremely unloving on His part not to punish before a hurtful act is committed, but this is not the way God operates. This might in fact be the best proof that God does not punish and that He allows evil to follow its course because interventions on His part would be violations of the freedom required to preserve love.

The problem with Eve was not so much the act of eating the fruit; that was only a symptom of the problem. The accommodation she made in her heart and mind that opened the door to self-serving attitudes was the real problem to be dealt with. It follows reason that the least level of "me first" attitude destroys trust for all, thus the problem is the attitude that produces the action, not the action itself. Indeed, all we have to do to destroy trust is to make it evident by our actions that we are willing to place our own interests ahead of those of others. What's more, when trust is destroyed because of the presence of a single untrustworthy person in a community, everyone in that community becomes immediately compelled to consider his or her own self-interests first or accept the risks associated with the untrustworthiness of others. It is for this reason that from one moment to the next all forms of life were plunged into mutual distrust. Like the domino effect, all forms of life were immediately affected by the deadly mind-set gone viral. In fact, no virus or other disease could spread with such swiftness or produce such immediate deadly consequences. The least lack of trust in a community destroys God's system of operation for all forms of life. As a result, life itself is inevitably threatened and ultimately destroyed. When God said that Adam and Eve would die He was not saying that He would kill them; He was saying that the foundation of life on which they were fully dependent would be destroyed and that this situation would ultimately destroy all forms of life. Unfortunately, we are well on our way. We worry about climate change, but the problem of evil is the central problem responsible for all ills.

As we consider this idea, we realize that it is not possible to change a person's mind-set or heart by changing rules or by creating new or more sophisticated laws and consequences for disobedience—what must change is the heart. Well-enforced rules and laws might prevent some undesirable behavior, but rules are external impositions; they are all powerless to change a person's heart, and they all chip away individual freedom. When there is lack of mutual trust everyone has to be suspected of potentially behaving in ways detrimental to others. All it takes is one thief in town for all homeowners to install locks on their doors.

Like the well-known domino effect, in matters of trust, the fall of one individual destroys trust for all. Likewise, the breakdown of trust in the Garden of Eden destroyed peace and safety for all forms of life, even for the animals God had placed in the safekeeping of humans. Sadly, some of them were killed to equip humans with adequate clothing (see Gen. 3:21). Perhaps more importantly, God did it to show humans who had never seen death that it is ugly, painful, shameful, unnatural, irreversible, degrading, and damaging to all other forms of life. It is difficult to imagine that the microorganisms needed to destroy cadavers were already in plentiful supply in the pristine Garden of Eden. The evidence may have remained for some time. Killing the animal(s) for their skins was not a sacrifice as some call it. A sacrifice implies that it is a gift made to God, which this was not. It was a slaughter intended to show not only the ugliness of death to people who had never seen it, but also to make it very clear in their minds that the consequences of putting one's self-interests ahead of those of others destroys life. Since an attitude of the heart has the power to destroy trust; it also has the power to destroy life itself, even the lives of those who are sinless and perfectly trustworthy, such as was Jesus.

With this outlook on sin we have reasons to question the traditions related to the reasons for which Jesus came to our planet. Indeed, He came to deal with sin in the world; that is biblical. But did He come, as so many say, to acquit the sinful acts, or did He come to help sinners think differently that they might overcome their propensity to sin? Clearly, the first resolves nothing, especially considering that the sinful act is not the problem; the thinking that preceded the act is the root cause of the problem. The nature of the teachings Jesus brought to a world in perdition suggests the latter. By considering the Cross as a forensic act of forgiveness and acquittal the real message of Jesus is overlooked.

Reading of Scripture Skewed by Human Concepts of Justice

There are several highly questionable translations and interpretations of the book of Genesis and others Scripture that have the potential to lead astray. This is because translators interpret God through lenses of human forensics and jump incorrectly to the conclusion that sin is an act, and that death is a punishment. Let us consider one text in particular. We read in Chapter Two that before they sinned: "The man and his wife were both naked, and they felt no shame" (Gen. 2:25). Indeed, since they were still pure of heart, considering that they lived exclusively with the primary desire to care deeply for the welfare and well-being of others before self, they could see nothing mutually menacing or potentially threatening by the fact that they were both naked. With the mind-set of God in their heart their greatest desires were always and unconditionally filled with the intrinsic need to serve one another without the least inclination to be self-serving. With such an attitude of heart they could not nurture the least desire to take advantage of one another or anyone else. They could be implicitly trusted. With a pure mind-set, mutual trust was unquestionable and recognized as the most basic requirement to maintain life in peace and harmony forever.

We can only assume that when God appeared to them in the Garden He appeared like another human being, and like them, He probably also appeared naked to them, or His appearance would have been unnatural, even mind-shaking or intimidating perhaps. In this passage the word translated "shame" is the Hebrew word *bush* meaning confounded, or confused. Indeed, it should be understood that Adam and Eve were naked but *they were not confused*. They could not have been confused because they had not yet willfully replaced the mind-set God had created in them with the mind-set of evil, which they willfully chose to adopt.

As long as Adam and Eve could look at one another's nakedness or that of God for that matter, and this without nurturing the least inclination for lust or the least desire to take advantage of another with intent to manipulate or possess that person, nakedness could not yet begin to confuse their divinely encoded minds. Before the first sin committed in the Garden a person could not possibly become the object of another's desires or manipulations; indeed, all people could only be viewed with such purity of heart that everyone craved the desire to enhance even more one another's already beautiful lives.

As long as they were in a state of purity of mind it could have never occurred to them to use, manipulate, or take possession of anything or anyone. After sin, everything changed. Even God's nakedness could have appeared to them as a threat, despite the fact that He probably looked just like another man (see Gen. 3:8). If He were different from Adam in general appearance God might have appeared intimidating, strange, or even haughty, not the image of a loving God. Nothing in the account suggests that God impressed them with the least level of superiority or authority over them. The text even goes so far as to specify that God produced typical human sounds. When He walked "the man and his wife heard the sound of the LORD God as he was walking in the Garden in the cool of the day, and they hid from the LORD God among the trees of the garden" (Gen. 3:8). Why did they think to hide? It is because they perceived the LORD God to be their equal in every way, One from whom it was possible to hide.

It is quite clear that God interacted openly with the first humans, even with Cain after he became a murderer. In all known interactive situations God kept everyone perfectly at ease, even the murderer. God never manifested Himself as a police officer or a judge. Unlike the pagan gods the true God did not intimidate, and with one exception at Sinai, He avoided representing Himself as a dominant authoritarian figure. We see it in His interactions with Abraham on several occasions (Gen. 17:1; 18:10; 18:17), or even much later when Jesus, whom the author of Hebrews called the "express image" (Heb. 1:3, KJV) of God, when He lived on this earth. When Adam and Eve chose to depart from the way God had programed their brains, they instantly became self-serving and were both instantly compelled to start focusing their concerns on their own personal survival—this because their entire environment had suddenly been contaminated by distrust.

It is possible that since God appeared to Adam and Eve as another man, as evidenced by the fact that Adam expressed the desire to have a mate (Gen. 2:20),[20] the broken trust caused Adam and Eve to perceive

---

[20]   Had God portrayed Himself as a female in the Garden, Adam might have been confused about wanting a mate.

the Lord as a threat. Their impulse to hide from their Maker may well have been because the only other Man in the Garden could have been a suitor for Eve. Even the devil did not try to appear as a potential suitor; he chose to appear as a serpent––cunning indeed. The only One Adam and Eve could possibly fear was their Maker. As a result they chose to become one another's mutual possession rather than God's. This was clearly the first case of idolatry. They were not ashamed with one another; no couple is ever ashamed of nudity. But Adam and Eve were indeed confused, and because they were confused they were afraid that their Creator might abuse them or cause their breakup or even kill one of them, or both.

Thus we can say that The Tree of Knowledge of Good *and* Evil could also have been called The Tree of Mental Confusion. Going where God told them not to go did not show our first parents the difference between "good" and "evil." It replaced the mind-set God had created in them with an opposite mind-set—one that could not sustain life long-term. Since then the two mind-sets have been on a permanent collision course in the same brain. A condition responsible for producing the intellectual chaos that leads to death. It is this condition of mind that Jesus came to alleviate all the way to the Cross, not to pay for sins in order to acquit sin, as tradition teaches.

The cocktail of intellectual confusion proved so lethal that it is far more damaging than any mind-altering drug known to science. It did not just put Adam and Eve in a dormant semiconscious state as drugs do; it destroyed their ability to maintain clarity regarding the unconditional altruistic mind-set of God that should also have remained their own. Worse yet, it did not affect just those two individuals in the Garden, it triggered a domino effect of undesirable consequences that would ultimately bring death to all forms of life. The line of demarcation between the "me first" attitude of evil and the "others always first" attitude from God became blurred to such a point that Adam and Eve chose to become one another's cherished possession rather than one another's gift of self to the other. The former is evil thinking because it reduced the couple to a form of mutual servitude, while the latter would have been the voluntary gift of self to the other that perpetuates unfailing mutual trust under the protection of perfect love. How is it possible not to trust explicitly a person whose only pleasures and desires are to perpetually enhance the lives of others at any cost?

As models of the gift of self to one another, Adam and Eve would have been a glorious model for all of humanity to recognize and admire. They would have been the perfect model of atonement understood as *at-one-ment,* as William Tyndale intended the word he coined to be understood. It is the coming together at-one of two individual people focused entirely on the unconditional gifting of self to the other that produces perfect oneness God desires for all His children. The descendants of Adam and Eve would have recognized marriage not as the possession of one another but as the model of being at one with one another as all humans should be at one with God and with one another. The concept would have been recognized as the only way to live in eternal harmony despite the fact that they died. Their descendants would have continued to die, but with the knowledge of how atonement is achieved and maintained, it would not have been possible for the mortals to stay in their grave indefinitely. For those who die with unconditional love in the heart that makes at-one-ment with others possible, as did Jesus, God would not allow them to remain in the grave much longer. Jesus who loved perfectly came out of the grave after three days.

Partaking of the Tree of Knowledge of Good and Evil should have never been considered forensically as involving a pronouncement of judgment of capital punishment for all people, guilty or not. Babies die in our world having never sinned, as did Jesus. Death is not a punishment; it is the product, or should we say, "the wages of sin." The Tree is the place where confusion of mind destroyed trust, and ultimately it is the lack of trust that produced the death of all forms of life, not God making a pronouncement of capital punishment. The destruction of mutual trust could not be without consequences because life is fully dependent on perfect mutual trust.

When mutual trust is absent from daily community life, pain, suffering, and death become inevitable. There is only one way to reverse the problem; it is called repentance. This word is often misunderstood as meaning feeling sorry for past sins. Instead it should be understood as accepting to undergo a 180-degree change of heart and mind by willfully returning to the mind-set God originally created in humans. Just as the departure from that mind-set was willful, the return to it must be willfully recognized and accepted by a sinner. Jesus came to show us the way. In other words, He came to show us the procedure that must be followed to accomplish this amazing feat. He showed us the way to choose willfully God's procedure that is never imposed on anyone. This is not righteousness by works because it amounts to doing the right thing thanks to having in us the right faith, or the correct mind-set.

Once persuaded, doing the right thing is not a chore or a duty; it is the sincerely desired and preferred course of action even when following that course might involve pain. God still deserves all the glory for this development. Without Him, and the willingness of Jesus who is His "express image" to show us the way all the way to the Cross, the human race would have been lost forevermore. The point is that we should pursue love with such enthusiasm that we would become ever more trustworthy. Jesus made the promise that a place is prepared in heaven (a universe made new) for those who are, or those who would be, willing to accept His way. He has prepared "many mansions" (Jn. 14:12) for us, He said. But He cannot take us in such a place before common sinners filled with the spirit of "me first" way of life yield their spirit to His Spirit, which is His way of life. Humans must prove to the universe that it is possible to change one's mind-set—something no religion has yet accomplished. Jesus is the only One who has. The capacity for ordinary humans to accept the divine mind-set and live it remains to be proven to the universe. This is how God will be vindicated. The foregoing is an attempt to shed some light on the procedure Scripture and Jesus have offered all along to dismiss the confusion.

It is because humans have corrupted the message from God that we have failed to recognize and understand the required procedure to overcome evil. We have always been confused regarding the extent to which a person should choose to serve self or consider the welfare of others first. This has become the dilemma of humanity ever since the first sin in Eden. All the confusion humanity faces when considering ethics is related to this very dilemma. Where should the line be drawn between me first and others first? How does one decide where the line should be drawn in a field of shifting sands? Where should the limits of self-serving acts be set to adequately protect the interests of society at large? Of course, we would first have to agree on what is acceptable, but how can that be determined, considering that no two humans agree? Legislators are desperately trying to find a platform of agreement regarding the level at which self-serving acts become improper, unacceptable, or intolerable, but answers continue to evade the most astute. The answers to those questions will continue to blow in the winds of confusion as long as humans fail to accept and understand the exact nature of God's message of truth.

In matters of self-defense for example, laws attempt to exempt from responsibility a person who kills another so long as it is in self-defense or to protect members of the household or even one's possessions in some cases. But things get confusingly complicated, because at what level of personal vulnerability in a scuffle does it become permissible and acceptable "by law" to kill an aggressor? As we shall see, God resolved that question long before Creation Week and long before sin occurred, but humans have repeatedly failed to listen to God. This explains why at the time of Noah, the world came so close to commit self-extermination. The worldwide cataclysmic event would have annihilated all life from the face of the earth, had God not intervened. He did not cause the Flood, though He is credited for it, but He allowed it because He does not interfere to prevent evil. However, He saved Noah and his family to give humanity yet another chance to understand His eternal Truth.[21]

Despite the errors of antediluvians and God's clear command never to cause the shedding of human blood for any reason (Gen. 9:5–6), humans managed to fail again and again. Rendering evil for evil is the rule of our judicial systems despite God's warning against such a practice (Rom. 12:17). It is a system that only has the power to perpetuate evil at the expense of goodness that should characterize the children of God. God attempted to get His message through to the descendants of Noah, and to put an end to violence, but once again they failed. Another agreement, or covenant was made with the descendants of Abraham in

---

[21]   Because of the author's contention that God does not kill, a matter briefly discussed later, Noah's Flood could not have been an act of God. Humans who were probably more scientifically advanced than we realize must have caused the conditions that produced the Flood. With their "me first" attitude they came to disregard the value of nature and life. According to Genesis 6:13 violence in the world was the root cause of the destruction. Though Scripture credits God for this act, we will discover that it was a false human perception of God founded on the pagan belief that the gods control everything that happens on the planet, good or bad. This view would also imply that God wanted humans to sin and become violent, which is preposterous. If He were really in total control of everything, no one would have ever been permitted to sin anywhere in the universe, but freedom would not exist, nor would love as a state of heart. We can deduct from the text that violence was indeed the root cause of the worldwide Flood of Noah, not God.

this regard, but again they failed. In the end God sent a final message of nonviolence to the world through the life and teachings of Jesus (see Heb. 1:1–2), but they utterly failed to heed His message. Jesus demonstrated unambiguously that serving others should always come first, and unconditionally, even at the expense of one's own life. God was trying to show humanity that it is better to accept one's own death than to break away from God's eternal and universal principle of unconditional love.

In this world we have intricate and sometimes painfully confusing rules of self-defense. They vary widely from country to country and even from community to community. The fact that there is no clear-cut code regarding such a basic issue of life and death is indicative of the confusion humanity faces in this regard. At what exact level of aggressive escalation does it become acceptable for a person to place self-interest of survival ahead of the lives of others? In other words, at what level of aggression does it become permissible to overlook the interests of others in our society?

This dilemma is ever present in the minds of translators of Scripture who believe in the rights of self-protection we should all enjoy. Thus it is understandable that they have often translated and interpreted the Holy Writ with forensic preconceptions. Examples of this flawed approach are present throughout Scripture and in all areas of interpretation. The entire sanctuary service has been interpreted as a judgment scene with confession of misconduct before the Great Judge of the universe in His judgment court. Instead, the sanctuary and its services were intended to convey God's unique approach to the resolution of evil through repentance as a radical change of direction on the level of one's heart. The ministry of the sanctuary was all about the new birth as it was later confirmed by the message of Jesus.

As we have said, it is not the fact that Eve took the fruit that brought the confusion in her heart and mind; the fact that she chose to go to the Tree was already an indication that she was confused. She had already placed her desire for self-satisfaction ahead of the interests of others or she would not have gone there in the first place, and the same could be said of Adam. However, by going to the Tree, they both made manifest their lack of trust in their Creator's way of life, which opened the door to the mutual distrust that afflicted all life-forms. Having lost a clear sense of God's system of life, humans developed an ever-growing appetite for self-aggrandizement and self-protection at all cost to others. Since our mental script determines our way of life, a script lacking mutual trust can achieve neither peace nor prosperity. As long as the mental script is focused on self, mutual trust will never be achieved, and peace in freedom will continue to be unattainable. The theory of evolution involving the survival of the fittest will prove totally flawed and ineffective.

Since sin was already present in Eve's heart when she chose to consider her own personal self-interests with less than sufficient regard for the welfare, comforts, and securities of others, we have all been in this boat from birth ever since. By eating the fruit Eve merely provided evidence before the entire universe that her heart was confused, thus, already sinful. This lack of concern for others was nothing less than a lack of love. Sin is always the product of a deliberate or unintentional lack of love, and the product of sin is unavoidable death (Rom. 6:23).

As we can see, the problem did not originate with an action; it all began with a state of mind, with a false faith. It allowed a departure from the divine principle of life founded on placing the interests of others first and foremost in all considerations of life, even when serving self. Indeed, serving self is necessary, but even serving self should always be part of our efforts to better serve others. With this in mind, we would actually do a better job of caring for ourselves, because we would soon realize that eating a good diet gives us more strength to serve others than eating junk food. We would realize that the way we dress and groom our bodies should never be intended to make a self-serving statement but to please and serve the greater number.

Could the case be made that Eve took the fruit to better serve others? The text is clear about that; she took it because "it was good for food and pleasing to the eye, and also desirable for gaining wisdom." All the wrong reasons to justify her action are listed in this statement. In other words, she did it entirely to please herself physically, considering that it was good food, to please herself mentally, considering that it was desirable to sharpen the eyes of her intelligence, and also spiritually, considering that it would make her wise "like God" (Gen. 3:5). But did Eve forget that she was already made in the image of God (Gen. 1:27)? How could anyone improve on that? And why would she want to? With a plentiful supply of everything in the Garden, the only reason she could have nurtured the desire to serve self was to accept a mind-set short on loving consideration for others.

Eve did not break a law; she disregarded an everlasting principle of life often called a law in scripture because of our forensically oriented mind-set. Shame was not the result of sin, but confusion of mind was the sin that produced the action. The principle Eve disregarded is that life eternal in peace and prosperity is possible only as long as all intelligent life in a given environment remains fully committed to valuing the interests of others before one's own. The instant a person departs from this immutable principle of eternal life the door of mutual distrust is left wide open for all to suffer its consequences. This breaks down harmony and ultimately brings chaos and death to all forms of life—it is just a matter of time. Adam and Eve did not lose their life instantly, but the principle required to maintain eternal life was indeed dead.

With stressed relationships, cooperation and collaboration between people suffer. Thus everyone suffers when there is lack of trust. Distrust spreads faster than the most virulent viruses. It is the broken trust that makes necessary the installation of locks on doors. What a waste of human resources! They could be better used to benefit others rather than to prevent theft. Today we need more than locks on our doors; we need electronic surveillance, police forces, huge arsenals of weapons of mass destruction, and huge armies. For eternal life to ever become possible absolute unconditional trust must be restored.

Some believe that the change will take place when the Lord returns, when we will be "changed in a flash, in the twinkling of an eye, at the last trumpet," as Paul affirms. "For the trumpet will sound, the dead will be raised imperishable, and we will be changed" (1 Cor. 15:51). Indeed, this resurrection at the sound of the trumpet will announce the beginning of a new kingdom of love. But the only change that will take place according to the text is that people will become incorruptible; that is to say, they will never decay ever again. For that day to become reality it must be demonstrated before the universe that a change of character is possible for sinners to accept. Jesus proved that point by living in human flesh. As we do, He had to learn by what He suffered (Heb. 5:8). God's kingdom of love cannot become a reality until it can be proven to the universe that sinners can also make the change. To do so we must listen to God. He has outlined the procedure in Scripture and Christ has demonstrated how this procedure transforms lives—the subject of another chapter.

CHAPTER 6

Our Mental Scripts Determine How We Live Our Lives

As we have seen, when Adam and Eve sinned it was not because they had broken a law or a command, it was because they willfully disregarded the mental script of life God had written on their hearts and minds when they were created. Their departure from the perfectly logical script did not bring about a punishment from God; they suffered the natural consequences of *willfully* disregarding the immutable principle of life God had engraved upon their hearts. God had warned them, but they did not heed His warning. If God could say of the work He completed on the sixth day of Creation that it was "very good" (Gen. 1:31), it was because Adam and Eve who were created that day were indeed "very good" down to the core of their hearts and minds. Since they were created in the image of God, their hearts and minds were scripted in the image of God's very own.

Didn't Jesus say to the Pharisees: "How can you who are evil say anything good? For out of the overflow of the heart the mouth speaks" (Mt. 12:34). The context shows that Jesus was not talking just about their words being the products of their hearts, but also about their deeds. He went on to say: "The good man brings good things out of the good stored up in him, and the evil man brings evil things out of the evil stored up in him" (Mt. 12:35). These declarations of Jesus begs an important question: Considering that the contents of our hearts make the difference between being a good or evil person, how much of our hearts' contents are we personally responsible for? This question begs yet another; if we are responsible for the good or evil contents of our hearts, are we not also responsible for the evil deeds generated from the contents of our hearts?

Perhaps another question would answer this last one: Why would Jesus say that good or evil thoughts and the actions related to these thoughts are the product of our hearts if we are powerless to control the contents of our hearts? We either have a responsibility in this regard, or Jesus is blaming the Pharisees for a condition they cannot be held responsible for, which would not only be unfair, it would be cruel. Worse yet, why would Jesus say that our actions are the product of our hearts if He, or the Holy Spirit Person of the Godhead, is the One responsible for the contents of our hearts? That would be like blaming Himself, or the other Person of the Godhead, for the problem. One way or the other, Jesus would be blaming God for the problem. What we must consider is that if God or the Godhead was indeed responsible for the contents of our hearts, Jesus could have simply said: "To be saved you must believe that I came to this world to die on a cross to pay for your sins. And if you believe that, the Holy Spirit Person of the Godhead will come to you and will fill your hearts with compassion and love toward all people, even for your enemies." But Jesus said nothing of the sort.

Obviously, Jesus never said anything remotely similar to this pagan-influenced concept propagated by the bulk of Christianity. If that concept were true it would have been a perfect opportunity for Him to disclose His message in terms no one could ever disclaim. But He never did, because it is simply not the way God operates. In fact, such a scenario would suggest a scandalous abuse of human freedom because it would destroy a person's sense of responsibility and would destroy love in its wake. If this were the way God operates, people would forever be subjected to the will of an external force, that of the Holy Spirit Person of the Godhead. If God should ever choose to control humans in such a manner humans would not be totally free, thus they would not be created in His image.

No one tells God what to do, yet he always does the right thing because His mind-set is polarized in one direction only: the welfare and well-being of others always first, never the other way around. In fact, logically speaking this is the only way God's system can achieve His purpose to make everyone king and priest. The problem is that in such a system there can be no exception, because the one exception would be the fallen domino that ruins life for all. Everyone's heart in the system Scripture calls the kingdom of God would have to be polarized as God's, just as the hearts of our first parents were initially created. Created in the image of God implies being self-governed. There is no way for a person who lacks a sense of responsibility can be self-governed, much less on the basis of serving others before self. A person created in the image of God could do no wrong and could hurt no one. All thoughts and strength would be dedicated to the sole purpose of making the lives of others even more wonderful than it is. Progress and prosperity in peace would be limitless. But for such a condition to become reality, not a single traitor could take part in the life of such a community, or trust would be broken for all. Once again, all people would suffer and be forced to return to the tyranny and inefficiencies of judicial systems because of the presence of a single "bad apple" in the group. As we all know, laws are for the bad apple, not the others.

Here is the problem however. Since love cannot be imposed, especially love for enemies (Mt. 5:44), any level of imposition would be tyranny. This view negates the traditional attributes related to the action of the Holy Spirit believed to be capable of supernatural magic to transform a sinner's heart. Indeed, that would be an imposition, and it would be tyranny.

This discussion has been going on since the first centuries of the Christian era and, more specifically, since the Reformation of the sixteenth century. If righteousness is by faith, what is the mechanism by which goodness replaces the evil in human hearts so that actions become the reflection of a transformed heart? Since the Reformation, a good number of Christians have come to despise what they like to call "righteousness by works," saying instead that sinners should simply believe in Jesus and His sacrifice on the Cross to be miraculously saved and transformed. Unfortunately for believers of this view, it does not appear to agree with Scripture.

Depending on one's understanding and definition of sin, the substance of Paul's statements related to righteousness being by faith can be understood differently. If love is perceived as a set of dos and don'ts from a judicial perspective, it either means that one must submit to the rules, which is righteousness by works, or that one is acquitted of sin by a higher authority, a concept generally viewed as righteousness by faith. The problem is that neither concept offers a viable solution to the problem of evil. As we have seen, the judicial outlook cannot resolve the problem of evil. The problem is that both of the above views are concepts derived from the perspective of human judicial systems. Either the law condemns sinners, or sinners are acquitted from observing laws. However, when sin is perceived as a flaw of rational thinking, rather than a wrongful act, a new perception capable of destroying previously held damaging preconceptions is needed. Faith capable of making this turnaround possible is the faith *of* Jesus that produces righteousness because it induces correct thinking that can replace or correct a previously held lapse of logic.

God's system to overcome evil bears no resemblance to the human judicial system at any level. It involves a totally different approach. God's system is never involved in judging actions; it only recognizes a flaw in the way sinners think, thus a problem with the human heart. At some point in the history of humankind here is what Scripture had to say about them: "Now the earth was corrupt in God's sight and was full of violence" (Gen. 6:11). Indeed, corruption engenders violence. But what causes the rampant corruption? During His ministry on earth Jesus said something significant about the last days: "As it was in the days of Noah, so it will be at the coming of the son of Man" (Mt. 24:37). But why are humans having such a hard time dealing with violence? It is only because they have a hard time dealing with its causes. The problem is not the act; it is the thinking that produced the act. God has been laboring with humans ever since they first departed from His way of life to rectify the problem, but there is an aspect of His method to overcome evil that humans have never managed to recognize, or perhaps they never wanted to.

Can a Persuasive Message Improve Hearts and Character?

We are all aware that perfectly logical messages can fail to persuade and that even a persuasion can fail to produce behavior compatible with the persuasion. A number of harmful behaviors are dictated either by the desire to promote self or to attain social acceptance. Cigarette smoking has been known to damage health yet many are willing to accept all the risks associated with the practice. The knowledge that extremely painful death often results from lung or tracheal cancer linked to this practice may not be a deterrent at all. While logical messages do not necessarily alter attitudes or behavior, it is also true that messages lacking sound logic and empirical evidence cannot change a person's behavior on rational grounds. When persuasions are held and acted upon in defiance of logic they are superstitions. The fear of breaking a mirror because of the persuasion that seven years of bad luck will follow is not founded on logic; therefore it is a superstition. Unfortunately, "faith," as Christians call rather broad portions of their belief systems tend to rest on similar levels of superstition.

The problem with religion stems from the refusal of religious authorities to subject their religious beliefs to sound logic. If logic is God's creation why would He expect created beings equipped with capacity for logic to depart from sound logic in their understanding of religion? If the problem of evil in the world is caused by lack of love, how can it be resolved by subjecting anyone to rituals unrelated to love, or involving pain, suffering, and death to pay for sins? The most pious Christians would simply answer that Jesus died to pay for sins despite the fact that paying for evil deeds cannot solve the problem. This line of reasoning fails to make the omniscient God of logic appear rational or loving. If God can take a sinner by the hand and require someone's painful death to resolve the problem, why did He choose to wait so long before giving His Son as payment? This fact alone betrays a lack of logic on God's part. If the blood of the sacrifice made on the Cross has the power to cleanse sin, why is it that the omnipotent God appears to lack the urgency to purify the believers' hearts, minds, and actions? Good logic suggests a follow-up question: If God can heal everything supernaturally, why did He need the shedding of innocent blood to grant the favor? Is that really how love is manifested? Something is clearly wrong with this view of God if indeed He is a logical and loving God.

With a theology falsely believing that healing from sin takes place because the Lord died to pay for them, we are compelled to examine this view in the light of Scripture. Paul contends that it is the life of the Lord that procures salvation, not His death (see Rom. 5:10). If the life of Jesus procures salvation we must ask ourselves an important question: Why would Paul say that it is His life that brings salvation and not His death? It is because the life He lived all the way to His death provides the message that saves, not a payment of death. If the life of Jesus has the power to save sinners, it should be their duty to study His life and how it saves, rather than focusing on His death. Sinners should strive to understand as clearly as possible the message conferred by His life. This is what Jesus calls seeking "the kingdom of God *and His righteousness*" (Mt. 6:33, emphasis added).

The idea that the death of Jesus was a payment can only have a soothing effect on sinners relieved that they have been pardoned. But God never fails to forgive. The death of Jesus was not required for God to offer a pardon; His death was only required to provide the clear and complete message of the paradigm of life sinners should accept unto death. For this reason Jesus said: "Anyone who does not take his cross and follow me is not worthy of me" (Mt. 10:38). What Jesus was saying is that anyone who is not willing to shed his or her own blood for the sake of living a life of love is not worthy of Him. The often-quoted text of Hebrews is not translated correctly. In the NIV we read: "Without the shedding of blood there is no forgiveness" (Heb. 9:20). This text should be translated to imply that without the willingness to shed one's own blood, as did Jesus for the sake of love, there is no *remission* of the sin disease. The King James translation of this text is better in this regard. Indeed, it is only when one's love becomes more important than one's life that sin can be overcome. The sin disease goes into remission only when a person is willing to love others so much that shedding blood unto death in the process becomes the acceptable outcome. The author of Hebrews confirms that view: "In your struggle against sin (or against lack of love), you have not yet resisted to the point of shedding your blood" (Heb. 12:4 parenthesis mine).

Thinking that a pardon or forgiveness is sufficient to obtain salvation gives a false assurance of salvation, but this is not faith, it is presumption. A pardon maintains open the doors of relationship with parties we have offended, but it offers no guarantee that the pardoned misdeed will not be repeated. That is why Jesus made it clear that we should not bother to count how many times we forgive others. On the other hand it is by recognizing the perfect logic and beauty of the message Jesus taught and lived in words and deeds that sinners can receive something far more powerful than just influence or a model to follow. What a sinner should understand is that the message from God follows logic sound enough to be persuasive, not merely influential. This is where the "Moral Influence Theory of Atonement" falls apart. The change in the life of a Christian might be somewhat influenced by the beauty and love manifested in the life of Jesus. But the change of heart comes from the soundness and logical persuasiveness of His message. This is far more than mere influence likely to stimulate one's desire to become a good Jesus impersonator.

Once clearly understood, the message of Jesus becomes a persuasion so powerful that it has the power to change the orientation of a sinner's thoughts and actions. If a sinner must rely on supernatural forces to be healed, how does he or she know that the supernatural forces at work are really from God? They could just as well be coming from the devil. He is cunning enough to instigate good deeds in order to mask the evil nature of the instigator. When the persuasion of logic is involved and recognized as coming from God because no human could have promulgated such a perfect message, the origin of the message cannot be mistaken.

This is a subtle but extremely important point. Scripture reminds us that the devil is not only very clever; he is also willing to take advantage of any situation that could benefit his purposes. If healing from sin is imposed on a sinner by a supernatural force the sinner must first be willing to relinquish his/her will and life to an outside force—a clear renunciation of God's privilege of freedom. The healing of the sin disease must take place in the heart; it can take place nowhere else. It is not done by submitting to a Person but by submitting to a perfectly logical message involving a procedure that also makes perfect sense. Right living is never accomplished by submitting to an outside force that destroys the freedom that makes love possible. Righteousness by faith is not a matter of submitting to a Person of the Godhead; it is accomplished by submitting to a principle of life that never endangers freedom because it comes from God.

God never imposes His will on anyone. He never pressures humans. He wants them to preserve their free access to love at any cost. He paid the dear price of the Son's life to preserve freedom for sinners by communicating the message of Truth that saves from sin. It is for that reason alone that Jesus went all the way to the Cross. God never changes; therefore He never reneges on His promises. Any level of pressure coming from an outside force acting on a person's heart or mind has to come from the devil. God wants us to change from within by receiving the Truth that has the persuasive power to change the worst among sinners. This is when the sinner's own persuasion becomes his or her faith. God calls this persuasive message the "Gospel." When correctly understood it has the power to change hearts, while a payment does not. In other words, it is the message of the blood and the Cross (see 1 Cor. 1:18) that has the power to change hearts, not His blood or His Cross, and much less, His death. There is no power in death, but in the clutches of suffering unto death our Lord clinched His message of persuasion.

Comedian Bill Maher rightly said about Christians and other religions: "Faith is the purposeful suspension of critical thinking."[22]

---

22   Bill O'Reilly interviewing Bill Maher, Sept 30, 2010 on Fox News Network.

Maher, a keen observer of the absurd, recognizes that the beliefs and teachings of Christians amount to a suspension of critical thinking. Christians have abdicated from logic and common sense in their consideration of God's Word. As already noted, the Greek word *pistis* usually translated "faith" really means "persuasion." But a persuasion must be logically demonstrable as true, or the concept cannot be called a truth, and it lacks the power of persuasion.

The author of Hebrews is often misunderstood when quoted to say: "Now faith is being sure of what we hope for and certain of what we do not see" (Heb. 11:1). Indeed, no one on this planet has ever seen a world where love reigns supreme. Yet with our physical eyes shut and our eyes of the heart wide open, it is relatively easy to imagine and become persuaded that a world of pure love could exist and that no eternal life would be possible without universal love. Life would be absolutely wonderful if unconditional love was the driving force in the hearts of every single person living on planet Earth. "Faith is being sure," affirms Paul; it involves a persuasion founded on logic, not a fairy tale involving someone dying to pay for sins. Faith is "being certain" of something on the basis of an invisible but indisputable persuasion. Though the cost was extreme because He died, God offers the persuasive message free of charge and without ever exercising the least pressure on anyone to follow or respect His message.

The Truth of God's message is unquestionably valid because it is self-evident and self-validating on the grounds of indisputable logic. How could a payment ever produce such persuasion in a person's heart? Has anyone ever attempted to satisfy the grief of parents whose child has been molested and murdered by a criminal? Would a payment of someone's death be sufficient? The resolution of a problem that causes death is not possible with a payment—not even the payment of perfect divine life. Only a change of heart, mind, and deeds can bring a lasting solution to the human condition, and God will ultimately take care of the child that died as well as the parents of that child. The incomprehensible aspect of faith is in the resurrection of the dead. That is incomprehensible to us mortals that we are. The procedure God has made available cost Him a great deal, but it is offered at no cost to the sinner.

The devil and his cohorts are always eager to take advantage of the freedom to think and act God has given humans—He has done it since Eden. On that basis we can ascertain that healing from sin has to take place on the merits of a powerful persuasion based on a powerful message; nothing else could possibly accomplish the purpose without abusing personal freedom. Since humans have now proven to the universe that paying for criminal acts improve neither criminals nor society, it is high time we listen to God.

Any guidance from a person claiming to have the powers of a supernatural spirit or that of a previously dead person should be considered as coming from the devil. These cases invariably end up controlling the subject. When a message is from God, it is conveyed through prophets who, when they have communicated their message to humanity, stand back and allow people to act in total freedom. When accepted, these messages have the power to change a person's heart, thus no credit should be taken away from God for the change. He is the author and the sustainer of His everlasting message of Truth. His message is also called "the eternal" or "everlasting covenant" (Heb. 13:20), depending on the translation.

Through these prophetic messages God conveys His detailed procedure to overcome sin. It is a procedure that never interferes with the will of a person. To preserve freedom, the only way the direction of one's life can be changed is by way of a message, not by way of an outside force telling a person how to think or what to do. Without God's repeated efforts to convey Truth, humans would have never recognized it, and they would never be in a position to benefit from a life guided by Truth for eternity rather than by laws or supernatural spirits. Without God's Truth we would all die never to be resurrected, and eventually the human race would disappear from the universe. Atheists would consider such a calamity a mere cosmic event. For them intelligent life is essentially meaningless and purposeless, but unfortunately it is not painless. Considering the pain and suffering that life brings in our world, it can only be considered a sad accident of nature! For believers in God such a state of life would be inconceivable, because even pain and suffering should be meaningful. It should be a signal for us that something is wrong and needs to be corrected.

The Lord's life and death is a historical fact backed up by historical accounts. He is called Savior and Messiah, thus He should also be recognized as the solution to the problem of evil. However, if His death is perceived as a payment, it is idolatry of blood and death, and the expectation to obtain salvation on that basis becomes mere superstition.

On the other hand, if the Lord's Life unto death is recognized as a message from God, it has to be a meaningful message——one that has the power to persuade from within sinners' hearts liable to change them for the better. Such salvation is the product of a persuasion, thus faith is not the product of a belief akin to fairy dust or Santa Claus.

When Christians believe that healing from sin happens through the introduction of a supernatural power in the heart, they fail to recognize the importance of their own participation in God's plan of salvation. This participation does not involve trying hard to keep the Laws of God, but it does involve a sincere appreciation for the Truth and the willingness to share it with others as the priests of old were expected to fulfill their Temple duties. However, to accomplish priestly duties, the message from God must first be cleansed of all pagan concepts it may still contain. God would never allow a sinner to be transformed into a remote-controlled robot, but the devil would. The life of a robot could not be called a life of freedom. For a free intelligent person it could only be the height of tyranny.

If life is the product of an omniscient, merciful God, He would never have created intelligent beings knowing that He would later have to take away their freedom-related privileges. He created life knowing His plan for the universe would succeed. It would have been cruel for a merciful God to create intelligent life fully equipped to handle all the advantages of freedom that makes love possible, only to decide later to take it all away forever. God preserves jealously the freedom He has granted. As the Second Commandment indicates, God is a jealous God. He is jealous of the way of life He has created because He knows that there is no other way to live eternally. He has entrusted intelligent beings with the greatest gift of all: love.

God would have never created a system of life bound for oblivion. He knew that ultimately the system would cost Him dearly because since the foundation of the universe He knew that someday He would have to come to the rescue of sinners, and this at the price of His life, a work for which He had been foreordained before the creation of the universe (see 1 Pet. 1:20). He went so far as to send Jesus who is the "express image" (Heb. 1:3 KJV) of His own self to our planet.[23] He did it to bring the

---

[23] More on this in our discussion about *Elohim* and *Yahweh* in the last two chapters.

message that will not only save the human race, but will also save the privilege of freedom and love for the universe, and He knew that He would have to do it at the price of His life. Indeed, Jesus did not come to die; He came knowing He would die. Is there anything that could be more important in the eyes of God than the preservation of freedom that makes love possible as a system of government for the universe? Someday, this divine kingdom will be reestablished in the universe. It will once again be founded on love.

To better understand that God is the great doctor of the universe who is in the process of solving the problem of evil while respecting and protecting freedom, let us draw a parallel between physical illnesses and the sin disease. If hospitalization were needed to overcome a known terminal ailment, it would be suicidal for a patient to refuse the diagnosis and prescription of expert doctors. This would be all the more insane if both the advice and the treatment were made available free of charge to the patient. With God the prescription and the treatment are both free of charge; no payment of any kind is or was ever needed. But as with physical illnesses, patients are never compelled to accept a prescription or the related therapy. In the religious world churches and temples should be spiritual hospitals for sinners dedicated to help them overcome the sin disease. Sinners attend with the desire to receive God's prescription and therapy, but all they get is a false assurance that because Jesus died, they are saved. Unlike physical illnesses, God, the great doctor of the universe, paid a huge price to make the prescription and cure available. Doctors are not expected to die to save their patients.

We all understand that a patient might not be willing to follow a treatment; some might even prefer death. The same is true with God's treatment of the sin disease. God never imposes His cure on anyone. Not only is the cure free, but patients suffering from the sin disease are also free to accept the cure or leave it. However, if the sinner wishes to be cured and live forever, such a patient better accept the full protocol of the treatment prescribed. Accepting just a portion of the treatment may not heal the disease and could even make things worse. Additionally, such a noncompliant patient would give the doctor and the hospital a bad reputation because the treatment would fail. Christians tend to do the same with God's treatment. Clearly, the treatment of the sin disease has thus far been a failure; is it any wonder that God's reputation is in jeopardy in our modern world? Unfortunately, this is what Christianity and Judaism have done with God. They are responsible for corrupting God's prescription and the related therapy, and the patients in God's hospitals are failing to go into remission. As a result, both God and the churches claiming to represent Him are made to appear powerless.

Now, let us imagine what the reputation of a doctor would be if he or she suggested that a healthy person should be slaughtered in order to transfer the disease from a patient to the victim about to be slaughtered. Even bloodletting would sound like a better solution, and it might even be less likely to bring a lawsuit against the doctor. Strangely enough, Christians claim that the great Doctor of the universe has done just that with sinners. He supposedly wanted the death of the Son so that the wickedness of humans might be transferred upon Him. Worse yet, Christians call that justice! Where are the texts in Scripture where such a treatment for sin is suggested? We are dealing with a human invention that makes God look worse than quack doctors or the devil. Is it any wonder that intelligent people refuse to accept their religion?

A church should not be a place for sinners to socialize and rejoice over the fact that Jesus made a payment of blood on a cross. It should be a place where God's message, which is His prescription and treatment of the sin disease, should be freely offered to all sinners. The ambience of modern churches would be totally different from what can be witnessed in most of them today. Like a hospital or a library, there might be more attention given to the learning the diagnosis and the seriousness of accepting the cure than the loud acclamations of gratitude for a price paid on an instrument of torture. Perhaps more tears of mourning for inadequacies should be shed along with a deep sense of grief for what the Lord had to endure to rescue His created beings. The emphasis should be on learning about the disease and its cure while making sure that sinners are made to understand more clearly how they can become more compliant patients and better students of the Word.

For a message to have the power to heal or change a person's heart and character, the message must be crystal clear. A superstition can only persuade gullible individuals inclined to believe fairy tales. If the message we believe to be from God fails to pass the test of sound logic, it is because it is not from God. And the only reason we have a fairy-tale-like message from God is either because it has been corrupted or incorrectly understood. The power of a message rests entirely on the soundness of its logic. Unlike patients of the past, today patients go to the hospital out of persuasion that the treatment suggested is sound. They accept the treatment with the assurance that it is the most hopeful course of action. Services offered by churches should be no different. If the treatment they offer on God's behalf fails the test of logic it is because it does not come from God.

For far too long the churches and temples of the world have claimed divine authority to offer salvation by teaching that forgiveness is all a sinner needs to receive God's gift of salvation. They claim it is obtained by confessing sins to a priest or to God, and they are brainwashed with the assurance that Christ came to die on a cross to make the forgiveness of sins possible.

If salvation is a simple matter of obtaining forgiveness it does little or nothing to suggest a cure involving a specific treatment. If God's plan of salvation were merely a matter of forgiveness it would cure neither suffering nor pain inflicted by offenders, nor the offenders' disease. Only the prescription from God along with its treatment would progressively alleviate the problem of evil. If a doctor told a patient: "I forgive you for having lung cancer," or worse yet, "I forgive you for smoking so much that you suffer from lung cancer," the patient would be horrified beyond words. Yet this is essentially what churches do and teach about the way God deals with the sin disease. The purpose of a church is not to belabor God's pardon, as important as that might be because He always grants it. What is really important is the cure. The church's job is to offer sinners God's prescription that will make the remission of sin a reality in sinners' life. The problem is that if a church does not know God's prescription it is likely to peddle God's pardon as the solution instead of a free admission to receive the cure that heals. If a church is not a hospital specialized in treating the sin disease it cannot be considered a church of the only true God; it is a "den of thieves" where quack doctors gain fame and respect for peddling "feel good" palliatives intended to numb the skulls of wrongdoers.

Only the remission of the disease can make possible the progressive enhancement of the sinner's character while also making the world a better place to live. All character flaws produce sin, and all sins are indicative of a love deficiency in the heart. The only solution is growing love in the heart, because it is the only way to produce remission of sin. Like all human diseases, such remission is progressive; it does not happen overnight. In fact, it is the work of a lifetime. As the remission progresses, good works increase because they are the product of faith in

God's infallible provided cure. Good works are not done to gain fame or to obtain eternal life; they are the product of a heart where love is growing. It is as natural a process as the growth of the seed that must be placed in good soil to grow (see Mt. 13:3–9).

Good works become an indication that a person's faith is not dead, but that a persuasive belief system from God is at work from within (see Jas. 2:17). The Bible teaches that the sanctuary is not so much a place where sinners are to gather to praise God or enjoy relationships with Him or with one another. It is a place designed to provide sinners with an ever-clearer understanding of God as the Great Physician who goes out of His way to communicate His system of government as the cure that will save the universe from evil. The only valid prescription against sin is the one that comes from Him who is Eternal, and makes eternal life possible for all who are willing to partake of His cure.

The problem is that God's prescription is available only if it is known in truth. A prescription that has been corrupted can only do more damage than good. As long as God's prescription remains hidden beyond a veil of religious confusion, churches will continue to offer mere shams. This has been the problem of humanity since the first sin in Eden. But times have changed; it is time to apply the logic we all learn in school to the Word of God. That logic is helpful to recognize that the current prescription is ineffective and to determine that it has been corrupted. Humanity has been illiterate long enough regarding the prescription; why do we accept to be illiterate in matters related to God and His prescription to heal society?

Indeed, why should the study of the Word of God be the only exception to the application of common logic in our modern world? Humans apply logic to advance sciences, technology, history, and philosophy, but they are resentful to apply it to Scripture. The "spirit of truth" that will guide at least some people into "all truth" (Mt. 16:13) Jesus predicted, is likely to be the capacity to study His Word with the help of modern sound logic; how else can truth be discovered? Truth has to be logically undeniable or it is not truth. Since scripture is still the object of strong disagreements from countless sides, deductive reasoning suggests that none of the current messages can be said to be undeniable; therefore they are not Truth.

This may come as a surprise to the reader, but the world has not had access to logical thinking on a broad scale until the application of logic to life made the industrial revolution possible. The mental process of reasoning from cause-to-effect and effect-to-cause was only popularized in a recent past. Modern schools and universities have been instrumental in popularizing critical thinking. This privilege was reserved for elites until the sixteenth century. Martin Luther popularized the idea that education should be provided to all people. His purpose was to make Scripture universally available.

It stands to reason that Jesus was talking about the popularization of logic when He spoke of a "helper" that would bring clarity to His Word of Truth. He links the event to a time near the end, when Jerusalem would cease "to be trampled on by the Gentiles" (Lk. 21:24). That event perceived by Jesus as a clear sign of the end did not take place until 1967.[24] It follows logic to conclude that the application of logic to the Word of God would not begin in a dominant way until the Gentiles are no longer in control of Jerusalem. What an amazing prediction of Jesus that was! If as Jesus said, the Truth will set sinners free, the Truth must be known sometime before the end comes or sinners will not be set free.

The reason children catch on so easily to the use of computers is because they have an advantage over adults who tend to remain trapped in thinking patterns of the past somewhat short on sound logic. Unlike children today, adults born before the computer age have not been systematically exposed to sound logic. The lives of the eldest among us continue to be largely guided by intuition and even superstition, especially as it relates to religious matters. Since the use of machines and computers require logic, it is no accident that the Apple Corporation calls the motherboards of their computers a "logic boards." The proper use of computers is entirely dependent upon a rigid application of all the rules and procedures related to sound logic.

What we are saying is that without the power of persuasion totally dependent on logic a freethinking and free-willed human being remains at a loss when it comes to understanding the logic of God's system of operation for the universe. It is not because logic is arduous that understanding the Word of God is difficult to understand; it is because in theological and religious circles logic has been banned in the evaluation and study of God's message. The fear is that if God's prescription could

---

[24]   There is much more to be said regarding the 1967 event that unified Jerusalem under Jewish rule for the first time in two millennia, a topic for another book.

be logically understood, faith would no longer be required for salvation, because faith ought to be about something humans cannot understand or it would not be faith. This is where a false understanding of the word "faith" has led religion.

The predictions of Jesus in this regard are stunning. He said that the "spirit of truth" would guide freethinking humans into "all truth" (Jn. 16:13). He was talking about the kind of Truth that persuades a sinner to harmonize his or her thinking with God's—the only Truth worth having because of its eternal all-encompassing value. Churches are more likely to teach from pulpits that it is not possible to know the Infinite God or His Truth than to encourage anyone to seek Him "in Truth" (Jn. 4:24) derived from sound logic. Jesus would not have insisted on the fact that salvation is obtained by knowing the Truth about God if such knowledge was unattainable. He did say: "Salvation is that they know you, the only true God" (Jn. 17:3). If such knowledge were not accessible to the human mind as God created it, Jesus would have been unscrupulous to even suggest the attainment of such knowledge.

Recognized by Scripture as the Creator (Col. 1:16), Jesus knows the capabilities of the human brain better than humans do. He went on to say that whatever we would hear from "the helper," which I believe is logic, "will bring glory to me (Jesus) by taking from what is mine and making it known to you" (Jn. 16:14). Whatever this knowledge is, humans will finally understand it exactly as Jesus meant it to be understood. Clearly, humans were not ready to understand all this while He was living on earth because of their religious superstitions. He told His disciples: "I have much more to say to you, more than you can now bear" (Jn. 16:12). Why could they not bear the information Jesus wished He could have shared with them? Most likely because they lacked sufficient reliance on logic to recognize that true religion must be entirely founded on logic, not the meaningless rituals they were accustomed to practice.

What Jesus is saying is that a correct knowledge of God will persuade many at the end of time. Many will embrace His solution to the problem of evil with a new understanding of the Word of God. This time humans will listen with the help of the "helper" that can be nothing other than sound logic, not a third Person of the Godhead. God's message understood in Truth will convey all the motivation needed to change sinners' hearts and characters in preparation for eternal life in a universe where His Truth will reign supreme.

The function of a church is not to pretend that all is well for sinners and that they should rejoice because Jesus died. The mission of the church is to become a rehab center for the human spirit specialized in the recovery from the sin disease. To accomplish this purpose the church must first clearly understand God's message without speculating on its meaning. The first thing that must be done to eliminate speculation is to remove all tenets lacking solid evidence from the standpoint of sound logic. The claim that the Lord's death is a payment cannot be a prescription; it can only be speculation based on irrational thinking incompatible with the message of Scripture. Again, a message from God cannot be irrational, or it is not from God.

When humans clearly understand that they sin because they suffer from an innate addiction to self that robs them from growing love in their hearts, they will realize at last that sin is a form of insanity that can be overcome only through the growth of love in the heart. All humans have inherited this addiction to self ever since Adam and Eve chose to place their desires ahead of the welfare of others in the Garden of Eden (Rom. 5:12). Lack of mutual trust has reinforced the law of survival. It is a vicious cycle from which a follower of Jesus must leap out. "Come out of her, my people" (Rev. 18:4) is God's last call in Scripture to accept a departure from the old and counterproductive religions of the past.

As previously said, to overcome the sin disease the correct cure must be known. While the church should become an emergency room for sinners overdosed on self, it should also be a rehab center offering a therapy that involves schooling these addicts in the knowledg of God's Truth. The knowledge of God is both the remedy and the rehabilitation. Truth alone can heal, strengthen, and prevent future relapses. The author of Hebrews likened the earthly sanctuary to heaven itself. As such, the Tabernacle and our churches should be a "sanctuary [or rehab shelter] and an exhibit of the way God's universe [which is heaven] operates" (Heb. 8:5 my translation).

One can well imagine that in the hot sunny desert sinners needed a shaded area where they could consult the road map that leads to God. This is where they were to recognize and accept God's cure, not a series of sacrificial offerings to obtain forgiveness for being sick. By learning that all sins are the result of an innate compulsion to serve self at the expense of others, peoples in churches should be led to realize that the solution implies a reversal of the natural instincts we all inherit from birth. It is because we are all born with the "me first" mentality of the survival of the fittest that we "all have sinned and come short of the glory of God" (Rom. 3:23 KJV). There is no exception to that rule. But the solution is not for someone to die to pay for this condition, it is to recognize the cure that God designed and inscribed in the rituals of the Temple.

When the sanctuary rituals were corrupted to become magic charms and fairy dust to obtain forgiveness and chase evil spirits away, the divine purpose for the temple was lost. Sinners who should have been led to gain the knowledge of God in order to become partakers of His nature (Mt. 5:48) became partakers of evil in the name of God. What could be more evil? The prescription that included a specific program of rehabilitation designed to produce the remission of the sin disease individually and collectively, became a useless sacred offering that only served to perpetrate evil and its consequences.

Heaven is what the universe was like before sin entered therein to create havoc throughout. Scripture tells us that heaven will be destroyed and restored to its original condition. None other than Jesus made the prediction: "Heaven and earth will pass away, but my words will never pass away" (Mt. 24:35). Jesus calls it "the kingdom of God," an expression found exclusively in the New Testament. But since God cannot impose His Kingdom or His way of life on free-willed beings, freedom-loving individuals must accept God's ways willfully by recognizing through perfect logic that the welfare of others must be placed before our own. It is the only way to live eternally in perfect peace and harmony. Thus, the universe cannot be restored to the status of "heaven" until the whole universe becomes a perfect sanctuary for all people once again. It has to be a safe place for free-willed intelligent beings determined to accept unconditionally that love has to be the immutable rule of life. If a free-willed individual fails to accept God's method and procedure to become loving, such a sinner would be unhappy to live eternally in the environment of heaven and would be a permanent menace to others; thus it would not be heaven.

The question that we must still answer in this book is the procedure a sinner must accept to be changed by choosing willfully to live eternally in harmony with God's ways. We shall explore this topic in the following chapters. As long as God's program to overcome sin remains distorted or veiled by superstitions and illogicisms, it will never fulfill God's purpose. Indeed, God's way to salvation cannot become a reality until the message of His Temple as well as the message of Jesus who is greater than the temple is "restored to its rightful place" (Dan. 8:14 RSV). They are both the true prescription. Before salvation can become reality for the universe, the Temple of God must once again become the genuine repository of His Truth.

Temple and Gospel Were Both Given as God's GPS to Salvation

It is only through the discovery of God's path to genuine love that created beings will ever access the genuine freedom from addiction to self. Scripture tells us that the destruction of evil in the universe cannot take place until some humans demonstrate through their words and deeds that they have found and accepted the way to genuine love. That message is subtle, but it is essentially found in the book of Revelation in the New Testament and in several of the prophetic books of the Old. This is how God will ultimately be vindicated before His accusers that include the devil and all his cohorts determined to reject God's principle of life. But the vindication of God's character and way of life must become visible in the life of fallen beings, or the universe may not believe that it is possible to overcome one's fallen condition by way of a persuasive belief system Scripture calls faith.

One of the most important adjustments that must be made to Christian theology is to recognize that God's purpose requires a clear understanding of the word atonement. This is essential because it means coming at one with God, or at-one-ment. Unfortunately the word atonement has been ill-treated for centuries. In our evaluation of this concept we must remember that it takes at least two to be of one mind, or to be in perfect agreement in the way they think; therefore atonement cannot be completed by a mere payment, even if made on a cross. The provision for the atonement to take place was completed on the Cross, but there is no at-one-ment until humans choose to share "the mind of Christ" (1 Cor. 2:16) with Him and with one another. That is true atonement. Such atonement can only be accomplished by coming at-one with God, which implies accepting His way of life forevermore. The repository of Truth, whether perceived through the Tabernacle or the Gospel message of Jesus is God's road map to salvation of which Jesus is the author as well as its Host.

God's Truth of the Tabernacle is identical to the Truth later proclaimed in the Gospel. The problem is that both were corrupted. This Truth could be called God's GPS to salvation. It was made available to humans at no cost to them, but Jesus paid a huge price to bring it to the attention of humans with unsurpassed clarity. Humans remain free to enter the address of their religious destination wherever they wish to go. It is up to them to follow the way of their fallen nature focused on self, or the way to God's destination founded on unconditional love for others. However, how could anyone ever decide to go anywhere if neither destination is clearly defined? Yogi Berra is credited to have said: "When you get to the fork in the road, take it." Funny indeed, but isn't that a bit how religion is presented to the world? As long as Truth remains ambiguous, like a destination that cannot be defined, it will fail to serve its intended purpose. As long as a GPS cannot be programed with a known destination, it cannot suggest a route, never mind reach a desired destination. This appears to be largely the condition of Christianity today.

Let us consider the destination from a practical angle. Would it be wise to accept drink or food from a stranger openly hostile to us? One would want to make doubly true that the food and drink is safe. More precisely, one would want to know the truth about the wholesomeness of the food and drink, as well as the truth about the giver's intentions. Yet when considering the teachings of God, many are willing to come to the table of spiritual foods irresponsibly. The food served on the tables of religions comes from a variety of unknown sources, notwithstanding the wholesomeness of the message itself. What if it is poisoned? It could easily contain hazardous ingredients. Scripture warns that Satan likes to pass himself for God. He even claimed superiority over the Creator in the wilderness where he encountered Jesus to tempt Him (see Lk. 4:5). All it takes to be fooled is to trust the more dazzling performers who are often satisfied with contaminating truth with just minute amounts of falsehood—just enough poison to be lethal. Suddenly the "water of life" becomes deadly. Jesus Himself cautioned His listeners in this regard: "Many will say to me on that day, 'Lord, Lord, did we not prophesy in your name, and in your name drive out demons and perform many miracles?' Then I will tell them plainly, 'I never knew you. Away from me, you evildoers!'" (Mt. 7:22–23).

This may surprise the reader, but ever since the Exodus of Israel from Egypt the sanctuary has been the repository of "all Truth," not just portions of it. It contained all the necessary information sinners needed to understand God's Everlasting Gospel in its completeness. All the Truth needed to gain freedom from sin was made clearly available. Enough knowledge was provided to help the Children of Israel to become true overcomers of sin. Nothing was left out, "not the least stroke of a pen" (Mt. 5:18), said Jesus who came to confirm and rectify the message Jewish Scripture contained. Nothing was to be abolished from Truth previously communicated through prophets and God's sanctuary (Mt. 5:17). The message of the Tabernacle had to reflect the exact same message of God Christ later lived and proclaimed in deeds and words, or it could not be said that God does not change (see Heb. 1:10–12). Though nothing was to be abolished from Scripture, the way it had come to be understood needed rectification.

Because He was conveying the most perfect version of God's message of Truth to the world, Jesus could say: "Thy kingdom come, in heaven *and* on earth" (Mt. 6:10, from the Latin Vulgate, emphasis mine).[25] This is a variant from popular translations, but this early translation suggests that both heaven and Earth had departed from the safety and protection of God's Sanctuary. Both are in dire need to regain the perfect knowledge of God that sets sinners free. Even those angels who remained true to God endure pain and suffering due to the presence of sin in the universe. Paul could say: "We know that the whole creation has been groaning as in the pains of childbirth" (Rom. 8:22). In the next verse he goes on to say that even those who accept God's Truth suffer: "Not only so," he writes, "but we ourselves, who have the first fruits of the Spirit, groan inwardly as we wait eagerly for our adoption as sons, the redemption of our bodies" (Rom. 8:23).

The cleansing of our religious belief systems must take place before God's everlasting peace can be restored in His universe. But if God expects humans to do the cleansing we better get to work fast. The groaning of the universe will continue until evil has been totally eradicated from the universe. But the eradication of evil cannot happen until fallen beings have proven to the universe that it is possible to overcome evil, as did Jesus through the means of His persuasion, "the faith of Jesus" (Rev. 14:12 KJV).

---

[25] The Latin Vulgate offers this variant: "veniat regnum tuum fiat voluntas tua sicut in caelo <u>et</u> in terra." (Underlining supplied by author)

The whole universe was once the Sanctuary of God's omnipresence, but now God's entire territory requires a total makeover. Paul is all-inclusive when he says: "The whole creation has been groaning." There is no room for exceptions anywhere in the universe according to this statement. If God is the Creator of all creation, not the least speck of space in the universe has been spared the pain and suffering that causes the groaning. Evil has brought sadness, pain, and destruction even in those places of the universe where sin may have failed to take hold. God Himself is groaning. Sin is like falling dominoes; the fall of one triggers damaging consequences for all others. It may seem unfair; all it takes is for one to fall to cause damages to all others. They all suffer, regardless of culpability. In the universe there are many innocent victims of the fall; they all suffer as much as the guilty, as did Jesus, the innocent One, taken all the way to the Cross.

Peter was looking forward to an entire universe made anew when he said: "But in keeping with his promises we are looking forward to a *new heaven and a new earth*, the home of righteousness" (2 Pet. 3:13, emphasis mine). This text is sometimes interpreted to say that only planet Earth will be renewed. But the text clearly states that heaven and earth will be destroyed before they are made anew. Jesus said the same thing before Peter: "Heaven and earth will pass away," He said, "but my words will never pass away" (Mt. 24:35). It should be noted that whenever the "new earth" is mentioned in Scripture, the "new heaven" is always mentioned as well, and it is always mentioned first.

As bleak as life might appear to be on earth today, God assures humanity that His plan of restoration will succeed. It will not be painless, nor can it happen without the willful participation of free-willed humans, but it will happen. Speaking of God's concern for humanity, Paul reassured his readers saying: "He made known to us the mystery of his will according to his good pleasure which he purposed in Christ, to be put into effect *when the times will have reached their fulfillment*—to bring all things *in heaven and on earth* together under one head, even Christ" (Eph. 1:10, emphasis mine). The future tense is used to announce the unconditional future fulfillment of this event. But who will be standing on God's side when this day comes to pass?

When He returns, who will be standing with the faith or the persuasion that was in the heart of Jesus while He was on planet Earth (see Mt. 25:32, 33; Jn. 14:2, 3; Lk. 18:8; Rev. 14:12 KJV)? Having the faith of Jesus in our hearts cannot become a reality until "all" the "truth" Jesus was speaking of is known and made available to the world. As long as it is only partly available it is not Truth because there is no such a thing as a partial truth. As long as it is not complete it is not the faith *of* Jesus.

When Paul talks about bringing all things "in heaven and on earth together under one head," he appears to echo the Lord's Prayer we just quoted from the Vulgate. He implies that the restoration of the kingdom of God involves a completely new Creation of both heaven and earth—a comprehensive renewal of the entire universe. The traditional reading of the Lord's Prayer (Mt. 6:10) suggests that the kingdom of God will be established on Earth *as it is* already operational in heaven.[26] The mention of a new heaven is not a new sky or a new layer of atmosphere around the Earth. Paul spoke specifically of "spiritual forces of evil in the heavenly realms" (Eph. 6:12). These evil forces are not in the sky; they are indeed located in God's universe marred by sin. Since the forces of evil have damaged the entire groaning universe, why should any portion of the universe be spared the promised reconstruction?

There will be no armistice day of the war in heaven until evil and sin, as well as their consequences responsible for causing the groaning are entirely eradicated from the universe. All traces of evil must disappear. All the dominoes of the universe must be reset in their upright position. Is it any wonder that it will all end in blazing fire? The Apostle Peter paints quite a picture of that Day of doom: "But the day of the Lord will come as a thief in the night, in the which the heavens shall pass away with great noise, and the elements shall melt with fervent heat, the earth *also* and the works that are therein shall be burned up" (2 Pet. 3:10 KJV, emphasis mine).

Current events taking place on planet Earth are observed by the entire universe, says Paul: "For it seems to me that God has put us apostles on display at the end of the procession, like men condemned to die in the arena. We have been made a spectacle to the whole universe, to angels as well as to men" (1 Cor. 4:9). The reason the universe is observing the events taking place on earth is because something ominous is taking place here ever since Creation Week.

Events taking place on planet Earth will have an impact of huge magnitude on the entire universe. Those humans who recognize and

---

[26] See most versions of Matthew 6:10 in English

value the importance of true love should count it a privilege to side with God in this effort despite the pain and ridicule they might suffer in the process. It is only by sharing unconditional love even with their worst enemies that sinners will prove God's system of government doable and desirable despite their fallen nature. By so doing, fallen earthly beings will demonstrate that they have willfully chosen to collaborate with God to bring about the salvation of a fallen universe dependent on the success of being revitalized by His Truth. They will do it by demonstrating that by His grace, which is His Truth given at the price of His life, mere humans can recognize and live the Truth they have received from Him, and thus come at-one with Him. Earth is the place where the demonstration will take place to prove that fallen created beings are perfectly able to voluntarily acknowledge and endorse God's Truth against all odds. This will be the demonstration beyond a doubt that mere fallen beings can be changed from self-serving to caring for others unconditionally, as did Jesus thanks to His persuasion that came to Him from the Father (see Is. 50; Jn. 15:15).

The Lord went so far as to predict something unthinkable: "I tell you the truth," He said, "anyone who has faith in me (or, who has My faith) will do what I have been doing. He will do even greater things than these, because I am going to the Father" (Jn. 14:12, parenthesis mine). These are sinners who will be changed by the "testimony of Jesus" (Rev. 19:10) that will finally be understood at the end of time. They will become living expressions of God's own character. This will demonstrate once for all that the sin disease can be set in remission sufficiently for the universe, "angels as well as men" (1 Cor. 4:9) said Paul, to recognize that with the mind-set of Jesus remission of the sin disease is possible. This will be proof positive that God was right in claiming that love can change a sinner to be transformed back into the image of God. They will not be gods, as some religions teach, but they will think as He does. They will share with God the beauty of His perfect humility that makes perfect love capable of mercifulness. They will finally reflect the character of God as the first humans did long ago when they were first created in His image.

If God does not change, as Scripture claims, Christianity has a serious problem. Many Christians claim that the message of the Sanctuary is different from the message of the Cross. We plan to show that they are in fact the same message. Time has come for humans to look at God and His message from a totally different perspective than ever before. Sound logic can be our "helper," and guide. The prophecy of Daniel Jesus quoted in this passage is of greater significance today than ever before (see Mt. 24:14 and Dan. 9:27; 11:31; 12:11). The return of Jesus will take place only after the cleansing of the sanctuary will have taken place. That cleansing is the purification of the message of the sanctuary as it is the purification of the "message of the Cross" (1 Cor. 1:18), which is the Gospel preached in Truth.

What we know for sure, is that two-and-a-half millennia after Daniel's prophecy was written, the evil forces of our world have grown exponentially with the capacity to exterminate all life on the planet. Serious signs of distress and calamities are looming. Cries of doom and gloom are resounding throughout the media. Economists, scientists, sociologists, and religious leaders are increasingly more vocal in expressing concerns and fear for the near term. Considering the compelling language of Daniel, his message begs a renewed interpretation. This is especially true if we bear in mind that the "cleansing" is to have a significant impact on the final events of world history. Could our freshly inaugurated twenty-first century be the last?

Importance of the Message

A false understanding of God leads infallibly to a false understanding of His love and His mercy. A false understanding of love and mercy leads to false understanding of the pathway He offers for His character to become ours. Salvation is all about restoring the image of God in humans. Any other definition of salvation does not involve a true healing of the problem of evil. Misgivings about God have also led to misgivings about His Judgment often perceived through the lenses of the human judicial systems that God views as aberration. These are central pitfalls of Christianity in general, as they were also pitfalls of Judaism. The only positive remaining out of the succession of erroneous outlooks of the past is that God's message is still available to us. That is in itself miraculous. The Holy Script still contains the message from God, but it is our job to untangle Truth from the corruption that contaminated Truth. Absolute Truth will not emerge from religious chaos until the falsehood that shrouds its perfect rationale is banished. God cannot force people to cleanse superstitious interpretations of His Word any more than

He could have removed idols from the worships of Israelites throughout their long struggles with idolatry. As long as humans fail to do their part in cleansing their religious belief systems they will continue to spread messages of delusion in the name of God. With faulty messages the reign of evil can only continue to be perpetuated. A perceptible remission of the sin disease will remain elusive until humans finally realize that they must first have access to the Word of God *in* Truth.

Theological disagreements abound. The prophetic statements of Daniel and Jesus regarding the abomination that will cause desolation are predictions that false belief systems will lead to widespread chaos on earth—all that because of a misrepresentation of God's message to humanity. Yet other prophetic statements indicate that the message of Truth will be fully unsealed before the end. This message will hold the key to the most pressing concerns of humanity in the last days. When properly understood, the Truth will bring peace to people's hearts regardless of the torments they may suffer in daily life. The most pressing questions regarding God and His plan of action to save His children for eternity will no longer be founded on presumption but on a faith that comes from God, solidly anchored on logical interpretations of His message of Truth. Even little children will be able to understand God's message with clarity.

God's message will finally be recognized as Truth. If this outlook is correct, it will be the first time since Jesus revealed the Father (Mt. 11:27) some 2,000 years ago that God's Truth will be once again revealed in its completeness to the world. This time the message will go "to every nation, and kindred, and tongue, and people" (Rev.14:6 KJV). This would not have been possible in the days of Jesus. Our next step in this study will be to recognize and understand the procedure God has designed for His children to restore in their hearts the image of God. It is nothing other than a portrayal of His kind of love carried to the world. Salvation is not a matter of choosing to do His will instead of our own; it is a matter of learning how to make His will, or His mind-set our own. Let us see what we can learn from the Holy Book to make His prediction come true in our lifetime.

CHAPTER 7

God's Procedure to Grow Love in the Heart

Scripture is clear; the final ministry of Jesus will be carried forward to the world from within His temple. But what is this temple of God? The author of Hebrews gives us a hint. Unlike the Tabernacle and the two Temples previously built by human hands in the desert and in Jerusalem, this one will have nothing in common with anything humans have ever built (Heb. 8:2, 3). Paul specifies that this particular temple will be "built on the foundation of the apostles and prophets, with Jesus Christ himself as its chief cornerstone" (Eph. 2:20). He goes on to say: "In him [Jesus Christ] you too are being built together to become a dwelling in[to] which God lives by his Spirit" (Eph. 2:22 brackets mine). Paul is actually saying that in this unconventional temple the Spirit of God will dwell within the human heart that God created. When at last this temple will become a reality in the world, God will finally be able to accomplish His purpose. The reason God will finally be able to achieve His goal for His children is because He will no longer be dwelling "among them" (Ex. 25:8) as He has ever since the Exodus from Egypt, but His Spirit will reside "in their hearts and . . . on their minds" (Jer. 31:33; Heb. 10:16). In other words, the last Temple of God in world history will be a temple "into" which God will dwell on the solid foundation stone of which Jesus is the "chief cornerstone."

On several occasions Daniel made reference to the Temple of Jerusalem as "the temple of God" (Dan. 1:2), and indeed it was. Just because it was located on planet Earth did not prevent it from being what should have been a microcosm of heaven, or a minuscule extension of heaven on planet Earth. The same will be true of God's last temple. Jesus will not only be "one better than the temple," but like Him His followers will be "better than the temple," but this only as soon as they will begin to reflect the Truth that sets sinners free as did Jesus before them.

With the identity of God's new temple established, recognizing that it will be a body of believers founded on the "mind of Christ" (1 Cor. 2:16), or the way Christ thinks, our next step is to consider what needs to be cleansed or "made right" in God's temple for it to succeed. Something was obviously wrong in the former man-made temples, or no cleansing would be needed near the end of time. Since we can affirm that the temple is the body of Christ's followers in the last days, the prophecy of Daniel is obviously about cleansing something that will have an impact on the faithful who constitute this group. This temple will be "the true tabernacle, which the Lord pitched, and not man" (Heb. 8:2), and this for two reasons: God is the Creator of the people who become the constituents of the new temple, and He will also be the Author of their belief system, which has become their faith, their persuasion. These people will not only have faith *in* Jesus, but they will be equipped with the faith *of* Jesus.

The only thing that needs to be cleansed in a group of humans destined to become the constituents of the new temple is their sin problem. But how can this to be accomplished? Did Jesus not say that the Truth would set them free? When Jesus made that declaration the Greek text could have been translated as follows: "When you will know the truth, then the truth will set you free" (Jn. 8:32, author's translation). This would imply that the message must first be understood correctly.

This clearly implies that to this day humans still fail to understand God's message correctly. As long as God's message is improperly perceived, it cannot be said that it proclaims Truth. It is only when sinners will be in possession of the absolute Truth that it will become possible for them to be set free. This suggests that when sinners attempt to gain the promised freedom on any basis other than God's Truth they can only be led to a faulty understanding of how righteousness can be made to develop in the heart of sinners.

Before the Reformation, official Christianity believed that fighting sin or evil was a matter of submitting to the will of the official church establishment and its leadership—a form of righteousness by works that Scripture condemns. This approach was similar to the traditional Jewish system Jesus denied in His day. Though the laws and regulations were different than they were for Jews, the process of acquiring salvation was by works through deeds and submission to ecclesiastical authorities. The form of worship and requirements were changed but not the means by which sinners are supposedly saved.

The Reformers recognized an important weakness in that system. They understood that salvation could not be attained by submission to external forces. The Apostle Paul remarked long before the Reformation: "Israel, who pursued a law of righteousness, has not obtained it. Why not? Because they pursued it not by faith but as if it were by works. They stumbled over the 'stumbling stone'" (Rom. 9:31–32). Paul is simply saying that one can only stumble over self by thinking that it is possible to improve a person's own heart by observing laws. This is a cop-out, because it gives the impression that doing right is possible without having to undergo a change of heart. Right doing had replaced right thinking through a changed heart. The only way to be improved from within is to adopt a belief system so persuasive that it becomes the guiding force of life. When this happens, a sinner no longer tries to overcome sin by observing laws but by accepting a belief system on the strength of its persuasiveness.

Israel tried to observe the Law of the Old Testament, but no matter how hard they tried, it did not make them righteous; the best it could do was to make of them a group of law-abiding people, for which they deserve credit. Many observe laws out of fear to get caught or condemned or out of concern to lose a "good" reputation or even salvation. Paul says that the problem of the Jews was not their lack of desire to submit to laws; it was their belief system that prevented them from adopting a sound persuasion he calls faith. Such a persuasion is the "faith" that should become the driving force of every follower of Christ, but following Christ is possible only if His Message is known as He meant it to be understood, in Truth. Jews and Christians both failed to recognize the persuasion that is capable of empowering them by way of persuasion. Instead they were driven by a conventional wisdom propagated by priests who demanded submission to religious laws, rituals, and other regulations as a requirement for salvation. As a result the general population accepted to submit to a plethora of rules and rituals that could not make them righteous inside, though they might have looked righteous from the outside.

Jesus encountered a rich young ruler whose understanding of religion was sincerely founded on this pagan-suggested system of blind submission to regulations imposed by religious authorities. He claimed to have observed God's Law since his childhood (Lk. 18:18–26). In effect, he was not observing God's principle of life; he was submitting to laws imposed by rabbis and scribes. We have no reason to doubt that the young man was sincere and that he was diligently applying himself to *doing* the right thing. But he was doing it out of submission without having to think about his need to be guided by the principle of life. He was not acting out of a powerful heartfelt persuasion founded on God's indisputable, flawless logic. Submission fails to empower or motivate; it only coerces. But a strong persuasion can be a strong motivator. Faith founded on persuasion is empowering, and it does not demand action; it empowers love from the heart.

A Tectonic Shift in Christian Theology Must Happen Soon

If we accept the idea that the new temple is the body of believers who have adopted a new mind-set, the cleansing in question will change how people think, which will produce changes of hearts and minds. The question is how?

A quick review of Christian history reveals that it has always suffered from a lack of theological unity. The disputes and divisions began soon after the departure of the Lord. Sometime between the years 50 and 60 of the Christian era, Paul opened his letter to the Galatians with a strident lament: "I am astonished that you are so quickly deserting the one who called you by the grace of Christ and are turning to a different gospel—which is really no gospel at all. Evidently some people are throwing you into confusion and are trying to pervert the gospel of Christ" (Gal. 1:6, 7). Other such examples from the New Testament are indicative of the fragmentation that was taking place in the church during the Apostolic Period. The movement led by Christ was not yet thirty years old. It was as difficult for Christians with Jewish backgrounds to abandon their Judaic traditions and practices as it was for early Gentile converts to let go of their cultural pagan heritage. Bart D. Ehrman credits the German philosopher Hegel for recognizing the existence of these two powerful social forces of which the synthesis of ideas led to a new conventional wisdom he calls, "catholic Christianity."[27]

The problem with "catholic Christianity" is that it became a consensus of religious hierarchal religion whereby a majority voice emanating from a body of handpicked theologians was accepted as the voice of God. In the same book, Ehrman evokes one of Hegel's students,

---

[27]   Ehrman, Bart D., *Lost Christianities: The Battles for Scripture and the Faiths We Never Knew.* New York: Oxford University Press. 2003 pp. 171

Walter Bouer, whose study of Christian heresy led him to the conclusion that by the second century not a single orthodoxy of Christianity had survived. He recognized that committee ruling was responsible for establishing a new orthodoxy. A majority decision established the official theology to be imposed on the rest of the Roman Empire.[28] The accusations of Jesus against the priests of Israel suggest a similar scenario going back to the Exodus. This perspective allows a rather unpleasant deduction: theological untidiness in Christianity might well need cleansing, but the elimination of the monumental confusion involved appears unfathomable.

Several books would be needed to cover the main points. The clutter of disparate and conflicting views appears impossible to untangle. Yet the prophecy of Daniel is clearly a prediction that the unfathomable will occur. On God's behalf, Daniel declares without reservation: "He said to me, 'It will take 2,300 evenings and mornings; then the sanctuary will be reconsecrated" (Dan. 8:14). The King James uses the term "cleansed," while other translations say that the Sanctuary will be "restored to its rightful state." Could it be that from the rubble of utter theological confusion the clarity of God's Everlasting Gospel will suddenly spring to light? Will it bring to modern believers staggering in a parched desert the equivalent of the refreshing water that sprung from the Rock Moses struck (Ex. 17:6)?

To revisit some of the most significant events of Christian history that have impacted the world, one would have to turn the clock back to the Reformation of the early sixteenth century. It was a powerful movement, but it may have only contributed a flicker of light on the ocean of theological darkness. It can probably also be said that the Reformation has raised more questions than answers. But this may well be a good thing in the long run. Jesus said: "Ask, and it will be given you; seek and you will find; knock and the door will be opened to you" (Mt. 7:7). Clearly, the prophecy of Daniel was not pointing to the Reformation, or more questions would have been answered. A cross-examination of the Word of God is a good thing. It challenges enquiring minds to seek Truth as God meant it, not as humans falsified it.

The current discords of Christianity over God's Everlasting Gospel need not be established. The fact that there are over 33,000 different

---

[28]   Ibid. p. 173

denominations worldwide speaks for itself. But what would happen if suddenly it were discovered that "the" Truth is so perfectly logical that it is manifestly undeniable? Would the Christian world be shaken to its core, or would most Christians choose to reject objective evidence in favor of subjective traditions?

It would seem, since the world has changed to become far more dependent on logic than ever before in history, that rational minds would be eager to consider the value of logical religious arguments. This would be particularly true if such arguments persuade the public that they are in perfect conformity with the message of Jesus. By so doing they would recognize a message that could only have its origin with God. With such a message many would be torn between choosing sound logic and antiquated religious superstitions. Sincere minds as well as earnest civil and religious entities would be compelled to take notice. Some of them would be compelled to accept Truth along with all the consequences their decision would bring, while others are predicted to hold on to religious traditions.

The most powerful religious organizations of our world would suddenly be proven inadequate and out of harmony with God. Some would probably accept to realign their views with the new doctrines while others would remain infatuated to their antiquated dogmas. Corporate religious pride would likely harden some hearts against the idea of accepting the use of sound logic to reevaluate religion. Many are likely to rebel against those willing to stoop so low as to accept God's Truth on logical grounds, rather than on what they call "faith." One thing is certain however; the Truth would bring unprecedented unity among those who choose to follow God on logical grounds, but it would increase disunity among those who refuse logic to settle matters of religion. The rejection of logic in matters of religion is bound to produce religious rifts such as the world has never seen. Religions founded on superstition will be infuriated against those whose religion is considered faithless because it is founded on logic.

The result will likely produce a socio-religious tectonic shift of such magnitude that it will bring unprecedented collisions of ideas and ideologies, not to mention unprecedented persecutions and wars. The foregoing scenario needs not be stated in the conditional tense. Such a conflagration of ideas would be as inevitable as was the Cross. If one Man could produce such commotion, is it possible to imagine what it would have been if there had been millions like Him? It is a reality that will confront the planet sooner than we can imagine, but not until the temple of God's theology has been cleansed of its misleading impurities.

Is the Key to Grow Love in the Heart Really in Scripture?

The answer to this question is a resounding yes. It can be said not only that Scripture contains the key to develop true love, but that it also contains the only key, because it is found nowhere else. As we have already stated, most, if not all, philosophers and religious leaders recognize that the problem of humanity is lack of love. But Scripture is the only human document that provides the cure––though humans have failed to recognize it. Both a lack of knowledge of God or a false knowledge of His message makes it impossible for a person to grow true love in the heart. The Apostle John stated the concept indisputably: "Whoever does not love does not know God, because God is love" (1 Jn. 4:8). Of course, John was not talking about a mere feeling of attraction to friends, family, or significant other in the traditional sense of the term. He was talking about true love, which is a principle less understood because it involves a commitment to others founded on a commitment to the divine principle of life. This kind of love is not necessarily pleasant. It must endure even when it becomes painful to fulfill the requirements of true love. Indeed, loving one's enemies can be painful in more ways than one.

The only way to reproduce the image of God in fallen humans once again since Eden is by accepting God's required procedure to be transformed back into His likeness. To accomplish this seemingly utopian goal of life Scripture warns that the required procedure must first be recognized, accepted, and endorsed, or love will fail to grow in a sinner's heart. The recognition and acceptance of the procedure that makes a person more loving is the Holy Spirit that God has gone out of His way to share with humanity, that they might finally understand what it is. The Holy Spirit is a holy state of mind because it is constantly at work to make a person more loving. Without the ability to develop a holy mind-set, humanity would be lost without hope of salvation, that is, without the hope of ever being restored to the image of God. Scripture is clear to say that this process must begin here in our life on earth. In a chapter about Trinity theology we will clarify this concept by showing that the

Holy Spirit is not a Person of the Godhead, it is the development of the mind of Christ in humans.

Despite the repeated invitations of God to recognize the procedure to grow love through the teachings of prophets who spoke on God's behalf (Heb. 1:1, 2), humans have repeatedly corrupted their messages. It is precisely for this reason that Jesus came to this world. The Truth that saves had already been communicated, but it could no longer save because it was corrupted. Unfortunately, despite the clarifications Jesus made, humanity has failed once again to recognize the procedure Jesus provided in words and deeds to grow love in the heart. There has always been among humans a sort of pagan obsession to earn salvation one way or another or, worse yet, by claiming that someone else earned it for them on a Cross, by substitution. Either way, a quest for the key to the development of true love became irrelevant because salvation had to somehow be earned. Salvation is not something we can earn; it is a change of heart that changes the way we think and act. Works cannot earn salvation any more than a pseudo-faith in the substitutionary works and death of Jesus can earn it for sinners.

The reason for the problem is that the religions of our world have been misguided by the intentional, or perhaps accidental, adoption of two basic false creeds. The Christian world is essentially divided between those who claim that righteousness is by works and submission and those who regard righteousness as unachievable, thus it is a gift received by faith implied to mean, by believing it strongly. The problem is that both groups believe that their sins must be paid for one way or another. The first group sees them paid by their own works while the second sees them paid on a cross. Either way, Christians want their sins paid for with the mind-set of Cain rather than recognizing salvation as a change of heart as did Abel. With such views, the search for another procedure to overcome sin is blocked.

For popular Christianity the search was blocked by the former concept for fifteen centuries and by the latter for the last five centuries since the Reformation. While the errors of the first are self-evident, if freedom is recognized as essential to the growth of true love, the mind-set of the latter opens the door to a very dangerous form of spirit-driven religion that also destroys individual freedom. We consider the latter dangerous because listening to a "spirit" can easily open the door to the deceptions Jesus warned against when He said: "Many will say to me on that day, 'Lord, Lord, did we not prophesy in your name, and in your name drive out demons and perform miracles?' Then I will tell them plainly, 'I never knew you. Away from me, you evildoer'" (Mt. 7:22). The only sure way to listen to the correct spirit is to consider the logic of the matter. Scripture provides all the necessary parameters needed to reach the correct conclusions but only if we consider them on the solid foundation of logic.

What Is the Key to Salvation God Offers to All Sinners?

There is no doubt that Luther was correct when he pointed out that righteousness comes by faith. His key text from the prophet Habakkuk in the Old Testament is quoted three times in the New—twice by Paul and once by the author of Hebrews.[29] It is most important to notice that two groups are contrasted in this text depicting an end of time scene: 1) The proud whose faith is inadequate, and 2) those whose faith comes from God.

Here is what God told the prophet Habakkuk as the updated NIV renders the text: "Then the LORD replied: Write down the revelation and make it plain on tablets so that a herald may run with it. For the revelation awaits an appointed time; it speaks of the end and will not prove false. Though it lingers, wait for it; it will certainly come and will not delay. See, the enemy is puffed up; his desires are not upright—but the righteous will live by his faithfulness; indeed, wine betrays him; he is arrogant and never at rest" (Hab. 2:2–5a, updated NIV).

Most of this text is straightforward. God was announcing something so important that He told Habakkuk to write it down for future reference. It is an end-time message that will not be proven false—probably because it will be proven unquestionably true. On the other hand, it appears that the exact meaning of the message will not be immediately clear; therefore a delay of understanding should be expected. Following the undetermined timetable of the delay, undeniable clarity will begin to shine through. When it does, the message will reveal God's enemies as puffed up people whose arrogance is tireless. An interesting deduction can be drawn from this passage: If God's enemies are puffed up and arrogant, by contrast His friends must be humble and meek. The

---

29   See Romans 1:16–17; Galatians 3:11; and Hebrews 10:38–39.

portion of this text that was dear to the heart of Luther may have been falsely interpreted because of the rampant biases that were still clouding God's Truth five centuries ago. Luther's Protestantism is credited for a popular doctrine known in Latin as *Sola fide*. Several popular clichés have emanated from this theology. Chief among them is the idea that "the just shall live by faith alone" or that "justification is by faith alone."

While the concept of living by faith is clearly biblical, the concept was tainted by the traditional understanding of the word "faith" that continues to be unclear to this day. Depending on the definition given to the words "faith" and "justification," the concept can offer unintended meanings. If "faith" is to be understood as a strong belief in a religious concept that humans cannot understand, then the word "faith" conveys an incorrect meaning because God would not communicate a message that humans cannot understand. Indeed, if faith is founded on logic humans can understand, then "justification by faith" should be understood in a manner humans can fully understand.

We face a similar difficulty with the word "justification." If justification is perceived through the human judicial system, it is immediately understood as a cancellation of debt. If justification is understood as acquittal or as paid in full, the faith involved is a matter of believing an irrational concept designed to deal with the sin problem without concern to overcoming the problem. Needless to point out, a payment made by someone else on a cross to pay for sins is a concept that defies all logic. The same is true of the concept that sins had to be transferred onto the Person dying on the Cross before they could be forgiven. Such beliefs defy both Scripture and sound logic. Yet this is what Christians preach when they claim that to benefit from a cancellation of sin the sinner must believe that the payment involved a transfer of guilt. In reality, the only way to really become righteous by faith is to be transformed by the powerful belief system that comes from God on the strength of its undeniable logic, a rationale so simple a child can understand it.

God's Truth can transform a sinner into a principled person whose guidance comes from solid rational evidence. The author of Hebrews confirms this view: "Now faith is the substance of things hoped for, the evidence of things not seen" (Heb. 11:1). How can anything not seen become evident? The only possible answer is that the transformation takes place on the basis of a message that is perfectly logical and undeniable even if its reality is invisible. As Jesus said to Nicodemus, no one can see the wind, but what the wind does everyone can see (see Jn. 3:8). Likewise, the invisible belief system of God anchored on the evidence of logic becomes the invisible force that produces visible changes in a person's life. This solid faith is capable of producing a change toward true love in a sinner's heart. Since humans are not born with sufficient love in their hearts, to acquire it they must submit to God's procedure that reverses the inherited natural inclinations we are all born with. The nature of our birth is responsible for sin. The required "new birth" implies the acceptance of the procedure we also call the prescription God offers. It is only by submitting to the healing of God's prescription that it becomes possible for a sinner to be transformed willingly by God's grace which is His Truth. This is salvation, because it heals the sin, it does not transfer the sin problem onto someone else.

What Is God's Procedure to Produce Love in a Sinner's Heart?

God's specific procedure to overcome sin is found throughout Scripture, but one must look for it. "Seek," said Jesus, "and you will find" (Mt. 7:7). The main hurdle to the discovery of the procedure is that both Judaism and Christianity have been driven off course by age-old presuppositions. Some of them have been particularly harmful. Old Testament Israelites came to believe that their sacrificial rituals were God's requirement to forgive sins and that forgiveness is sufficient to insure salvation. Likewise, Christians have long held the belief that Jesus came to die on the Cross to forgive sins that they might have salvation. Jews and Christians have both failed to recognize that God grants forgiveness without precondition and that it is always free. But both groups have also failed to realize that forgiveness is not the equivalent of salvation.

Forgiveness is extremely important, but it does nothing to correct delinquent behavior responsible for breaking down relationships. Salvation is not only the establishment of a relationship with God; it is also a commitment to healing the sin problem responsible for all relational breakups in our world. For a relationship to succeed, it must be fully engaged on both sides of the equation. Forgiveness and growth of love are two sides of the same coin. As soon as a sinner disengages from one side or the other, the relationship suffers. The same is true of our relationship with God. God always keeps His promises, but humans have a tendency to be satisfied knowing that they are forgiven, not realizing that if one side of the coin is missing it is of no value. Having God's unconditional pardon is not sufficient for salvation. Forgiveness is important because it keeps on reopening the door to a relationship, but if love fails to grow daily nothing is gained. This is what Paul calls "the perfecting of the saints" and "the edifying of the body of Christ" (Eph. 4:12 KJV). Forgiveness does not produce love in the heart; it only opens the heart to the growth of a relationship.

The problem is that translators and interpreters of Scripture have all been influenced by long-held preconceptions. They all believe that a confession and a price paid on an altar or in the form of good deeds brings automatic forgiveness, and thus salvation. The fact of the matter is that with forgiveness the process of growing the seed of love in the heart has not yet begun, it has only been given the opportunity to sprout. The wording translators use betrays their biases. Most of them thought earnestly that the Sanctuary's slaughter rituals and the Lord's death on the Cross were requirements of God the Father to forgive sins. They totally failed to realize that God is unconditionally merciful; this means that He forgives without precondition. Neither the death of an animal nor that of His Son on a cross was required to forgive sinners. Both were important but not to procure forgiveness; they were intended to procure the message that heals the sin problem. The animal's death on the altar as well as that of the Lord's death on the Cross was intended to show sinners the way to overcome sin, not to forgive them. Jesus made it clear; He said: "I am the way," (Jn. 14:6), He did not say, "I am the payment for your sins by substitution."

Salvation means healing, not setting aside sins as though they could be swept under the rug through substitution, forgiveness, or acquittal. Salvation is all about overcoming the sin disease. But how could a person be interested in overcoming a problem of criminality without the assurance that the crime has been so totally forgiven that it will never be brought up again? Clearly, forgiveness and acquittal are an important part of the process, but neither forgiveness nor acquittal can change a criminal's heart. On the other hand, forgiveness could offer a serious encouragement for criminals to accept a rehabilitation program to correct their disgraceful behavior. The privilege to undergo such a program knowing that their reputation remains unscathed should be a huge motivation to undergo a change of life. As previously clarified, forgiveness can only open the door to salvation; it does not guarantee it. It offers the sinner the hope and motivation to undergo the required change of heart that is capable of curing the behavioral problem. For the change of heart to occur however, God's prescription must be accepted along with the required rehab treatment. Forgiveness is the acceptance of the diagnosis of sin God forgives freely; but God's truth is the prescription to ovecome He also offers freely. Compliance with the prescription is the patient's prerogative because he or she is free, but God also offers help to remain compliant––through the weekly church services. In the end, salvation is entirely thanks to God.

The idea that misdeeds are no longer a problem because they have been forgiven is never an admissible reason to dismiss a case in a court of law; why should it be acceptable to God? A killer who has been forgiven by the family of the victim is not released without consequences. That person still poses a threat to society. But some would claim that God's forgiveness is sufficient because He is God, and thus He can do whatever He wants. Such misconceptions have had devastating effects on humanity. Religions portray God as working with a different logic, but it is the religions of humans that He calls "rebellion that causes desolation" (Dan. 8:13). All human preconceptions responsible for veiling the true nature of God's love are idolatrous. How can the religious world improve as long as they continue to perceive God as requiring a payment on a cross to expunge sin? Such an assumption is not only illogical and irresponsible, but it also keeps the knowledge of God hidden behind the veil of presumptions grounded on superstitions.

If a sinner believes that offering an animal brings salvation because his or her sins were transferred onto the animal and that forgiveness is granted because the animal was slaughtered, such a person will needlessly continue to slaughter animals superstitiously forever, because it will not cure the problem. The same could be said about the Cross. As long as Christians remain persuaded that forgiveness is salvation obtained by the transfer of the sins of the world onto Jesus who died to pay for them, they have no reason to look further for God's solution to the sin problem. Such a religion is indeed rebellion because God's procedure to overcome sin is willfully neglected and overlooked. Why should anyone seek a procedure to overcome sin if all they need is the assurance that their sins are forgiven and that forgiveness is salvation?

Humans should clearly understand that it is because God forgives unconditionally that He is so intent on sharing with them the only procedure available in the universe to regain access to eternal life. If God failed to forgive, what could a procedure to overcome sin accomplish? Nothing! Paul wrote: "All have sinned and fall short of the glory of God" (Rom. 3:23). Indeed, we should all be thankful for God's forgiveness because without it a procedure to overcome sin would be meaningless—we would remain guilty forever. God offers both forgiveness and the prescription to heal free of charge that we might someday enjoy eternal life together.

One of the most often quoted Bible texts in Christianity has been abused beyond recognition. Some Christians actually claim that it is the only text sinners need to know in Scripture to be saved. These words of Jesus were recorded by John: "For God so loved the world, that he gave his only begotten Son, that whosoever believeth in him should not perish, but have everlasting life" (Jn. 3:16 KJV). This text is so rich that an entire book could be dedicated to its analysis. There are a number of problems with traditional interpretations, not the least of which is a false understanding of what Jesus meant when He said to "believe in Him." If believing in Him was a matter of believing that He came to pay for sins, then the next question ought to be: Which text in Scripture affirms that Jesus came to pay for sins? Since there is none, the next question ought to be: What did Jesus really imply then, when He said that humans should believe in Him?

Jesus answered that question in plain language. Did He not say: "I am the way and the truth and the life" (Jn. 14:6)? Jesus could just as well have said: "I am the payment that pays for your sins that you might have eternal life," but He did not. By saying that He is the way, Jesus was saying that He offers the demonstration for the whole world to see that He is the pathway to the only true procedure that brings healing. Without the way to get to the Truth there is no access to Truth, and without Truth there is no eternal life. In this short statement Jesus was making a reference to the path of the high priest through the sanctuary on the Day of Atonement. The journey of a high priest takes him all the way beyond the curtain into the Most Holy place of the sanctuary. It is also the path Christians must learn to follow if they wish to be saved, because only then can they become instrumental in the salvation of others. We will analyze this pathway in more detail in the next chapter.

But the idea that John 3:16 implies a payment for sins is a snare of the devil. Mention of payment is made neither in the text nor its context. Some Christians request baptism on their deathbed, as did Constantine the Great in the fourth century CE, thinking that baptism insures forgiveness of sins and thus the assurance of salvation. Little did he realize that forgiveness is only God's open door to salvation as it was the open door to the sanctuary! With the assurance of forgiveness sinners are only reassured that past sins will not be held against them. At this point the sinner is ready to take the first step which involves the first stage of the cure toward a salvation. Though God's forgiveness is never declined, it is not salvation. It is because sinners know that they are forgiven that they have the courage to venture into a healing relationship with God. Patients would not return to a physician that has maltreated them in the past because they failed to comply with the prescription. How could such patients have the assurance that the physician would do his or her best to save their lives? The moment a sinner wishes to enter into a relationship with God he or she is on God's territory, in His sanctuary, that is, in His safekeeping. It is in the course of the relationship with God in the sanctuary of the human heart that a sinner learns how to overcome sin to become a priest.

In this context Christians should study attentively the methodology Jesus presented transparently in the opening statements of His ministry. His first sermon begins with The Beatitudes. These eight short statements were not only intended as God's greetings to humanity with a promise of salvation, but they also offer a challenge to all intelligent life in the universe. With a little rationale intelligent people are invited to recognize Him and His message as the only way to the Truth that gives eternal life. These eight statements are woven in the same fabric of God's teachings given to humanity since Creation Week.

Like the daily and yearly services of Israelites in the Tabernacle and later in their Temples, the Beatitudes were intended to retrace God's pathway to salvation just as He had always outlined the process. Since God does not change His message designed to heal the sin problem has never changed, as we shall see.

We should remember from the first chapters of this book that God's purpose has always been to make priests and kings out of every citizen in His kingdom. Although God is always more than willing to forgive, He never communicated the idea that sinners should consider forgiveness the ultimate goal of spiritual growth; it is only the open door to the growth of love in the heart.

To undergo the spiritual metamorphosis God desires that we might become kings and priests, one cannot remain a spiritual babe; spiritual growth is mandatory. A seed does not become a tree if it does not grow. Likewise, when a butterfly's egg hatches, only a devouring caterpillar is born. This hungry self-seeking monster must be transformed into an adult butterfly or the species would die out. The newborn human is not unlike a self-seeking caterpillar. We are all self-centered individuals from birth. As Paul said: "All have sinned and fallen short of the glory of God." It is for that reason that we are all invited to be born again into other-centered priests in God's sanctuary. The sanctuary of the last days will be the body of those who share the mind-set of Jesus. The difference is that a caterpillar has no choice in the matter; the transformation happens. Humans are free beings, thus it is their prerogative to choose if they want to remain caterpillars or become butterflies. Unlike butterflies, humans can refuse to become pupas, which for the butterfly is a temporary state of nothingness. Humans must accept to become nothing in order to be changed; this is the humility required for transformation to take place. The cocoon stage of spiritual life is God's gift of forgiveness accepted with humility. It is the stage that opens the door to the transformation of heart. The cocoon stage is akin to the death of the old selfish self before the final transformation into adulthood. But for a sinner, such a change can only take place when God is known in truth. Scripture makes it clear that there are several levels of transformation required for the process of growth of love to take place successfully in the heart. The transformation is complete only when the full length of the divine pathway through the sanctuary has been completed, all the way into the Most Holy Place in the presence of God.

The demonstration that such a metamorphosis is possible for sinners must take place in the sight of the entire universe (see 1 Cor. 4:9). This is important, because unlike God the inhabitants of the universe called angels cannot read or evaluate the state of a person's heart—they must see evidence that the transformation is taking place. Created heavenly hosts cannot be persuaded that it is possible for sinners to undergo a change of heart as long as they cannot see it happening in the reality of their actions. The change of heart can only be revealed by the change of behavior and attitudes toward those who are difficult to love.

Unlike Jesus who knew that the thief on the cross next to Him would have undergone the change of heart that would have changed his behavior, the angels and other humans must see it happen to believe it. Ultimately humanity will reveal to the entire universe that when a sinner has access to God's Truth it is indeed possible for that person to undergo a willful change, and that it is possible for them to live a life in harmony with the kind of love that makes eternal life possible. By their change of behavior sinners will establish that living God's way can become reality, and that it is the greatest privilege one could possibly wish to enjoy for eternity. With such a complete change, a former sinner would never again be threatening toward anyone in all of eternity. Sinners who understand God's plan and His procedure to overcome sin become increasingly eager to follow His pathway with an ever-increasing desire to overcome any lack of love that might remain in their hearts.

It is always lack of love that causes sin. It is not possible to sin any other way. With perfect love in the heart it is impossible to sin. The quality of a person's character is always proportional with the level of love in that person's heart. As far as God is concerned, it is not the level of love attained that counts most for salvation, it is the fact that it is growing. A tree is perfect at every stage of its development; likewise, as far as God is concerned the sprouting love in a heart is just as perfect as the towering love of a totally merciful mature heart. Jesus was calling for high standards of love when He said: "Be perfect as your Father in heaven is perfect" (Mt. 5:48), and implied the same concept when He said: "Be merciful, just as your Father is merciful" (Lk. 6:36). Since God's perfection is manifested by His infinite capacity to serve others at any cost to Himself, the perfection sinners should seek with all their heart, mind, and strength (Mk. 12:30) is likewise to serve others before self ever more intensely. It is not until love becomes difficult or costly to self that love becomes mercy. When this happens, love has to grow even more to accept lovingly the attacks of those who hate us. This growth of love to the point of mercifulness can only be the result of a powerful persuasion God alone could have placed in a human heart, because sinners are never born with that persuasion—this is the kind of persuasion Scripture calls "faith."

Jesus talked about this higher level of faith in His first Sermon on the Mount when He said: "If you love those who love you, what reward will you get? Are not even the tax collectors doing that? And if you greet only your brothers, what are you doing more than others? Do not even pagans do that?" (Mt. 5:46, 47). As Paul points out to the Church of Rome: "Consequently faith comes from hearing the message" (Rom. 10:17). He was obviously talking about the message of Jesus, because no one before Him had been so insistent regarding this highest level of love called mercy. Paul also said that we must all "press on toward the goal" (Phi. 3:14) as long as we live on this planet. That goal is love capable of mercy.

God knew that in the last days a new nation entirely composed of priests and kings would arise on planet Earth. These kings and priests are not those who seek to be served as we traditionally know them on our planet; they are kings and priests who have become experts at serving others in love capable of utter mercy.

These kings and priests are sinners who may not have overcome all sins in their lives, but because they love so much, they are recognized to slowly reduce the sin factor in their lives. They are people who are visibly demonstrating that a change of heart does not occur through the pressures of authorities or legal systems, nor through the action of supernatural powers of doubtful origin. These are people who have clearly recognized that love capable of mercy can only come as the product of a persuasion that comes from the Truth God has proclaimed through the prophets and later through the life and deeds of Jesus. This concept is found nowhere else in human literature. They become priests of the only true God because they live and proclaim His powerful Truth, and they are kings because no one has to to tell them how to think, act, or behave. The soon-to-be formed new nation of priests and kings will be made up of men, women, and children who have all fully accepted to follow God's path that leads to utter selflessness while also leading them to the ultimate care and concern for others before self. Thus they will become God's true representatives on the planet. In other words, these are humans who are not born selfless, but they are born-again selfless thanks to the Truth that will make them increasingly more loving and merciful as long as they live.

Jesus appeared in Person on the scene of a totally dysfunctional human family because their religious system and its rituals had become meaningless. His purpose was to correct the message of Truth that was lost in the course of the previous millennia and a half and before that in the course of time since the Creation. So misrepresented were the symbolisms of Temple rituals that it became imperative to discard them entirely and replace them with a new set of symbols. Central to the required change of symbolism was the erroneous understanding that a confession made just before the slaughter of an animal procured pardon and salvation at the price of a blood offering. It was not pardon that was offered through the symbol; it was the remission of the sin disease. Humans had totally failed to understand that God never requires anything from sinners to grant them a pardon. His forgiveness is always unconditional, but it is not salvation. What God requires, is for humans to recognize that His pardon opens the door to a journey with Him through a sanctuary of learning that teaches how a sinner's heart can be changed.

Indeed, forgiveness is always free—no confession is ever needed. The confession of sin was not a condition to be pardoned, it was a condition to begin the journey with God to overcome sin by learning what love is, how to love, and how much to love others. Here again, traditions stand in the way. They have influenced a faulty translation of Scripture. What happens when a confession is made is not forgiveness; it is God's required first step required to make possible the *remission* of the sin problem. Forgiveness and remission of sin are not synonymous despite the appearances conveyed from the various translations of Scripture and countless Christian theological treatises. Jesus is quoted as having said: "The Christ will suffer and rise from the dead on the third day, and *repentance and forgiveness* of sins will be preached in his name to all nations, beginning at Jerusalem" (Lk. 24:47 NIV). Interestingly, the KJV translates: "*repentance and remission* of sins." Unfortunately, even the KJV is not consistent with its translation of the Greek word *aphesis*. In Acts and elsewhere it is often incorrectly translated "forgiveness." In this book Luke is translated as having written: "repentance for Israel, and forgiveness of sins" (Acts 5:31). Here the KJV should have translated *aphesis* with the word "remission" as it has in just a couple of other places. By using the word "remission" the text suggests a progressive diminution, or reduction of the sin problem, not a pardon of acquittal intended to alleviate the conscience or guilt of sinners.

When the King James Version of the Bible was translated in the seventeenth century, the English word "remission" meant "reduction" or "healing," as it is often used today in the medical world. A disease is said to be in remission when healing begins to take place. The problem is that most Christians have attributed to the word "remission" the idea that the penalty of sin is reduced, not a reduction of sin. Clearly, it should have been understood as remission that leads to a reduction of the sin problem, which is God's only purpose for His plan of salvation. As we have said, salvation is all about recreating the image of God in humans, not a free ticket to heaven because Jesus died. The ticket to heaven is free because Jesus gave us the way to the truth that gives life in heaven at the price of His life, not to pay for sins. Obviously, with a reduction of the sin problem in the world, there would also be a reduction of the consequences of sin, and the world would become a better place to live.

What Christians have always had some difficulty understanding is that there is no penalty for sin; there are only consequences that result from sin. Contrary to common belief God does not penalize or punish sin, but He allows its consequences to be manifested. If someone chooses to jump off the Golden Gate Bridge, God would love to intervene and prevent the inevitable consequence, but He does not because that would be a bold interference with free will. If we can hurt ourselves without interference from God, we can also hurt others without His interference. The context of all references to forgiveness in Scripture need be reevaluated. Remission implies the progressive removal of sin through a new persuasion, whereas forgiveness is falsely interpreted as the removal of consequences for sinning. Remission is the willingness to deal with the sin problem, whereas forgiveness falsely implies a mere reduction of penalties associated with sins.

The consequences of sin are irreversible despite the fact that God always forgives. Thus repentance implies the acceptance of a procedure intended to produce a reversal in the heart. It is the reversal of the way we think that makes it possible for a sinner to overcome sin. Christianity is far too concerned with removing remorse for sins, but that was not God's purpose.

Once activated, true repentance prepares the way for the remission of the sin problem, not the forgiveness or acquittal of sin. Forgiveness is automatic, but the remission of the sin problem is not. This is because remission is entirely dependent on the reversal of one's mind-set, which is a personal decision. It has to be based entirely on the freedom God grants all His children. Scripture calls this reversal of mind-set, repentance. As previously mentioned, neither the Cross nor the Sanctuary were about forgiveness; they were both God's attempt to convey a message intended to bring about the remission of the sin problem on planet Earth. The problem is that God's plan is activated only if or when humans choose to listen to His plan exactly as He meant it to be understood. A false prescription, or a false understanding of the prescription cannot produce remission. Humans have corrupted the prescription multiple times, which explains why the plan is not yet accomplishing God's purpose, with the exception perhaps of few individuals, but not a gathering of people devoted to study Scripture as God meant it to be understood.

Time has come for sincere students of Scripture to cleanse the corrupted prescription so that people might be able to recognize it as coming from God and accept to embrace it as the only solution. Only then will there be a gathering of people about whom God will be able to say: "No lie was found in their mouths; they are blameless" (Rev. 14:5). This text could just as well have been translated to say: "In the message they convey there is no false doctrine, thus they become blameless." The Greek word translated "lie" is the word "decoy." Thus it could be said that in their expression of God's message there is no decoy, no corruption, no incorrect interpretation. Consequently, they are proclaiming a message that progressively renders them blameless of conveying lies about God or His message. The Truth is changing their hearts into the likeness of God's.

It is because Almighty God grants unconditional forgiveness that the sinners of old could feel secure to encounter Him at the Broad Gate of the Tabernacle, or Temple. Let us remember that the ancients had great fear of the gods, and Israel was no exception following centuries of slavery in pagan Egypt. But we must recognize that the reason they were to confess their sins at the entrance of the Sanctuary was not for God's benefit; it was for their own. Confession is the sinner's first expression and recognition that he or she lacks love, or sin would not have occurred in the first place. Confession is the acknowledgement of a flawed heart, thus it is an act of humility. It is only because lack of humility prevents the growth of love in a sinner's heart that God requires a confession, not because it is a condition to obtain His pardon. God merely gives the sinner an opportunity to recognize and accept the fundamental truth that a sinner must recognize that sins are due to lack of love. Since self is the only obstacle to growing love, the old self-centered self must yield to a new others focused self. Since lack of humility implies lack of love, it is also true that only the lack of love is responsible for making the remission of sin impossible. God does not need a confession, but the sinner needs it because it is the first step in the process of salvation. It is the spirit of humility that makes possible the growth of the spirit of love in a sinner's heart.

In His parable about the seed that falls on the pathway, in rocky soil, among thorns, or any other undesirable place, Jesus insists on the fact that the seed must fall on "good soil" (Mt. 13:3–23). It is clear from the context that the seed represents the "message about the kingdom" (Mt. 13:19). Let us never forget that for a gardener "good soil" is always the plot in his garden that was carefully prepared to receive seeds. Several steps are involved in the preparation of the soil. Likewise, one's spiritual soil must be prepared before it is suitable to receive the seed; like the good ground a person's character needs to be broken down and softened before placing in it the seed of love, or it cannot grow. The tilling of the heart is the recognition that it is either filled with stones or weeds and thorns that must first be removed. This prepares the heart for a new way of life with the recognition that conversion is essential. This is humility. It begins with the confession that stones and thorns must be removed before learning from God can proceed, or the seed of love will die prematurely.

When a student believes that he or she is more knowledgeable than the teacher, what could such a student accept to learn from the teacher? It is the acknowledgement that the teacher has something to teach that brings a student to class. It is likewise with God. He has a procedure to teach that must be followed if the sinner is sincere about cultivating the seed of love in the heart to its fruition. Nothing happens if the heart is not prepared to receive the seed. In the parable of Jesus the soil that requires tilling represents the heart that must accept to be broken down in contrition. The thorns and stones must be removed, or growth may occur, but not fruition. Indeed, the cry of the psalmist indicates that he also understood this principle when he wrote: "The sacrifices of God are a broken spirit; a broken and contrite heart, O God, you will not despise" (Ps. 51:17). A broken-down heart is required to accept the seed of Truth that will grow to produce love first and mercy later.

It is imperative for all sinners to understand that the first step toward salvation is to recognize that they have a faulty heart from birth. To make it new the old heart must be broken down before the birth of the new loving heart can take place. Lacking such persuasion, a sinner cannot access the first level of salvation, which is humility. Without humility the journey with God that makes the new birth possible is aborted. This humility step is the preparation of the loam of the heart. God had taken great care in conveying this concept throughout the Old Testament. But having failed to understand that the Sanctuary is a place where sinners were to receive God's prescription to cure sin, the priests were satisfied with advocating rituals corrupted by meaningless pagan dogmas. The conditions required for the remission of the sin problem were lost only because God's prescription became the reflection of pagan views and practices, rather than a reflection of God's character. Sins were believed forgiven and salvation granted at the entrance of the Sanctuary.

The remission of sin will always be proportional to the growth of love in a sinner's heart. But humility alone is not sufficient. The solution is not a fight against sin; it is the acceptance of God's unique prescription to grow love in the heart—it is a fight against evil, a fight against the lack of love that produces sin. As long as love fails to grow, the remission of sin stalls. Paul preached this doctrine. Speaking of the body of Christ, which Paul describes as His church that needs to be built up, he said that it would not happen "until we all reach *unity in the faith* and in the knowledge of the Son of God and become mature, attaining to the whole measure of the fullness of Christ. Then we will no longer be infants, tossed back and forth by the waves, and blown here and there by every wind of teaching and by the cunning and craftiness of men in their deceitful scheming. Instead, speaking the truth in [or, regarding] love, we will in all things grow up into him who is the Head, that is, Christ" (Eph. 4:13–15, emphasis and brackets mine). My translation of the last verse is a little different: "When spreading the truth about growing true love, let us grow into Him in every way, including His head (or mind-set), indeed, that of Christ."

Let us consider the procedure to grow love in more detail. Scripture provides us all the clues needed to accomplish the purpose.

CHAPTER 8

The Beatitudes Restate God's Prescription to Heal Sin

With His Beatitudes Jesus retraced for His Jewish listeners the journey sinners should have taken all along if they had been taught a correct understanding of the journey through the Sanctuary. With the correct understanding, the people would have been changed and their character would have once again begun to reflect the image of the Creator God. The plan of salvation is a plan designed to return humans to the mind-set God had given them at Creation. It is a program designed to heal the problem of sin, not a plan designed to forgive sin without resolution. If God's plan fails to resolve the problem itself, it is of no value at all, and religion becomes a mere formality. Unfortunately, the current doctrines of Christianity are more geared to expound on forgiveness of sin than its resolution. Indeed, the God's plan is of no value if it fails to include a process by which growth of love that destroys sin can be achieved.

God's real plan to achieve His purpose is least touted among Christians. The symbolic rituals, some of which included the slaughter of animals, were intended to draw humans closer to God and thus to one another. In Hebrew these rituals were called *korban*. A careful study of that word in its original usage makes it clear that rituals were never intended to be offerings made to God. Indeed, all rituals were *korban*, intended to draw humans closer to God and thus to one another. From its root *krv* the word means "coming close," not offering. Pagans are known to approach their gods with gift offerings, including various foods and, in some cases, slaughtered animals or humans. Self-mutilations are also practiced to offer God or the gods a distorted form of self-sacrifice. This pagan approach to their gods is responsible for the shift of meaning that occurred on several occasions in Israel. Over time the meaning of the word *korban* was altered by the Israelites who had always been flirting with pagan practices and mentalities reported in some detail by OT prophets. As a result the word *korban* was altered over time to mean offerings made to God in pagan fashion.[30] We must remove from our minds the idea that God ever wanted offerings for anything, regardless of the way Jews in the days of Jesus understood this term. No wonder Jesus quoted the Prophet Jeremiah when He denounced the Temple of His day, calling it "a den of robbers" (Mt. 21:13 and Jer. 7:11). In both Testaments the word translated "robbers" should have been translated "plunderers." These are people who create havoc and destruction in order to loot. When Jesus made the statement He was clearly implying that the religious leadership had initiated the confusion that destroyed the Word of God in order to take advantage of the situation for their financial and political gains.

Scripture is clear to say that forgiveness and salvation are absolutely free. The Temple rituals instituted during the Exodus were never intended to be offerings made to God; they were God's offerings to humanity. Indeed, God was giving sinners a second chance by teaching them how to regain the mind-set of God. To do so, and partly because most of them could not read or write, God offered them to engrave the procedure in their minds through meaningful symbolic rituals. Each of the symbols represented the various stages of the sinner's journey through the gates of the sanctuary. Going in they were to draw ever closer to God before encountering Him in the Most Holy Place and coming out a born-again new creation.

For reasons we have already discussed, in the Israelite system one had to be a priest to enter the Holy Place and a High Priest to enter once a year the Most Holy Place. As we have seen, all the symbolism was changed when Jesus reinstituted the idea that His people were to become a priestly kingdom. All followers of Christ were invited to become priests, just as God wanted all Israelites to become priests (Ex. 19:5, 6). All Christians are urged to become priests and thus to journey with God through the Courtyard and beyond, all the way to the Most Holy Place. However this will not happen as long as we have a false understanding of what *korban* means. Jesus came all the way from heaven to restate its true meaning. While the followers of Christ are encouraged to follow

---

[30] The word *korban* is found in the NT, in Mark 7:11, where it is spelled *corban*. The discrepancies between the various translations of that text are an indication of the confusion that surrounds the true meaning of that word. The explanation given in parenthesis in the NIV is clearly wrong and was probably added by scribes.

Him all the way to the Holy of Holies, they can only do so with a correct understanding of the symbolic journey involved.

In God's plan sinners were to be led beyond the Veil because they were to be symbolically standing in the very presence of God as they received from Him the final message of transformation. This is where they were to receive the final refinements needed to become priests. It is only when the sinner symbolically reaches the presence of God in the Most Holy that the anointment to the priesthood is received from Him. This is where the fullness of the Truth that makes everlasting freedom possible is accepted (Jn. 8:32). The discernment of the message God conveys at the Mercy Seat transforms a sinner into a priest ready to share with others the true message of *korban*. It is in the presence of God that a sinner begins to be re-created into the image of the Creator.

However, to reach this ultimate goal the sinner must scrupulously follow God's prescribed procedure in the proper sequence. Attempting to skip a step is bound to compromise the healing process. Throughout the journey the sinner is led to desire the death of the old selfish self as a condition for the new birth to take place—this process is clearly outlined in The Beatitudes, and they are further explained in the rest of the Sermon of Jesus on the Mount.

The First Beatitude

"Blessed are the poor in spirit, for theirs is the kingdom of heaven" (Mt. 5:3). My translation is a little different: "Consider the growth potential of those who crave the mind-set of the kingdom of heaven."

The Greek word *makarios* translated "blessed" may not convey the meaning Jesus intended. Because the Greek prefix *mak* implies "becoming long or large," or perhaps, "becoming better, or greater." The rest of the word implies the person who becomes better. Thus we prefer to say: "Consider the growth potential of those who . . ." The word "blessed" has acquired a mystical meaning. It tends to imply the action of a supernatural power involved in the bestowment of "holiness" without necessarily involving the sinner's direct participation. Yet as we have seen, because we are free the improvement of life and human character must be motivated by a powerful persuasion that comes from God, not an external supernatural force at work in one's heart. The Beatitudes are all about changes that should take place in a person's heart and life thanks to the motivating force of a persuasion we have been calling faith. Righteousness is by faith because it is motivated by a rational persuasion. Jesus is calling His listeners to imagine what would happen to people who are persuaded that life as we live it on earth is not all there is to life. Indeed, there is much more in the kingdom of God, but when a sinner is satisfied with the life of this world there is nothing better to look forward to. Such a person is not "poor in spirit" but satisfied with the status quo and falsely believes to be rich in spirit—as were Jews compared to pagans and as were the Temple leaders compared to other religions. If a person does not feel poor in spirit that person never bothers to look to God for a better way of life.

Jesus is not talking about material poverty in this statement. He has a far more crucial message in mind. A person who is "poor in spirit" recognizes that the way humans think and live from their natural birth is flawed and that there must be something better to seek and look forward to, if indeed there is a God who created the universe. It is time for humans to realize that the environment they have created is not sustainable and fails to be heading toward a solution but toward doom.

The crowd listening to the Master's words must have been shocked when Jesus told them that poverty could be a good thing. Indeed, knowing that we are poor is like knowing that we are sick. A patient does not go to a doctor for advice unless he or she knows that advice is needed. Likewise, a person does not go to God if he or she believes to be spiritually fit and rich. One may wonder what the Jewish public understood when they heard these words. But let us remember that Jesus spent days with them. He had plenty of time to clarify and explain what he meant.

This statement of Jesus is all the more surprising that the Jews were the only people on earth who recognized the existence of the only true God. Thus they were the only people on the planet who had reasons to believe that they were spiritually rich and secure. Yet it is to them that Jesus was addressing these words as if to say: "Be careful, dear people, don't take God for granted just because you are descendants of Abraham and believe in the only true God." Was Jesus suggesting that spiritual humility is preferable to prideful spiritual wealth? The most spiritually affluent nation of the world was actually in a pitiful state of spiritual poverty, as is Christianity today.

Ironically, it was precisely because they were Jews that Jesus could talk to them as He did. These words would have been meaningless to people of other nations. No nation was more proud of its religious affiliation with God and Abraham than were the Jews; they were God's official descendants of Abraham in the flesh. Was it not their religious national pride that Jesus was attempting to purge? Was not Jesus trying to feed the Jews a little "humble pie" that they might recognize their state of spiritual poverty? Only the recognition of their spiritual poverty could open their hearts and minds to the saving grace of God's Truth Jesus was attempting to convey. Jesus was the doctor telling His patients that they were sick and that they urgently needed to change the treatment they were receiving from their religious leadership. Instead of seeking the solution from the Word of God they subjected themselves to useless religious rituals in blind submission to superstitious beliefs that could resolve nothing. These relatives of Jesus were the fulfillment of Isaiah's prophecies, when He predicted that they would be "devoured by the sword" (Is. 1:20) and would end up "like a garden without water" (Is. 1:30). Sadly, the last two millennia have proven the prediction all too accurate.

In order to develop love in the heart, personal and religious corporate pride had to be broken down first—like the "good ground" of the parable. In fact, religious pride can be even more damaging than personal pride because it instills a false sense of security regarding salvation. Knowing that they were God's chosen people, the Jews developed a sense of religious pride unequalled until Christians appeared on the scene of world history and managed to outdo them in matters of religious pride. The importance of developing a sense of corporate humility to develop corporate love cannot be overstated. As long as any form of pride remains in the teachings of a group the door to further growth remains shut. Such pride has not only been a stumbling block for religions, but it has also stalled the growth of past civilizations. This may sound a bit strange, but pride involving religious and national identity must be banished, or further growth is immediately impaired. As long as people remain persuaded that their nation or religion is superior to that of others they are not only stalled in their growth, but they also become enemies of those they denigrate. True brothers and sisters are people of all religious and ethnic backgrounds who remain steadfastly devoted to follow God's path to greater love in all humility. All other paths to religion are false doctrines responsible for building up religious and national pride responsible for the exclusion of others and at their expense. This is not the religion Jesus taught to His Jewish brothers and sisters in need of a new mind-set founded on love rather than hatred for their Roman autocrats.

For pure mutual love to grow, pride in all its forms must be banished. Jews became persuaded that God had given them a universal monopoly on religion, but that was not God's intention. While it is true that God gave them His eternal Word of Truth on multiple occasions, it is also true that they repeatedly corrupted His message beyond recognition. Instead of producing humility in their hearts, their corrupted religion produced unprecedented levels of religious corporate and individual pride. Christianity fell in the same trap, and Islam may well be a close rival. It is difficult to imagine that any pagan religion might have ever reached a level of pride that equals or surpasses that of the three so-called monotheist religions of our world. What a crying shame, because with pride love cannot grow!

The first and perhaps most pressing mission of Jesus was to enlighten His spiritually conceited Jewish fellow citizens regarding the importance of humility. In their case it was particularly important for corporate religious humility to precede their personal humility. As long as their Temple and its teachings were considered with pride their minds would remain closed to the gems of truth Jesus had in store for them. How does one address a people persuaded that they already have God's absolute Truth? Events leading up to the death of Jesus indicate that the pride of the nation had not yet waned.

The Messiah they were anticipating to deliver them from political tyranny had to first deliver them from a much greater foe, a false theology responsible for producing impervious pride. They thought themselves rich spiritually, without realizing that their long-held false doctrines had made them poor. Jews today are still proud of a religion Jesus denounced, but unfortunately they have plenty of company among other religions. This prideful condition characterizes the Church of Laodicea mentioned in the book of Revelation (Rev. 3:13–22). It remains persuaded that it is rich and in need of nothing, a perfect portrayal of the religions of our world today.

When Jesus was talking about the spiritual poverty of His Jewish siblings He was concerned about their individual lack of the kind of spirituality that comes from God. Most of His listeners had probably come to realize that Judaism was divided into sects and that all the existing divisions had failed to resolve the problems their nation was facing. They were probably aware, as we are today, that conditions could only get worse. The deplorable condition of the Jewish nation must have caused them to wonder why God appeared to be so indifferent to their plight. Little did they realize that God was indeed with them, in the person of Jesus, and that the religious authorities were feeding them a poisoned dish of unscriptural dogmas on a daily basis. The same condition already existed in the days of Isaiah the prophet. He lamented prayerfully: "No one calls on your name or strives to lay hold of you" (Is. 64:7)! As in the days of Isaiah, God said to them: "Where is the house you will build for me" (Is. 66:1)? Notice the future tense, considering that in the days of Isaiah they still had the Temple of Solomon standing proudly in Jerusalem. The Children of Israel had not yet understood that God did not wish to "dwell *among them*" but that He wanted to dwell *in them* through the persuasive message of His Truth. The new order of God's temple made up of His people was yet to be built. Because of the failure to build such a temple Jesus had to come. He thus became the Alpha and Omega of a new order of priesthood and a new temple. This new temple is to become the final living repository of God's Word of Truth.

In this first of eight Beatitudes Jesus was warning His listeners that the most important thing the Jews could do as a people, was to realize how "poor in spirit" they really were. Just because their religion originated with a call from God to Abraham did not mean that they had nothing more to learn or that their religion had faithfully remained pure through the centuries. Their prideful leaders were called teachers, scribes, and doctors of the Law (Lk. 5:17). But they chose to substitute the priestly duties God had ascribed, which was to heal the sin problem, with a self-ascribed merchandizing scheme of salvation sold at the price of useless counterfeit sacrificial offerings. Their duty should have been to listen to God and to "reason" with Him (Is. 1:18) that they might clearly understand how to pass on to all people the Truth that saves from sin. Instead they chose to become salesmen of bloodstained "indulgences" burnt on the altar of God.

Had they taken the time to seriously reason with God about the message of Truth His rituals were intended to convey, they would have recognized the healing beauty of His message on the strength of its perfect logic. They would have discovered a practical approach to salvation that motivates a genuine change of life, not a useless payment made in exchange for forgiveness at the price of blood and death on a religious altar. Had the rituals been recognized as meaningful exercises designed to convey a message that changes lives they could not have been corrupted and sold to the people as "meaningless offerings" (Is. 1:12–13). Indeed, the Truth contained in the original OT rituals was to convey the exact same Truth later proclaimed when Jesus lived it all the way to the Cross. God does not change. The message of the Cross, said Paul, "is the power of God" (1 Cor. 1:18). The message of the rituals was no different. Had they understood the message rather than submit to vain rituals, they would have all become priests of a message that changes hearts.

The very fact that the Jews were willing to listen to Jesus, a man from Nazareth, a place of disrepute, where there were no religious leaders, was symptomatic of the disregard some people had for their Temple and its teachings. If the Temple of Jerusalem had been proclaiming the Truth that makes sinners free, why would people come in droves to listen to the Son of a carpenter from Nazareth? There was hunger and thirst in the parched land of Judea, hunger for solid spiritual food and thirst-quenching drink. No existing synagogue or temple was teaching Truth any more than do our churches and temples today. In the days of Jesus the people had access to priests of the Temple rather than priests of God. All that was to change when Jesus made the announcement that He was greater than their Temple (Mt. 12:6) and the cornerstone of a new one (Mt. 21:42). The new Temple made up of followers of Jesus are, like Him, called upon to become *"merciful* and faithful *high priest"* in service to God" (Heb. 2:17, emphasis mine).

Love cannot grow or survive where humility is lacking

Spiritual poverty is the realization that true religion has to be more real, more desirable, and more relevant than the religions we have in our world today. Such a religion would be united in its search for truth rather than united in its belief that truth can be found only in their ranks, which makes them prideful. Such a religion would have a greater impact on changing people's characters to make them more loving and merciful. With the current events of our world we all hear and witness, we all know that something is wrong almost everywhere we look. No area of life is spared overwhelming problems. In fact, we all recognize that while religions preach love there is an obvious lack of it in the land, in the world, in the churches, and in our own hearts. Where we all tend to fail spiritually is in our inability to recognize that the lack of love is entirely due to a serious lack of humility at all levels of life on this planet.

A person dejected and "poor in spirit" has to acknowledge that if there is a God there also has to be a better message, one that would produce the "fruit of the Spirit, which is love" (Gal. 5:22). They are dejected over the fact that all religions fall short of providing valid and relevant answers to the real problems our world is facing—if anything the religions of the past century appear to have done more harm than good, and that, mostly because of pride.

Where is the answer to the decaying human condition? Sad to say, only those who truly seek answers in all humility will realize sooner or later that God's Truth sought on the grounds of logic alone can offer real solutions. They will also recognize that to seek God they will have to follow Him all the way to the Most Holy Place where they will finally get to see God's character face to face. His Most Holy Place is the only place where real answers can be found. Any journey with God that fails to reach the Most Holy will also fail to produce true love. The problem is that so far the priests of our current temples have all failed to offer access to God. Instead they have been offering the people an empty and meaningless message that does not come from God. By so doing they are preventing the people from entering God's territory beyond the Brazen Altar of the Courtyard where religions have been stuck for millennia. Many enter by way of the wide gate and broad way that leads to death, said Jesus. Only a few enter the "narrow gate" (Mt. 7:13), the one that "leads to life" on the other side of the Veil in the presence of God. Jesus adds: "Only a few find it" (Mt. 7:14).

Indeed, the clergy of today's Christian churches appear to be proud and protective of their prestige in society. They are perfectly happy to maintain their monopoly on the priesthood, but this will change. They want exclusive access to the Holy and Most Holy Places of sanctuaries. This restriction should have been lifted long ago. God wants an entire "kingdom of priests" (Ex. 19:6), not a priesthood of whose attitudes Jesus can say that they "shut the kingdom of heaven in men's faces." They themselves have failed to enter and prevent from entering those "who are trying to" (Mt. 23:13).

Where is the heavenly sanctuary God has promised? When will His sanctuary be cleansed of its corruption that humans might replace their temples of stones, wood, and concrete? Where can the people receive real comfort from God beyond obscure and fruitless method of forgiveness by payment offered to a demanding God? Is there a place where sinners are welcome to enter and meet their God in Truth? If so, where is the real church of God today?

We should remember with Paul, that Jesus was "the firstborn among many brethren." He indicates in the same passage that God who knows the heart "foreknew," and "foreordained" others "to be conformed to the likeness of his Son" (Rom. 8:29 ASV). If they are conformed to the likeness of the Son they are clearly called upon to become high priests. They are invited to become both the structure of His new temple on Earth and its priests. Today the world is still waiting for both the theology that comes from God and its priests. They will proclaim the cleansed and purified message of God. This newly cleansed temple will not be made by human hands because God will build this new temple with people He made, and once again it will reveal the true power of God's saving message of Truth.

We live in a world today where many have given up on religion because it lacks the foundations of sound logic. As a result humanity hungers for answers and solutions that will make a real difference. Strangely enough, logic is the light that shows them the inadequacies of today's religions, and the same logic will eventually show them the way to the Truth the gives life. The prophet Amos wrote nearly 28 centuries ago: "'The days are coming,' declares the Lord, 'when I will send a famine through the land—not a famine of food, or a thirst for water, but a famine of hearing the word of the LORD'" (Amos 8:11). God has the solutions to the world's problems, but when will the people listen to the Truth He proclaims rather than to the superstitions they choose to hear?

Before God can satisfy the hunger of the people for spiritual food His message must be cleansed of all corruption that renders it undesirable to people unwilling to accept irrational rhetoric. Theological temple cleaning is imperative and it will happen soon. Only then will the Lord have a sanctuary where the Everlasting Gospel of Truth will reside in the minds and hearts of His people and will be clearly demonstrated in their deeds, as was Jesus. Only then will there be a real sanctuary and real priests. Only then will there be a people on earth that can be called a Priestly Nation where people are observed to grow into the likeness of God. The world hungers for the cleansing of God's temple. Incongruous promises of salvation made on the basis of inexplicable concepts of pagan origin will become intolerable for sincere seekers of God.

Christians must realize that as long as they fail to teach God's perfectly coherent Message of Truth the fulfillment of His last-day promises of salvation will not come to pass. God is waiting for His people to do the cleansing because He cannot do it for them anymore than He can destroy idols and idolatrous beliefs without abusing individual freedom. Indeed, the sanctuaries of today have once again become "dens of thieves" where priests rob the people of the very salvation they promise under false pretenses. If humans fail to cleanse the Message of God, they will all end up suffering the fate of the kid goat for Azazel on Yom Kippur. They will all be taken down the path to the wilderness of evil that leads to unavoidable oblivion. Indeed, "the wages of sin is death" (Rom. 6:23). What the world needs more than anything else is a sanctuary where God's Truth reigns supreme and where Christlike priests spread the Everlasting Gospel to a spiritually impoverished world starving for Truth. Otherwise, "men will" continue to "stagger from sea to sea, and wonder from north to east, searching for the word of the LORD, but they will not find it" (Amos 8:12).

To begin the journey with God, both individual sinners and the organized religions of the world must have the courage to approach the Main Gate of God's Courtyard with a contrite heart willing to encounter God on the solid grounds of logic. If established religions remain unwilling to recognize that something is dreadfully wrong with their teachings, a new religion will sprout from the dust of this tormented world. How soon will the religious leaders recognize that the Message must be cleansed before hearts can be changed! The wrong prescription will never heal the disease. Once prostrate on the threshold of humility, God Himself will take by the hand those individuals or religious groups seeking His kingdom. He will lead them through a prayerful study His Word and will take them all the way to the healing presence of God in the Most Holy Place. He is the only medicine that has the power to set sinners free.

Sinners who at the end of time will choose to complete the journey with God all the way to His presence will reach a level of healing never before witnessed or achieved by a nation or group of people. Their journey will transform them into the likeness of Jesus because they will be guided by the same persuasion that guided Him. It is a persuasion that grows one's devotion to love on a daily basis. Each step of the journey with God takes the sinner to a new level of understanding and love. Love grows in the heart as the understanding of Truth grows in the sinner's mind. Like a plant, every day brings a new level of desire to grow upward toward light and remain on course regardless of the winds and storms of pain and suffering. Jesus said: "If anyone would come after me, he must deny himself and take up his cross and follow me" (Mk. 8:34). This statement implies that for such a person, having love in the heart has become more important than having life itself. Even death by torture becomes preferable to denying the love by which Jesus lived.

The point of this First Beatitude is clear: It is not possible to entertain the desire to journey with God as long as sinners and religious organizations fail to recognize the poverty of their spiritual condition with humility. Only then can sinners be motivated to encounter God at the Gate of His sanctuary. From that point forward "the kingdom of heaven is at hand." As Jesus illustrated the concept in His parable of the Prodigal Son, the sinner finally "came to his senses" (Lk. 15:17); he realized that he needed to humble himself and consider a solution in the presence of his Father (see Lk. 15:11–32). To the sinner's surprise, the Father is always more than willing to welcome His sons and daughters back home. A sinner must go through the process of which this first Beatitude only represents the beginning of the journey—the transformation of mind and heart will follow.

The Second Beatitude

"Blessed are those who mourn, for they will be comforted" (Mt. 5:4). Again, my amplified translation is a little different: "Consider the potential of those who are sincerely regretful that they are flawed, for they shall be shown how to overcome them."

The first sign that a sinner is sincere about accepting God's prescription to cure the sin disease is manifested by the mournful sorrow that comes from realizing that we are all born flawed. The word "mourn" is a translation from the Greek *pentheō,* which means to grieve, or feel badly, not necessarily mourning the loss or death of a loved one. When the reality that the prideful character we are born with is the problem, only then can a sinner recognize the need for a change. The discovery that we are born with a serious flaw that requires a 180° change of orientation is a painful realization. We are suddenly made to realize that we have been a part of the problem of evil ever since our natural birth. This is especially true when sinners come to realize that it is the unwillingness to overcome self-centeredness that causes all the problems in the world. Such unwillingness to change is unwillingness to be born again. A new light has to be turned on in one's brain to feel remorse for having been part of the problem for so long. But only then are sinners likely to seek a solution from God, and if they do, God is sure to bring them the "comfort" and support needed to make the necessary changes.

The sadness of heart comes from the realization that we are all caught up in the same vicious cycle of evil. Realizing the importance of turning to God for the solution is the beginning of wisdom. God alone has the solution, but His solution must be accepted. A statement from the pen of Paul needs to be recognized correctly. We have already quoted it as saying: "For all have sinned, and come short of the glory of God" (Rom. 3:23). Many are those who think this text to imply that there is nothing a sinner can do to reverse sinfulness. The assumption is that since nothing can be done to overcome sin, a sinner should leave the problem entirely in the hands of God. While this is true because God does it all, we must never forget that God has already contributed His part to the solution on multiple occasions. He has given the key to salvation to the prophets, and since humans failed to accept the key of understanding from them, Jesus came to proclaim it once again all the way to the Cross.

When reading that text we must keep in mind the fact that we are all born sinners and that we are indeed all contributors to the sin problem on earth. But unlike the conclusions reached by many, this does not mean that we are left helpless in a hopeless situation. On the contrary, it is because we are all born with a flawed mind-set of self-centeredness that we must be born again with a new and totally different mind-set. This new birth experience is the acceptance of a totally different faith to live by than the one of our natural birth. We all have faith in something, whether or not we believe in God. Indeed, we all have a modus operandi, or we could not function, but we are called to adopt the one and only true faith that comes from God because no other faith can sustain eternal life. The way God thinks is the reverse of the mind we receive from our birth in a world where survival through self-preservation is the rule of life. A new and opposite rule of life should replace the one of our birth. We should all be depressed and mournful when we realize that we were born flawed. It is painful to recognize that there is something wrong with us. Parents feel bad when a child is born with a birth defect, but we rarely consider the minds we are born with as birth defects. It is worse than a doctor telling us that we have a terminal cancer because the flawed mind of our birth is indeed a terminal disease.

But we should take heart over the fact that with God's prescription the natural flaws of mind can be healed through the new birth. With God's prescription we are left neither helpless nor hopeless. With Him there is hope and solution, but only if we are willing to accept the only cure available to reverse the natural inclinations of our hearts. God's cure offers a new birth because it creates in us a new mind-set and a new heart. It is a new spirit that Scripture calls "holy" because it stands in opposition to the natural spirit of our birth—it is from God, and it sets apart those who accept it from those who do not.

God cannot inject the new spirit into our minds; that would be abuse of our God-given freedom. As long as sinners fail to recognize that there is lack of love in their hearts and that this condition is a birth defect, the sin problem cannot be addressed with a sufficient degree of desire to correct the problem. If sinners fail to become sorrowful for their condition it is only because they have failed to realize the lack of love in their hearts. Such sinners are in no position to seek the cure from God that opens the door to a new birth. The mournful attitude triggers a state of readiness for the change God alone can operate in a sinner's heart. Mourning one's past lack of love opens the heart to the healing hand of God.

Here the translators of Scripture may again have used the wrong term. At the entrance of the sanctuary sinners were not mourning the death of a lamb, but it is difficult to imagine a tearless sinner confessing a lack of love while slaughtering a lamb. The Sanctuary and its services were all intended to help sinners understand this principle. A person cannot enter the Broad Gate without acknowledging sorrowfully that sins are due to lack of love and that they have devastating effects on all forms of life. Such an admission of guilt for having lived a life lacking love is essential. Not because confession is a condition for pardon, but because it is an admission that the lack of love must be reversed or it will continue to produce immeasurable damages to self and others.

True confession is the acknowledgement at the altar that love has been lacking and that such lack of love causes the death of all life, including that of the most innocent and blameless among us. It is for that reason that a perfect young lamb was used to illustrate the point. The innocent animal is a victim placed on an altar to illustrate the ugliness of death caused by lack of love. Let us remember that when God instituted the slaughter ritual it was not intended to be an offering. Humans did not know what death was, and they needed the graphic image of a perfectly innocent life dying because of their sins. Cain and Abel had never seen death when they practiced their ritual. Through this ritual they were to acknowledge that the minds and hearts of their natural births were flawed. This fact alone should bring heartfelt mournful tears of surrender to God's cure. The lamb on the altar dies to demonstrate the ugliness of sin as well as the fact that the most innocent among us also die because of sin.

The death of the animal was never intended to be a payment for sins, as commonly believed. The death of Jesus on the Cross was no different. No Scripture implies anywhere that the death on the Cross was a payment for sins. Only false interpretations of Scripture convey such a pagan concept. The death of the Lord proclaims the exact same message the death of the lamb was intended to convey: Sin causes the slaughter of all people, including that of the most innocent. It is the pride of humans unwilling to listen to God's cure that caused the death of the Son of God who had lived the most innocent life ever lived on our planet. Jesus understood that sad reality when He said: "Forgive them, for they do not know what they are doing" (Lk. 23:34, cf. 1 Cor. 2:8).

At the Altar of the Outer Court the journey in the sanctuary has not yet begun. But the sinner has accepted the idea that the lack of love in his or her heart is the problem that must be corrected. The process of confession is the recognition that a failure to change can only perpetuate death, including that of innocent victims. Confession is the groundbreaking experience of humility that prepares the heart for the seed of God's love. The seed that falls on good ground is a seed that falls on ground that has been prepared. Following that first step comforting help is offered. The subsequent steps in the Sanctuary of God's miraculous transformation will open the other two remaining gates of access to the miracle of growth. In the Holy place the plant will grow, but in the Most Holy it will reach fruition.

The breakup of the old heart prepares the sinner for a new one. What a comfort it is to know that God can transform a heart from self-seeking to perfectly loving. A lack of sorrow would betray a lack of acknowledgment that love is the lacking element in a sinner's heart. Thus we could say that the sorrow of the sinner at the altar is indicative of the required brokenness of heart that comes with the realization that a change must take place and that the seed of love must grow. Details of the transformation will take place in the other two compartments of the Sanctuary. The sinner has the assurance that God's grace will make the change possible.

The Third Beatitude

"Blessed are the meek, for they will inherit the earth" (Mt. 5:5). Otherwise translated: "Consider the potential of people who recognize the importance of gentleness born out of humility, for they shall astound the world."

Here I choose to translate the Greek word *praus* using a phrase, because the word "meek" fails to render the concept Jesus had in mind. He was not talking about the traditional human understanding of "mild mannerism," or "meekness" we sometimes impose on ourselves. Indeed, plenty of gentle mild-mannered people lack true humility. Jesus used a term intended to convey a specific kind of meekness, the kind that grows out of genuine humility. For many the mild treatment of others is by design, to project an image. False meekness is always an attempt to manipulate. Unfortunately the human vocabulary does not distinguish between self-serving gentleness and meekness born out of humility. The latter is genuine; the former is premeditated and manipulative.

This third step in God's procedure to transform sinners back into His own image required mournful sorrow on the part of sinners for having failed to understand sooner that humans are not born with a loving heart but must acquire it. Some would say that this is righteousness by works, but it is not; it is righteousness by enlightenment that comes from God, which is the faith of the new convert. It is a distressing insight to suddenly realize that we are flawed from birth. In the first step sinners chose to seek God for answers, in the second they recognize mournfully that the mind-set received at birth is inadequate, and in the third there is an outpouring of genuine grief for their past lack of love. This grief opens the sinners' hearts to God's recommendations; it is the softening of the heart that becomes malleable. Repentance is sometimes believed to be a willingness to confess wrongdoing, but it is much more than mere recognition of sin. Humility of heart brings about openness to a complete reversal of attitudes from a life focused on self to serving others. The grieving is an indication that humility and contrition has begun to take effect. It is an indication that the course of a sinner's life is about to change.

Humans must all face an important choice at some point in their life. They can either choose to remain on the path of survival based on natural instincts received at birth or recognize the worthlessness of such instincts and opt for a change by accepting God's pathway. When left unchecked, the natural instincts are given free course to rule a sinner's life. This is the main difference between human and animal life. Thankfully, many humans recognize on the strength of logic alone that yielding to natural instincts can be damaging. It is for this reason that many agnostics and atheists are far more humble and loving than proud religious people persuaded that they have the only truth worth having. Humans have a built-in capacity to change what they are from convictions formed within their hearts. The strength of their beliefs changes their lives, but animals are powerless to escape their natural instincts. This may well be the best proof that humans are not descendants of animals. We could even say that if humans were unable to change their natural instincts by forging ahead with a new mind-set, the Word of God would be of no value, and the Cross would have been for naught. A study of God's Word shows that it has always been intended to help humans escape the natural instincts of their birth to forge new ones. The sinful nature acquired after sin must *willfully* yield back to the nature God gave humans before sin.

True meekness of heart is never manipulative, and it is never judgmental. It is the continual expression of unconditional and selfless devotion to others. The Apostle Peter talked about the inner beauty that should characterize true followers of Christ. The "inner self" of such a person should express the "unfading beauty of a gentle and quiet spirit, which is of great worth in God's sight" (1 Pet. 3:4). He goes on to admonish: "Finally, all of you, live in harmony with one another; be sympathetic, love as brothers, be compassionate and humble. Do not repay evil with evil or insult with insult, but with blessing, because to this you were called so that you may inherit a blessing" (1 Pet. 3:8–9).

While sincere sorrow is essential for genuine change to take place, it is only the beginning of the process to change a sinner's instincts and character. Cain must have felt the need to do something about his lack of kindness or he would not have bothered to implement a ritual involving the acknowledgement of wrongdoing. Of itself confession is not a manifestation of meekness or repentance; it could be the opposite. The only meekness God recognizes as genuine must be born out of genuine humility, or it is pretend meekness. In Cain's case, he was willing to acknowledge his wrongdoing as a problem, but his intention was to buy leniency and avoid God's requisite for a change. Cain just wanted to pay up and move on unchanged.

Confession involving recognition of wrongdoing at the Brazen Altar is not sufficient to rid a sinner of self-centeredness. Mournful sorrow out of regrets for past lack of love is the only adequate preparation for a sinner's heart to accept the cleansing that follows. The priest having to wash his hands and feet at the Laver on behalf of the sinner after the slaughter symbolized willfulness to have a change of heart and mind. Washing hands represented the cleansing one's actions, while washing feet symbolizes a complete turnaround of direction in life—toward God's Sanctuary rather than away from it.

The sorrow demonstrates a genuine acceptance of meekness as the mainstay of life. The step-by-step procedure is required, or love cannot grow in a sinner's heart. This third stage in the sinner's life might best be described as his or her willingness to go into the womb of God this time around, to receive from Him the new birth. This time however, it is the sinner who has chosen the place of incubation, not earthly parents. The growth in the womb of God requires a gestation period that leads to the genuine new birth for eternity despite the fact that death of body will occur, as it did for Jesus. Just as Christ left the majesty of His divine status to enter the womb of a human mother, a sinner must accept to become once again a very small embryo of submissiveness to God's mind-set for eternity. With the understanding that comes from Him, self becomes increasingly more irrelevant while others become increasingly more the focus of care, love, and mercy. This is a major turning point in a sinner's life. It is a life now dedicated to radiate daily an ever-growing expressions of God's kind of love.

This is where Cain failed. In his corrupt mind he assumed that a mere confession made at the price of an expensive gift to God would be sufficient payment to deserve His generous grace. What presumption on his part to think that God would be swayed by a generous gift! This attempt on Cain's part is a clear indication that God was not intimidating to him in the least. On the other hand, Cain had neither humility nor the submissive meekness required for true love to sprout in his heart, much less for love to reach fruition. Cain's offering was not a heartfelt expression of a gift of self that would have made possible the germination of love. Thus Cain could not be accepted of God as long as he remained unwilling to give up an attitude of heart from human birth that could not resolve the sin problem. His lack of contrition failed to lead him to the womb of God wherefrom his spiritual rebirth could have ensued.

By contrast, Abel's offering was an expression of humble disposition to accept God's makeover of heart that leads to new birth. The importance of focusing on the well-being of others that the "Lamb of God" later exemplified by giving His life for the sake of others had already become the focus of Abel's life. He had understood and accepted God's message of eternal Truth. As a result, Abel was accepted of God. Abel's sacrificial offering was not viewed as a gift to God but as the expression of his gratitude for God's willingness to give sinners a second chance. The sacrificial ritual was not a gift for God on an altar; it was, as were all the rituals of the Temple, a lesson study intended to grow love in the heart. But the change is possible only for those who accept true humility as the motivational force to genuine meekness. It is the first indication that a sinner is on God's path to recovery and inheritance of His kingdom on the New Earth.

At the Laver of the Outer Court the sinner's heart begins the healing process in a rather peculiar way—the blood of past life is washed and made to disintegrate into humble nothingness. Jesus made that observation when He talked about the kernel of wheat: "I tell you the truth," He said, "unless a kernel of wheat falls to the ground and dies, it remains only a single seed, but if it dies, it produces many seeds. The man who loves his life will lose it, while the man who hates his life *in this world* will keep it for eternal life" (Jn. 12:24–25, emphasis added). Indeed, only a person who hates the self-serving lifestyles we inherit from life in this world can live forever, because keeping that lifestyle is incompatible with eternal life. The kernel must die and become nothing before it can grow and bear fruit. The message of the Laver is analogous to that of John the Baptist. Confession opens the door to humility that produces genuine meekness. It is the beginning of God's cleansing of the old self through baptism of water.

Many who end up in the grave before the return of the Lord will be saved, as was Abraham, "on credit" (Rom. 4:3–5). However, as long as God's kingdom of priests is not present on earth, no proof will have been presented before the universe that humans can become a faithful kingdom of priests. As long as this does not happen, God's disposition of heart cannot be vindicated by His created beings. Before the return of the Lord some humans must demonstrate to the universe that it is possible to be transformed back into the image of God. As John the Baptist indicated, the baptism of fire and Holy Spirit had yet to come, but he did not say when it would. Jesus gave a hint when He said that the spirit of truth would someday guide us into all truth (Jn. 16:13). In the same passage Jesus made it clear that He would first return to the Father. The expressions He uses to talk about those end time events are strikingly similar to the words He uttered in this third Beatitude: "I tell you the truth," He said, "you will weep and mourn while the world rejoices. You will grieve, but your grief will turn to joy" (Jn. 16:20). Jesus goes on to say that the grieving will be so intense that it will be similar to the pain of a woman about to give birth. Indeed, these are people who will grieve the fact that Christianity had been so blind for such a long time that it failed to recognize the procedure involved in the new birth. From the context it appears that the principles involved in the new birth will be understood just before the return of Jesus to earth, because only then will the message of Truth be correctly deciphered.

These first three steps represent the sin-stricken patient who has come to realize that he or she is suffering from a terminal disease. The grief that comes with such a discovery is painful to bear. But the patient is willing to accept the temporary death of anesthesia before the heart surgery. The patient has accepted a period of total submission and abandonment into the hands of the Master Surgeon. These are three required steps that must be taken before the least change of heart has begun to take place in terms of growing greater love in the heart. The skillful Surgeon must still perform the surgery that will require the patient to bleed. But this is no ordinary surgery. The complete redo from head to toes requires a period of rehabilitation. The remission of the disease continues over the rest of a lifetime. The daily rehabilitation efforts will slowly produce a total re-creation of the sinner into the image of the Creator (see Col. 3:8–10). Since the Creator is infinite, the growth of love never ends.

From this point forward a sinner's life is no longer focused on survival but on the need to grow ever-greater love. Out of the hands of God the former sinner is progressively rehabilitated to a life focused on serving others at any cost. The kernel has died in the ground and a life of love born out of humility and meekness is about to burgeon. God's forgiveness was not granted because of the change, but it made the change possible. Thanks to God's unconditional forgiveness the sinner accepts the required surgery of heart. There are no conditions to receive God's forgiveness, but there are conditions involved in accepting to be transformed. The transformation is salvation, eternal life the reward.

All the enemies of Jesus were forgiven at the Cross but not all of them will necessarily be saved. The only reason some will not be saved is because humility that produces meekness was rejected, though meekness was right there, visible for all to see, bleeding, naked, and dying on a Cross. Let us remember that it was not Cain's gift that God rejected, it was Cain himself (Gen. 4:7). He was rejected because he rejected the humility and grief required for a heart to be changed, not because God was unwilling to forgive him. It is true that Cain's choice of gift was a clear expression of his arrogance. Indeed, he practiced a worthless ritual. Nothing in his ritual expressed the willingness to shed his own blood for the sake of serving others in love all the way to the death. Cain failed to recognize that the growth of love in a sinner's heart is thwarted only by a lack of humility—it closed the door to meekness that sprouts love and he proved it by killing his brother.

The Fourth Beatitude

"Blessed are those who hunger and thirst for righteousness, for they will be filled" (Mt. 5:6). Why not say: "Consider the potential of those who hunger and thirst with desire to become loving, for they will grow in uprightness."

The author's translation might be a little surprising. However, righteousness is love; the word "love" is just as fitting, if not more so. Protestantism was propelled into existence when a few sincere church leaders became aware that unscriptural traditions had insidiously infiltrated the belief system of the self-proclaimed official Christian church. Their concerns for questioning the tenets of the church earned them the infamous label of "heretics." The objections, trials, and persecutions they endured did not dissuade them from pursuing their mission. Their goal was to rid theology of unscriptural dogmas.

Unfortunately the violent clashes and harassments they endured slowed their work, and eventually the Reformation came to a halt. A few revivals attempted to rekindle the fire of protest; some were positive while others contributed only greater confusion. Much remains to be done. The object of this book is to expose some of the most fundamental dogmas of Christianity this author considers unscriptural to this day. Shaking off the dust of superstitions and mystical interpretations lacking logic is no easy task. When Jesus advised some disciples to "shake off the dust that is on your feet" (Mk. 6:11), He never intended that they should reject people because of their belief systems or religion. He remained emphatic in saying: "Love your enemies, do good to those who hate you" (Lk. 6:27). But He also told His disciples to shake off the dust on their feet and move on if their message was rejected.

Unfortunately, a great deal of fairy dust has settled on the message of Jesus over time. Preachers of all Christian religions are guilty of casting a fair amount of this dust on their parishioners. It is a level of mysticism that fails to reflect the true character of God and often casts Him in a negative light. Countless theologians and clerics attempt to validate the dust of pagan origin on scriptural grounds. But the more they do, the more they turn the Word of God into sludge of deceit. As a result churches have gotten bogged down instead of liberated, because only God's pure truth can set sinners free.

Since righteousness cannot exist without the Truth that makes freedom from evil possible, recognizing Truth for what it is in truth has become the most urgent task of last-day Christians. Jesus made it clear, "that very word which I spoke will condemn him at the last day" (Jn. 12:48). God or Jesus will condemn no one, but the Word of Truth that came from God will condemn those who refuse to recognize Truth. The task cannot progress as long as hunger and thirst for Truth continues and Truth continues to be lacking among Christians as long as they remain more dedicated to fairy dust than to the message of Jesus. The idea often preached that God's Truth is unattainable is contrary to the words of Jesus. He made it quite clear that the "Spirit of Truth . . . will guide you into all truth" (Jn. 16:13). To accomplish this goal the sludge of theological deceit responsible for clogging the arteries that bring Truth to the heart of Christianity must be surgically removed. As long as people are deprived of Truth, progress toward righteousness will remain trapped with their genie in the bottle.

In the fourth Beatitude the Greek word *dikaiosune* is probably incorrectly translated "righteousness." This word is translated "justice" in the NLT[31] and other translations with the implication that the sinner is "justified," thus "declared just." In reality, despite the fact that theologians tend to disagree, this word should probably have been translated, "to become just, or righteous" as opposed to "declared just, or righteous." The text would read: "Blessed are those who hunger and thirst to become just (or, those who seek God's way to become just), for they shall become upright." In other words, their hunger for truth will eventually bring them to the Truth that will set them free. Since Truth alone can provide a sure path to freedom, the very freedom we all yearn for will remain unattainable as long as Truth remains hidden beyond the Veil of pagan thinking. There are no shortcuts to becoming righteous; it is entirely dependent on Truth, but all truths, including God's must be established on logic.

When the LXX was translated from Hebrew to Greek in the third century before Christ, the Hebrew word *tsâdaq* was translated *dikaiosune* as we have it in the NT Greek. Daniel used this word when he predicted the cleansing of the sanctuary.[32] While *dikaiosune* implies acquittal for pagan-minded Greeks who had no knowledge of the only true God, I have reasons to believe that this Greek word fails to communicate accurately God's original meaning of the Hebrew *tsâdaq*. Thus the word *dikaiosune* was probably chosen by default, because a Greek equivalent for *tsâdaq* did not exist for good reasons.

The lack of Greek counterpart words follows logic. We must remember that in those days Hebrew was the only language in the world that benefited from the influence of prophets whose instructions came from God. This fact is confirmed in Scripture: "In the past God spoke to our forefathers through the prophets at many times and in various ways" (Heb. 1:1). At the time of Jesus no other religious group could have made that claim.

A careful study of Scripture shows that God's definition of *tsâdaq* fails to correlate with the Greek *dikaiosune*. The original Hebrew meaning should have been explained because the word *dikaiosune* that

---

[31]   New Living Translation. Copyright© 1996, 2004, 2007 by Tyndale House Foundation.

[32]   Daniel 8:14, KJV.

was coined by a pagan culture is totally inadequate to convey a principle from the only true God. We must remember that before Christ all the languages of the world were derived from pagan concepts and customs, with the exception of Hebrew. To translate Hebrew correctly, some Hebrew words would have required explanatory sentences to convey their correct meanings. Unfortunately this might have appeared suspect and condescending toward the Greeks whose language was considered the most advanced in the world at that time. Why should Jews, often considered inferior by Greek standards, have benefited from words nonexistent in other languages? With a lack of clear explanations and definitions, translations of Hebrew into other languages could only betray God's intended meaning. Scripture makes it clear throughout, that the word *dikaiosune* here translated "righteousness" implies "becoming just," as does *tsâdaq,* not "declared just or acquitted." In God's sight righteousness is never a pronouncement of acquittal; it is always the sinner's recognition that transformation of heart is required to overcome sin by becoming more loving.

It is true that God considers righteous even those who still commit sin so long as they recognize their need to progress on the path to righteousness, which is the path to ever-greater love. They may fail to reach the fullness of righteousness before dying, but as long as they are on God's path they are growing and they are considered righteous—just like a plant is perfect at every stage of its development. If aware and persuaded of the Truth that heals, sinners continue to manifest a failure to progress it can only be because they have chosen to reject Truth. By so doing they are committing the sin against the Holy Spirit. They are rejecting the spirit or mind-set that makes a person grow in love that God calls holiness. Jesus made that clear from the Cross when He said: "Forgive them, for they know not what they do." It is because their perception of God's Truth was corrupted, thus false, that they murdered a perfectly innocent man. Had they known and accepted the Truth as God intended it to be understood they could not have done such a thing. In fact, many did not participate, but there were no public outcry of protest when they were about to crucify Him while favoring the release and acquittal of Barabbas.

Jews and Gentiles at Calvary were all acting according to the way they were conditioned to act. Though they knew of God they had no practical knowledge of Him in Truth. Their understanding of religion was essentially mystical. Those who claimed to know God only knew the falsehoods propagated about God by Temple leaders who had been misguided for centuries. By contrast with ancient Hebrew culture,[33] when Moses could talk with God, Greeks, Roman, and other pagan cultures considered their gods vindictive, which led them to develop rules and rituals designed to appease them. The fact that Jesus, a mere human, dared called Himself Son of God was an affront and an insult to them, especially considering the message He taught. Appeasement or propitiation was for them the only way to "earn" divine favors, yet Jesus is not reported to have offered any sacrificial offerings in their Temple. Gentiles had to propitiate with gifts offered to their tyrannical gods to circumvent calamities, punishments, and to earn their favors. They knew no other way to deal with their gods. But their attitudes toward their gods had also become that of the Jews at the time of Jesus.

All known ancient cultures and languages were founded on pagan views of their gods. They entertained relationships with these gods that were wholly incompatible with the way the only true God wants to interact with His children. Contrary to the gods of pagans the true God never requires payments or offerings of appeasement to forgive misconduct or to rescue sinners eager to overcome evil. The prophet Jeremiah made that point very clear when he wrote: "For I spake not unto your fathers, nor commanded them in the day that I brought them out of the land of Egypt, concerning burnt offerings or sacrifices: But this thing commanded I them, saying, Obey my voice, and I will be your God and ye shall be my people . . . But they hearkened not, nor inclined their ear, but walked in the counsels and in the imagination of their evil heart, and went backward, and not forward" (Jer. 7:22–24 KJV).[34] The LXX appears to imply even more implicitly that God wanted no part at all of slaughtered burned offerings. What then did the true God want?

The answer is found in the Old Testament as well as the New. In the dialogue between Jesus and a teacher of the law Jesus quoted the Old Testament. Here is the account from the Gospel of Mark 12:28–34 in the NIV:

---

[33] We are not talking about the Jewish culture as it was at the time of Christ. That culture was already highly paganized, as Jesus affirmed in words and actions when twice He cleansed the Temple of Jerusalem.

[34] Some translations, such as the NIV, cannot be trusted with this text. The RSV and KJV are acceptable.

28 One of the teachers of the law came and heard them debating. Noticing that Jesus had given them a good answer, he asked him, "Of all the commandments, which is the most important?"

29 "The most important one," answered Jesus, "is this: 'Hear, O Israel: The Lord our God, the Lord is one. 30 Love the Lord your God with all your heart and with all your soul and with all your mind and with all your strength.' 31 The second is this: 'Love your neighbor as yourself.' There is no commandment greater than these."

32 "Well said, teacher," the man replied. "You are right in saying that God is one and there is no other but him. 33 To love him with all your heart, with all your understanding and with all your strength, and to love your neighbor as yourself is more important than all burnt offerings and sacrifices."

34 When Jesus saw that he had answered wisely, he said to him, "You are not far from the kingdom of God." And from then on no one dared ask him any more questions.

In this dialogue, Jesus was quoting Deuteronomy 6:4, 5 and Leviticus 19:18. It is clear that even the teacher of the law considered the sacrificial services of secondary importance. Since love is given prime importance in this account one could ask, why were the sacrificial offerings given so much consideration at the Temple, and why was so little said about love while mercy was considered counterproductive? This teacher of the law appears to have been on to something very important: if love is most important, could it be that the rituals were also intended to teach something important about God's kind of love?

Indeed, true religion should concern itself exclusively with teaching people how they can grow God's kind of love in their hearts. It should be entirely about the love of God and how His kind of love should also become the love of humans for one another. Unfortunately the rituals had lost their intended meanings. They were no longer teaching love; they were teaching a message that painted God as demanding, controlling, and unwilling to forgive unless gifts of bloody animals were presented to Him. The teachings conveyed by their sacrifices could do nothing to portray God as loving, nor the way to foster love capable of mercy toward neighbors. If God is the model of love the message of their rituals could only convey that God is all about control and that to be like Him humans had to be likewise forceful and demanding of those who broke His laws. With a false perception of God comes a false perception of love, and the meaning of true love is lost. This was the dilemma of humanity at the time of Jesus, as it is once again the dilemma of Christianity today.

God wanted the people to listen to Him for answers to the problem of evil, but it was difficult for them to hear His message in Truth. The lambs slaughtered on altars were not intended to be sacrificial offerings of appeasement; they were supposed to be educational in nature to help sinners draw closer to God. Likewise, the death of Jesus on the Cross was not a sacrificial offering to satisfy God's anger against sinners; it was a statement made about love on behalf of God to draw humans closer to Himself. As Paul said it so well, it is not the Cross that represents the power of God, it is the message of the Cross, because it draws sinners closer to God and the correct understanding of love (1 Cor. 1:18). Jesus said: "But I, when I am lifted up from the earth, will draw all men to myself." Being God, He was drawing all men to God when He showed them that love is unconditional and boundless. Only death can put an end to love.

Jesus offered Himself in sacrifice to teach humanity what love is, how to love, and how much we should all be tutored by God to love. We say that He offered Himself because unlike any of us He could have come down from the Cross. He proved it when He resurrected Lazarus. Indeed, He demonstrated that the kind of love that comes from God goes all the way to that last drop of blood and the last breath of life. When properly understood, the slaughter ritual God originally instituted contained this very message of salvation for sinners, but it became so corrupted that it no longer provided sinners with a correct understanding of the word love. Since the message the rituals were to convey failed, Jesus came to bring us the intended message in Person. The rituals were not intended as payments or offerings to God for sins. These were pagan interpretations.

Unfortunately the pagan interpretations prevailed and are responsible for leading both Jews and Christians astray. Christians distorted the meaning of the Cross by comparing its message to the falsified understanding of the sacrificial system, as Jews understood it incorrectly at the time of Jesus. From that time forward it became increasingly difficult to understand why Jesus came to this world. The false theology of the Cross destroyed God's intended message, thus it took people away from a message intended to grow love in a sinner's heart.

The new birth is all about accepting a new disposition of heart. It is the growth of love that enables "righteousness" understood as: "becoming increasingly more just." Scripture sometimes calls this process the "remission of sin." Unfortunately the concept of remission is all too rare in our translations of Scripture. The word "remission" is found primarily in the KJV rendition of the New Testament because of Tyndale's influence. It is regrettable that the word "remission" has often been translated "forgiveness" in modern versions of Scripture. This substitution is a corruption of God's intended message.

To illustrate our point, let us consider a well-known statement from the author of Hebrews who writes: "Almost all things are by the law purged with blood; and without shedding of blood is no remission" (Heb. 9:22 KJV). Since the NIV substitutes "remission" with the word "forgiveness," it invites an interpretation implying that the bloodshed on the altar or on the Cross was a payment made to obtain God's acquittal. Instead, God wanted people to understand that sins confessed before slaughtering the animal are responsible for all deaths. Additionally, the victim on the altar represented what the sinner deserved because of his or her own sins: death. The sinner was conveying his or her willingness to shed his or her own blood for the sake of love, because the remission of the sin disease is possible no other way.

The message of the slaughter ritual was no different than the message of baptism—indeed, God does not change. Both are a symbol of the sinner's willingness to end the former self-centered life in order to open the way for the development of a new nature. The author of Hebrews confirms this interpretation a bit further in the text: "In your struggle against sin, you have not yet resisted to the point of shedding your blood" (Heb. 12:4). We could understand the text to say: "In your struggle to grow love that you might avoid sin, you have not yet accepted your own blood to be shed if necessary." Clearly, the author of Hebrews focuses on the importance of healing the sin disease in this context, not its forgiveness or acquittal.

In pagan Greek culture the word *dikaiosune* was always intended to mean "legally justified." Since their legal systems are the only tools pagans possess to control human behavior, they are entirely dependent on the applications of rules and penalties adjudicated by magistrates. Unlike the Hebrews, pagan cultures did not have access to a process designed to help sinners reduce and overcome misconduct on the basis of a persuasion coming from God. They did not possess a divine message or religion designed to convey a transformative persuasion. By contrast the Hebrew word *tsâdaq* implied the idea of "becoming increasingly more just" through a change of heart that involves the voluntary gift of self to fellow humans, not a gift intended to appease God. It is unfortunate that by and large Christianity has failed to recognize this vital difference between God's intended approach to evil and that of pagans.

The late Thomas F. Torrance, a leading twentieth-century Scottish theologian, made an interesting observation, but I agree with his observation only in part. Here is what he wrote: "*Dikaiosune* goes back mainly to the Old Testament *tsedeq* and *tsedaqah*. In the Septuagint, *tsedeq* is rendered by *dikaiosune* 81 times and *tsedaqah* by *dikaiosune* 134 times, but *tsedaqah* is the word for the positive act of righteous mercy, meaning succor, help, and therefore is often translated as *eleemosune* to be a positive act of divine deliverance in mercy and truth, as in the Old Testament expressions."[35] If we can appreciate the information related to the translations of the Hebrew words *tsedeq*, it is regrettable that some translations have included the Greek word *eleemosune* to reinforce the false notion that God's acquittal saves sinners. Clearly, the Hebrew word *tsedeq* was meant to imply that by coming close to God and His mind-set, sinners are given the opportunity to know God and to become increasingly more righteous and merciful. It is not just a relationship with God Christians should entertain; it is a oneness of mind that could be called a oneness of spirit. It is literally the *atonement* of coming "at one" with God. This at-one-ment, a word coined by William Tyndale, is the required event that makes possible the re-creation of humans in the image of God. It is for this reason that Jesus could say: "Be merciful, just as your Father is merciful" (Lk. 6:35), implying a perfect oneness of mind and purpose, not a mere relationship. Everything in the sanctuary was designed to accomplish this lofty purpose, as later did the Cross.

The above paragraphs suggest that translators of Scripture are often subjected to guesswork. They often lack the appropriate vocabulary as well as the proper understanding of the culture, religion, and mentality of the people whose language they translate. They are often trapped by the limitations of human language. Translators and commentators of

---

[35] Thomas F. Torrance, *Atonement: The Person and Work of Christ*, InterVarsity Press, 2009, Downers Grove, IL. USA. p. 101.

Scripture should always keep in mind that the Children of Israel were the only people on the planet who received information directly from the only true God through prophets until 2,000 years ago. No other nation or religion can make that claim.

The reason Abraham was called to begin a new national and religious identity and mentality was to circumvent the fact that all the nations of the world had completely lost their connection with God as well as the vocabulary to communicate the uniqueness of His nature and ways. Any attempt to use pagan words with their pagan definitions to express information related to God or His message can only lead astray. The fact that through the prophets God communicated a way of life diametrically opposed to that of pagans impacted the usage and meanings of key Hebrew words. The problem is that Israel failed to listen to God. Failure to listen to Him was viewed as rebellion against Him because it involved a rejection of the way of life He suggested to the Israelites. This caused them to revert to pagan definitions of some of their own words.

Moses expressed the importance of listening to God on multiple occasions, but history and the prophets made it clear that Israel and Judah failed to listen. Among others, Isaiah sounded a loud warning call in this regard: "If you resist and rebel, you will be devoured by the sword" (Is. 1:20a). Indeed, the Northern Kingdom of Israel fell under the sword of Neo-Assyrians, and a century later Judah fell under the sword of Babylon. Despite the rebellion of Israel confirmed multiple times by the prophets, a vocabulary all their own had developed over time, but unfortunately, it also mutated under various pagan influences. God's messages had a direct impact on the mental process and vocabulary of early Israelites, but it appears that whenever God's truth might have been recognized, it was short-lived. In fact, it is quite amazing that after four centuries spent in Egypt, the Israelites still had any knowledge of the Hebrew language. It rarely takes more than two generations for immigrants to America to forget their native language. Whatever knowledge of Hebrew the Israelites might have retained must have been minimal at best. This gave God an opportunity to introduce new words with unique meanings in their vocabulary and to assign new meanings to existing words. As a result, the meanings of several distinctively religious Hebrew words are totally incompatible with the vocabulary of other nations.

Unfortunately, as in all languages the meanings of words change over time. As a result of their interactions with pagans, the meanings of many Hebrew words began to convey traditional pagan understandings of life and religion. Thus it stands to reason that the secular vocabulary of Gentiles is not always adequate to convey accurately certain aspects of Israelite Scripture without providing additional background information. Word-for-word or so-called literal translations of Scripture do not work, especially when equivalencies of vocabulary are missing. On the other hand, misguided paraphrasing can sometimes be even more damaging, especially when translators fail to understand God and His message, in truth. Only God's definitions of words and concepts should be acceptable, but this would have been a departure from acceptable protocol, because who has a lexicon from God?

For translations to be accurate one would have to know the God of Israelites as He is, not a paganized perception of who He is. When no word exists to convey accurately God's message in the original language, a new word needs to be coined with its definition. The alternative would be to provide longer explanations whenever such a word from the original language is used, but that could be fastidious.

William Tyndale Coined Words to Fill Some of the Gaps

It is for this reason that William Tyndale coined a number of English words. In fact, William Tyndale is considered the greatest contributor of all time to the English language, even more so than Shakespeare who shares with him the same given name. Most of Tyndale's contributions are related to his work of translating Scripture. When translating the OT into English he soon discovered that a number of Hebrew words and concepts could not be directly translated into English or other pagan-based languages. Among other words he created, he is credited for having coined the word "atonement."

Interestingly, he did not coin that word until he attempted to translate the Old Testament from Hebrew. He had previously translated the NT from Greek, from which text he had not encountered the same difficulties because English and Greek are both pagan languages. Equivalencies appeared to be available in English. However, the intended meanings of some pagan Greek words might have been understood with a different meaning when the early Christianized Jews of the Apostolic Church used these words. This might explain why Christianity flourished first among Jews. They might have recognized that some elements of their own religion had been paganized. To a certain extent, they might have recognized that Hebrew words had been assigned pagan meanings and that Apostolic Christianity had corrected such departures from God's truth. Later in time however, Christianity managed to re-corrupt God's message.

The foregoing should give us substance to understand why Tyndale did not coin some of his new English words until after attempting to translate the Old Testament. Before translating from Hebrew Tyndale freely used such terms as "propitiation" and "justification." But when he attempted to translate from Hebrew he realized that his earlier translations of the NT contained conceptual errors that needed to be corrected. Unfortunately his life was cut short. He was made prisoner because of his beliefs considered highly heretical because they denied some pagan applications to God's messages. He died strangulated while being tied to the stake where he was to be burnt alive along with his most recent manuscripts.

As mentioned, it is not until Tyndale translated the Old Testament that he came to realize that some Hebrew words had no Greek or English equivalent. Such was the case of the Hebrew word *korban*. When Tyndale realized that all Temple rituals were called *korban* and that this word literally means, "coming close to," he had to be stunned, considering that he had previously translated all these concepts by such words as, sacrifices, offerings, or sacrificial offerings. Indeed, contrary to his former belief, the rituals of the Temple were never intended to be offerings, much less offerings of propitiation to please God by giving Him slaughtered lambs or bulls. These *korbanot* (Hebrew plural of *korban*) were to be understood as meaningful learning exercises designed to bring humans closer to God and thus to one another. Tyndale had to study the word extensively before realizing that none of the rituals were meant to be offerings of propitiation despite the fact that Judaism had considered them as such for centuries. The Temple rituals were never intended to appease God; they were *only* intended to draw sinners closer to Him. With this realization Tyndale probably attempted to find a word suitable to convey a religious notion that existed nowhere else in the pagan world. The reason such a word was missing is relatively simple to explain. Because pagans perceived their gods as demanding disciplinarians unwilling to be approached by mere sinful humans, they supposedly wanted gifts, just as Cain attempted to offer gifts to God. The gods were supposedly insistent on being offered a plethora of slaughtered animals and sometimes human beings in exchange for forgiveness and blessings.

Since there were no words in pagan cultures to express the desire of their gods to be approached and consulted to show humans how to become more loving in character, Tyndale had to invent a new word. Considering the professed character of demanding and eager-to-punish pagan gods, who would nurture the desire to become more like them? There was no vocabulary in pagan languages to express the concept because no one would have nurtured the desire to become like them; humans are bad enough. They were perceived as tyrants, not loving and long-suffering or merciful. Tyndale faced a dilemma because the words propitiation and expiation both imply offerings made to appease these horrific gods to obtain their mercy. Thus he was left with no other choice than to coin a new word.

It is true that Tyndale probably considered the possibility of using the word "reconciliation" which he had already used when translating the NT. He must not have been satisfied with the meaning of that word however, or it would not have been necessary for him to coin the word "atonement." The likely reason the word "reconciliation" was not suitable is because it implies that an attempt is made to rekindle a broken relationship. But Tyndale may have understood that sinners are born flawed, lacking at birth both the knowledge of what love is, and the knowledge that coming close to God is the only way to repair the damages of evil upon the human heart. Thus a nonexisting relationship with God could not be rekindled; it was not existent therefore it needed to be established. One cannot be reconciled with a person with whom there never was a relationship, as it is the case for all naturally born human beings in need of new birth. The new birth requires a growing knowledge of God and the understanding that unlike the pagan gods He goes out of His way to contact humans to teach them the nature and importance of true love.

Baptism is the new birth ritual that implies a commitment of the sinner to "come close" (*korban*) to God. Not unlike the rituals of the Temple, baptism is a *korban*, as are the rituals related to the Last Supper. They are rituals designed to bring humans and God ever closer to one another through meaningful educational rituals. They involve recognizing that we must abandon the mind-set of our birth and accept a new mind-set that God teaches us through His rituals as through the gift Jesus made of His life to humans, for the sake of their education. They open the door to a new way of life that involves a sincere devotion to the welfare and well-being of others. The egocentric instincts we all inherit from birth are counterproductive in terms of relationships, thus they must be given up. As we have said multiple times, God does not change, and His way to salvation has always been the same: It is the restoration of the character of humans to the image of God. The only problem is that humans have repeatedly corrupted the meanings of rituals that were intended to educate, not to subject them to the will of an authoritarian arbitrary God. A false understanding of the rituals keeps people from coming ever closer to God and one another—thus the atonement is thwarted.

Since the words "propitiation," "expiation," and "reconciliation" did not fit Tyndale's intended meaning gleaned from translating Hebrew texts he chose to coin a new word. He called it: *Atonement*. Breaking up this word gives us *at-one-ment*. The suffix "ment" comes from the French. This suffix implies a continuity of fact. Most English words ending with this suffix come from the French language, with the exception of the word "atonement." Such words as govern-ment imply the continuing reality of governing. Likewise, at-one-ment implies the continuing reality of coming ever closer, or "at one" with God and fellow humans.

Unfortunately, it is difficult to explain why, with the passing of time, the word Tyndale coined for a very good reason reverted to a meaning no different than propitiation and expiation. Today we use Tyndale's word incorrectly when we say for example, "It is time for him to atone for his mistake." In this case "atone" implies making someone pay for mistakes by doing penances or payments, not at all the usage Tyndale had in mind for this word. When today we say that Jesus died to atone for our sins, we are in fact saying that He died as a propitiation offering to appease God. Tyndale would turn in his grave if he could hear such usage of a word he coined for a very specific purpose. When we say that Jesus died to atone for our sins with Tyndale's understanding of the word we should recognize that He died *to bring us closer to God's and His character,* by developing love that eradicates sin. To accomplish God's purpose, the process involves the practice of several *korbanot*, or rituals with specific meanings. Coming close to God, or *korban*, is accepting the only methodology available to grow His kind of love in the human heart.

It is often because they examine God's intended meaning of Hebrew words through tradition that exegetes and translators tend to bring confusion to their interpretations of sacred texts. By failing to consider God's own definition of words they assign incompatible secular meanings to Hebrew concepts of divine origin. All the languages of our world are by-products of people's religions, mores, traditions, and philosophies of life. To make matters even more confusing, over time Jews have had a tendency to assign secular pagan meanings to their own ancient Hebrew words.

In any pagan or secular setting the only way a person can be justified is by pronouncing that person justified through a process of acquittal in the face of accusation for wrongdoing. In pagan and most other religious settings, acquittal is obtainable through series of propitiatory offerings, penalties, or penances. God's approach to correct evil behavior is not only incompatible with the judicial approach of humans, but it also teaches the exact opposite. God requires absolutely no offering, penance, or penalty whatsoever. He only requires sinners to recognize the obvious: that the only reason they hurt people is because they lack love. Thus the only way to remedy the situation is to seek God's method to increase love in the heart to become increasingly more just. Justice for humans is to get even, but for God it is to become just. As we said, salvation is the restoration of the image of God in humans. Jesus called the search for a solution to the problem of evil, "hunger for righteousness." Regardless of a sinner's past experience, when God's method to develop a new heart is accepted, the past becomes irrelevant. Only the sinner's earnest desire to overcome sin by growing love matters to God.

Paul, who was a highly educated Jewish cleric from the school of the Pharisees must have changed his mind about the meaning of the word *dikaiosune.* He had probably encountered it multiple times in his study of the Greek LXX Septuagint of his day. It is clear that before his conversion Paul understood the word *dikaiosune* as did all Hellenized Jews of his time. By the time Jesus manifested Himself in Paul's life experience, the general understanding of Judaism was that God required burnt offerings for sinners to be forgiven and saved. He had probably offered many such sacrificial offerings. The Jewish approach to religion and salvation was mostly founded on rituals that could do little or nothing to change sinner's hearts because they had become meaningless.

Paul's conversion had to involve a radical change in his understanding of salvation. His interpretation of the LXX Old Testament, the Scripture available at the time, must have changed dramatically following the enlightenment he received from God on his way to Damascus and shortly thereafter. Not a single book of the New Testament was yet in existence when his transformation took place. His life-changing encounter with God, his *korban* one might say, along with newly acquired knowledge of Jesus Christ helped him to recognize that the Old Testament should be read in a different light. Considering that Paul's religious education came from Pharisees, known to be the most conservative branch of Judaism, and that he had an excellent knowledge of Scripture, the only thing he could have been missing was *a correct interpretation* of God's Word.

Considering the disapproval Jesus expressed about Judaism, it appears obvious that over time the Hebrew word *tsedeq* was assigned the same meaning as the secular Greek word *dikaiosune*. Instead of meaning "becoming more just" it was understood as a divine pronouncement that the sinner was acquitted thanks to the practice of offering rituals. The shift in meaning had obviously taken place sometime in history, a question best left for expert philologists and historians to answer. But it is entirely possible that the translators of the LXX in the third century BCE had already lost the correct meaning of the Hebrew word *tsedeq*. Not only had the Jewish nation and its religion been Hellenized for well over three centuries, but other pagan nations had strongly influenced various aspects of Jewish theology long before that time. Considering Nehemiah's report in the fifth century BCE that the Jews had lost respect for their religion and their Temple, it is more than likely that two centuries later the translators of the LXX had already lost God's intended meaning of the word *tsedeq*. In fact, the change could have taken place long before, perhaps already in the days of the Judges, shortly after the Exodus, if not during the Exodus.

We know that five centuries after the Exodus David still had at least some understanding of God's intended meaning when he wrote: "You do not delight in sacrifice, or I would bring it; you do not take pleasure in burnt offerings. The sacrifices of God are a broken spirit; a broken and contrite heart, O God, you will not despise." (Ps. 51:16, 17a). What is certain is that at some point in time the Children of Israel began to regard their rituals involving slaughters of animals as offerings of appeasement and acquittal, not the *korban* or "atonement" they were designed to produce in the hearts of sinners. As a result, slaughters that should have taken place once or twice in a person's life were overdone out of fear and overzealous piety, not from a sincere desire to *come close* to God or His mindset. This view can be verified by the message God later gave Jeremiah the Prophet. As discussed earlier in this section, God never intended these sacrifices to become offerings, much less a way to appease Him through propitiatory gifts. Only a false knowledge of God could allow such a conclusion.

Jesus came primarily to correct a false understanding of *korban*

It is primarily for this reason that Jesus had to come from heaven to set the record straight. As long as people could be made to believe that offerings of slaughtered animals were gifts to appease God, it was no longer possible for them to know God in Truth. Jesus came to restate the Truth as it was originally intended to be understood, but this time He would restate His Truth so perfectly that the purpose would be accomplished "once for all." Jesus knew that He would die in the process, but the price of His life would not deter Him from God's ultimate mission. All other avenues had been attempted but failed only because humans failed to listen to God who had spoken through the prophets. Having corrupted the meaning of the word *tsedeq*, the Children of Israel had lost the meaning of the most important word and concept of their religious vocabulary and creed. Under the circumstances God's Truth was irretrievable and humanity would have been lost sooner or later. It is for that reason that Jesus had to come and had to teach what love is, how to love, and how much to love in words and deeds that would take Him all the way to the Cross.

God has always wanted sinners to become "more just" thanks to a process that motivates them to become increasingly more other-centered. All other cultures of the world were limited to dealing with social issues forensically, on legal grounds. They had two legal choices: 1) the administration of penalties to punish criminals, or 2) a pronouncement of acquittal because criminality could not be proven, or through governmental mercy. Pagans assumed that their gods practiced the same human style of justice. Jesus came to correct the pagan concept that Jews had come to worship in their Temple with the assumption that the legal system came from God. No wonder Jesus called the Temple a den of thieves. They were merchandizing salvation at the expense of sinners instead of showing them God's ordained way to grow love, which in the end, would have probably brought far more Temple riches.

Paul's fellow Jews believed that their sins were acquitted by offering sacrifices to their God. It is precisely to correct this flawed perception of how salvation is obtained that Jesus came. He made it very clear that no payment of any kind would ever be necessary to open the door to salvation. God's forgiveness and prescription to overcome sin are free, but God cannot force anyone to accept the prescription. Since the prescription is not a command to do anything, it is not a matter of obeying laws; it is a matter of accepting to think a certain way only because it is logical to think that way. What God requires is the knowledge of the correct prescription, because only the correct formula and procedure can be persuasive enough to change sinners' hearts. In God's vocabulary, becoming just is a matter of becoming increasingly more blameless because true love is growing in sinners' hearts and minds. Such was the original meaning of the word *tsedeq*. This word was never intended in the least to imply any level of penalization or acquittal for the sake of a human style of justice, as does the Greek word *dikaiosune*.

It is clear that before Saul (meaning: prayed for) of Tarsus began to be known as Paul (meaning: small), he was persecuting Christians because of their unacceptable outlook on salvation. It totally betrayed the Pharisaic approach that required sacrificial offerings. In fact, after his conversion, Paul was compelled to teach a message diametrically opposed to the message he had been trained to convey. He understood that sinners must become increasingly more just to be saved and that mere offering rituals would never accomplish God's purpose in this regard. He also understood that subjecting oneself to keep laws does not make a sinner better and that no sacrificial gift made to God could bring pardon or acquittal. He championed the idea that sinners are not under a forensic judicial system because they are under God's grace (see Rom. 6:14). To him, the grace of God is knowing God's Truth, because it is both empowering and transformative. He understood that God's pardon is never in question and that only the transformation of a sinner's heart to become more loving can bring about a resolution of the human condition. He defended the triviality of ritualistic circumcision and other rituals because only a clear understanding of God's intended symbolism contained in these rituals was important. But he understood that their corrupted ritualized interpretation was of no effect. The message of the circumcision ritual was not a mark of belonging to a given nation or race; it originally involved the idea of humility similar to that of a contrite heart willing to bleed if necessary to live God's kind of love all the way to the death (Rom. 2:25–29). Indeed Paul said: "For in Christ Jesus neither circumcision nor uncircumcision has any value. The only thing that counts is faith (or persuasion) expressing itself through love." (Gal. 5:6, parenthesis mine).

Sinners must recognize, as did Paul, that true salvation is about accepting God's Truth because it provides the only correct mental undergirding and procedure to overcome sin God has ever prescribed. Scripture calls the recognition and acceptance of this simple procedure, the Truth. This Truth is so powerful that it motivates all the positive changes in people's lives, even when they fail to recognize that the principle involved comes from God. Considering that Paul's teachings were entirely based on Old Testament Scripture and the testimonies of Disciples who knew no other Scripture, we are led to recognize that existing Scripture contained all the necessary Truth entrusted to the care of Israel. Jesus came to rectify the errors of a corrupted message that no longer qualified as Truth; therefore it could no longer save humans.

The New Testament did not begin to surface until decades later, though a few writings may have been known. The Four Gospels and the diffusion of these writings took time and had to overcome huge political and religious obstacles. However, it can be clearly deduced that the Old Testament corrected by Jesus contained all the information Paul needed to preach the message of Truth. Let us remember a key statement of King Solomon regarding this error of understanding: "Acquitting the guilty and condemning the innocent—the LORD detests them both" (Pr. 17:15). If the Lord detests those who acquit the guilty, why should anyone presume that God wanted the innocent Man Jesus to die as payment to acquit the guilty? The fact is that God did not require the death of Jesus to pay for sins, but His death was required to bring to the light of Truth once again the message from God that heals sin. Jesus died for our sins, but not to pay for them. Could God and Jesus be considered guilty of detestable deeds Scripture condemns? The point of this discussion is to recognize that God never intended to acquit the Israelites through their bloody offering rituals any more than He intended to acquit Christians through the bloody death of His incarnated Son.

Paul was fully aware that Truth alone has the power to set sinners free and that it is the only way God can relieve people from the sin problem without abusing their freedom. So persuaded was he that he said: "But thanks be to God that, though you used to be slaves to sin, you wholeheartedly obeyed *the form of teaching to which you were entrusted.*

You have been set free from sin and have become slaves to righteousness" (Rom. 6:17–18, emphasis mine). Here Paul makes it crystal clear that it is not a payment that saves; it is a teaching—in other words, God's unchanging message to humanity.

Through the first four Beatitudes we have recognized that they each represent a stepping-stone on God's path to righteousness. The first step is the recognition that all humans are contaminated with the sin disease from birth, thus they need the enlightenment to perceive that they are poor in spirit. This is a condition to seek something better and to progress toward the healing of a chronic condition from birth. A sinner must first acknowledge the fact and he or she needs help from the source of life, or healing cannot take place. The second step involves sorrow for past mistakes that leads to a firm decision to deal with the sin problem proactively by accepting God's own prescription for the disease. The third is the recognition that sin is always caused by a lack of love that cannot be cultivated in the absence of genuine meekness or humility. It is the acceptance of the fact that humility is the key to the development of love in the heart. The fourth step brings the realization that since humans are born flawed, sinners need spiritual nutrition that comes from God because no human entity can provide an accurate account of what love is, how it grows in the heart, and how far it should be taken. The newly acquired appetite for love causes sinners to hunger and thirst for divine guidance and knowledge that grows genuine meekness and love in their hearts.

It is regrettable that most of Protestant Christianity has been afraid to consider the possibility that God transforms sinners by motivating them to become righteous by means of a persuasion of which God is Himself the Author. It is probably a pagan understanding of the word "faith" that has led them to believe that righteousness by faith means believing strongly that God declares righteous those who believe that Jesus paid the price of their sins on the Cross. They fail to realize that when a sinner is persuaded by a divine message to become loving, God is still fully "the author and finisher" (Heb. 12:2 KJV) of that person's faith. The change that occurs and the resulting good works are the product of a belief system that comes from God, thus a faith from God.

The Greek word *dikaiosunē,* as did the Hebrew word *tsedeq,* imply a strong commitment to Truth that produces uprightness. Using the upper case "T" when mention is made of God's specific "Truth" is fitting because it is a persuasion that could have come from no other source other than God. When ethics and morality are in question, God's Truth fills all the gaps of understanding. If an action is unconditionally in the best interest of others, how could we possibly fail to fulfill the requirements of good ethics? It is impossible to be unethical or immoral when perfect love governs a person's heart and life. It is only because love fails that humans are confused about ethics and morality, a fact that brings them to legislate morality, not realizing that morality imposed by laws destroys morality that should emanate from the heart. Of course, there are problems for the world with this approach to ethics, because in a world of survival of the fittest the principle is also applied to a family, a clan, a tribe, or a nation. Thus morality implies accepting to go to war or acting with violence for the protection of the group. The problem with this approach is that it can only perpetuate evil, thus it can only fail to break the vicious cycle of hatred and death in the world.

It is for this reason that Jesus said: "The world cannot hate you, but it hates me because I testify that what it does is evil" (Jn. 7:7). Jesus was talking about the mentality imposed on all of us by the inborn mind-set of survival, the very mind-set that must be challenged to break the cycle of evil and death.

When true unconditional love reigns in people's hearts all questions of ethics disappear. With the God principle of life in the heart it is not possible to be judgmental about other people's beliefs and actions. Wrongdoers would be encouraged to recognize love as the only solution, not punishment, penalties, or hurting others in self-defense, all of which perpetuate evil. God's paradigm of life changes people from wanting to live longer self-serving lives to living potentially shorter lives focused on breaking the cycle of death and hatred as did Jesus. But eternal life awaits those who love regardless of how short their life on earth might be. Paul shows that he understood this reality when he wrote: "Do not repay anyone evil for evil" (Rom. 12:17). Peter echoes the same message: "Do not repay evil with evil or insult with insult, but with blessing, because to this you were called so that you may inherit a blessing" (1 Pet. 3:9). Clearly, to repay evil accomplishes nothing; it only prolongs and expands the agony of evil for planet Earth and the universe. God's judgment is entirely about love and lack thereof. One difference must be noted however. God knows the hearts; therefore He knows whom He should bring into His kingdom.

With love we might live a shorter life on earth, but eternal life is guaranteed. With lack of love life on earth might well be prolonged, but it is a way of life "that leads to death" (Pr. 14:12; Rom. 6:16). In fact, it is the "abomination that causes desolation" (Mt. 24:15). The final desolation of the world will be the natural outcome of lack of love, not a punishment that God imposes on those who fail to love Him. The same has to be true of the desolation of the universe; lack of God's kind of love will cause the destruction of the universe. A literal translation of a passage in Ezekiel would read: "A fire from your midst will devour you and will turn you to ashes upon the ground" (Ez. 28:18). God does not punish evil; evil punishes evil by its consequences.

The world is overwhelmed with good actions lacking love. Such actions are not only deceptive, but they also serve to confuse both givers and beneficiaries. Good deeds lacking love are manipulative, and they can only serve to perpetuate opportunism, not love. It is not the right of any human to judge actions to determine if they are the product of love or opportunism. But certainly, it is documented that people have been fed religious food intended to fatten them spiritually like cattle prepared for the slaughter. The only hope for humanity is to recognize true love as the product of God's Truth that brings change of heart inclined to righteousness out of love. This is the only kind of justice God knows. It is designed to make people more loving and thus increasingly more just. It is not God that will judge the world; the Truth will bring judgment. Those who refuse to accept God's love in their hearts will end up on the side of those who will suffer the consequences of evil. As John said, "Whoever does not love does not know God, because God is love" (1 Jn. 4:8). God need not judge anyone because His Truth brings love, and the rejection of Truth brings indifference, hatred, and ultimately, death. Since humans cannot read hearts, God alone can read the motivations of people's hearts and decide to what degree they are inclined to accept Truth that leads to love. God does not have to judge because He already knows the hearts. In other words, it is God's system of operation for the universe that does both the judging of those who manifestly reject it and the creation of love in the hearts of those who accept His Everlasting Gospel of Truth. The only viable solution to the problem of evil is to sit at God's table of knowledge and to partake freely of His "bread of life" (Jn. 6:48) and His "water of life" (Rev. 22:17).

Only sincere conversion can bring a person to genuinely "hunger and thirst" for the Truth that leads to righteousness. God's prescription must be recognized as the power of God that grows love in a sinner's heart, or who would bother to willfully accept the redemption it procures? With a sincere desire for a change of heart manifested by a sincere confession of guilt for lacking love at the Altar, the desire to cleanse the old self of its self-centeredness is confirmed at the Laver where the hands and feet of former deeds are washed away. From this point forward the sin disease will be set in remission if the sinner continues the journey through the sanctuary. Like a patient whose disease is in remission after a prolonged illness, the sinner's appetite for wholesome spiritual food begins to grow. Increased appetite is often the best sign that the remission of a physical disease is taking place. Jesus called it the "hunger and thirst for righteousness." Righteousness is not what we do; it is how we think. The only way to change how we think is to eat the "bread of life." "Then Jesus declared, 'I am the bread of life. He who comes to me will never go hungry (spiritually), and he who believes in(to) me will never be thirsty (for water of life)" (Jn. 6:35, parentheses added).

The hunger Jesus talks about was represented in the Sanctuary by the showbread that was placed on the table in the Holy Place. That table represents the learning that must take place from God's Word of Truth. The more a person learns from God about His system of love with a contrite heart, the more insatiable the sinner becomes for Truth. In fact, the sinner's greatest desire is to live permanently in the Holy Place of life, as did the high priest for several days before The Day of Atonement—the Day of Coming-At-One with God and fellow humans. Some consider that this day represented the day of God's Judgment. In a way it did, but it is not God who does the judging, it is the Word of God that separates people into two camps depending on their willingness to come at-one, or not. In the Holy Place sinners receive the bread at the light that shines from the Seven Branch Chandelier, the Word that later came to the world in human flesh (Jn. 1:14). Though God always provided the necessary light to understand His Word, Jesus is that final beacon of light that opens the heart to true wisdom and understanding. Love that grows thanks to the Word of Truth that comes from God makes it clear that sinners do not change on their own, but only thanks to God.

Because humans failed to recognize or accept God's everlasting Truth despite 2,000 years of communications through the prophets,[36] Jesus Himself came to correct the problems related to the way humans

---

[36] The period from Abraham to Jesus represents about two thousand years.

understood His Truth (see Heb. 1:1–2). He is the Seven Branch Chandelier made of solid gold in the Holy Place of the Sanctuary. He is the One who enlightens the mind of sinners that they might begin to comprehend the Mind of God, as it should always have been understood. Jesus brought all the light necessary to educate all willing sinners for the priesthood. These are converted people willing to carry the torch of Truth to the four corners of God's Heaven-bound Temple on Earth. The requirements for becoming priests are completed only when the journey outlined by the Beatitudes is fully completed. But we are only at the beginning of the learning process involving the cleansing process. The symbolism has changed, but not the message. Three more steps are required to complete the journey. Let us remember that when the Children of Israel first entered the desert of Exodus, God communicated a very important precondition to become priests: "If you listen to my voice, you will become for me a kingdom of Priests" (Ex. 19:6, translated from the LXX).

This ancient prophecy dating back to Moses stating that God is preparing a kingdom of priests is not yet fulfilled. Thankful for the priceless discovery of God's Truth that was made unambiguously possible when Jesus brought it to light once again in human flesh, sinners are now in a position to enjoy a new level of at-one-ment with God. They become one of His priests, not through a mere relationship of friendship with whom we may disagree, but through a clear understanding of His message they fully approve and endorse. It is from the Altar of Incense also located in the Holy Place that the Word of Truth brings the "pleasing aroma" to God. This is the aroma of a sinner in remission, healing from the sin disease.[37] Could there possibly be a sweeter fragrance than the fragrance of love that grows in sinners' hearts to produce perfect rest and freedom that everlasting love makes possible? The perfume of righteousness ascends to God and spreads its fragrance well beyond the Holy Place. The pleasing restful aroma of sinners' hearts in mutation prepares them for the long awaited "at-one-ment" of humans coming close to God and one another. Indeed, true atonement is the hand of God at work in the sinner's heart

---

[37] It should be noted that in the original Hebrew, the word translated "pleasing" in Genesis 8:21 is the word *niykho-akh*, which means "restful." It may not have been pleasing to God because of its smell but because it symbolized people seeking God's rest, which implies healing from their separation from God.

to heal it and return it to the image of His own likeness (Gen. 1:26) as it once was. Through this process God's ways are literally taking residence in the heart, but the process is not yet completed. The scent of God's atoning work also spreads throughout the camp. Other sinners enjoying its fragrance are inspired to embark on their own journey with God in a quest that will take them to the throne of His mercy.

The Fifth Beatitude

"Blessed are the merciful, for they will be shown mercy" (Mt. 5:7). Again, we could say: "Consider the potential of those who become merciful, for they will be shown the true meaning of mercy."

It is only by changing the polarity of their hearts and minds that God's Truth has the power to change the lives of sinners. Nothing else needs to be changed, because the new polarity changes everything. The polarity from birth on serving self is evil because such a person cannot be trusted unconditionally. It is the focus on self that must be changed to the opposite polarity, a focus entirely dedicated on the welfare and well-being of others. The only way absolute mutual trust can be established is by having a society entirely composed of people whose hearts are unconditionally focused on the welfare and well-being of others before their own. None of us have ever experienced life in such a society. The reason such a society does not exist on planet Earth is because the process to make the change possible has been overlooked, neglected, and even disparaged. For the change to occur, humans must openly and sorrowfully admit that they were born with a heart of which the polarity points toward self. They must admit to themselves that only a new birth can change the polarity of their hearts toward others. They must realize that eternal life is possible no other way. Considering that from birth we are all bent on serving self, we must realize that a place where everyone remains with such a polarity of heart, peace and eternal life will never be possible. People must come to realize that a different persuasion (faith) powerful enough to change the orientation is an absolute necessity. It is thus imperative to demonstrate to the universe that such faith and such a change of polarity of a heart is possible thanks to the Truth that comes from God. When this happens on earth among those who accept God's polarity of heart, God's system of government for the universe will be vindicated at last.

Genesis tells us that we were created in the image of God; thus with His character, no other resemblance is possible. Considering that we *willfully* departed from His character we should also understand that to restore His image in us we must *willfully* begin to reproduce His character here on planet Earth. So far Jesus alone has proven that it is possible to live in the flesh of humans and still manage to live a life with God's polarity of heart.

The change of polarity transforms self-serving hearts into merciful hearts entirely focused on the best interests of others at any cost to self. When love can endure pain with genuine concern and care for others it is called mercy in Scripture. For God mercy is not a matter of forgiving sin; it is about becoming merciful. It is the ultimate level of love because it is love shared against all odds. In our world expressions and displays of love may appear genuine and sometimes they are, but unfortunately love can be simulated. But mercy is never bogus. It is not possible to fake mercy so powerful that even extreme and unfair administration of pain and suffering from enemies is endured with sincere love for them, and sadness for their unloving behavior, as Jesus did. God alone knows when love is genuine, but acts of mercifulness are an open book for everyone to recognize.

Who can know for sure that a sympathy card, a birthday wish, or a kiss is a sincere display of love and affection? Unlike those who simulate expressions of love to manipulate, true mercifulness cannot produce pretend acts of mercy. It is not possible for mercy to be a forgery because love displayed in the face of utter abuse and adversity stands in stark opposition to the natural instincts of human birth. Many humans are willing to die for a cause. But if they accept to risk death to advance a personal, political, or religious agenda while killing or hurting others, their actions cannot be considered acts of love or mercy. In a way, the same could be said of many professions, such as firemen, lifeguards, and police forces. They risk their life because they have accepted the duties and responsibilities of their profession; we are all thankful to them for their dedication and services, but when they suffer death it can be an act of mercy because they refused to kill an enemy, but it can also be done out of duty, not love for enemies.

According to Jesus, the least display of anger is akin to killing someone (see Mt. 5:21 KJV). On the other hand, accepting mistreatments from enemies while lovingly caring for their welfare is the height of unconditional love—it is the mercifulness to which we are all called. Such grace is not possible without accepting the change of heart that comes from adopting God's own modus operandi that denies all impulses to serve self at the expense of others. To display such grace, which is the product of mercy, a human being must accept to abandon all natural instincts of survival in favor of love so genuine that it is powerful enough to produce unfathomable mercy.

Without Jesus who made Himself the "Word," or "expression of God" in human flesh (Jn. 1:14), we would fail to realize that He accepted all the limitations and inadequacies of natural-born humans. Without Him at-one-ment with God would not be possible and the human race would perish. The Message of the Mercy Seat in the Sanctuary would have remained beyond the Veil forevermore. It would have remained a mystery hidden beyond the Veil of human disbelief, false beliefs, and contempt against God. It is only because Jesus was willing to take "the very nature of a servant" (Phil. 2:7) in human flesh "made like his brothers in every way," that He became "a merciful and faithful high priest" (Heb. 2:17). He showed how to live mercy born out of a renewed heart to demonstrate not only that humans can be changed, but also to show us how. He was baptized to demonstrate publicly that He too had to undergo the process of heart repolarization through the new birth.[38]

Mercy is so contrary to the natural human disposition of heart that despite all the help and teachings the disciples of Jesus received they remained incapable of understanding His Message of eternal truth from His words alone. Even His life unto death remained a mystery to them until Pentecost, fifty days after His resurrection. They were compelled to go through the incomprehensible experience of His death and resurrection as well as several visits to explain what happened before they began to understand. The correctness of their enlightenment was confirmed when God sent "tongues of fire" (Acts 2:3) above their heads. This was God's way to let His disciples know that they were finally on the right track. They were finally beginning to understand that the Cross teaches the true meaning of love capable of mercifulness. Previously they had a friendly relationship with Him, but they had failed to connect with Him on the level of His love capable of mercy, which is the only change of heart that really matters to God. The brief visit of Jesus made

---

38   See Chapter 3 of this book.

it possible for humans to access all the Truth necessary to eliminate from their preconceptions the countless false notions about God that kept them from recognizing Truth that heals evil.

God's Message had been fully communicated through the prophets and the sanctuary rituals, but the visit of Jesus lived the teachings of the Sanctuary all the way to His death, as the perfect demonstration of pure mercy. The Cross was the event they needed most, because it helped them to connect the present Truth they had just lived with God's Message of past centuries. By His life unto death Jesus made it possible for mere humans to decipher at last God's intended meanings of former defunct rituals. They could now understand why Jesus said five times in His Sermon on the Mount: "You have heard it said . . . but I tell you" (Mt. 5:21, 27, 33, 38, 43). Jesus was not contradicting previously conveyed Truth; He was rectifying the way it had been falsely interpreted.

For all of fifteen centuries the Children of Israel were looking at a Veil in the Temple thinking that their High Priests were the only ones allowed to enter the Most Holy Place. Little did they remember God's desire to make of every one of them kings and priests that would someday prepare His return. They had thus far totally failed to figure-out a way to fulfill God's intent to establish a kingdom of priests. They did not understand that by becoming priests they would all have to enter the Most Holy Place of God's presence that they might become beacons of light for the entire world to recognize God's way of life. Had God's wish been fulfilled by the Israelites, the Veil and all the rituals of the Temple would have been discontinued because the symbols and practices they represented would have outlived their usefulness. The Children of Israel would have become priests with full access to the Message of the Mercy Seat in Truth rather than in symbol, and the symbols needed to teach Truth would have become obsolete. Instead, they became obsolete because Jesus came to offer a message "greater than the Temple." Indeed, a message so complete and perfect that God would never again have to repeat His teachings.

The unfortunate reality is that although the Veil itself no longer exists in a Jewish Temple, it is still dividing Christianity. It continues to keep away from the presence of God many who yearn to know Him. As long as humans fail to understand the reason for the separation between the Holy and the Most Holy Place they will continue to misunderstand how God is to take residence in their hearts. This does not mean that they are lost, but it does mean that humans are not yet ready to prove to the universe that it is possible for the merciful character of God to reside in human hearts. Only those who are willing to become merciful by providing tangible evidence will open the way for humanity to end their problem with evil on planet Earth. Humans have long been invited to recognize the Message of the Mercy Seat, but thus far they have failed to realize that the Veil remains a symbol of their pagan mind-sets that prevents them from seeing Truth.

It is their pagan minds that kept both Israelites and Christianity from recognizing the importance of becoming merciful, as God is merciful (Lk. 6:36). The Temple Veil only symbolized the pagan mind-set. It was daily sprinkled with the blood of innocent victims to show that as long as humans would fail to recognize the importance of mercifulness the blood of innocent victims would continue to be shed. Jesus emphasized that concept more than once during His ministry on earth. Speaking of Himself He quoted Hosea 6:6 as He attempted to enlighten the Pharisees: "If you had known what these words mean, 'I desire mercy, not sacrifice,' you would not have condemned the innocent" (Mt. 12:7). Since Jesus never sinned, the only reason He went to the Cross was because humans had failed to understand the importance of mercy to the point of killing innocent victims such as Jesus. But God cannot confer upon sinners any level of mercifulness of heart as long as they fail to seek it with genuine yearning. As previously said, God never imposes His will on anyone.

As long as humans fail to recognize the importance of mercy for one another with the sincere desire to live mercy, they will never become merciful. While God has always been boundlessly merciful with humans, we have yet to produce a nation of priests ready to recognize that God is waiting for such a group to demonstrate that understanding the Truth can make people merciful. Humans have failed to apply God's level of mercy to one another despite the call of Jesus to become merciful "as your Father is merciful" (Lk. 6:36). The only reason they have not is because, so far at least, they have failed to recognize the only Truth that empowers a change of heart.

Ever since the departure from God's modus operandi in the Garden of Eden, God has taken humanity by the hand to lead them toward the Truth that saves. He has done everything that could be done to guide them toward the understanding that mercy is the ultimate goal of spiritual life. Jesus was expressing His concern in this regard when He raised a question: "When the Son of Man comes, will he find faith on the earth?" (Lk. 18:8). The faith He was talking about is the persuasion that produces mercy in the hearts of sinners, not an irrational pagan-induced belief that Jesus came to pay for sins.

The symbolic significance of the sculptured cherubim that were set on the cover of the Mercy Seat is not revealed in Scripture. However, considering their posture of reverence over the spot where God manifested Himself in the form of light during the night and a protective cloud during the day, we are led to assume that they were conveying indebtedness, respect, and gratitude toward Him. They recognized that all intelligent free beings should be like God only in that they should become active participants of His boundless mercy, as He manifested it daily toward the Israelites.

Let us remember that the Hebrew word "Satan" means accuser, or adversary. It is one thing to accuse and quite another to accuse with an adversarial attitude. Only those who lack mercy are prone to be adversarial to the point of wanting to destroy their opponents because of their beliefs. It is acceptable to oppose someone's views or beliefs, but it is never acceptable to become adversarial toward a person or group of people. Jesus accused the Pharisees for their hypocrisy, but He treated them with respect born out of love and compassion. He never attempted to hurt them for their misguided beliefs, but He condemned all belief systems responsible for perpetuating evil and death.

The day is coming when the entire universe will recognize that the message of the Most Holy Place involving the Mercy Seat of God is the message Jesus proclaimed by going to the Cross. It is the key to unconditional universal mercy. This ultimate level of love we have called mercy in this book will someday rule the universe. The irony is that when mercy will be demonstrated, mercy will no longer be needed because no one will nurture the least desire to accuse or abuse anyone else. For now, while on earth it is important to demonstrate to the universe that there are humans willing to value love to the point of becoming merciful as was Jesus. Mercy born out of love is the only weapon needed to make the change permanent for the entire universe. As soon as mercy will become reality for some on this planet, the promise of Jesus to return will take place. When that time comes, one group will remain adversarial by refusing God's definition of love and mercy, the other group will demonstrate their faith in God's system by accepting pain and suffering at the hands of their adversaries. In the words of the psalmist: "You prepare a table before me in the presence of my enemies. You anoint my head with oil; my cup overflows. Surely goodness and love (mercy in KJV) will follow me all the days of my life, and I will (future tense) dwell in the house of the LORD forever" (Ps. 23:5, 6 parentheses added).

God's unconditional mercy toward rebellious beings, including Satan, is simply amazing. Humans are not the only beneficiaries; angels also share the benefits and promises of His mercy. But someday God's followers will share His model of mercy with their foes, thus proving to the universe that fallen beings can be changed to recognize and accept mercy as their own modus operandi as does God. By so thinking they will act in ways that demonstrate the faith they have developed thanks to God's clear messages. They will demonstrate that it is possible to recover the mind-set received at Creation and that fitness for eternal life is founded on a persuasion Scripture calls faith. They will recognize and demonstrate that this fitness comes entirely from God. As long as humans fail to demonstrate that they are capable of the mercy they have recognized in Jesus all the way to Calvary, they will fail to persuade the universe that humans can be made fit for an eternity of bountiful love. When we consider the current status of Christianity, and even my own as the author of this book, we have reason to wonder if this day will ever come. But fortunately the Word of God brings assurance of victory.

The universe of God's Kingdom will be composed of individuals fit to live eternally. Outside observers (1 Cor. 4:9) of the universe will recognize this reality through the merciful deeds of some humans at the end of time. Something else will happen. Humans will finally realize that with perfect mercy in the heart it is no longer possible to break the Law of God. This does not mean that they will be living sinless lives, but the fact that they are overcoming sin will show that they are on their way to become sinless, perhaps later in heaven. Better yet, they will realize that it is no longer necessary to worry or try hard to keep the Law, because with their focus on the welfare of others they will keep the Law without trying. How could a person be hurtful toward others when perfect love becomes so strong in the heart that dying at the hands of aggressors becomes preferable to breaking from love?

With that new faith it will also be understood that the only supernatural power responsible for making mercy possible is God Himself. Righteousness will never be imposed on anyone by a Third

Person of the Godhead. The Holy Spirit will be recognized as the Spirit God has placed in humans through His Word of Truth. By focusing on the message of Jesus countless sinners will choose to grow love that produces mercy in their hearts. Jesus said it Himself in plain language: "The words I have spoken to you are spirit and they are life" (Jn. 6:63). Why are we waiting for the Holy Spirit to come in our hearts when all we have to do is to listen to the plain words of Jesus?

It is probably because God knew that the Children of Israel would idolize the tables of stone inscribed with His Law that He gave them clear instructions to hide the precious document in a box. Since that was not sufficient, He told them to place a heavy lid of gold on that box and to place the precious cargo beyond a Veil where no one was to ever open that box ever again. God made it clear that He was sitting on the heavy lid called His Mercy Seat to make sure no one would ever dare open the box. The box itself, but not its contents, was to be seen by only one pair of human eyes once a year for just a few minutes.

Why did God do that? The answer is not given to that question, but it is likely that they were instructed to do this until they would finally understand the eternal value of the universal message of the rituals. They were intended to teach the priests first, and later the people, all of whom were called to become priests. Had the people of God acquired the correct understanding of the Mercy Seat as a nation, they would no longer have need for the Law written on those tables. The Veil that represented the reason for their lack of mercy would have lost its significance, as well as the tables of the Law hidden in the box. All the false religious beliefs of humanity were represented by the Veil sprinkled daily with the blood of innocent lives. Such a comprehensive understanding of the procedure to produce love in the heart would have removed all risks or temptations to idolize the sacred symbol of God's presence. They would have finally known God so well that they would have understood that His presence was to be invited into their hearts, not an object to be celebrated or worshiped. In His wisdom God told them to keep these objects out of reach to avoid corrupting symbols meant to convey Truth.

As precious as were the tables of stone for the Israelites, God demanded that these priceless treasures remain hidden under a heavy lid called the Mercy Seat. Theologians have speculated that Martin Luther and William Tyndale had no reason to call the lid of the box His Mercy

Seat. While we don't know how they both arrived at that conclusion, it is clear that Samuel understood that it was the seat of God. When he "sent men to Shiloh" to bring "back the ark of the covenant of the LORD Almighty," he specifies that God "is enthroned between the cherubim" (1 Sam. 4:4)?[39] Even modern X-Ray vision would fail to see the Law through the heavy golden lid! To make the box all the more impenetrable, God Himself chose to sit on it, as did the Egyptian Pharaohs on their Barks.[40] Who would dare disturb God? He had forbidden to open the box or to see the Law written in stone until humans would finally get over

---

[39] Hebrew *kapporeth* means: cover, or to cover. Sometimes this meaning has been associated with covering sin, but that notion is implied nowhere in Scripture. God does not cover sin; His purpose is to help humans overcome sin or to recover from sin. Covering sin is not a solution to the sin problem; it only perpetuates it. The idea of covering sin is associated with the notion of propitiation understood as an offering made to obtain from God the favor to cover sin, or to ignore sin by way of acquittal. This non-Scriptural traditional interpretation is also at the heart of a fundamental Christian belief that Christ had to be nailed to the Cross as a payment for sins in order to cover or acquit them. The concept of covering is falsely perceived as an act of Jesus to cover or hide sin and sinners from God's view and His wrath. We should understand that it is the Law written on stone that was hidden in the Most Holy Place, not the sins the Law reveals. Considering that God was aware of Israel's propensity to idolatry He made sure that the document written by His own finger would never become the object of open worship, and it never was, at least not as an object. It is sad to observe however, that although the Children of Israel never worshiped the object itself, they continue to worship the legal message engraved upon the tables, which is equally as idolatrous. Christians have taken a different outlook but are every bit as idolatrous, if not more. Citing Hebrews 9:22 they worship the payment of blood as the agent responsible for covering sin, making the blood shed on the Cross the solution. To this day humanity as a whole is obsessed with the notion that "laws" resolve human problems and that the purpose of religion is to cover sins, as though they could be swept under the rug. This assumption has proven inadequate to change hearts. God's solution is logically the only acceptable way to overcome sin because it involves changing the natural human heart into a heart re-made in the image of God's own.

[40] Barks were very similar to the Hebrew ark of the testimony. It was also located in the most holy portion of Egyptian temples, and was used on special occasions to transport the Pharaoh on a symbolic journey among the people. The Pharaohs sat on it as they were transported by pole bearers, not unlike the ark of the testimony on which no one but God was to sit.

their temptation to idolize the precious document, as indeed they did despite all precautions. Humans have always been obsessed with the idea that religion should be approached either mystically or legally, as they still do. This may explain why the precious documents are still hidden. They will continue to be hidden until their intended message is correctly understood. It is a sad statement to make, but humans today would be far more likely to worship the Ark of the Covenant and its contents than the perfectly rational message of love and mercy the covenant was created to convey. Preparations are currently underway to rebuild the Temple of Jerusalem and to reinstate the sacrificial system. Clearly, humans are proving that they are indeed incorrigible.

But perhaps more importantly, God has discreetly been telling the human family something extremely important: "Always put mercy ahead of the Law and never the Law ahead of mercy!" It is the failure of humans to recognize and understand this fine point of God's truth that caused Jesus to be hung on a cross. He had broken no law of man and no Law of God. But because Jesus did not fit their preconceived model of God, or that He came to convey the message they had missed, their lack of mercy in the face of perfect innocence wanted His death as an imposter. Had Jesus not told Philip: "Anyone who has seen me has seen the Father" (Jn. 14:9)? Indeed, the passage of Isaiah should have been translated to say: "He was pierced *by our* transgressions, He was crushed *by our* iniquities, and this (unfair) punishment brings us peace" (Is. 53:5, emphasis and parenthesis mine), but only if we understand why He accepted humans to abuse Him. Although the word "unfair" is supplied here, it is understood in the context of a man suffering a punishment unfairly, like a lamb taken to the butcher. Yet it is thanks to this unfair punishment that God demonstrated for all times that His kind of mercy should also become ours.

Along with other misinterpretations of God's eternal Message of truth, the Law of God became more important to the religious leaders of Israel than mercy. In our modern societies solidly anchored on the "rule of law," we find all too often that modern justice is no different. The idea that laws and law enforcement has the power to control humans should be recognized as an archaic system of social control. It has proven ineffective to serve the purpose ever since its conception in the mind of Cain. Where in today's religions or political systems do we find that they are father figures like the "Father of Two Sons" (Lk. 15:11–32) in the parable of Jesus? One of the two sons was an overt rebel, the other a

law-abiding covert one. Both were sons of the same father and neither was
rebuked. Both were wrong in different ways, yet both benefited fully from
the unconditional mercy of the father. The merciful heart of the father
in this parable should be the hallmark of the messages preached in the
Most Holy Place of God's Modern Temple—the body of His believers.
If His followers are the body of Christ of which He is the cornerstone,
as a group they make up the corporate Temple of God on earth (1 Cor.
3:17). Boundless mercy for one another should become the theme of all
teachings in His Holy Temple. True followers of Jesus should become
unconditionally merciful. It is only when mercy will be written in the
hearts of believers that God's Law will be indelibly written in the heart of
every individual claiming to belong to Him (see Jer. 31:33).

When Jesus was hanging on the Cross, His parting words contained
the most powerful expression of mercy ever uttered by human lips:
"Father, forgive them, for they know not what they do" (Lk. 23:34). Until
those words were articulated, no one on this planet had fully understood
the true meaning of the word "mercy," as God defines the word. From
the Cross, Jesus did not request the mercy of God for Himself; He
demonstrated the purest form of mercy toward all His persecutors!
Sinners are so eager to receive the mercies from God and so reluctant
to bestow mercy upon others. Mercy is the maturation of unconditional
love. Love starts with perfect humility; it grows and develops by studying
the true meaning of love as God defines the word, but such love is
fulfilled and manifested in the sinner's life only when he or she begins to
manifest unconditional mercifulness toward all others, regardless of race,
belief system, age, gender, or social and financial status.

There is no true love without mercy for those who live in a world of
sin. Mercy is the gauge by which the level of one's love in the heart is
measured. "If you love those who love you," said Jesus, "what reward will
you get" (Mat. 5:46)? In other words, what have you proven about the
level of your love for others? Jesus was trying to show that mercy toward
those who hate us is the only *visible* expression of true love. I sometimes
say: "We only love God as much as we love our worst enemy."

When the essential truth regarding the meaning of mercy was
revealed to the universe for the first time in its fullness from the Cross,
unlike other humans, Christ could have saved His own life. Instead He
chose to lay it down (Jn. 10:18) so that no one could ever be in the dark
as to how far God expects mercy to be taken—to the death. At that

crucial moment, when death was imminent, God was revealing the key to His eternal truth to a confused world. The thick Veil hiding the Most Holy Place of the Temple was torn down from top to bottom by an invisible divine force (Mt. 27:51). This was to reveal in no uncertain terms the true meaning of the message related to the Most Holy Place where the Mercy Seat had been located. Jesus was indeed merciful all the way to His death, and all His created beings were offered access to the persuasion or faith that love capable of mercy is the key to eternal life and that His followers must like Him, be willing to take up their cross and follow Him all the way.

The requirement for participating in God's promised eternal life was revealed in its completeness from the Cross by God Himself and for the entire universe to witness. But this was not enough. The events surrounding this tragic moment on Calvary also revealed the unavoidable reality of evil in all its ugliness. Evil, or sin, produces death, just as Paul said (Rom. 6:23). On the Cross God's Word of Truth was made so evident that to make it even more palpable the Veil in the Temple could no longer hide the mystery; it ripped without human intervention by a true act of God. The Veil was a symbolic time capsule from God. It revealed that humanity would remain forever incapable to comprehend the mystery of true love on their own despite all the help received through the prophets. God proved that even with His help humans remained incapable of recognizing the value of mercy on their own or to find the key to eternal life without the graphically morbid demonstration of true mercy from a Cross. It is while giving His last breath on the Cross that Jesus revealed to the entire cosmos "once and for all" the full range of God's perfect beauty and depth of character now exposed for all to see. Evil is indeed merciless, but love that comes from God is boundlessly merciful.

All the faithful angels of God recognized in this ultimate gift of self a level of mercy never before witnessed anywhere in the vastness of the universe. Unfortunately, two millennia later, humans still remain essentially clueless. Traditions and superstitions along with a host of meaningless and erroneous religious views must be discarded from Christian theology, or these false doctrines and dogmas will continue to blind the most sincere of heart. Are the modern doctors of biblical knowledge keeping the people from entering the territory of God's Temple, as did the Pharisees Jesus rebuked (see Lk. 11:52)?

Receiving God's mercy implies becoming unconditionally and indiscriminately merciful toward all people. It is not a virtue we can achieve on our own. Jesus alone was able to demonstrate this divine truth in its completeness. No other philosopher or religious leader has ever come close to making such a demonstration. Humans could have never found the key to the kingdom of peace on the strength of their own rationale. This is proven by the fact that in spite of God's amazing help through His prophets, humanity still managed to fail utterly to understand the message that saves. Jesus presented it with clarity in words and deeds stained with His own blood and sealed with His own death. Without Him humanity would still be forever lost in the darkness of their meaningless traditions and cults. We owe it all to God who through Jesus made it possible for us all to become divinely merciful by His grace, and "shhhhh," no need to boast about it and no need to assess our own level of perfection (1 Cor. 1:29–30), that would be self-centeredness, not the self-irrelevance required to grow ever greater Christlike love in our hearts.

The Sixth Beatitude

"Blessed are the pure in heart, for they will see God" (Mt. 5:8). To use our formula we could say: "Consider the potential of people whose heart is pure, they will see God."

The passion to serve and be merciful unconditionally, as Christ was, is the only way to live eternally:

When sinners begin to reflect the divine mercy of Christ in their own lives, their life experience changes dramatically. Because their focus of life has shifted from serving self to serving others they become increasingly less concerned with their own sinfulness as they focus more intensely on serving others. Indeed, their sinfulness is being replaced with a clean heart. As self becomes less relevant, life is increasingly focused on serving and loving others. When true love is applied to daily life its ultimate purpose is to journey in the presence of God in His Most Holy Place, the Sanctuary of His immutable Truth. With mercy in the heart life becomes increasingly more altruistic because it is no longer obsessed with serving self. "Blessed are the pure in heart," for their inner eyes shall "see God" with such clarity that their own hearts will emulate His loving character evermore adequately. The shift of focus from self to others is the "faith of

Jesus" (Rev. 14:12) that all of us should seek. As the shift occurs, God's own finger writes His Law on the hearts and minds (Heb. 10:16) of those who become His children. With true mercy in the heart, sinners are prepared to take on their duties as priests of God in His Heaven-bound Temple here on earth. They see His character as the only character worth having; thus they see God in His true light.

The Seventh Beatitude

"Blessed are the peacemakers, for they will be called sons of God" (Mt. 5:9). Could we say: "Consider the potential of people willing to lose everything for the sake of peace, for such are people born again into the family of God."

Only true love shared unconditionally and universally can bring lasting peace. All it takes is one exception to disturb the peace for all.

When God's mercy is written on a sinner's heart it is cleansed and that person's greatest desire is for love to reign in his or her heart. Such people love peace so much that they are prepared to die if necessary for the sake of safeguarding love in the universe. Such people do not seek salvation because they want to benefit from the promise of eternal life; they are simply people willing to live a life of love at any cost because it is the only rational way to live. The motivation for loving is not driven by the hope of eternal life; it is driven by a persuasion that comes from Truth that emanates from God. For them nothing is more important than love, not even life. With such an agenda written on the heart, sinners become true "peacemakers."

Indeed, with this agenda in mind sinners become members of God's family. They become guardians of God's system of government based on love as a universal way of life. This is what God requested Adam and Eve to do when He placed them in Eden; they were to guard (Gen. 2:15) the very system of life that would have made possible the expansion of the life they received on the whole planet. Sinners who become priests are people who change so much that they become true peacekeepers of God's cosmic sanctuary. There is no greater reward or greater joy than to hold and safeguard the key of God's eternal kingdom. Upon completion of the most enlightening journey of sinners that has taken them all the way to the presence of God in the Most Holy Place, they have indeed seen God's true character with the spiritual eyes of their hearts. When such sinners become priests it will only be because they have undergone a complete cycle of rebirth through the womb of God's Spirit.

Having reached the presence of God, sinners are finally ready to face the world, regardless of what destiny awaits them. The pain and suffering that might await them is totally secondary to their mission, as it was for Jesus. He came to planet Earth from the flanks of the Father in Heaven to show us the way to the truth that gives life. For the first time priests are covered with God's white garb of humility because they have become His true representatives on earth. Although not yet perfect in character, these priests are ready to bring the message of freedom and salvation to their fellow humans still wandering aimlessly in the wilderness of life. Like the kid goat for Azazel, priests who fail to become lamblike are doomed to remain in the wilderness of risks and perils.

Sinners who have become priests have undergone a metamorphosis like the pupa that becomes a butterfly. This priesthood is attainable only through the merits and enlightenment received from Jesus. He showed the way to the presence of God. This is where it is demonstrated for the universe to see that love is so deeply ingrained in the heart of these former sinners that they are more willing to give up their own life than to deviate from pure love. The radiance of this understanding can only be received at the foot of the Cross. With His act of total self-denial Jesus inaugurated the "ministry of reconciliation" that "He has committed to us" (2 Cor. 5:18–19). Jesus was the Alpha of a new priesthood of which the sons and daughters of God must become the Omega in His name. Children of God must inherit from Jesus the priesthood of reconciliation He began. The secret of the "at-one-ment" in the sense of coming together of one Spirit with God will finally become reality, and that Gospel of the kingdom will be preached to the whole world (Mt. 24:14). This is the Everlasting Gospel that will be preached "as a testimony to all nations" just before the return of the Lord. It is the message that will bring healing and peace to those who are willing to recognize it in a world where the torments of evil appear to reign more visible than ever and appear to have gained the upper hand (Heb. 2:17; 2 Cor. 5:18). The promise of Scripture will not fail: "But where sin increased, grace increased all the more" (Rom. 5:20). It is when sin will reach its pinnacle that the grace of God's Truth, which is mercy, will also reach its summit.

The Eighth Beatitude

"Blessed are those who are persecuted *for the sake of righteousness*, for theirs is the kingdom of heaven" (Mt. 5:10 KJV, emphasis supplied). How could we translate that one? Here is an attempt: "Consider the potential of people willing to be merciful in the face of persecutions, for the kingdom of heaven already belongs to them."

Salvation becomes reality for sinners when nothing matters to them more than sharing God's kind of love against all odds, even at the ultimate price of their own lives.

Jesus made it clear that it is ultimately His Truth that will transform sinners from living a life controlled by evil to a life of genuine love that produces true freedom. This transformation becomes evident when sinners are prepared to live the closing statements of Jesus in His Beatitudes: "Blessed are they which are persecuted for righteousness' sake" (Mt. 5:10 KJV). The battle is all about righteousness or lack thereof—there is no middle ground.

The willingness to accept persecutions to safeguard love as the modus operandi of the universe is the righteousness Christ came to teach and demonstrate. The righteousness of Jesus teaches three fundamental elements of righteousness in the order in which they must occur:

1. Humility is the required springboard of true love.
2. This change is no ordinary miracle, because the kind of love humility produces is no ordinary love.
3. It is love so powerful that it is capable of bestowing unconditional mercy on all people regardless of who they are and no matter what they do—even when they choose to hurt us.

Suddenly, the meaning of "righteousness by faith" takes on a new meaning. A "new birth" has occurred, a "new mind" is burgeoning, and a "new heart" has seen the light of "the Sun of Righteousness" that soon "will rise with healing in its wings. And you will go like calves released from the stall" (Mal. 4:2). The journey to the Most Holy Place where sinners reach the presence of God involves the whole process that releases them from their stalls of contempt to the healing womb of God. When healing begins to occur, sinners become priests ready to return to the pernicious prejudices of the "real" world. This is where they will share the

Testimony of Jesus, presenting it as a complete system of faith that must be propagated to others at great risk. The return to the pernicious world is risky indeed; the message from God has nothing in common with the mentality of this world. All the newly born into the kingdom of God's mercy make of His message the centerpiece of everything life is worth living for—nothing else matters. It is only when a person has recognized and espoused the "faith of Jesus" (Rev. 14:12) that true happiness can rule in the heart even under unjust persecutions. God's definition of "righteousness" is simple. It is nothing more and nothing less than unconditional mercy born out of love so powerful that it can only be the product of genuine humility.

Christ chose to demonstrate God's eternal principle of life by safeguarding love at the price of His own life (see Ps. 63:3). This must also become the everlasting commitment of those who wish to be called children of God. John begins his Epistle with these words: "Yet to all who received him, to those who believed in his name, he gave the right to become children of God—children born not of natural descent, nor of human decision or a husband's will, but born of God" (Jn. 1:12–13). Here John makes a clear distinction between the natural birth and the new birth out of God's womb. Receiving Him is not a matter of believing that he exists or that Jesus died on a Cross to save humanity. It is a matter of persuasion regarding the importance and power of love; the same persuasion that motivated Christ. Righteousness has to become the product of a powerful persuasion called faith, identical to that of Jesus. That faith alone has the power to produce righteousness.

The Epistle to the Hebrews was probably intended to explain to a Jewish public the link of rationale that can be established between the former rituals of the Temple and the Message of Christ. Since God was clearly understood both by Jews and the Apostles that He does not change, it was important to show that He had not. Unfortunately the translations of that letter were made with preconceptions responsible for a great deal of confusion. We cannot take the time to review these instances, but one statement is worth pondering: "The Holy Spirit was showing by this that the way into the Most Holy Place had not yet been disclosed [or was not yet understood] as long as the first tabernacle was still standing" (Heb. 9:8 brackets mine). The word "standing" is translated from the Greek *stasis* of which the primary meaning is: "the cause of an uproar." When there is an uproar people are compelled to stand on their feet and take notice. In other words, as long as the theology linked to the first tabernacle remained in a state of confusion because of its corrupted theology, the "Way" to the Most Holy Place where mercy is to be found in the presence of God would remain inaccessible. But all this has changed. The message that was inaccessible because it had been corrupted before Jesus came was made accessible thanks to the new information He brought from God. To bring clarity to the message that was corrupted, Jesus had to accept to die on the Cross to show humans the correct meaning of the word "mercy." He did it by showing that true love does not end until death occurs, even if it occurs at the hands of enemies.

Like Jesus, the remnant of the last generation will accept to follow Jesus at the risk of persecutions, but the persecutors will be loved as long as they have life to persecute. Since the refusal to render evil for evil is the only way to insure the everlasting survival of love capable of mercy, following Jesus is not only a great privilege, but it is also the only way to cast our "vote" in favor of God's universal kingdom against evil. It is accepting the duties of the priesthood in a world evermore unjust and evermore threatening. What a complete message of hope Jesus has brought to the world! His pristine robe of righteousness will soon replace the tattered sackcloth covering the shameful nakedness of His church yet unfit to proclaim the last message to the world (see Rev. 3:18).

Conclusion

"Blessed are you when people insult you, persecute you and falsely say all kinds of evil against you because of me. Rejoice and be glad, because great is your reward in heaven, for in the same way they persecuted the prophets who were before you" (Mt. 5:11–12). Could we just say: "Imagine the potential of people who are willing to accept insults, persecutions, false accusations, and even utter rejection because of me. Indeed, they should rejoice and be delighted, because they will enjoy all the rewards of heaven along with the prophets of the past who suffered similar oppression."

When Jesus tells the crowd that they would consider it a blessing to suffer "because of me," He is not talking about suffering because of the mere belief that He exists or that He died to save humanity. Many will believe just that without suffering persecutions. Those who will be persecuted because of Jesus will suffer because they have chosen to become as merciful as Jesus. It is on this very point that the rubber meets the road, as the saying goes. Because they accept to be mistreated at the hands of their enemies they will be considered utterly out of their minds. Their decisions to love their enemies at any cost to them will be considered insanity deserving of punishment and even torture. These are true children of God who have clearly understood that unconditional mercy is the product of true love and that true love is the product of unconditional humility, even in the face of enemies. Indeed, many will say: "Lord, Lord" (Mt. 7:21), but they will have failed the test of God's love and mercy. This is when the Lord will tell them: "Away from me, you evil doers!" (Mt. 7:23). What will be the nature of their evil? They will persecute the followers of Jesus who preach and practice unconditional nonviolence on the strength of a persuasion identical to the faith of their merciful Father (Lk. 6:36).

Summary of the Journey with God in His Last Temple

To understand the Truth God was attempting to convey through the rituals of the two Temples of Jerusalem and the Tabernacle, it is important to consider them within the framework of the Beatitudes. Since God does not change His requirements for salvation do not change either. With the Beatitudes Jesus was giving the people an insight as to why the Temple had been given them in the first place, as well as the Truth they should have understood from the Temple's message. Unfortunately, the message God had given the Israelites to convey understanding regarding His methodology to overcome evil had been corrupted to such a point that it was no longer valid. It could no longer convey the Truth that could have set the Children of Israel free. With God's Truth they had all been called to become priests qualified to teach others how to become priests, but that function will be offered in the last days to the true representatives of God's kingdom.

The mission of this last generation of priests will be to teach the gospel of the kingdom in Truth and to demonstrate to the universe that God was perfectly correct when He instituted a government founded on love and free will. Let us remember that the last Temple of God on this planet will not be made by human hands but by God Himself. Since God made humans and since the incarnated Jesus said that He was the cornerstone of a new temple, those who willfully choose to follow Him constitute the other stones of His temple. It is for that reason that the cornerstone of the Temple in Jerusalem was not to be shaped by using tools made of iron. This was to symbolize that the cornerstone was not to be shaped by human hands. By contrast, the cornerstone already prepared to build the Third Temple of Israel was cut using diamond instruments, rationalizing that only diamond is precious enough to cut the significant stone. This stone is already made and ready to be placed on the Temple Mount, but every time the attempt was made, the attempt led to a Palestinian *intifada*.

Here are a few parallels to be considered between the Beatitudes of Jesus and the message of Truth that will be proclaimed by the final temple not be made by human hands:

1. Those who are poor in spirit are discouraged because they realize that something is wrong with the way things are going in this world. They try to put their confidence in money, education, politics, big business, or the legal system, but they soon realize that there is pride, egocentrism, and greed everywhere. Mutual trust and fairness is nowhere to be found. Discouraged, they consider religion as a possible solution, but here again, they are discouraged for the same reasons. Yes, even the religions of our world could use a dose of humility. However, there is hope; being dissatisfied, they look intensely for something better. As they do, they are bound to be surprised as they begin to discover that the message of Jesus is by far more beautiful than Christianity has presented it for centuries. In their search for Truth they recognize the importance of leaving their egocentricity at the Broad Gate. This is imperative to continue the journey all the way to the presence of God in the Most Holy Place.

2. Those who are regretful for the lack of love that caused them to hurt others will be comforted by their discovery that there is a valid and logical way to change a lackluster heart. Upon entering through the symbolic Broad Gate of the Temple where the egos of sinners have been dropped off, they accept the reassurance of God's forgiveness. Indeed, it is not God who grants forgiveness; He always does. It is sinners who must accept God's forgiveness. Lacking such assurance of forgiveness sinners could never face the One they have wronged. At this juncture in the journey

with God sinners are already saved, but failure to continue the journey would indicate that forgiveness was all they wanted, nothing more. These are sinners who have failed to recognize the importance of developing greater love as the only solution to the problem of evil. Jesus lamented the fact that many enter the Broad Gate, but few are willing to make the journey with Him all the way to the straight and narrow that leads to the Mercy Seat. They fail to realize that they cannot regain a character in the image of God without meeting Him in the Most Holy Place where they become merciful, as God is merciful. Only then will they begin to be restored in the image of God; this is healing. It is salvation.

3. Having recognized that lack of love is the problem, sinners become meek, gentle, and more submissive to God's ways in order to grow His kind of love in the heart. Now they choose sincerely to submit to the only solution, the one that comes from God. The procedure that follows will take them to a better understanding of God's meaning of the word "love." By so doing they recognize that to cultivate true love in the heart they must continue to cultivate humility of heart. Confessions are never for God's benefit but for the sinners' own, recognizing that lack of love responsible for all sins must yield to ever-greater love. As they progress along the way, they become increasingly more thankful to God who offers all sinners a second chance to seek His healing through His prescription that produces the remission of the sin disease.

4. Now aware that to obtain victory over sin, love in their hearts must continue to grow, sinners accept the cleansing of their former character at the Laver where self-centeredness of the past must yield to a reversal of orientation. Interestingly, the Laver of the Tabernacle was made out of bronze collected from the women in the camp. They donated their mirrors to be smelted down into a laver for the cleansing of past egocentric self-contemplation (Ex. 38:8). The symbolic message is clear: True cleansing of the heart is a matter of looking at the well-being of others before our own.

5. Now that they symbolically ender the Holy Place sinners begin to learn God's meaning of love. They soon realize that love must develop in the heart all the way to mercifulness. At this stage

in their journey, sinners realize the importance of focusing all their energies on the welfare of others before their own. True healing from the forces of evil begins to occur. Now that healing is taking place, a healthy appetite develops in the heart. They want to learn all there is to know about love; what it is, how it grows, and how far it must be taken to become like God's. The Table where the bread is representative of the Bread of Life it is ingested as should the information found in the Word of God. Sinners soon realize that God's kind of love is unconditional and that bleeding at the hands of persecutors is no reason to end one's love for enemies. Only the sinner's own death can bring an end to love. The more they learn about love from God the more they want to continue the journey that must begin on Earth, knowing that it will be continued in heaven for the rest of eternity. To grow, the symbolic bread of life, representative of God's character, must be eaten daily, just as one's need for daily food. On the Sabbath, special attention should be given to the Word. The priests of old ate the showbread placed on the table of the Holy Place every seventh day of the week. This "bread of life" transforms the sinner progressively into the character of God.

6. As love grows in the hearts of sinners they realize that true love transcends all known natural bonds of love for family and friends. Studying the word at the light of the Golden Candelabra, which is light coming from God through Jesus, sinners begin to understand the truth that will set them free. When this happens a sweet scent begins to rise toward God pleased to see the progress made in hearts being purified. The unnatural divine brand of love grows and matures to the level of mercy. Mercy is love that grows against the grain of human nature. For that reason even friends, family, and others not making the journey disapprove and reject those whose hearts are being purified by God's message of love. The promise is clear: blessed are those whose heart is being purified, for they will see God.

7. It is not possible to recognize the importance of mercy without becoming a peacemaker. Once a true peacemaker unwilling to ever perpetuate evil by rendering evil for evil, sinners become sons and daughters of God. They become members of His family. Once in His presence in the Most Holy Place where the Throne

of Mercy is located, God personally pronounces them born-again member of His eternal family. They have accomplished the goal proposed by Jesus when He said: "Be merciful, as your Father is merciful" (Lk. 6:63). Now sinners who have reached this personal encounter with God share His character with Him. They are children of God and no longer children "of the evil one" (Mt. 13:38). Only now can it be said that they are ready for the new birth into this world. They are new priests of God about to go out into the world regardless of the risks they might encounter, just as did Jesus. This is in fact what He meant when He said: "If anyone would come after me, he must deny himself and take up his cross and follow me" (Mt. 16:24).

8. The kind of peacemaker the followers of Jesus are called to become leads them to suffer persecutions. It is clear that this eighth Beatitude implies that the righteousness of the children "of the Most High" (Lk. 6:35) brings out the worst out of those who remain "sons of the evil one" (Mt. 13 38). However, to interact with the sons of the evil one, those who have been transformed to adopt the character of God must come out of the heavenly (heaven-like) Sanctuary. There is only one way out, through the Broad Gate from which they entered. At that moment, they are once again in the presence of enemies. But this time they are no longer like them. It is difficult for them to preach that rendering evil for evil will never resolve the problem of evil. Coming out of the Sanctuary after a personal encounter with God is the new birth Jesus was talking about to Nicodemus in the third chapter of John's Gospel. Anyone led to believe that the new birth takes place at the Brazen Altar or the Laver is misled to believe that baptism is an end-all experience with God. The Brazen Altar is only the beginning.

Once born again out of the womb of God, sinners are filled with the most unnatural need to love enemies against all odds. It is a change of character they hunger for more than anything else in the universe. This kind of love can only be the result of a "one on one" encounter with God. This kind of love can be communicated to produce such powerful persuasiveness in sinners' hearts that they are equipped to dispense it freely to all people, even their worst enemies. This kind of love becomes the best proof that true divine mercy is obtained from God, because it could have come from no other source. This gift is made available only at the Mercy Seat where God's mercy becomes the sinners' own without pressure or coercion from any external or supernatural forces.

It all stands to reason. If a person on this planet can be persuaded in the absence of sound logic that he or she should kill infidels and accept to die in the process, why should the opposite persuasion fail to produce the fruit of the Spirit of God? Why would a person persuaded on the strength of sound logic fail to accept death as Jesus did, for the sake of preserving forever the benefits of love and mercy? The difference is entirely a matter of education. One comes from God; the other does not and cannot be rationally debated to be from God.

The incoherent invitations made from pulpits to "come to the foot of the cross" are overused and meaningless when they are associated with receiving God's forgiveness at the Cross. Jesus did not die to forgive; He died to make possible the remission of the sin disease. Humans are always forgiven. Forgiveness is a free gift, but it only opens the door to mercy if the gift is accepted, and the demonstration that it was accepted is made by accepting to go all the way to the presence of God. Once on the road to recovery sinners recognize that God's unconditional gift of Himself to His created beings must also become the sinners' unconditional gift of their own self to others. This is the only way sinners can show to what extent they cherish love.

God has given us a beautiful illustration of the entire principle. The eggs of butterflies hatch on this earth as self-serving creatures, devouring caterpillars eager to eat everything on their way. They suddenly realize that they must change. To do so they hang themselves on a tree to become a pupa of which the substance is a formless paste. Exposed to the sun, a transformation they cannot explain eventually takes place. The adult butterflies begin to appear. They are not only totally inoffensive, but their colorful dashes of beauty bring joy and happiness to the lives of many. They are now ready to begin a new cycle of life. The ultimate goal of a Christian life is for love in the heart to grow on the level with Christ's. Despite the power He had to destroy His enemies, even as He was dying on the Cross He demonstrated unconditional love and mercy to the very end. He gave the demonstration from heaven that it is better to die loving than to hate and destroy the enemies of God. The utmost level of mercy was made visible for the entire universe to see as He hung on a cross before being placed in a tomb. His resurrection was also heaven's demonstration that those who die loving have nothing to fear; they will be resurrected.

Mercy gives access to eternal life thanks to the metamorphosis true love makes possible. Death is the inevitable maturation of sin (James 1:15) resulting from a refusal to recognize the importance of change. Once equipped with the divine gift of mercy, sinners begin to realize that like the seed that must die in the ground before new life can begin to germinate, the death of the body must be accepted just as was the death of the old self at the Brazen Altar and the water of baptism.

CHAPTER 9

What Went Wrong with the Religion Jesus Brought from Heaven?

J esus warned His disciples and the people on several occasions that there would be trouble ahead. He knew that the message He had come all the way from heaven to share at great price with humanity would soon be corrupted. False prophets and false teachers, even false Christs were predicted to arise (Mt. 24:24; Mk. 13:22) and sow seeds of confusion. John goes so far as to call them Antichrists. "Dear children," he writes, "this is the last hour; and as you have heard that the antichrist is coming, even now many antichrists have come" (1 Jn. 2:18). A bit further John makes it clear that the apostasy had already begun: "This is the spirit of the antichrist, which you have heard is coming and even now has already come" (1 Jn. 4:3). The predictions of Jesus that confusion would arise came sooner than could have been expected. The Apostolic Church was hit very hard. The Apostles were compelled to confront vigorously the false teachings that were arising in various places, but they had no idea what was coming, especially after their deaths. They did not dwell on the nature of the false teachings they had to confront in their lifetime. Mere hints are provided. Perhaps no book of the NT provides a more concise expression of concern for the erroneous theological concepts that were infiltrating the Apostolic Church than does the short narrative of Jude.

Jude Sounds the Alarm

In the context of our discussion about God's Truth and its power to change peoples' hearts, the way Jude introduces his message is worthy of note. Here is how he introduces his narrative: "Jude, a servant of Jesus Christ and a brother of James. To those who have been called, who are loved in God the Father and kept for Jesus Christ: Mercy, peace and love be yours in abundance" (Jude 1:1, 2).

Jude provides his readers with an indirect statement of his own identity. In humility typical of the Apostles, he makes it known indirectly that he is a brother of the Lord. He identifies his own brother as a brother of the Lord without mentioning that he was himself a brother of the Lord. The powerful introductory statement that follows identifies him as a true bearer of the message of Christ. His reference to peace, love, and mercy is indicative of His unwavering dedication to the message of the Lord. This statement is so different from those made by the philosophers of this world. Clearly, Jude identifies himself not only as one eager to receive the peace, love, and mercy from God, but also as one who shares and lives these persuasions with others, as did Jesus his Lord all the way to the Cross.

By and large, translators, interpreters, and preachers tend to insist on a unidirectional dispensation of mercy; we received it from God. Meanwhile insufficient emphasis is placed on the fact that followers of Jesus should grow to become like Him in this regard. The idea that James was talking about the love and mercy his readers should manifest toward others is not clearly established. Christians go to church to receive God's mercy, not so much to learn how to become unconditionally merciful with others. The preaching of tolerance is a good start, but preaching mercy implies that tolerance is unconditional and boundless. The last sentence could read as follows: "May love and mercy that produces peace abound in you." Since Jude's readers had a clear understanding of the message of Jesus this statement identifies for them the authority of the writer as a true follower of Jesus, recognizing him as a boundless devotee to the uniqueness of Christ's message.

The most updated research regarding the dating of NT books places Jude roundabout 68 CE. This is important because although the destruction of Jerusalem had not yet occurred, the persecutions of Christians under Nero had reached its pinnacle. The atrocities of this Roman Emperor against Christians in various arenas of the empire need not be recounted here. Unfortunately, such massacres were also commonplace in city streets and houses where Christians worshiped. Paul and Peter were both executed by orders of this fierce enemy of Christianity.

Historians and commentators often overlook an important question: Why was the Roman Empire so intolerant of Christians? Why was this peaceful religion so savagely persecuted by the Roman Empire known for its unprecedented tolerance toward religious diversity, including Judaism? Anti-Judaism had been quite common for centuries throughout the Greco-Roman world, but the dislike of Jews was not comparable with the hostile contempt against Christians. There was something about Christianity that was more offensive and more distasteful to the Roman authorities than all other religions. The antagonistic attitudes toward Christians were all the more surprising that Paul and other Apostles preached the importance of respect toward all cultures, authorities, and religious affiliations. For them "there is no Greek or Jew, circumcised or uncircumcised, barbarian, Scythian, slave or free, but Christ is all, and is in all" (Col. 3:11). In many ways Christians were far more culturally integrated than were the Jews who loved to flaunt their religious identity. They dressed and behaved differently. They even refused to eat meals with Gentiles or to buy meat sold in their markets because their animals were slaughtered in the names of their pagan gods. Christians actively minimized such rifts of culture, just so long as they could remain faithful to their God. "Meat is meat," says Paul, regardless of which gods were implored during the slaughter. "Eat anything sold in the meat market," said Paul, "without raising questions of conscience, for, 'the earth is the Lord's, and everything in it'" (1 Cor. 10:25; Paul quoting Ps. 24:1).

Why were the Roman authorities so intolerant of Christianity? Why should Christians have been singled out as practicing a disruptive religion considering that they were unconditionally devoted to love and mercy that produces peace? The fact is that they were considered fanatic in their preaching and devotion to nonviolence. They were also known for respecting authorities without ever presenting the least threat to Roman leadership at any level. Paul went so far as to say: "Everyone must submit himself to the governing authorities, for there is no authority except that which God has established. The authorities that exist have been established by God" (Rom. 13:1). Why then did the Roman authorities resent Christianity with such a violent passion?

Roman historian Tacitus reported the cruelties of Nero who eventually blamed the fire of Rome on the Christians. Indeed, Nero suggested that Christians' failure to honor Roman deities caused their deficient protection of Rome. During the first three centuries following the Cross, no less than ten periods of brutal government led persecutions against Christians are documented. However, dislike of Christians was widespread throughout the period even when persecutions were not officially mandated. But again we ask, why? What could these peaceful people have done to merit such derision, especially considering that Jews and pagans continued to convert to Christianity exponentially despite such persecutions?

While the answer to the question is not all that nebulous, historians have generally preferred to put the blame on Christian monotheism and their allegiance to one single God. This was alleged to be the curse responsible for the decline of the Empire. Christians were perceived as worshipers of an insufficient number of gods! Not only was the decline of the Empire blamed on them, but also was the social unrest, wars, and famines that ensued. The fact that the population might have disliked Christians because of their single God is somewhat understandable. However, this fact alone fails to explain the fierce hostility of Roman officials toward Christians. Indeed, a much deeper motivation for their unfavorable attitudes toward Christians is often overlooked. At the time the Empire was tolerant toward more than two hundred pagan religions and several factions of Judaism. All the factions of Judaism were monotheist, as were the Christians, most of whom were coming out of Judaism. Yet the leniency toward Jews was not extended to the followers of Jesus.

A study of history suggests that leniency was granted to religions that did not interfere with the willingness of its members to serve in armed forces and fight against enemies of the Empire. It is known that the pagan religions of the time attributed high honors to warriors willing to sacrifice their lives for the survival and expansion of the Empire or return from war either dismembered or with horrible scarring. Monotheist Jews were tolerated because they were willing to join the Roman armies and fight enemies. This allowed the Jews to maintain some administrative autonomy as well as their Temple in Jerusalem, along with a significant number of synagogues throughout the Empire. Early Christianity did not fit that mold. Faithful to the principles of life Jesus had taught them, they were deeply devoted to peace. As such they were unwilling to hurt or kill anyone, including the enemies of the Empire. They systematically refused to "render evil for evil" (Rom. 12:17) under any circumstance.

Indeed, as it was when Jesus was nailed to the Cross, in the eyes of the local secular and religious authorities Jesus had committed the unpardonable sin. Their accusations of blasphemy were merely a pretext to kill a Man unwilling to bear arms. The crowd openly demonstrated a preference for a Jewish militant named Barabbas, a rebel willing to bear arms even against the Roman occupation. Though a fierce activist, he was released from prison (see Mt. 27:15–37) while Jesus was persecuted and tortured because of His open dedication to peace at all cost. His followers later suffered a similar fate at the hands of Jewish and Roman authorities. It is documented that Christians were unwilling to join the Roman armies until Constantine the Great came to power, and even then, severe persecutions continued under Diocletian and Galerius from 303–324 CE.

Historians generally agree with this perception of the facts but they often fail to recognize Christian pacifism as the main reason for which they were disliked and rejected: "During a considerable period after the death of Christ, it is certain . . . that his followers believed He had forbidden war, and that, in consequence of this belief many of them refused to engage in it, whatever were the consequences, whether reproach, or imprisonment, or death. These facts are indisputable: 'It is easy,' says a learned writer of the seventeenth century, 'to obscure the sun at midday, as to deny that the primitive Christian renounced all revenge and war.' Of all Christian writers of the second century, there is not one who notices the subject, who does not hold it to be unlawful for a Christian to bear arms."[41] While refusing to participate in cultic rituals of Imperial religions was punishable by execution, countless Christians were in fact persecuted for their refusal to join the Imperial armies.

As mentioned, something changed unexpectedly under Constantine the Great (272–337 CE). The many contradictory historical versions and interpretations of his alleged conversion to Christianity suggest that similar confusion is responsible for clouding that entire period of history. We know that Constantine's mother, Helena, claimed to belong to the Christian faith. But by then several factions of Christianity had already managed to corrupt the message of Jesus. The groups most faithful to the Lord's authentic message were banned and persecuted by apostate Christians. It is also known that some Christians were spared persecutions because they accepted to dilute the message of Christ with pagan concepts. Considering that the stories related to Helena are full of conflicting legends, the accounts related to her search for the Cross of Jesus are so mystical in nature that they could not possibly be representative of the authentic message of Jesus. The Cross she is

---

[41] Dymond, Jonathan, *An Inquiry into the Accordancy of War with the Principles of Christianity* (1892), p. 80. The following site provides further information: http://www.heraldmag.org/olb/contents/doctrine/ecvowams.htm

credited to have found with the help of Jews in Jerusalem was said to have supernatural healing properties and even the power of resurrection. Even the dirt into which the Cross had supposedly been planted was said to replicate such powers. Some stories affirm that she was able to distinguish the Cross of Jesus from all other crosses by putting it to the test of healing and resurrection. This alone is indicative that she was probably not a true follower of Jesus. It is not the Cross that heals, it is "the message of the Cross" (1 Cor. 1:18). The Cross was an instrument of torture, not an instrument of salvation possessing supernatural powers. Only pagan assumptions could yield such a conclusion.

We cannot take the time to develop the subject here, but considering the influence of his mother and Constantine's ambiguous back-and-forth friendships with theologians holding opposing views of Christianity, it is difficult to imagine that Constantine could have been an eager follower of Jesus. He befriended anti-Trinitarian Arius, until he realized that Trinitarian theology might offer an alternative more amenable to the pagan populations of the Empire. At that point he had Arius exiled until well after the Council of Nicaea and sided solidly in the camp of Trinitarians Athanasius, and Alexander of Alexandria. Constantine's religious ambitions were probably more motivated by his political ambitions and eager pragmatism to unify and expand the Empire than by the teachings of Jesus. It is generally believed that his close friend Eusebius, historian and bishop of Caesarea, baptized him on his deathbed. But one has to wonder why so late, whether or not it was a mere nominal conversion, and what might have been his real motivation to accept a Christian baptism. Considering his illness, we are also led to question whether or not Constantine was fully willing or conscious of his decision. The fact that he was baptized is still disputed by some, as are several traditional accounts related to the lives of both Constantine and his mother, Helena.

Constantine Rescues a Flailing Empire

Constantine's main objective was to insure the survival and expansion of his Empire already near bankruptcy and embroiled in political turmoil. Anxieties from all sides were serious enough that he would have been delighted to avoid dealing with Christianity, a problem that was quickly taking center stage. The last thing Constantine wanted was to spend time, resources, and money on a mere matter of religion, yet doing nothing could only make matters worse. He had no choice in the matter; he had to tackle the situation head-on with all the resourcefulness available. As fast as noncombatant Christianity was growing in the Empire, he could anticipate the day when his armies would be depleted of soldiers willing to fight because of their Christian persuasion. This was deemed unacceptable. Constantine came to realize that the Christian attitude toward his military forces had to be reversed at any cost. He was fully aware that it was no longer possible to prevent Christianity from growing regardless of repressive actions taken against them and that if the reversal of their religious belief system should fail, the days of his great Empire would be counted.

The genius of Constantine was multifaceted. He certainly proved himself highly competent militarily. But he also demonstrated that he had remarkable skills as a diplomat and as an administrative strategist. With the experience of his predecessors who had done everything under the sun to derail the expansion of Christianity, going so far as to inflict inhumane restrictions and gruesome tortures, Constantine realized that a new strategy was needed despite a critical lack of funds. Great tactician that he was, he did the unimaginable. As dispassionate as was the Roman Empire in matters of religion, he decided to legalize Christianity as a first step, with the intention of making it the State religion. All previous empires of the planet had previously operated on the strengths and passions of religion. Kings, Pharaohs, and Caesars were all religious leaders who imposed their religion on the people. Constantine clearly understood that when it is not possible to fight a group, it is better to join them and assimilate them. He still had to overcome a huge handicap however: Christians were peaceful and intensely opposed to war. Since the noncombatant stance was unacceptable to maintain world supremacy, the Christian religion would have to be transformed from within. The best way to accomplish the purpose was to become a central figure of the Christian religion. By convening the Council of Nicaea as its chairman in 325 CE, Constantine was in perfect position to influence the outcome of the deliberations. But how could he expect to turn on its head the most central tenet of Christianity? No minor undertaking, for sure! This is where the malignant genius of Constantine reached its pinnacle. He managed to subtly change the tenets of Christianity in such a way as to bring them to accept enrollment in the armed forces.

Unfortunately the mosaic of Christianity contained too many pieces, each with a different outlook on the Person of Jesus. Since the teachings of Jesus were in dispute, Constantine had the luxury to choose segments of each to serve his purpose. Considering the fact some groups had already accepted some levels of compromise with pagans to avoid persecutions, it was a matter of assembling the elements needed to create a hybrid religion acceptable to the greater number. It is difficult to establish a clear factual account of the proceedings because those who participated in the changes of Christian tenets were also the historians who reported the changes. Needless to say, the conflicts of interests were blatant. Anyone who opposed the views of the council had to be wrong or, worse yet, were considered and treated as heretics and enemies of the new church. A key figure in this process provides circumstantial evidence that the council was rigged. Indeed, historian Eusebius of Nicomedia provides sufficient evidence that new tenets were likely imposed. Historian "Gibbon[42] refers to Eusebius as the 'gravest' of the ecclesiastical historians,[43] he also suggests that Eusebius was more concerned with the passing political concerns of his time than his duty as a reliable historian.[44]"

While Gibbon is severely criticized, he could not have been wrong about everything he wrote. What is certain, regardless of historical claims made in favor of, or against Eusebius, is that this entire period of history is extremely difficult to piece together. The accounts vary widely from one historian to another. Even the matter of Constantine's baptism is disputed as to who baptized him, why he was baptized, and whether or not he was in fact baptized.

---

[42] http://en.wikipedia.org/wiki/Eusebius

[43] "The gravest of the ecclesiastical historians, Eusebius himself, indirectly confesses, that he has related whatever might redound to the glory, and that he has suppressed all that could tend to the disgrace, of religion." (History of the Decline and Fall of the Roman Empire, Vol. II, Chapter XVI)

[44] "Such an acknowledgment will naturally excite a suspicion that a writer who has so openly violated one of the fundamental laws of history has not paid a very strict regard to the observance of the other, and the suspicion will derive additional credit from the character of Eusebius, which was less tinctured with credulity, and more practiced in the arts of courts, than that of almost any of his contemporaries." (Ibid.)

Ultimately the original devotees to the message of Jesus were labeled as heretics only because they refused to accept Trinity theology. They were monotheist on the strength of Jesus's own admission when He said, "I and the Father are one (being)" (Jn. 10:30, parenthesis mine) and spoke extensively about "the only true God" (Jn. 17:3). Christians who remained faithful to both OT and NT declarations that there is only One God were persecuted or exiled for not accepting the new Trinitarian tenets imposed by the official church in the third and fourth centuries CE. It is clear that followers of Christ were strict monotheists long before the teachings of Arius became known. Most of them were of Jewish background or they were Gentiles who had converted to Judaism. Yet because staunch monotheist Christians held to the monotheism of Judaism they were labeled Arians regardless of whether or not they knew anything about Arius. These people had been monotheists for three centuries before Arius came along. Since God does not change there is no reason to believe that He changed His mind with the advent of Jesus. Jesus would have clearly proclaimed the change to a Trinitarian view of God, but He only reinforced Jewish belief in this regard.

When Trinitarian theology was partly accepted at the Council of Nicaea, the original followers of Christ who had been monotheists since the days of Jesus were suddenly labeled Arian heretics, though they had never heard of Arius. They were persecuted because they were followers of Christ, not because Arius had exercised heretical influences on their theology. In fact, being monotheists of Jewish tradition founded on Scripture, they did not necessarily agree with Arius in every way, especially as it relates to his views regarding the divinity of the Son of God. But despite the marked differences of theology between early Christians and Arius, they were indiscriminately accused of Arian heresy. Historians would be hard-pressed to demonstrate that Arius's missionaries managed to bring his theology throughout Europe and areas of North Africa within the time frame of a couple decades or less, as they often suggest. How can it be explained that monotheist Christianized populations in distant places could have heard of Arius in the first place. Christian monotheists were all over the areas today known as Spain, southern and northern France, northern Europe, vast areas of northern Italy and what is today's Germany, and Switzerland as well as vast areas of northern Africa. The majority of Christians were then firm in holding a Jewish monotheism while also accepting the divinity of Christ, but not a Trinitarian view of God in three Persons.

Instead of suffering persecutions at the hands of pagans, the most devoted of monotheist Christians were now persecuted unofficially at first, and officially later, at the hands of Trinitarian Christians, and this, for centuries to come. Napoleon Bonaparte should be credited for subduing papal power between 1798 and 1812. This event brought the suppression of most such persecutions, though the Inquisitions continued till 1834.

Arius and at least two or three of his disciples in the days of Constantine suffered such persecutions and exile. It is clear that Trinity theology suited the agenda of Constantine far better than the monotheism of Arius and other Christians who at that time still represented a vast majority. It is true that Constantine vacillated between the two theologies. He had made peace with Arius and even appeared to lean toward his views, even after the Council of Nicaea. In 328 CE he recalled Arius from exile and in 335 he officially sided with Arius and exiled Athanasius to Trier. But the new Emperor Contantius sided with the Trinitarians and released Athanasius, sending him back to Alexandria in 337. Several anti-Nicene councils followed during which period Athanasius was exiled three times. It is not until 381 at the First Council of Constantinople that the controversy was settled in favor of Trinitarian theology. Can we believe for one instant that if Trinitarian theology was the original theology of the Apostles there could have been so much opposition to Trinitarian theology? Would it be conceivable that Trinity theology would end up having to be imposed on people by force? Clearly, early Christianity was not Trinitarian.

As for Arius, he was apparently poisoned to death in the city of Constantinople under suspicion that high-level Trinitarian authorities were responsible for his death. He suffered a dreadfully painful death. Unfortunately, the word "suspicion" should be removed from the narrative of this story.

Let us remember that Constantine was no saint, as many historians and church authorities would like us to believe. He was directly responsible for the death of one of his sons and one of his wives among others. Indeed, monotheism was viewed with contempt in the pagan world of the time. Trinity theology was adopted only because it offered a practical solution to unify the Empire by changing the tenets of true

Christianity. It is only through the suggestive power of "faith" that Three Persons could be considered equal to One, and One equal to Three. First grade math denies the concept. Indeed, faith falsely understood allows unreasonable departures from logic and from Scripture. Bad math has nothing in common with God or misapplied faith or logic. The persistent departures from logic have opened the doors to false Christianity ever since. Faith falsely understood has the power to mislead people to the highest levels of insanity along with the immense irrational power to incite egregious acts of violence.

Pagans were persuaded that a single God could not possibly be powerful enough to face all the problems of the world. It is for that reason that pagans believed in the supernatural actions of multitudes of gods, but interestingly, a trinity of gods was believed responsible for leading all others. The Roman leadership considered far more attractive the Trinitarian approach to Christian deity, especially considering that saints could be named for each day of the year to help the triune God who would otherwise be overwhelmed. The names of the gods changed one more time in the history of polytheism, but this time they were given Hebrew and Christian names. Unfortunately, with Trinity theology the pagan mentality remained strong, and perhaps this time, even more violent than ever before.

False teachers and false prophets whose theologies Jesus predicted would produce thorns rather than good fruit are known to have spread their falsehood throughout the Empire, mostly by force, or by ignorance. Some of the false teachings were already causing problems among the followers of Jesus within a couple of decades after the Crucifixion. Here is how Jesus expressed His concern: "Watch out for false prophets. They come to you in sheep's clothing, but inwardly they are ferocious wolves. By their fruit you will recognize them. Do people pick grapes from thornbushes, or figs from thistles" (Mt. 7:15–16)? The mention of "ferocious wolves" was Jesus's way to portray a spirit of violence. Likewise, the thorns and thistles were not the announcement of a period exempt of bloodshed. Jesus also predicted that the false prophets would deceive many people, causing an increase of wickedness and tragic outcomes. So much so that "the love of most," He predicted, would "grow cold" (Mt. 24:11–13).

Unfortunately for the world, State churches also in control of central governments imposed forcefully the false teachings of Christianity that they might serve in the military with good consciences. The false teachings spread unimpaired, because they were imposed by force. True Christianity continued to be persecuted and driven to caves in mountains. Meanwhile, Christian rifts continued to multiply in the name of Jesus. The false teachings are responsible for unparalleled bloodshed throughout the Empire and well beyond. Eventually the theological disagreements managed to split the State church, a split known as the East-West Schism. More bloodshed ensued, and Islam was born in apparent protest against Trinity theology and the failure of Christians to explain the difference between the invisible Infinite God, His visible Image as Jesus, and the Spirit of God, which is the way He thinks. They failed to show that Jesus is the Image of God that came in human flesh to bring the Truth that saves, not a Truth that merely forgives. This purpose could have been achieved no other way without violating human freedom. The idea that a payment for sins was made from a cross to save sinners was the extension of additional pagan concepts of salvation made possible only by Trinity theology—a religion that clearly lacks the power to produce fundamental changes of hearts.

Among all the schools of thought available from Christianity in the fourth century, after evaluations and reevaluations the authorities settled for a list of dogmas most likely to amalgamate Christianity under the banner of pagan religions. The tenets of the new State Religion opened the door to military service as well as the sincere devotion to killing enemies for the sake of Christ. The architects of Trinity theology provided a splendid opportunity to develop the new hybrid religion. While there is a great deal of disagreement about the way Trinity theology became a fundamental tenet of Christianity, please forgive me for offering my succinct views on the subject. But since the architects and propagators of Trinity theology wrote this chapter of history we have very little concrete information available from opposing camps often tortured and exiled, and whose manuscripts were often burnt. Circumstantial evidences remain our most reliable guides. The claims made by bishops and historians who personally benefited from their collaboration with Constantine's agenda were often forced into submission against their will.

Indeed, the fact, or the legend that Constantine had a vision of sort has been well publicized, though the origin of the vision is debatable. Many Christians see it as a message from God, but God is not the only one capable of communicating with humans through dreams and visions. Eusebius reports that Constantine saw a cross above the sun while a voice was urging him to conquer by this sign. There are disagreements regarding the nature of the cross or Christogram that was seen in the vision. Constantine required the sign to be displayed on all shields and banners of his soldiers. But the fact that the sun was represented alongside the cross may have suggested the amalgamation of Christian beliefs with the pagan cults of the Sun, *Sol Invictus*. As it turns out, Trinity theology became the Trojan horse of the new religion.

How Did Trinity Theology Come About?

The subject is far too complex to be explored academically within the framework of this book. What is important to realize is that even if while on earth Jesus and the Father could be perceived as two separate Persons, for reasons we shall explain later, it remains clear that the Holy Spirit was never considered a third Person of the divinity. Jesus would certainly have prayed to the Holy Spirit if "He" were one of the Holy Three, but He never did, nor did any of His New Testament disciples and followers. This alone should provide food for thought. Just because the Holy Spirit is an attribute of God that Jesus proved compatible with human flesh does not make it a Person.

The Holy Spirit is the Spirit of God that Jesus acquired while on earth to show that human flesh does not disqualify a human being from accepting to think as God would, in terms of relationships. This Spirit was also in Adam and Eve from the moment of their creation until their departure from the Spirit of the "only true God" (Jn. 17:3) in whose image they were both created. Salvation is entirely a matter of restoring the image of God, or the way God thinks, in fallen humans. Thus salvation is clearly a matter of restoring the Spirit that God had created in Adam and Eve when He created them. While they demonstrated that humans could depart from God's Spirit, Jesus came to demonstrate the opposite. He showed that it is not the flesh that inhibits the restoration of God's Spirit in humans, it is the focus of people's own spirit on their own flesh that blocks holiness of thought (see Rom. 5:17). John quoted Jesus as saying: "The Spirit gives life; the flesh counts for nothing" (Jn. 6:63a). In other words, to have life it is vital for sinners to acquire the Spirit of God. Having His Spirit allows sinners to operate with a mind that works like His, but only as it relates to mutual relations with all other beings created in the image of God. With such a mind-set that comes from God the sinner grows progressively away from sin. It is the focus on serving self at the expense of others that inhibits sinners from accepting the Spirit of God in their hearts.

One early Church Father, as they are commonly called, is credited for the first use of the Latin word *trinitas* in his description of God's attributes. The Latin word has since been translated, "trinity." However, he did not use this word to imply that God is made up of three Persons; on the contrary, he used it to describe three fundamental realities related to God. He was talking about a trinity of divine attributes. He called them "God, His Word, and His Wisdom." He was implying that God could communicate in words, or by means of "the Word" (Jn. 1:1) His message of wisdom that saves—not three different Persons. Thus, Theophilus of Antioch who made this observation round about the year 180 CE; was reinforcing the idea that God has the power to share with humans His ultimate message of wisdom, which is His Spirit, or the Holy Spirit.

It follows reason that if God is the infinite eternal being Scripture describes Him to be, He has to be unexplainable and unreachable. As such, He would remain forever invisible and out of the reach of finite beings. While finite beings cannot understand or touch an infinite reality, He is able to communicate Truth and wisdom to them in their own words and on their own physical and mental level. In fact, He has gone out of His way to convey vital Truth to His free-thinking created beings while pointing out the eternal vital importance of adopting His everlasting wisdom. His message is so contrary to the natural quest for survival of this world that having access to His truth and wisdom through His finite Envoy is nothing less than miraculous. The problem is that the world has not yet accepted the Message of God's Envoy called Jesus, who is the finite image of His infinite reality. So far humans have only managed to corrupt His message, which also caused them to lose track of the perfect rationale of His wisdom.

We must come to understand that the Infinite God cannot communicate with humans or other finite created beings without having access to a *finite material* image of His own Infinite Person. Thus Jesus is not another Person but an extension of God Himself. How else could He link finite beings with the infinite immortal Person that He is? The required linkage with humanity was something that the Infinite God alone could accomplish. No finite being could ever hope to bridge the finite with the infinite, but the Infinite God suffers no such limitation.

He can have an image of Himself to interact with finite realities precisely because He is infinite and omnipresent.

God managed to bridge the infinite gap thanks to His "express image" (Heb. 1:3) in the person of Jesus, through whom He maintains a link with all the finite reality of the universe. This is how He has also managed to communicate the most important element of His wisdom our fallen world needed; it is called "the Holy Spirit." A Holy Spirit is a mind that operates with the wisdom of God. God is known to have communicated through His Image with Adam and Eve, with Cain and Abel, with Enoch, and with Noah, before the Flood. Later He communicated through His Image with Abraham, Jacob, Moses, and a number of prophets. But as long as God's Image was a nonhuman metaphysical expression of the Infinite One, He was somewhat limited in His communications because God's physical expression being an extension of the immortal God was also immortal. Thus the Image of God could not come to this world to show mortal humans that love must be a way of life that death alone can interrupt. Indeed, since the Image of God was not mortal He could not come to this world and live the entire life span of human life all the way to His death. For that reason the Word, or the Image of God, had to become mortal human flesh. This was the only way the physical Image of God could become mortal. An immortal image of God would have remained incapable of demonstrating a concept totally unnatural for humans to understand. Indeed, God wanted to show that love could inhabit even the spirit of a being even if that being is made of flesh. To accomplish that purpose, He had to show humans that love must go all the way to the death and that love remains incomplete as long as it remains incapable of becoming unconditionally merciful toward enemies all the way to the last drop of blood and last breath of life.

The incarnation is that moment when the Image of God became human flesh in the history of the universe. The finite metaphysical Image of God became for the first time the Son of one of His own created beings—thus, at that moment He became both Son of man and Son of God. Indeed, as we are told in the book of Hebrews, it is the finite Image of God that created everything in the universe, including Adam and Eve and thus He is the Father of all their descendants. When the Image of God was born human as one of His own created beings He became both Son of man and Son of God. Before that He was neither Son of God nor Son of Man, He was the only eternal visible image of the only true eternal, infinite, and immortal God. It is not until 2,000 years ago that Jesus became the Son of humans of whom He was indeed the Father.

We cannot understand the Person of Jesus if we fail to recognize His role as the Image of the Infinite God throughout the infinity of time. In His dealings with the inhabitants of planet Earth God had expressed Himself through His Spirit by communicating with prophets. It is only on special occasions that He expressed Himself through His infinite express Image. When all other avenues of expression had failed, because humans kept corrupting the messages received, the express image of God became human to get the job done "once and for all" (Jude 1:3). Previously He had been the expression of God that morphed Himself to communicate with all the realities of the finite universe. He has not always been Son of God but He has always been God's finite expression that created every finite realities of the universe (Jn. 1:1–3; Col. 1:16). Jesus proved who He was when He multiplied baked bread and cooked fish (Mt. 14:17–22) and later resurrected Lazarus (Jn. 11:43–44) and others. For the Eternal Image of God to become human, He had to be "begotten of God" (Jn. 1:14 KJV). We know this by His own admission: Jesus preexisted His incarnation into human flesh (Jn. 6:62). He was not yet Son of God at that time, but He was already the express Image of the invisible God.

When it became necessary, because humans kept misunderstanding God, He became the only Son God ever begat, and since a human gave him life He became Son of humans, or Son of Man. He became Son of His own creation, thus He is both Father and Son, just as Isaiah 9 describes His birth and mission: "For to us a child is born, to us a son is given, and the government will be on his shoulders. And he will be called Wonderful Counselor, Mighty God, *Everlasting Father*, Prince of Peace" (Is. 9:6, emphasis mine). Who is this Savior if He is not the Counselor we call the Holy Spirit, if He is not the Mighty God we all call God, if He is not the Everlasting Father we try needlessly to separate from the Son as a different Person, and if He is not the Prince of Peace the Dead Sea Scrolls call, "Prince of the peaceful ones."

We must remember that Scripture used the word "man" as a generic term for all humans of all genders and all races. Jesus being an extension of God is not a separate Person, but He is the only visible Image of the Infinite One. He is the finite Image of God who had to accept to become human "like His brothers in every way" (Heb. 2:17), or else He could not have lived the full and complete version of God's message all the way to the last breath of life. It is only while He was showing humans the Way of life that He lived like all humans do and endured all the trials of humanity all the way to the worst possible death by prolonged torture. While human, Jesus never took advantage of the power He had from also being the Father. Jesus never took advantage of the divine power to serve His own Person as a human being. For Him, that would have been sin, because if He had taken advantage of the divine power to avoid sin He would have proven to the universe that humans are indeed incapable of overcoming sin. The Truth He accepted from the Father (see Is. 50), is Truth available to all humans. It is the faith, the persuasion of Jesus that kept Him from sinning; that persuasion is the Holy Spirit of God, not a supernatural power that makes us do the right thing. Just like all humans, He lived as a human. He suffered all the temptations, pain, and trials that we are all subjected to endure and much more because of who He was. Humans could not have made bread out of stones or come down from the Cross, but He could have, and demonstrated in more ways than one that He could have. What a temptation that must have been! Which one of us could have withstood such temptations?

It is not possible to affirm that in 180 CE Theophilus understood the concept of God as I try to explain it here. However, it is clear that he was on track and that if he had been aided by the logic of our Modern Age, he might have reached the same conclusions. Let us remember that he lived at a time when it was sacrilegious to apply any level of logic to religion, a sad reality still true today. It is for that reason that Jesus had to tell His disciples: "I have much more to say to you, more than you can now bear" (Jn. 16:12). Time has come for modern humans to lift the curtain of confusion still standing in the Temple of God by accepting to consider His message objectively. We cannot understand God, but we can know and understand His heart rationally, and thus, His character. All this is revealed to us with clarity through the Everlasting Gospel of Jesus, but only if we are willing to consider His message rationally. Speaking of the Spirit of Truth required to understand mentioned in the following verse, Jesus was probably talking about the time when the spirit of logic, which is the spirit, or thinking that reveals truth. Emphasis on logic is relatively recent and has yet to be applied to religion. The application of logic did not become widespread until the industrial revolution along with the expansion of human educational efforts with a focus on logic. The divide we have between religion and education is largely a matter of logic. Unfortunately, sometime science is as unwilling to apply logic to their own research, as are the religions of our world.

Here is what Theophilus appears to have understood by the word trinity (*trinitas*) as he applied it to God:

1) God is the *invisible* all-powerful Person who is the fullness of the infinite single divinity of the universe (Col. 1:15; 1 Tim. 1:17; Heb. 11:27).

2) His Word, or Jesus is the Finite Tangible and *visible* expression of the infinite invisible God. He came in the flesh as a human, but we are told that in Him the fullness of God resided (Col. 1:19; Col. 2:9).

3) His Wisdom is the Truth that reveals the only mode of operation by which free beings of the universe can remain eternally alive and in peace with one another. What greater wisdom is there? We are all invited to participate in the wisdom of God's Truth. Only the Wisdom of His Truth makes it possible for us to "be filled to the measure of the fullness of God" (Eph. 3:19b). It appears quite clear that Theophilus envisioned the Wisdom of God as His Holy Spirit, not another Person of the divinity. The Holy Spirit being the Spirit of God or His mind-set, we could say that it is His Wisdom that should become ours as we grow in the Truth that produces true love capable of mercy. Only then can it be said that we are filled with the Holy Spirit, which is the wisdom of God.

If the position of Theophilus can be said to reflect the general monotheistic views of Christianity prevalent until roughly the year 200CE, the same cannot be said of Tertullian. He managed to shoot a poisoned dart deep into the most fundamental principle of Scripture and teachings of Jesus. It is not until about the year 212CE, that Tertullian, a man credited for being the founder of Christian theology, used the word "trinity" to designate a Godhead composed of three separate Persons: Father, Son, and Holy Spirit. Tertullian's view of trinity was in sharp contrast with that of Theophilus's, some thirty years before. At that time all true followers of Christ probably disapproved of a three Persons view of the Godhead. But persecuted and scattered at the hands of Christians disloyal to the message of Christ, they could only find refuge by hiding away from mainstream society where their voices were could not be heard.

This is not surprising. The Lord as well as Apostle Peter and others had predicted this outcome. In his Second Epistle Peter writes: "But there were also false teachers among the people (among the Jews), just as there will be false teachers among you (among the Christians). They will secretly introduce destructive heresies, even denying the sovereign Lord (singular) who bought them—bringing swift destruction on themselves. Many will follow their shameful ways and will bring the way of truth into disrepute. In their greed these teachers will exploit you with stories they have made up" (2 Pet. 2:1–3a; parentheses mine).

While translations of the above text vary, it is clear that false teachers would do two things to falsify God's message: (1) defame God's word, His message, and (2) abnegate His personhood, His sovereignty. With the false theology God's Lordship is not renounced or denied; that would be too blatant a lie and too easy to identify as a false teaching. The personhood of God is merely altered for the purpose of deceiving and manipulating people, as the Greek word *arneomai* suggests. The text predicts that an ominous deceptive method of teaching would be fixated on transforming both the nature of God, done through Trinity theology, and His message, by calling it a payment for sins. What better way to deceive people who had a rather limited knowledge of Scripture and a vague understanding of the religion of Christ? These people who had lost contact with true Christianity in hiding were manipulated by making it appear as though the Christian message is similar to that of pagans. By manipulating the nature of God His message is immediately perceived through a false paradigm. Trinity theology accomplishes both deceptive goals in one fell swoop. By dividing the nature of God into Three Persons the message of Truth can be falsified with ease.

Interestingly, Tertullian who can probably be credited for inventing Trinity theology is also credited for having redefined faith by saying: *"Credo quia absurdum"*—"I believe because it is absurd!" Since this is the traditionally paraphrased citation found in history books, here is what Tertullian actually wrote, though the meaning remains the same: *"Prorsus credibile est, quia ineptum est"*—"It is wholly believable, because it is incongruous" (*De Carne Christi*, 5.4. Tertullian). Quite an incredible statement for a man considered the father of theological studies. As far as Tertullian was concerned, the philosophy of Athens had nothing to do with the religion of Jerusalem. To Him, the logic of Athens was irreconcilable with religion. True, there were pitfalls with the logic of Athens because they were unable to separate their logic from pagan traditions, but at least, they were seekers of logic. At the same time Tertullian was supposedly defending a religion on the basis of rejecting logic. As we have observed, incongruous beliefs related to religions remain the stumbling block of religious and social progress to this day. Under the pretext of rejecting falsehood and heresy, Tertullian and those who agreed with him were actually guilty of mystifying the Gospel Jesus wanted His followers to understand through sound logic. In the name of guarding the religion of Jesus pure and free from unorthodoxies, they multiplied the heresies related to His message of Truth that requires logic to be properly understood.

What is officially known about the development of theology related to the Three separate Persons of the Godhead is nebulous and fragmented. We have already touched on the problem. What is certain is that the theology of One God was widely prevalent for the first two centuries following the Cross. In the duration of that time period there was not even a hint of Trinitarian theology in the Christian world. How the distinction was made between Father and Son is unclear, but it slowly led to a distinction of Persons from a third, the Holy Spirit.

The first Christians were all Jews, and certainly a change of understanding from a One-Person God to a Trinity of Persons is nowhere to be found in the New Testament. There was no reason to depart from a position dating back to Moses and even Abraham. God made this point very clear in His first three Commandments and the *Shema*, a prayer repeated twice daily at the opening and closing of the Temple. Here is how this prayer begins: "Hear, O Israel: the LORD our God, the LORD is one" (Deut 6:4). Jews and Gentiles already converted to Judaism were the first Christian followers of Jesus on the face of this planet. It is not until Trinity theology was introduced and imposed by force on all people that Jews became reluctant to become Christians. Without the Jews and their unconditional dedication to a strict monotheistic understanding of God Christianity would have failed; it is that simple. Indeed, if Jews had not endorsed Christianity, no other religious group would have. This is why the gospel was to be preached in Jerusalem first, then in

Judaea and Samaria, and only then unto the "uttermost part of the earth" (Acts 1:8). Why would God have gone out of His way to teach the Israelites that there is only one God, a message they reluctantly accepted, only to change His mind in the New Testament where the concept of Trinity of Persons is nowhere to be found?[45] When carefully analyzed, the deductions supposedly made from Scripture to arrive at a Trinity of Persons of the Divinity are all twisted rationalizations.

Although discussions about God in Three Persons only began round about the year 200, it is not until the Council of Nicea in 325CE that the groundwork for the acceptance this theological concept began and was partially accepted. It was fully adopted as a fundamental tenet of the church in 381 at the Council of Constantinople, of which little or nothing is known about the deliberations. The history of this development is so convoluted and surrounded with so much controversy and hidden agendas that it is not possible to draw conclusions from simple readings of contradictory traditional history. What appears certain however is that when the topic is studied in depth, Constantine appears to have hijacked the religion of Christ, even if he might have been remorseful later on.

The Council of Nicaea had a devastating impact on Christian theology. Instead of resolving theological issues it had multiplied the arguments needed to create confusion. Christianity has yet to recover from the blow. The 318 or so representatives called to participate to the deliberations of the Council of Nicaea were obviously handpicked. It is clear that the Empire subsidized copiously the expense accounts and salaries of the delegates. The same could be said of the 1,500 guards planted throughout the Council for the three months' duration. These were the very same guards who had previously administered persecutions on Christians. Everything had been preplanned to guarantee a majority vote in favor of Constantine's agenda regardless of prevalent Christian

---

[45] Here is how Encyclopaedia Britannica introduces the subject of Trinity:
Trinity, in Christian doctrine, the unity of Father, Son, and Holy Spirit as three persons in one Godhead.

Neither the word Trinity nor the explicit doctrine appears in the New Testament, nor did Jesus and his followers intend to contradict the Shema in the Hebrew Scriptures: "Hear, O Israel, The Lord our God is one Lord" (Deuteronomy 6:4). http://www.britannica.com/EBchecked/topic/605512/Trinity

beliefs at the time or the teachings of Jesus. Historical data that confirms this assertion is scarce for obvious reasons, but circumstantial evidence is overwhelming and speaks for itself. It is known that even Eusebius who was clearly of Arian conviction ended up voting in favor of Trinity theology. Could it be that the guards were so daunting that they could forcefully sway the voters one way or the other?

This subtlety of history is conspicuously shaded. Whenever prevalent historians such as Gibbon suggest that the integrity of key members of the Council such as Eusebius can be considered with suspicion, the opposing camp is quick to refute the objection. Yet the official conclusions of the Council are revealing. It appears that not a single Council attendee viewed Jesus as the "express image" (Heb. 1:3 KJV) of the Father, and that Jesus and Father are indeed just One and the same Person, as Jesus claimed (Jn. 10:30). The image of a person is not the image of someone else. This fact alone should be significant enough, considering that the true followers of Christ all believed that Jesus was the Creator, thus that He was God who had temporarily accepted all the limitations of a human nature.[46] Although it is true that most Christians today endorse the Trinitarian view, it is clear that the majority of pre-Council of Nicaea Christians were in opposition to that persuasion. In fact, long after the Council until the sixth and even the seventh century,

---

[46]   See Robert McQueen Grant, *God and the One God, p 156,* The Westminster Press; Philadelphia, PA. 1986. Although Robert M. Grant was himself a Trinitarian, his study of early Church history clearly indicates that the concept of Trinity gained popularity and acceptance round about the Council of Nicaea and later. Speaking of pre-council authors Grant says: "What we find in these early authors, then, is not a doctrine of the Trinity—a term we reserve for a doctrine that tries to explain the relation of the three Persons to the one God-but a depiction of the three Persons. In other words, we find the materials for such a doctrine but not a doctrine as such."

It is Grant's view that the material for the doctrine of "three Persons" was present in Scripture, but he recognizes that not everyone shares that view. He states further that: "Arianism: Before Nicaea, Christian theology was almost universally subordinationist. Theology almost universally taught that the Son was subordinate to the Father, but Arius expressed this kind of Christology in a provocative way. . . ." (Ibid. p. 160). It is clear to me, that the finite expression of God, as I call His visible expression in this book, is later the Person of Jesus who was subjected to the infinite, invisible reality of the only true God while on earth in human flesh.

the majority of Christians were still hostile to Trinity theology. Whenever one side was in power, the other was persecuted. Both Trinitarians and Arians have blood on their hands. As time went on, both groups were led to consider the benefits of political power at the expense of the message of the Lord, along with the Truth that produces peace He advocated. Discussions relative to Arianism and Trinitarian theology are far from settled to this day. When two or more views are wrong about a given topic, discussions and debates defending them over centuries fail to resolve anything. At the end of the day, they are still all wrong about their conclusions. Instead of finding unity by searching for Truth in love and serenity, these groups remained divided because of their prideful devotions to false beliefs from which they remain unwilling to depart regardless of evidence to the contrary. Christianity suffers the fear of confusion by facts.

Both Arian and Trinitarian Theology Are Problematic?

There are several variations of Arianism and Semi-Arianism, none of which agree with the teachings of Jesus or the Apostles. By and large their theology is presented as claiming that the Father created the Son at some point in the infinity of time. This claim makes of Jesus a being created at some point in time during His preincarnation existence, which is not in agreement with the declarations of Jesus. John quotes Jesus as saying: "What if you see the Son of Man ascend to where he was before!" (Jn. 6:62) Before what? we should ask. Before He came to earth, clearly, but also before He became Son of Man. Indeed the preexisting Jesus was always the visible extension of God as His "express image" (Heb. 1:3; 2 Cor. 4:4; Col. 1:15), thus eternal and immortal. With the belief that the preincarnated Jesus was Son of God before His incarnation, Arians are led to believe something Scripture does not say. A *created* Image of God is immediately perceived as inferior to Almighty God, thus He cannot be considered eternally and infinitely divine, but this is an error of perception. The disciples of Jesus show no indication that they ever doubted the eternal preexistence of Jesus, or His power as equal with the Father. They never doubted that Jesus preexisted His incarnation eternally and never said or implied that He was in any way inferior to the Father. Not so well understood is the affirmation from Scripture that the preincarnated Jesus was indeed the Creator of the universe, before the creation of humans in Eden. Nothing in Scripture implies that humans were created at the same time as the rest of the universe.

While Arians are correct to deny the personhood of the Holy Spirit, they fail to recognize Jesus as both Father and Son. Jesus became the incarnated Image of the very Image of the infinite He was previously. He is the God that created the universe and later became the product of His own creation at the incarnation. Thus Son of His own creation. This made Him both Father and Son, a concept in perfect agreement with Isaiah, as discussed in this chapter. In this passage the child our Savior is also called, future tense, "Mighty God," "Everlasting Father," and "Counselor" (Is. 9:6). Why should we ever doubt that the Infinite God should lack the capability to fulfill all those purposes? Was that not the argument that opposed pagan-minded Christians to monotheist Christians for centuries?

When the preincarnated Jesus is viewed as created, He is also viewed as inferior to the Infinite God. What Scripture tells us is that He was for all eternity the only finite image of God. How confusing it would be if God had several images of Himself? Whenever the divinity of Jesus is in question, a gap is immediately created between Father and Son. Unfortunately, Trinitarians have also allowed such a gap to creep into their theology despite their assertion that all Three Persons are One and divine. When Trinitarian theology teaches that Father and Son are separate Persons, that fact alone places a gap between them—they cannot be the same person. The gap is then exploited to imply that One came to plead the case of sinners before the Great Judge of the universe. If the Advocate and the Judge are One and the same Person the Advocate would not have to plead the sinners' case before Himself! Again, logic should come to our rescue and help us to clarify some such theological ambiguities. Why are so many theologians reluctant to consult the wisdom of logic to clarify passages of Scripture? Is not logic the wisdom of God?

While there are several versions of Trinity theology, we focus here on the most common and most universal points of the dogma. Trinitarians are correct to consider Jesus divine; Scripture is clear about that. But they are wrong to think that Jesus is of the same "substance" as the Father while He is also a different Person. The image of God before the incarnation might well have been of the same substance, thus it was immortal. After the incarnation it could no longer be said that Jesus was of the same substance, because it is clear that the human substance was mortal. The only finite immortal Image of God chose on His own volition to cloak Himself with human flesh identical to that of all humans. From that point forward Jesus was made of the same substance as His brothers (Heb. 2:17; Rom. 8:3), a material substance made from elements found in the earth (Gen. 2:7). God was not made of that earthly substance; in fact, God was never made, He is, and has always been, and always will be, since before there was substance of any kind. The same could be said of the preincarnated image God projected for the finite universe to see. He created all finite realities through His finite Image (Rom. 1:20).

Also lacking biblical support is the Trinitarian idea that Jesus was always the Son of God from all eternity. The Gospel of John 1:14 makes it quite clear that Jesus was not always flesh; He became flesh, thus He was not of the same substance as the Father while on earth. Since Jesus is also the Father who created all the finite realities of the universe including Adam and Eve, He is our Father because He created us. By becoming Son of humans whom He created, Jesus then became Son of His created beings, thus He became the Son of people of whom He was the Creator and Father.

Before becoming Son of Man Jesus was the Image of the Infinite invisible God who created humans. He is called both Son of God and Son of Man multiple times in the New Testament. If Jesus had always been Son of God, He would indeed be a Person different from the Father. And as Arians believe, He would have been created at some point in time before coming to this planet in human flesh, a concept Scripture denies. If He were created as Son, He would not be eternal, thus He would not be equal with the Father. On this point, both Arians and Trinitarians are in disagreement with Scripture. Worse yet, Trinitarians are in disagreement with their own teachings, because they claim Jesus to be divine, yet a separate Person who shares with God the same substance. If God is immortal, so would Jesus be if He were of the same substance, yet we know that He died on the Cross.

Trinity theology "defines God as three consubstantial persons,[2] expressions, or *hypostases*:[3] the Father, the Son (Jesus Christ), and the Holy Spirit; 'one God in three persons'."[47] Unfortunately, the Greek word

---

47   See http://en.wikipedia.org/wiki/Trinity. [2] The Family Bible Encyclopedia, 1972 p. 3790. [3] See discussion in "Person." *Catholic Encyclopedia*. New York: Robert Appleton Company. 1913.

hypostasis has strong pagan ties and was used primarily in philosophical discourses related to abstract notions. In the fourth century BCE, Aristotle and Plato used it to discuss the underlying substance and essence of reality. The concept involved called Platonism is far too confusing to be discussed as it could only be misleading to our discussion. Unfortunately a Christian version called Neo-Platonism brought back Plato's philosophy along with the word *ousia*. This was roundabout the third and fourth centuries CE. It appears that the resurgence of Platonism in Christianity was an effort to validate Trinity theology on the strength of existing pagan philosophy.[48] Through time philosophers disagreed and often contradicted one another's premises, especially under Neo-Platonism. The confusing rhetoric involved was probably intended to demonstrate that even the highly regarded academic landscape of the time favored the idea of God as a Trinity of Persons. Thus, Christian academia became the hotbed of Trinitarian propaganda, but sadly, many were forced into submission, as was Eusebius who was of Arian persuasion, yet voted in favor of Trinity at the Council of Nicaea.

For the followers of Jesus the underlying substance and essence of everything, visible and invisible, animate and inanimate, is a moot point. Everything has its origin with the Infinite God who throughout eternity has always manifested Himself through His finite image. Later the Image of God came in the flesh to communicate a Truth with humans that they would have never understood unless the extension of God Himself came to live it all the way to His death. A relationship between God and the finite realities of the universe could not be established without a finite expression of Himself, of which there was only one. For the followers of Jesus the explanation given by the author of Hebrews should provide ample clues: "By faith we understand that the universe was formed at God's command, so that what is seen was not made out of what was visible" (Heb. 11:3). My translation might be helpful: "Our persuasion (faith) is that the finite realities of the universe were formed by God's (*rhēma*) utterance, or essence. This explains why that which is visible no longer appears as God made it."

---

[48] In philosophy the word *hypostasis* is a term used to discuss the metaphysical properties of underlying realities in terms of their substance and essence. As for *ousia*, even philosophers disagree on the meaning. Generally it is believed to mean: substance, essence, or the nature of a thing or person in a state of being.

Paul conveys the same concept when he exclaims: "For by Him all things were created: things in heaven (entire universe) and on earth, visible and invisible," (Col. 1:16a, parenthesis mine). Everything bears the signature of God despite the degeneration and disorderly realities of the universe that sin has marred. Not only has our planet Earth suffered, but also the rest of the universe. All three Gospels quote Jesus as saying: "Heaven and earth will pass away, but my words will never pass away" (Mt. 24:35). No conditional tense is implied here. What God says is clear: His Word will never change or pass away, but heaven (the universe) and earth will indeed pass away.

As followers of Jesus we have no reason to disbelieve that the entire universe suffers the effects of sin and that as Jesus predicted, it will ultimately all disappear. What a big bang of disappearance that will be! Angels sinned long before humans did and caused the progressive destruction of the universe in the process. When God made humans, Satan who already existed was allowed a place of influence in the Tree of Knowledge of Good and Evil. Paul clarifies the matter as follows: "We know that the whole creation (that includes the entire universe) has been groaning as in the pains of childbirth right up to the present time" (Rom. 8:22). The only reason the universe continues to groan is because of the devastation sin has brought everywhere; there can be no other reason. The reason planet Earth was "formless empty and dark" (Gen. 1:2) when God came to bring order and beauty was likely because sin had destroyed the original beauty of this planet. We know from Jude that angels had to depart from their abodes because of sin. (see Jude 1:6). In the following verse Jude goes so far as to compare those angels to the inhabitants of Sodom and Gomorrah who likewise lost their places of residence.

The assumption that God and Jesus could be perceived as two separate Persons while Jesus was incarnated in human flesh is understandable, because during that time Jesus was living like all other humans. He relied entirely on the infinite invisible God whom He called Father, and whom He alone had ever seen. Because the expression of God had become human He had to learn everything from the Infinite immortal One. The appearance is given that two Persons were involved. But Trinity theology gets in deeper trouble when the suggestion is made that the Spirit of God is yet another Person of the so-called Godhead.

The word "spirit" is another concept that has been highly paganized through the millennia. It is used to imply a person's thinking when we say: "I will be with you in spirit." It also refers to a person's mind and emotions, when we say: "She had a broken spirit." But the word "spirit" is also used to imply phantoms or ghosts perceived as having special powers and the ability to vanish. The Bible calls this latter category, necromancy or divination. They are supposedly the spirits of dead people returning to visit the living, but they are evil angels. The Bible strongly warns God's people never to communicate with such spirits. It is as wrong to communicate with such phantoms, as it was to take the Fruit in Eden. Pagans claim, as did the serpent in the Tree, that something in a person's makeup never dies and that once dead a person continues to enjoy some level of awareness. Our mention of Plato and Aristotle regarding the word *hypostases* was related to this concept well known in pagan circles, but Scripture denies that the dead know anything or that they can communicate with anyone after death. The dead are dead, says Scripture; they "know nothing; they have no further reward, and even the memory of them is forgotten. Their love, their hate, and their jealousy have long since vanished; never again will they have a part in anything that happens under the sun" (Ecc. 9:5b, 6).

Mediums and spiritists are known to help the living to communicate with the dead, but here is what Scripture says about them: "When men tell you to consult mediums and spiritists, who whisper and mutter, should not a people inquire of their God? Why consult the dead on behalf of the living? To the law and the testimony! If they do not speak according to the word, they have no light in them" (Is. 8:19–20). Many other references from Scripture could be supplied here, but the message is simple: Beware of spirits, especially if they fail to speak in accordance with Scripture.

The reason for the warning is simple. The dead who "know nothing" do not have active spirits. The spirit is a person's ability to understand, think, reason, and make decisions, but this is no longer possible after death. When a person is dead that person's spirit is also dead. The only thing that survives is the memory of that person in the mind of God. In a way, it can be said that their spirit, as to who they are and have accomplished, is still with us and still with God, but only because the living remember them for their contributions or for their destructiveness. It is because God remembers them that He can resurrect them on the last day. What goes back to God is the memory of the unique person they were while living. When Lazarus, a friend of Jesus had been dead and buried, Martha, his wife, exclaimed to Jesus: "I know he will rise again in the resurrection at the last day" (Jn. 11:24). Jesus answered in the future tense: "I am the resurrection and the life. He who believes in me will live, even though he dies; and whoever lives and believes in me will never die, do you believe this" (Jn. 11:25–26)? Both the first and second statements are in the future tense. If they believe, they will live, in the future, and they will never die again, in the future.

If the dead could indeed communicate with the living, why would Jesus have bothered to resurrect Lazarus? On the other hand, would it not be confusing if a host of spirits of dead people could communicate with us at any time? We would be placed in a situation where it would not be possible for us to recognize voices from dead people, devils, or that of God. It is for that reason that the voice of God is heard only when absolutely necessary, and only when humans reach an impasse of understanding. When the information we need is clearly available from the voices of prophets, Jesus, and Apostles, there is no further need for God to speak directly to individuals. It is for this reason that Jesus said: "seek first his kingdom" (Mt. 6:33), and "seek and you will find" (Mt. 7:7).

God does not want us to be confronted or confused by a multitude of voices regarding the only Truth that matters in the universe. Even with a good knowledge of Scripture confusion would be difficult to avoid. This is especially true when Scripture itself is not clearly understood or when it is considered in the framework of misleading traditions and interpretations. God wants us to seek from Scripture the common denominator of the Truth it contains. Scripture is not the Word of God; it only contains it. It is for us to find it. This is one of the ways God protects freedom. If it were not necessary to seek the Truth that sets sinners free, because it is all there to be perfectly understood without having to search, Jesus would not have urged upon the people the importance of searching for Truth. On the other hand, if Truth were available without effort and if it were presented in plain words, we would no longer have Scripture today. Indeed, humans would have found a way to destroy it long ago, because it teaches unconditional love and nonviolence, a concept naturally born humans cannot accept. The narrative of the Old Testament is the story of a people who failed to listen to God. Unfortunately, Christianity promptly made the same mistake.

The knowledge of God that gives eternal life (Jn. 17:3) provides the necessary understanding of Truth that sets sinners free (Jn. 8:32). It is only when the process of finding freedom begins to take place that the Holy Spirit begins to germinate and grows in a sinner's heart. The Truth is not difficult to understand or hidden, but it is presented in such a way as to be *available only to those who want it and are willing to search for it.* The search is not righteousness by works because righteousness is the product of the correct understanding of God and His message. That understanding is the faith of God, which is also the faith of Jesus that all Christians should seek. It is knowledge that must make sense to a logical mind or it could not possibly be called "knowledge." Irrational knowledge is never useful knowledge. God's knowledge has to be understood intellectually just as the merchant of pearls of the parable recognized thanks to his knowledge that a particular pearl was priceless (Mt. 13:46–47). Jesus did not say that the Holy Spirit spoke to him to tell him which pearl he should buy. The merchant recognized all other pearls as lacking something despite their similarities of appearance—this one had invisible characteristics that changed his life, just as the true religion of Jesus should change ours.

If we fail to understand that the Spirit of God is the way God thinks and that this particular orientation of thought is also called the Holy Spirit, we also fail to recognize the Holy Spirit as a person's immutable focus on the welfare and well-being of others. Any deviation from that understanding produces immediate confusion as to the Truth regarding God's method of government of the universe for eternity. The moment we expect the Holy Spirit to be a divine Person rather than a disposition of mind and heart that should be similar to that of God, we are in danger of thinking that the Holy Spirit is a third party that must somehow take control of our minds and hearts.

Expectations of supernatural powers dispensed to humans by the Holy Spirit along with special blessings are a false understanding of the way God operates. The disciples of Jesus who clearly received the Holy Spirit were not favored with riches or protected from persecutions. What they received was not a Person of the deity in their hearts; what they received was a clear understanding of the message of Jesus who taught and lived God's mind-set to save humanity. It is because they understood and accepted the mind-set that God empowered them as He did Jesus to perform the miracles. It is not because they were empowered that they understood; it is because they understood that they were empowered. It is dangerous to expect power or favors from the Holy Spirit, as so many preach from pulpits, because understanding the mission of Jesus, which is a communication of the mind-set of God, has to be accepted first. When expectations are based on a false understanding of the Holy Spirit, failures can produce discouragement liable to produce a permanent detachment from God. If the Spirit of God were a Person who talks to us, how could we know if the spirit in question is from God? It could just as well be that of an evil angel masquerading for a dead friend, relative, or an angel claiming to be from God?

God has not changed through the millennia. The problem is that humans are slow to understand the message from God. He has given us all the information we need to cultivate His Spirit in our hearts and minds that we might be Spirit-filled. As Jesus Himself made it clear: "the Spirit gives life . . . The *words* I have spoken to you are spirit and they are life" (Jn. 6:63, emphasis mine). If the Spirit of God is a message in words, it is not a Person. Yet in a way, it is God Himself speaking to us because He is responsible for conveying Truth. In this text the second word "spirit" should also be capitalized, because they both refer to the Spirit of God, which is the Spirit, or mind-set, that should also be in us. Without it eternal life is not possible. Fortunately God knows the hearts, thus He knows who would have accepted His Spirit if they had been exposed to His Truth.

Jesus is clear about the knowledge and understanding needed to create the final separation between those who follow Jesus because they have His faith, or His Spirit, and those who refuse His Spirit, and thus fail to think and live His modus operandi. He said: "For there is nothing hidden that will not be disclosed, and nothing concealed that will not be known or brought out into the open" (Lk. 8:17).

We hear it said sometimes that the Holy Spirit is the voice of God in the heart. In a way it is just that but not because God or the Holy Spirit is a Person that speaks to us, but because with the correct knowledge of God we are prompted from the heart to act as He would. Jesus, who was the full expression of God's character on the planet never acted as though He was superior to anyone else. The "Word," whose actions washed the feet of His disciples, is a clear example of God's style of interaction (see Jn. 13:15). He demonstrated in action the message of unconditional service to others without expectations of blessings from God or repayment from those whom He served. This manner of service was shocking to His disciples, because it is totally foreign to the way humans think and behave. This was a time when they fully expected Him to *impose* Himself on them as His subordinates and to impose Himself on Romans authorities. They expected Jesus to dominate the world in a "Divine" show of power and authority, not to serve in a spirit of unconditional love. Far from them the idea that God would stoop down to the level of their dusty feet to wash them. They totally failed to recognize this act of humility as the expression of His power and His unique form of government for the universe.

Jesus treated His disciples as though they were already kings in His kingdom of kings and priests. This is the way it will be when sin will have been abolished from the universe. But the only way this can happen is by recognizing and adopting the true Holy Spirit, God's mind-set in whose image we were created. In a way the Holy Spirit is a Person, because it comes from God, but not another Person who shares divinity with God. With the understanding that the Spirit of God is the way He thinks and that His mind-set must become ours just as it was in Jesus, it will be possible to demonstrate before the universe before our Lord returns that humans can indeed improve thanks to the Spirit of God that lives in them. This is how God and His way of life will be vindicated before the devil and those who oppose Him.

Objections to key Bible Texts Used to Validate Trinity

It is important to recognize that there are very few texts in Scripture that Trinitarians can use to validate their persuasion that the Godhead involves three consubstantial persons. A review of these statements will show that they either fail to prove Trinity, or they are misinterpreted. Considering that God does not change, in the face of Trinitarian theology it is always difficult for me to side with God who claims that He is One because it places me at odds with the bulk of Christianity. But the more I study Trinity theology the more I consider it the mother of theological confusion. When the idea of Three Persons in the Godhead is dismissed most theological issues are resolved, especially those lacking sound logic. A dismissal of Trinity also dismisses irrational dogmas. We shall review statements from both the Old and New Testament.

Old Testament Statements Presumed to Suggest Trinity

The first OT text that comes to mind when the subject of Trinity is brought up deals with Creation Week. This is where the word *Elohim,* a plural noun in Hebrew, is translated "God," a singular. Trinitarians suggest that the Hebrew plural for God is a clear indication that God is not a single Person but three. Of course, Trinity theologians dispute that point with Jewish scholars who despite the plural defend the singularity of God as a single entity, not three. When Jews translate Scripture in modern languages they never use the word "God" or its equivalencies in other languages.

A superficial read of interlinear translations of Scripture provides readers with the immediate realization that translating Scripture can be very subjective. In his personal library, a friend of mine who collects English bibles has counted over a thousand translations of Scripture. Why so many translations? It is only because there is failure of consensus on the meaning of ancient texts. And since no original manuscript of Scripture still exists, proving authenticity is difficult. What we have is small fragments of ancient copies of copies of copies, and even those are so ancient and tattered that very little remains. This is true of the New Testament, of which the lost originals date back less than 2,000 years. But the same is also true of Old Testament Scripture of which the originals would date back 2,500 to 3,500 years if they existed. The NT was written over a period of about 50 years, while the OT was written over a period of about twelve centuries, from Moses who wrote before about 1,500 BCE to the last books of the OT written round about 400 BCE.

Considering the subjectivity of translations we must accept the fact that the paradigm of prophets who wrote may not correlate with that of their translators. Since by the Bible's own admission the message of God has been repeatedly corrupted, it is very likely that the original message should be reconsidered with different pairs of eyes. A passage from the prophet Jeremiah is seldom if ever quoted by Christian theologians, priests or pastors, and it is shocking for those who discover it for the first time. Here God is speaking and saying to Israel: "How can you say, 'We are wise, for we have the law of the LORD,' when actually the lying pen of the scribes has handled it falsely" (Jer. 8:8). The context confirms the statement, implying that everything we read in Scripture is indeed sufficient for our understanding of God, but not necessarily entirely true. Scribes have manipulated texts, and interpreters run away with false ideas and teachings. A word-for-word reading of the first line of Scripture shows that it is subject to interpretation. Since all translations are interpretations they always reflect the translator's understanding of statements, not necessarily the original writer's intended meaning.

The first line of the Bible is generally translated to say: "In the beginning God created the heavens and the earth" (Gen. 1:1). When reading word-for-word translations in interlinear renditions of Scripture the same passage reads: "In beginning he created *Elohim* the heavens and the earth." No punctuation is provided here because none existed in Hebrew. But since there were no separations between words and no punctuation in ancient texts and because their grammar was somewhat limited, the sentence could have been translated to say: "In the beginning He created *Elohim*, the heavens, and the earth." This sentence would then convey the idea that when the universe was originally created, He, singular, whoever He might be, created a plurality of intelligent created beings called *Elohim*, as well as the heavens and the earth. This could imply that "he" stands for an unnamed singular entity responsible for creating a plurality of entities called *Elohim,* as well as the entire universe that includes the earth. If that is the way this text should have been translated we need to identify the subject "he" and identify the meaning of the plural word *Elohim* that appears to be the primary product of Creation, but not the Creator God who may well include Himself in that group since they are created in His image.

Before answering those two questions we find that the next statement may well offer an interesting clue. Creationists usually fail to recognize this clue because of their dogmatic persuasion that the entire universe was created when humans were placed in the Garden of Eden. In that verse the interlinear suggests the following: "And the earth she *became* chaos and vacancy and darkness over surface of abyss (water) with *spirit* of *Elohim vibrating* over surfaces of the waters." We immediately note that the earth *became* chaos, suggesting that it had not always been in a state of chaos, and that it was probably not always "vacant" of life and that it had not always been in a state of permanent darkness. If it became chaotic it was not because God created it that way or because God caused it to become the expression of something a perfect God would never create. Indeed, when God does something, it is beautiful, orderly, life-giving, perfect, and fully completed, not half-done, much less in a state of empty chaos. Thus it is clear that the surface of this planet was marred, rendered disorderly and lifeless by the action of forces that were not from the action of the "he," here unidentified. The only thing that causes harm to animate and inanimate realities of the universe is the evil that produces sin and destruction.

It should also be noted that the word translated "spirit" from the Hebrew *rûach* could also be translated "breath" or "life." In other words, the spirit could well be all the life of the universe that shares the image of God. The "he" could well be the Creator of all that life, but includes himself in their number of which "he" has always been a part on an equal basis and has always been in their presence.

It appears that there is another way to understand the first sentence of OT Scripture. The singular "he" could well be the God who created the heavens and the earth, as well as all inhabitants made in His own image. *Elohim* must therefore include the Creator along with His entire family of all the living life created in His own image. We are told that one-third of these beings fell to sin, which means that contrary to God's way of life always focused on the welfare of others, they chose to care for self before others (see Rev. 12:4).[49] That third of fallen angels, or "stars" of heaven, are probably responsible for causing all the chaos visible throughout the known universe. Modern science depicts for us dangerous asteroids causing destruction as well as incomprehensible black holes of oblivion. There are signs of lifelessness and defacement on all planets in the cosmos.

This line of reasoning is not contrary to Scripture because Jude talks about angels who were forced to leave their dwellings; these were probably planets (Jude 1:6), as discussed earlier in this chapter. Our planets may well have been in a state of active chaos, more than any other. This one became utterly worthless and uninhabitable but not in the hands

---

[49] Speaking of the tail of the dragon representing the devil, in the symbolic language of Revelation 12:4 states the following: "His tail swept a third of the stars out of the sky (or heaven) and flung them to the earth. The dragon stood in front of the woman who was about to give birth (mother of Jesus) so that he might devour her child the moment it was born." Clearly these are not the physical stars of heaven; they are stars that trashed themselves. The expression "flung to the earth," implies that they became trash, as something one would throw away. These are the created angels who chose to side with the mentality of the devil.

of God. In the vastness of the universe this speck of dust called planet Earth is the place where God chose to give all of His already existing intelligent beings a sandbox demonstration of the utmost importance. Not only would God demonstrate what salvation is and how it can be achieved, but He would also provide a clear understanding of what evil does and how it leads to self-obliteration. It is for this reason that Jesus could say emphatically: "Heaven and earth shall pass away" (Mt. 24:35). This is a serious prophetic statement that many Christian leaders fail to heed. Indeed, the entire universe has been contaminated by evil and has suffered the worst possible consequences of sin.

We have further evidence of this view a little further in Chapter 3. We find that following the first sin, the Creator who is designated as *Yahweh* has reason for concern. The NIV translates the passage as follows: "And the LORD (*Yahweh*) God (*Elohim*) said, 'The man has now become like one of us (plural), knowing good and evil. He must not be allowed to reach out his hand and take also from the tree of life and eat, and live forever'" (Gen. 3:22, parentheses mine). Could this probably have been translated to say: "*Yahweh* told *Elohim*, humans have become like us, they are now familiar with both good and evil." Here the understanding that there are consequences for evil is implied already familiar to the intelligent inhabitants of the universe.

Christian scholars of the Hebrew language will likely disagree with my suggestion, but Christians could have been entertaining a false understanding of the plural *Elohim* as it relates and compares to the singular *Yahweh*. This of course allows them to conclude that God is more than One Person. Such a conclusion may imply that we have been misled regarding the events that are taking place between heaven and planet Earth. While in Chapter One of Genesis the plural *Elohim* is clearly mentioned as being present during the event of Creation, in Chapter Two *Yahweh* is also mentioned alongside of *Elohim*. Does this suggest that both were in some way involved in the work of creation?

It is not until we read the Fourth Commandment in Exodus 20 that confirmation is provided with clarity. In this statement regarding the importance of the Sabbath day on which the children of God were to seek holiness, or separation from the ways of an evil world and universe, four verses beg for attention. In the NIV they read as follows:

"Remember the Sabbath day by keeping it holy. Six days you shall labor and do all your work, but the seventh day is a Sabbath for the Lord your God. On it you shall not do any work, neither you, nor your son or daughter, nor your manservant of maidservant, nor your animals, nor the alien within your gates. For in six days the Lord made the heavens and the earth, the sea, and all that is in them, but he rested on the seventh day. Therefore the Lord blessed the Sabbath day and made it holy" (Ex. 20:8–11). A word-for-word translation of the passage yields something very interesting. We quote only verses 8, 9, and 11: "Remember day of the Sabbath to hallow Him. Six days you shall serve and do all work of you, but day the seventh is to YAHWEH, the ELOHIM you are shall do no work . . . Because in six days made He, YAHWEH, the heavens and the earth . . . so He, YAHWEH, set aside the seventh day as a Sabbath for you to keep with (or close to) Him" (punctuation mine).

Here *Yahweh* is given full credit for the work done during Creation Week. During that week He created another group whom He also calls *Elohim* probably because an addition was made to His family. This *Elohim* is located on planet Earth. The *Elohim* present during Creation Week were the sum total of God's or *Yahweh's* divine counsel made up of all the intelligent beings created before the Creation of planet Earth in disarray took place. As already noted, Paul speaks of events on this planet as on display before the entire universe. This was not just since the time of the Cross; this is a reality that has captivated the attention of all intelligent beings since Creation Week: "For it seems to me," Paul wrote, "that God has put us apostles on display at the end of the procession, like men condemned to die in the arena. We have been made *a spectacle to the whole universe, to angels as well as to men*" (1 Cor. 4:9, emphasis mine).

God created intelligent beings because He wanted them to enjoy contributing endlessly to the development of the universe. But the plan could work only as long as perfect love and cooperation endured. Everyone knew that such a development would immediately be halted if evil should ever appear, and this is exactly what happened. The moment evil entered the universe the forward movement was halted and reversed. Only destruction and chaos could be the result. We have no way of knowing how long all this was going on in the universe before God (*Yahweh*) brought together His Divine Council (*Elohim*) to re-create the earth. He populated it with humans also created in His image—thus also members of His family whom He called *Elohim*.

The reason evil has had the upper hand so far in the universe is perfectly logical. If a group of truants is intent on taking advantage of peace-loving pacifists unwilling to hurt anyone out of perfect love and mercy, we all know that the outcome can only be at the expense of those who love. Degradation is predictable and inevitable. However, those on the side of love know that rendering evil for evil can only produce ever-greater evil. The only way to protest evil is to refuse to render evil for evil, just as Jesus taught us all the way to the Cross. He proved that doing so should be done fearlessly, because even if death should occur, the resurrection to everlasting life is a certainty, because in the end, the love of the everlasting God is more powerful than the power of self-annihilating evil.

It is rather surprising that Jesus quoted one of the most One of the most thought-provoking and controversial statements of the Old Testament when He was accused of blasphemy for saying that He was Son of God. Reading from the NIV He is quoted to respond: "Is it not written in your Law, 'I have said you are gods?' If he called them 'gods,' to whom the word of God came—and the Scripture cannot be broken—what about the one whom the Father set apart as his very own and sent into the World? Why then do you accuse me of blasphemy because I said, 'I am God's Son'" (Jn. 10:34–36)? The statement from the Psalms Jesus was quoting is translated as follows: "I said, 'You are 'gods'; you are all sons of the Most High" (Ps. 82:5). Going back to the Hebrew we find that here "gods" is a translation of *Elohim,* while the "Most High" is obviously *Yahweh.* These are humans created with the accord and participation of the entire council of God called *Elohim* in Hebrew. Both the statement of Jesus and that of the Psalms identify *Elohim* with the Council of God. These are all the created beings *Yahweh* has created throughout the universe to participate in the aggrandizement of His universal Kingdom.

A significant number of statements in the Old Testament suggest that Jesus and God, as we refer to Him, are both One and the same Person. Let us review just a few:

The psalmist writes: "O Israel, put your hope in the LORD (*Yahweh*), for with the LORD (*Yahweh*) is unfailing love and with him (singular) is full redemption. He himself (singular) will redeem Israel from their sins" (Ps. 130:7–8, parentheses mine).

In his *Messiah,* George Frideric Handel draws from Scripture. Performed for the first time in 1742, it has been heard and performed ever since during the Christmas season in all Christian neighborhoods.

In it, a section drawn from the messianic writings of the prophet Isaiah is quoted from the King James Version: "For unto us a child is born, unto us a son is given: and the government shall be upon his shoulder: and his name shall be called Wonderful, Counselor, The mighty God, The everlasting Father, The prince of Peace" (Is. 9:6 KJV). Indeed, the child Jesus is the Messiah who is also the Spirit of the Holy One called Counselor. He is also the mighty God, as well as the everlasting Father and the prince of Peace. All these titles belong to the same Person who is *Yahweh,* later incarnated in human flesh as Jesus, thus the Son of *Yahweh,* or *Son of God.*

Hosea the prophet makes the same claim. Quoting God he writes: "But I am the LORD your God, who brought you out of Egypt. You shall acknowledge no God but me, no Savior except me" (Hos. 13:4). Of course, based on the foregoing I would translate: "I am *Yahweh* of you my special *Elohim,* the One who brought you out of the Land of Egypt. Do not acknowledge a Savior other than Me."

The prophet Zechariah echoes these prophets when God requested him to record His words about the soon coming of Jesus: "'Shout and be glad, O Daughter of Zion. For I am coming, and I will live among you,' Declares the LORD (*Yahweh*)" (Zech 2:10, parenthesis mine). The prophet reinforces the oneness of *Yahweh* adding: "Many nations will be joined with the LORD (*Yahweh*) in that day and will become my people. I will live among you and you will know that the LORD Almighty has sent me to you" (Zech 2:11). How much plainer could the prophet of God say it? *Yahweh* is the Almighty God of which there is but One. All created beings made in His image called to become participants in His work of creation are all called His *Elohim.*

All that being said, although there are more texts worth reviewing in the OT, one more is key to our discussion. In Deuteronomy Moses makes a baffling statement on God's behalf: "See now that I myself is He! There is no God (*Elohim*) besides me. I put to death and bring to life, I have wounded and I will heal, and no one can deliver out of my hand" (Dt. 32:39, parenthesis mine). Since the word *Elohim* is here translated "God," how can the Speaker who is *Yahweh* say that there is no *Elohim* in Him, or with Him? He, *Yahweh,* the singular God was probably saying to Moses that in some cases He acts alone without involving *Elohim,* the Divine Council that includes all His intelligent created beings. Unfortunately, the rest of the text is probably mistranslated. Here is my rendition: "As you can see, I myself is He (the singular God *Yahweh*). Aside from Me no *Elohim* can bring life out of death or heal the wounded while delivering them with a single hand." This verse informs us that the Creator *Yahweh* who later became Jesus in human flesh, and thus Son of *Yahweh*, created humanity in concert with the Divine Council *Elohim*, but when it comes to saving them, He (*Yahweh*) is on His own. What an amazing God!

New Testament Statements Presumed Evidence for Trinity

The purpose of this discussion is not to dispute biblical fact. As we have seen, God is so infinite that He cannot reveal Himself in Person to a finite being. The Infinite God is invisible and will remain invisible for eternity for good reasons. If the Infinite God were visible we could see nothing else, because He is also omnipresent, and we would not survive the impact, because He is all-powerful. As Jesus made it clear, when speaking of Himself He said: "No one has seen the Father except the one who is from God; only he has seen the Father" (Jn. 6:46). Indeed, the Infinite God is the Father who expressed His infinite Self-existence (or Self-being) through His one and only image called *Yahweh* until the birth of Jesus in human flesh. There is a self-imposed difference between *Yahweh* and Jesus. *Yahweh* being a visible living fragment of the Infinite God was just as immortal as the Infinite God. When He became human, Jesus later called the infinite immortal God, Father. We sometimes think of the self-sacrifice of Jesus as being made on the Cross; but who can begin to evaluate the infinite enormity of the self-sacrifice involved in going from being the immortal *Yahweh,* to accepting to become the mortal Jesus. He became mortal knowing that He would die to prove a point to humans whom He knew would listen no other way. This self-sacrifice is far greater than mere humans can begin to imagine. It would stand to reason to think that the self-sacrifice of Jesus going from divine to human was far greater than His self-sacrifice as a human in His prime who accepted torture and the grave willfully.

This aspect of the self-sacrifice of Jesus is rarely if ever considered. Many Arians are reluctant to say that Jesus was divine because while living on earth He lived a human life in the absolute sense of the term, from conception to the grave. He appeared to have no advantage over any human being because He refused to make use of the advantage He could have called upon. He even appeared to lack knowledge about certain things, but only because He knew only that which the Infinite God had revealed to Him.

For example, about the timing of the return of the Lord, which deals with His own return to our planet, He said: "No one knows about that day or hour, not even the angels in heaven, nor the Son, but only the Father" (Mk. 13:32). He made it clear on several occasions that what He was sharing with humans was only that which the Father had revealed to Him—nothing more and nothing less. Had He wanted to obtain more information from the Father while human, He could have, but He accepted to submit to the Father throughout His life and ministry as though He were human, which He accepted to be through His death. If the Father had not revealed something to Him, it is because it was irrelevant to Him and to the world at that point in time. Imagine if Jesus had responded, "Oh, you will have to wait at least twenty-five centuries before my return," who would still be talking about Jesus or trying to spread His message today?

The point is that He was not Son of God before His birth from the womb of Mary, but like all of us humans, He became Son of God when He became human. We are all His children because we are all born of the couple of which He was Himself the Father when He created them and placed in Eden. The *Yahweh* who created Adam and Eve in the presence of His *Elohim* is the One who implanted himself in the womb of Mary to become human. He is the One who, on the eighth day, was brought to the Temple to be circumcised and named Jesus (Luke 2:21). This Jesus was fully human. He had to learn who He was from the Father and also had to learn from Him the nature of and motive of His mission (see Is. 7:16–17; 50:1–8). The Father gave Him His education on a daily basis, nothing more and nothing less than the basic knowledge required to communicate the Truth that saves to a dying world. He had no advantage over other humans. As Paul said: "And being found in appearance as a man, he humbled himself and *became* obedient to death—even death on a cross" (Phil. 2:8, emphasis mine)!

That image of God is not a separate Person from the Infinite God Jesus called His Father. Like pictures on driver's licenses or passports, they are images of people identified on the document, not someone else. That document fits in the back pocket. Likewise, *Yahweh* who later became Jesus is a living finite visible portion and expression of God.

Thanks to this image of God finite beings can enjoy the privilege to see Him, thus He is not another Person. He said to Philip: "Anyone who has seen me has seen the Father. How can you say, 'show us the Father'" (Jn. 14:9b)? Since both the Infinite God and His finite expression are the same Person, that person has a mind. We can only call God's mind His Perfect Spirit, or the Holy Spirit. It is a mind that can only think in terms of unconditional love. "God is love" (1 Jn. 4:8, 16). It is indisputable that God is One Person. However, that Person is at the same time the Father of humanity who became the Son of God when He was born out of the womb of Mary, and the Son of humans whose Father He was. God thinks flawlessly because the way He thinks is the only way a person can think to preserve life eternally. Thus God is Father, Son, and Holy Spirit, just as Scripture describes Him, but not three different Persons. The concept of Three Persons is a human invention. If God were Three Persons, none of them would be infinite. There is only one infinite space, not three. The moment space is divided it is no longer infinite.

Humans go out of their way to believe in either a Trinity of gods, as do far too many Christians, or a multiplicity of gods, as do pagan religions. An old adage comes to mind: To usurp God's authority and sovereignty that should be His alone, humans have attempted to divide Him to conquer Him. Unfortunately, they have almost succeeded. When stated in terms of world politics the adage is even more telling; it would be stated to say: divide and rule. Dividing God accomplished the purpose some human clerics have always sought to accomplish. It has opened the door for churches to usurp God's authority and leadership in order to impose their authority on people's lives. One has to go out on a very thin limb to prove Trinity, because with an honest reading it is nowhere to be found in Scripture. Why are Trinitarians going through convoluted and irrational mental processes to prove that John did not really mean to say that "In the beginning was the Word, and the Word was *pros,* Greek for, 'a part of' God, and the word was God" (see Jn. 1:1)? Could John have said that God is one with more clarity? Unfortunately the mistranslation of the Greek *pros* implies that the Word was "with" God rather than a part of Him as the only visible part of God. Trinitarian translators and interpreters of Scripture have a tendency to separate God from His Word and His own Spirit.

Consider the translation of verse 18 in the same first chapter of John's Gospel. Reading from the NIV we have the following: "No one has ever seen God, but God the One and Only, who is at the Father's side, has made him known" (Jn. 1:18). It should be observed that the King James Version uses the expression "the only begotten Son, which is in the bosom of the Father." This translation is clearly more accurate because Jesus was begotten, just like humans are begotten. The process of human reproduction produced the birth of Jesus. We have the entire genealogy of Jesus in the Gospel of Luke to demonstrate that He was a descendent of these people. When the NIV implies that the Word was "at" the Father's side, the word "at" is not in the Greek. A correct translation should read: "the one who is the Father's side." These lapses of translation are typical of Trinitarian renditions responsible for leading readers astray.

The problems with dividing God into Persons will be further discussed in the next chapter of this book. It is interesting to note that many texts Trinitarians use to prove Trinity are also used by non-Trinitarians to prove the absence of Trinity. When Trinitarians say that Father and Son are one in purpose but not in Person they are definitely not saying that the divinity is one single divine Person. The one and only finite image of the Infinite God was but a visible "sliver" of His Person, but the same Person nonetheless. This "sliver" of the Infinite God detached itself from God at great sacrifice to become a mortal human. When the "sliver" became Son He lived "among us" (Jn. 1:14) to bring us the message that saves. At some point in time He had to return to the place He occupied before coming and had to take back His position *as* the Father's side, not *at* the Father's side (see Jn. 1:18).

Let us focus on some of the key statements Trinitarians use to suggest the notion that three Persons rule the Godhead and see if there is substance for their belief in those texts:

Let us first consider the statement of the New Testament most commonly used to prove Trinity theology; it is now clearly known to be a counterfeit. So bogus is this Trinitarian statement that it is no longer included in the newer translations of Scripture. Here it is from the old King James Version where it was fraudulently inserted in the First Epistle of John: "For there are three that bear record in heaven, the Father, the Word, and the Holy Ghost: and these three are one" (1 Jn. 5:7 KJV). Since this text is no longer found in modern versions the NIV has an explicative margin note stating: "not found in any Greek manuscript before the sixteenth century." What a shame that Christian scholarship had to wait so long to correct such an important error in a book they call the Word of God. The text is found in the Latin Vulgate however, which suggests that it was probably introduced in that version in the heat of the Arian Controversy at the beginning of the fourth century CE. Somehow the add-on was inadvertently introduced in the King James Version, probably because its translators made extensive use of the Latin Vulgate to help their early translations of Scripture into the common languages of the world. This extraction should have dealt a serious blow to Trinitarian theology because it was the only explicit text on the subject in all of Scripture, but it did not. The manipulation of Scripture demonstrates to what extent Trinitarians were desperate in trying to impose their false teaching on Christianity. No other passage of Scripture can be found to be as declarative on the subject, yet for centuries Christians have assumed that this text was divinely inspired.

Let us consider the second most important statement used to suggest a Trinity of Persons. Here Jesus was telling His disciples to go and baptize in the name of the Father, Son, and Holy Spirit. This is clearly another foundational linchpin text of Trinity theology. Jesus was making His final remarks face to face with His disciples minutes before returning to heaven: "Therefore," He said, "go and make disciples of all nations, baptizing them in the name of the Father and of the Son and of the Holy Spirit, and teaching them to obey everything I have commanded you" (Mt. 28:19–20a). Let us first note that Jesus never *commanded* anyone to do anything, nor did He ever require *obedience*, not even to be saved. Both concepts suggest obedience to an external force or authority, which God never requires. God wants the authority to come from within, making it possible for His followers to become kings and priests of His kingdom, as previously discussed. Indeed, God does not want any of us to answer to an external authority, or the free will He has given intelligent beings would be violated. The authority that comes from God must also become the authority that rules our lives. The Greek word *tereo* implies service, not submission. Thus the text should be read: "Therefore go and make disciples of all nations, baptizing them into the name (singular) of the Father and the Son and the Holy Spirit, to serve others as I have shown you."

The problem with this text, as it relates to Trinity theology, is that it may appear to imply the involvement of Three Persons in whose name(s) new disciples were to be baptized, though it does not implicitly say that. Interestingly, the text implies a singular name, not names in the plural.

Though grammatically incorrect, that singular may well be considered somewhat defensible on the basis of a Trinitarian paradigm of thought, because for them God is One in purpose but Three in Persons. The problem is that nothing in this text clearly suggests a plurality of Persons. It could just as well imply that God is Father, Son, and Holy Spirit, all in One Person, and thus one name. The Person we call God is indeed *Yahweh* who is our Father because He created humans. But the same *Yahweh* also "became flesh" (Jn. 1:14). When He did He became both Son of *Yahweh* and Son of Man. By becoming Son, Jesus has been able to provide humans with the knowledge of the Infinite God Jesus called Father all the way to His death. By so doing He conveyed to humanity the way God thinks; this is the Holy Spirit we must acquire to restore the image of God in us. This is how God's children will be set apart from those who remain indifferent to such restoration.

There is another difficulty however. Considering that these were the last words of Jesus, His last stated wish, why did His most influential and most devoted disciples fail to fulfill His wish to the letter? Were they not told to baptize "in the name of the Father and the Son and the Holy Spirit?" We must ask, why then have Peter, Paul, and others never baptized in accordance with this last wish of their beloved Master? Could it be that they were careless or had forgotten His specific request? Not likely! They are all recorded to have baptized in the name of Jesus, while never including the name of the Father or the Holy Spirit.

In Acts, Peter was encouraging his listeners to "Repent and be baptized, every one of you, in the name of Jesus Christ for the forgiveness of your sins. And you will receive the gift of the Holy Spirit" (Acts 2:38). Peter could not have forgotten to baptize in the name of the Holy Spirit; he mentions it in the context. On the other hand, another problem should be mentioned to avoid a false understanding. Baptism is not a ritual intended to bring forgiveness of sin or impart any kind of special power. It is a ritual that confirms the sinner's intent to walk in a new direction of life, away from the ways of the world and toward the ways of God. Propelled by the perfectly logical mind-set of God Scripture calls the Holy Spirit, sinners demonstrate publicly their decision to "walk in newness of life" (Rom. 6:4 KJV). This walk with God brings *remission* of sin, not *forgiveness*.

Forgiveness is never in question with God, but the remission of the sin disease is entirely dependent on the individual's acceptance of God's message of Truth that transforms a sinner's mind and heart. Could three thousand people have been baptized in the name of Jesus Christ (v. 41) because the disciples had forgotten to baptize them in the name of the Father, Son, and Holy Spirit? Let us not be naïve.

Three possible conclusions can be drawn:

1. The three names are indicative of three Persons sharing divinity over the universe. This is not likely because Jesus would have made sure to clarify the change. He would have said, "You have heard it said that there is only one God, but I am here to tell you that there are three . . ." His monotheist Jewish followers would not have been left in the dark on such an important issue. He talked about Father, Son, and Holy Spirit, but never once implied that they were three Persons of the divinity.

2. Not unlike the bogus text previously mentioned of 1 Peter 5, this statement of Jesus in Matthew could also have been manipulated during the Arius Controversy. Unfortunately, we have no remaining fragments of this portion of Scripture dating back to a time before the controversy; thus this assertion cannot be verified. However, once again, circumstantial evidence does not favor Trinity theology.

3. The expression "in the name of" comes up between 28 and 30 times in the NT, depending on the translation. It is only in Matthew 28:19 that the expression "in the name of the Father and the Son and the Holy Spirit" is found. The Greek *onoma* translated "name" is not necessarily a reference to a Person's name, but a person's character and/or authority. It is clear that through the Son the Father was made known. This was necessary to make it possible for sinners' to have a change of heart and character. Such a change is possible only through the renewal of one's mind-set retrained to reflect that of God. Since the Father is also the Son, as explained above, it follows logic to assume that the Holy Spirit is the logical mind-set by which the Father who is also Son operates, and by which mind-set humans are also called upon to operate. Unquestionably, the Spirit is that of a Person, and that Person is God who is both Father and Son, and whose Spirit is Holy.

As Philip preached, we also find that he baptized in the name of Jesus Christ (see Acts 8:12), as did Paul (1 Cor. 6:11). In this passage Paul makes an interesting assertion: "But you were washed, you were sanctified, you were justified in the name of the Lord Jesus Christ and by the Spirit of our God." Here Paul uses the word "washed" to imply baptism in the name of the Lord Jesus Christ. His use of the word Spirit is the Greek *pneuma*. Though this word is related to the word "air" and "breath," it is used to designate a person's rational mind. Why should it be different when speaking of God? God is perfectly rational, and His rationale is key to living His kind of life. His rationale should become our rationale. But if we fail to know God we cannot acquire the rationale of someone we do not know. When the rationale of God becomes our rationale, we become increasingly more just, but we are not justified or acquitted, as a human legal interpretation would suggest. God's justice is to make sinners more just, not to acquit the sinner of His sins, because God always acquits unconditionally. Acquittal does not mean salvation however. As previously stated the acquittal is automatic with God; it is never in question, but it only opens the door to salvation, if we understand that it is the restoration of the image of God in humans. Becoming just is entirely dependent on receiving the message of Truth from God, which is the Holy Spirit that sanctifies us, makes us holy. As Jesus said: "Now this is eternal life: that they may know you, the only true God, and Jesus Christ whom you have sent" (Jn. 17:3). A failure to know God leads to a failure to know how He thinks and a failure to develop the mind of God, which is a failure to receive the Holy Spirit and a failure to understand the true meaning of love.

If the spirit is the mind of a person, the Holy Spirit is the mind of a Person, indeed, but that Person is none other than the Only True God. The mind of God is not another Person in the Godhead. Why should God need another Person to be His Spirit? Is God not allowed to have a mind of His own? This concept of a Person called the Holy Spirit makes no sense at all. The few texts used by Trinitarians to suggest that the Holy Spirit is a separate Person are all subject to highly disputed interpretations; they never explicitly state that the Spirit is another Person. And since Trinitarians are the original translators of Scripture into the common languages of the world, many statements are translated with their biases.

Perhaps the most egregious bias expressed in translations has to do with the personification of the Holy Spirit through the unwarranted use of singular personal pronouns such as He, Him, who, or whom. This is apparent in several places of the NT; however, in one rather surprising exception, the personal pronoun "he" is correctly translated. Apparently, John, its author, intended the personification. Here John is quoting Jesus as saying: "But when he, the Spirit of Truth, comes, he will guide you into all truth. He will not speak on his own; he will speak only what he hears and he will tell you what is yet to come" (John 16:13). The fact that in this case "the Spirit of truth" is intentionally personified has bothered me for a long time. Why this exception? Because the personification is clearly established in this statement, Trinitarian translators have considered acceptable to personify the Holy Spirit as well as the advocate or helper elsewhere in the NT. Why would the "Spirit of truth" be clearly personified while the personification is highly questionable elsewhere, except perhaps in one statement of the Apostle Paul?

If the Holy Spirit is a Person, why is the personification not consistent throughout? My personal view is that when Jesus is talking about a future event related to the arrival of the Spirit of truth, He is talking about a time in the future when humanity will have access to the method required to arrive at truth. When Newton saw the apple fall to the ground from the tree, he inquired why and how and decided to apply pure logic to his search and he arrived at conclusions that were universally accepted as truth about gravitational pull. Instead of thinking, as would the ancient that the gods are responsible for such occurrences, Newton wanted to understand the whys and wherefores. Though some level of logic was available to the world before Newton, it was not until the age of science that humans began to apply logic to all their activities. Since pure logic is a gift from God made available only to His intelligent created beings, when God breathed in them the breath of life He also breathed in them the breath of pure logic.

When Jesus discussed this future event with His disciples, He was talking about a return of the human mind to the logic God had given them initially. This is a progressive reality that is still taking place. It is a progressive return to the way God thinks in terms of logic. Till then logic had not been applied systematically to the sciences, and to this day, it is not yet applied seriously to the study of God and Scripture. Jesus was predicting that this would change, but not until the value of logic would be recognized, because without it truth can never be attained. When the logic of God, which is the Spirit of Truth, is applied to His communications, a new message begins to emerge from the chaos of Christian confusion. In fact, the emerging message is not new; it is the message God had been communicating all along and the message Jesus had come to communicate to the world. Without the help of logic even the message of Jesus could not be fully understood. It is only because logic failed to be applied to the message of Jesus that it could be corrupted by the predominant superstitious religions of the Middle East and Europe. Indeed, superstitions have nothing in common with logic.

What was Jesus telling His disciples in this passage about the Spirit of truth? It is interesting to reconsider the Greek because it yields interesting alternatives. Allow me a paraphrased translation: "But when the Spirit of Truth will come He will guide you into all truth because He is the Spirit of God's perfect logic. His Spirit of logic that leads to truth will not bring you a false message; He will reveal only that which makes perfect sense and has yet to be understood." God being the author of logic, He is the Spirit of Truth. When we consider issues on the basis of sound logic, the Spirit of Truth who is God leads the way. Jesus said: "I am the way, the truth and the life." We all know that Jesus is not a thing, and yet He calls Himself the Way, the Truth, and the Life.

Another argument sometimes used to personify the Holy Spirit is based on Scripture telling us that the Spirit did certain things. How can a thing do anything unless it is a Person? Yet it is not uncommon for things to be personified in Scripture. We are told that the blood of Abel is crying from the ground and that the blood of Jesus is speaking a better word (Gen. 4:10; Heb. 12:24). Even the rivers are said to clap their hands (Ps. 98:8), and the wind blows where it wishes (Jn. 3:8). Who was Jesus talking about when He said: "But wisdom is proved right by all her children" (Lk. 7:35)?

In the story of the birth of Jesus Luke reports that the Holy Spirit came upon Mary saying that "the power of the Most High will overshadow you. So the holy one to be born will be called the Son of God" (Lk. 1:35). Here again the Holy Spirit is that of the Most High; it is not another Person associated with God. Let us also make note of the fact that the child "will be called Son of God," because He is not yet Son of God, nor is He yet, Son of man. Likewise, when Peter said to Ananias that Satan had filled his heart and caused him to lie "to the Holy Spirit"

(Acts 5:3), a bit later Peter said to him, "You have not lied to men but to God" (Acts 5:4). Clearly, when Scripture talks about the Holy Spirit, it is that of God; therefore it is God.

Far too much remains to be said on the subject, but the intention here is not to persuade, but to challenge readers to think logically and accept where logic takes them with regard to God and Scripture. The only true God of the universe is not three Persons. He is one God whose finite expression was made visible to His finite creation and whose logical mind is unconditionally focused on loving. This is the Holy Spirit of God and sinners are called to accept the importance of thinking like God. His Spirit in us is the only way to restore holiness in the confused hearts and minds of sinners for eternity.

CHAPTER 10

Trinity Theology Could Well Be the Mother of Theological Confusion

Trinitarian Christians will probably feel that the title of this section is misguided. I cannot blame them because Trinity theology is rooted in a long string of traditions going back to all major pagan cults since antiquity. These cults were largely responsible for holding back the tide of progress. Early Christians wanted no part of polytheism. By the fifth century, Trinity theology was imposed on all Christians who risked severe persecutions over a period of a thousand years or more. It is a theology that has established the faulty paradigms by which we read, study, and try, perhaps in vein, to understand what the Bible is all about. Trinity theology has only contributed greater confusion.

If there is a question that begs an answer in Christianity, it is this one: Why is there so much theological confusion, considering that all Christian denominations claim the same source of religious authority? They have all found ways to interpret the same document in a wide variety of ways. At the center of their disputes we find God. Who is He, one or three Persons? What does He do and how does He really interact with humans to save them? Not to mention other questions subject to a variety of interpretations, largely because of Trinity theology. The struggle to explain God should be telling, because any false interpretation of the only true God represents one form or another of idolatry. Indeed, idolatry is any incorrect representation of God. Most if not all the theological issues responsible for separating Christians are related to the way God is perceived, which means that Christianity must be bathing in idolatry.

Since the vast majority of perceptions of God are founded on Trinity theology, countless doors of confusion are left wide open, especially if Trinity theology happens to be one of the false teachings Jesus predicted. Variances of perception related to each of the three Persons of the divinity contribute exponential possibilities of interpretations, which is probably the reason Scripture insists in both Testaments that there is only One God. With Trinity theology a consensus of thought about God is impossible. So impossible is the consensus that any attempt to reach a consensus on theological grounds has long been abandoned.

To remedy the problem and for the sake of "unity" the latest trend in Christian religion is to accept any and every doctrine and dogma because disagreements over these matters are futile. Since it is no longer possible to agree on any particular point of doctrine related to God or salvation, Christians are in the process of unifying on the sole belief that Jesus is their Savior. Considering that this sole belief is enough to save them by faith in the Cross why should they bother to compare notes about the nature of God, the role of Jesus, and how He saves sinners? Utter tolerance of all theological views has become the new religion, because confusion is such that any attempt to understand contradictory views brings increased confusion. The US military's "don't ask don't tell" applied to gay and lesbians in 1994 is now applicable to all Christian doctrines, just so long as Jesus is recognized as the Savior. Why and how He saves no longer matters.

Christianity is fast becoming a social club where people meet to celebrate Jesus their Savior and to organize social actions to help the less privileged in the community. Such actions are good, but didn't the Savior say that eternal life is dependent on the knowledge of "the only true God" (Jn. 17:3)? We have discussed this point in previous chapters, but the knowledge of the only true God being corrupted; people's mental image of God is likewise corrupted and has become an idol for worshipers of such false images of God. If we are wrong about God, we are likely wrong about everything else related to Him, including the salvation He offers through Jesus. Recognizing Jesus as the Great Healer does not make Him my Healer until I allow Him to work on my broken heart. Identifying the Person of the Godhead that saves does not make Him anyone's Savior any more than identifying a heart surgeon can heal a person's the heart. Believers of utter tolerance can be legalist or not, Trinitarian or not, perceive Jesus on the Cross as a payment or not, as a substitute or not, believe that He brought a message from God or not, that He was truly human or not; nothing really matters. All such discussions are considered divisive, unproductive, and unchristian. But all these differences produce different images of God in people's minds and as many idols.

Is it not important to consider the fact that since idolatry is always a false image of the only true God, any attempt to divide Him into three Persons creates an image of God that limits the power and mission of each? If Christians had access to the single correct perception of the "only true God," they would find that there is only one possible interpretation of God and only one possible interpretation of His message offered through the ministry of Jesus on planet Earth.

As Jesus said, while in the flesh praying to the Infinite Invisible Almighty One He called, Father: "I have made you known to them, *and will continue to make you known* in order that the love you have for me may be in them and that I myself may be in them" (Jn. 17:26, emphasis mine). In this prayer Jesus clearly says that it is the love that comes from the Father that will unify His followers, but this will happen only when Jesus "may be in them." He is not saying that the Holy Spirit would be in them, but clearly it is the mind-set of Jesus that must be in us, not the physical Person of Jesus. Though my human father has been dead for over a decade, the way he thought and behaved is still very present in my mind, as is the content of his book. I can therefore say that the spirit of my father is still with me. Likewise, the Spirit of Jesus is the His Holy Spirit that should inhabit our being, thus our thoughts and actions.

I cannot adopt the spirit of my human father if I don't know what he taught, believed, or lived throughout the course of his life. Likewise, I cannot receive Jesus or His Spirit if I fail to know anything about Jesus or the Infinite God He came to reveal.

The disparity of paradigms associated with Christianity is entirely due to false teachings that have infiltrated and contaminated the religion of Jesus. If we could eliminate all false teachings either because they lack the support of sound logic or because they promote superstitious concepts, we would go a long way toward unifying Christianity. Doing so would set the stage for a change of heart such as the world has never witnessed. Let us review a few points associated with Trinity theology that have contributed, not only to the confusion, but also to the waywardness the confusion has engendered:

1. "The only true God" is One Person, there is no boss in heaven

It is because Trinity theology splits the Father and the Son into two different Persons that this dogma has opened the door to countless false interpretations of the teachings of Jesus. First to come to mind is the false idea that one Person of the divinity had given orders to another to come down to this dark world. Indeed, Jesus did say: "For God so loved the world, that He gave his only begotten Son, that whosoever believeth in him should not perish, but have everlasting life" (Jn. 3:16, KJV). Let us remember that Jesus was not Son until He was begotten of God in order to come to our planet in human flesh. Before coming He was *Yahweh*, the Creator (Col. 1:16), thus He was the Father of all created beings, including the human family whose Son He became. Indeed, the Creator was only the finite "sliver" of the invisible and immortal God who created everything in the universe. It is only that "sliver" of God that chose to become mortal because the Infinite God is immortal. He went through this ordeal only to show in Person how sinners should come to understand God. By coming in human flesh born of a woman He became His own Son (Heb. 1:5). The Father and the Son are the same Person, just as Isaiah 9:6 makes it crystal clear.

It cannot be said that the Infinite Immortal God ordered another Person of the divinity to go to planet Earth. Only the finite expression of the infinite immortal God came to earth; that was *Yahweh*, there was none other in the deity. Just as Jesus became Son, the Father became Father after the Son was born. One did not tell the other to go save humanity. He has always been and will always be the Infinite God's only hands and feet as well as His only mouthpiece. The expression of God is not limited to the words He brought us; it also includes all His deeds. John calls "the Word" that portion of God that was His arms, legs, and mouthpiece. Only the expressiveness of God chose to detach itself from God to become mortal, because being a part of God His visible expression was immortal. The message from God could be brought to humanity in its entirety no other way. The message had to be complete. It had to convey Truth all the way from a natural human birth in human flesh all the way to the death and even the Resurrection. A superior God did not give commands to a lesser one to come to earth; He came because He alone was the expression of God since the beginning of all eternity.

Paul goes so far as to affirm that the "grace was given us in Christ Jesus since before the beginning of time" (2 Tim. 1:9). The only reason this is possible is because the visible expression of God was God's only expression ever since before the beginning of time. *Yahweh* was, is, and will always be the only visible expression of God. On earth, in His mortal reality He was called Jesus, because calling Him *Yahweh* would have totally confused the Jews who should have recognized *Yahweh* in

Jesus. The fact that He was the Creator was revealed later in the ministry of Jesus. He is the One who had been given the responsibility to create all the finite realities of the universe and to communicate with them on God's behalf ever since before time began. No one else in the Divinity could come and communicate the message of God in words and deeds all the way to the death because there is only One God and that God only has one mouthpiece, *Yahweh,* who later came as Jesus. By creating two, and even three, Gods, it is possible to perceive one as boss over the others, which is an incorrect understanding of the "only true God" Jesus was talking about. Only while Jesus was on earth was the Father His teacher and guide, but that was necessary precisely because He was now human and had to depend on the Infinite God as we all do. That is why He later had to return to take His place as the mouthpiece of the Father in heaven, the portion of the Infinite God He once was had not been there for a while. He told His disciples before His death and Mary Magdalene after His resurrection that He would return to the Father (see Jn. 13:1; Jn. 20:17).

2. The Father is the infinite reality of the finite Son of Man

By splitting Father and Son into two Persons the Father is made to look demanding, cruel, and even a murderer and an executioner for demanding a payment of the blood and death for the sins of the world—a concept not found in Scripture. Any rational person would rightfully ask: Why didn't the Father volunteer Himself to bring the good news of salvation to humanity? Why the Son? Wouldn't a rational, loving Father prefer to spare His Son the agony of death? The reason is simple; the eternal God could not have a Son until His own visible Image became the Son of humans, thus also, Son of God. It is the Father of humans who became Son of humans, and, by so doing He also became Son of God. By becoming Son of His own created beings He became Son of His own Creation, thus, though He became Son He is the Father of all things that were ever created. By becoming the product of His own Creation he became His own Son, thus the Son and the Father are One and the same Person, One and the same God.

Why is this important? A simple reason: because it should never be said that the Father wanted the Son killed. The Father chose to become Son so He could offer the message at the risk of His own life.

3. The Father is falsely accused of wanting blood and death

Things get worse with Trinity theology. By creating a split between Father and Son the Father is falsely accused of demanding the blood and death of His Son to pay a debt, because supposedly, sin cannot be allowed to go unpaid. That is human justice, not God's. Retribution for misconduct is the way humans settle their misguided accounting of misbehavior. By attributing to God the retributive approach to dealing with sin, the Father is portrayed not only as demanding, but also as totally unreasonable. Nowhere in Scripture is it stated that Jesus died to pay a debt to satisfy or appease the Father or anyone else for that matter. Unfortunately, an explanation is in order here, because some statements of Scripture have been translated or interpreted with the human retributive bias of payment. The split Trinitarian theology has created between Father and Son is largely responsible for the acceptance of this widespread Christian dogma of pagan origin.

One common statement quoted when the subject of God's requirement of death penalty for sins is discussed comes from the pen of Paul in his Letter to the Romans. A reading of the statement as we have it in the NIV and other versions provides a false understanding. Paul supposedly wrote: "God presented him (Jesus) as a sacrifice of atonement, through faith in his blood. He did this to demonstrate his justice, because in his forbearance he had left the sins committed beforehand unpunished—he did it to demonstrate his justice at the present time, so as to be just and the one who justifies those who have faith in Jesus" (Rom. 3:25, 26, parenthesis mine).

What is wrong with this statement? It does appear to say that God offered Jesus as "a sacrifice of atonement" to pay for sins, or as the King James renders it, "a propitiation," which is a sacred offering to appease pagan gods. At first glance we assume that Paul is talking about a retributive God whose system of justice is no different than that of humans. The difference is that God appears to want a perfect specimen of humanity to die for the sins of humanity—a rather unjust pronouncement of itself. However, on the basis of the paradigm presented in this book, the word "atonement," or "propitiation," should not be understood as an offering made to God; rather, it is an exercise of coming at-one with Him.

When reading this statement from various translations it becomes clear that translators treat both the words "atonement" and "propitiation" as though they were synonymous. As explained in Chapter 8 of this book, this was not Tyndale's intention at all when he coined the word "atonement." If the two words were synonymous he would not have bothered to coin a new word. When we correctly understand that "atonement" implies a meaningful and educational "coming close to God moment," as opposed to appeasing Him by way of offerings involving blood and death, we immediately get a different picture of God. If at the same time we remember that God understands justification as "becoming just," not as "pronounced just," a paraphrased version of this text could read as follows: "God's purpose was to have Him (Jesus) demonstrate that His persuasion (faith) lived all the way to the shedding of one's own blood produces at-one-ment (coming at-one with Him). By so doing He showed that the One who does not hold our sins against us by punishing, demonstrated instead how it is possible for sinners to become just. He showed that from now on becoming just is possible for those who have the faith *of* Jesus (the persuasion of Jesus, not a mere belief in Jesus)."

Having in us "the mind of Christ" (1 Cor. 2:16) is having "the faith of Jesus Christ" (Gal. 2:16 KJV) or having the belief system of Jesus in us. It is the only way to have Jesus in us. It does not happen by the intervention of a supernatural force called the Holy Spirit. Knowing Jesus and how He reasoned is the only way to learn how to reason like Him. Calling on the Person of the Holy Spirit to come to our help is meaningless, especially if there is no such Person—we should ask God for help. Indeed, we should be asking God to open our eyes and hearts to the Holy Spirit, which is asking Him to help us learn to think as He does, and of course, as Jesus did, so that He might be in us.

We must understand that developing the "faith of Jesus," which is the way Jesus thinks, is the only way to develop in us the mind of God in whose image we were originally created. Thinking like Jesus is the only way to restore in us the image of God; in fact, it is the only salvation worth pursuing. It is a restorative salvation, not a salvation unjustly acquired at the price of innocent blood on a Cross. Having access to the way God thinks is indeed the ultimate gift from God, Jesus went all the way to the Cross to share with us the secrets of thinking like Him, that we might have everlasting life. We would not have access to eternal life if Jesus had not shown us the value, importance, and beauty of God's mind-set. He showed us that like Him we should be unconditionally dedicated to love, even if such love leads to the Cross. It is a mind-set we should want to develop because nothing in life should be considered more important than love. "Blessed are you when people insult you, persecute you and falsely say all kinds of evil against you because of me" (Mt. 5:11), said Jesus.

4. The Theology of Substitution requires splitting Father and Son

It is interesting to consider some of the stories of Scripture that have been interpreted to imply that Jesus came to this world to die a substitutionary death. Substitution theology also implies that for substitution to work, sins have to be transferred onto the sacrificial victim—yet another pagan concept. Scripture supports neither theological conclusion. In fact, it is logically impossible to arrive at such conclusions unless Father and Son are perceived as two distinctly different Persons of the divinity. Substitution and transfer theology are deeply rooted in pagan cults. Pagans are known the world over for their beliefs in transferring luck, diseases, misfortunes, and even sins for which the subjects seek acquittal or lesser penalties. This can be done with the aid of sacrificial offerings or on the basis of other requirements made by witch doctors. If there were only one Person of the divinity it would be absurd to think that He or She would want to die on the Cross just to satisfy Himself that sins were finally paid for, and that Divine justice was finally served. As for the idea of God wanting the transfer of sins to be uploaded onto a sinless Person, one would have to consider the idea insane and useless.

Garments of skin

Many consider the story of God providing Adam and Eve with "garments of skin" (Gen. 3:21) an example of substitution. The idea advanced is that innocent blood had to be shed to spare the lives of sinners. Nothing in Scripture suggests such an interpretation of this story, thus the idea might well be a matter of jumping to conclusions. It is true that God was probably showing Adam and Eve that sin has its consequences and that it produces death, even that of innocent victims. But that does not mean that the victim was God's way to apply His justice. On the contrary, it was a demonstration that sin should not be considered lightly, because it always leads to bloodshed and death. God wanted Adam and Eve to consider the ugliness of death and blood that sin produces, something they had never seen. By doing so, God was opening for them the door of repentance, hoping that they would ask for help in overcoming the problem. God was simply suggesting that they should return to the mind-set given them at Creation rather than to remain on track with their newly found mind-set focused on self, regardless of consequences. God made a similar attempt later when He attempted to lead Cain to repentance. As explained previously, God did not want an offering; He wanted a demonstration that sinners understand, not only that sin is a problem, but also how it should be remedied. Abel's heart was changed, not by an offering, but by a ritual that was meaningful to him in that helped him change his disposition of heart.

A ram in the thicket

Another story of Scripture purported to show substitution is the account of Abraham whose son was rescued when God prevented the slaughter and provided a ram in a thicket. It is interesting that this story should even be considered as an example of substitution, considering that a ram was provided, not a lamb. There is not a shred of evidence from Scripture that this story should be understood as it is traditionally interpreted. The fact that God provided a ram should be telling, because Jesus is represented as "the lamb of God" (Jn. 1:29, 36), not a ram. God was not telling Abraham to look forward to the death of Jesus as a substitute; in fact there is nothing in Scripture to suggest that Abraham knew anything about the forthcoming advent of Jesus. What God was probably telling Abraham is that he should not consider killing his son as an offering to God as did the pagans of the time but that he should destroy and even burn the idols of the land, of which the ram was the most dominant god.

All through Egypt and Asia Minor, the ram was the great protector of the land. To this day there remain countless statues of Pharaohs protected by the ram god. The ram was considered the protector of all prominent monarchs and empires of the time, all the way down to the Roman period. It is not surprising therefore that male lambs were to be slaughtered just before the Exodus of Israelites out of Egypt. By slaughtering them and painting their blood on lintels of their doors, families were manifesting their disapproval of worshiping Egyptian gods. They openly denigrated the most important god of Egypt to show them that only *Yahweh* should be worshiped. They were demonstrating that the Egyptian gods were powerless to protect anyone, even the Pharaoh and his family. Only One God in the universe has the power to save people from their sins.

It should be noted that the same pagan divinities were later placed on the brazen Altars of God's Tabernacle and the two Temples. The ritual's purpose was to burn in the minds of God's people that false gods as well as the mentalities these false gods produce should be slaughtered and burnt. Ridding themselves of false gods and the mentalities false gods generate was the only way they would eventually reduce bloodshed resulting from sin. The slaughter and burning of future rams and bullocks were intended to increase the Israelite's resolve to detach themselves from idolatrous practices of Egypt wherefrom they came, as well as Canaan's EL, the bull god father of Baal, where they were to settle.

If the story of Abraham's attempt to offer his son to God means anything else it is only because the story has been corrupted by pagan thinking. It is true that Isaac carried the wood, as Jesus carried the Cross. The major difference is that in God's mind the wood would be necessary to burn the most important idol of the time, the ram, unlike Jesus who was never burnt. If substitution were God's intended message in the story of Isaac, He would have provided a lamb, not a ram. The substitution version of this story becomes meaningless and could not possibly imply that the God of Abraham wanted a sacrificial offering of blood to satisfy a frivolous requirement of divine justice to be served. Such perception of justice serves pagan justice that lacks divine justice, not God's. In God's Holy Book justice is never served by rendering evil for evil even if His people resorted to such methods. God's justice is never retributive; it is only restorative. Retributive justice fails to show sinners that there is a way to be restored to the image of God. Any attempt to draw pagan conclusions from the story of Isaac on the Altar falls apart if God is recognized as One Person, as He should be. Indeed, the "only true God" could not have attempted to persuade Abraham that another Person in the Godhead would later come to pay the price Abraham was willing to pay to appease God. God does not look for appeasement; He only wants progress toward the restoration of heart and mind, because in God's Book, that is the true meaning of salvation—it heals people; it does not punish them.

It is also true that Isaac was willing to lay his life down, as later did Jesus. But here again we should recognize that Isaac, like Jesus, is the victim of a pagan mind-set, that of his earthly father Abraham who has yet to know and understand God in Truth. By intervening to prevent the pagan slaughter of which Jesus will later be the victim, God was indeed sending a message to Abraham. He later reiterated the concept during the Exodus in the form of a Commandment: "Do not bow down before their gods or worship them or follow their practices" (Ex. 23:24a). Following their practices includes conforming to the mentality of bloodshed all pagan worships foster.

The only conclusion that can be drawn from the story of Abraham on Mount Moriah is that he totally misunderstood God. His pagan mentality demonstrated that he still had a long way to go before understanding God. God did not ask Abraham to offer his son as a burnt offering. Here again an interlinear translation can be helpful. A word-for-word reading of the Hebrew reads as follows: "Go you for you to land of the Moriah and up you him there for ascent on one of the mountains which I shall say to you." I have deliberately left out the word "offering" because it is not in the Hebrew text. The idea that rituals involving slaughter and burning were offerings made to God was already a corruption of the sacrificial ritual in the days of Abraham. God needs no offerings, except that of the renouncement of self in order to recognize the value of God's ways that are always in opposition to pagan rituals and mentalities.

The Hebrew word *alah* has consistently been translated: "offer as a burnt offering" despite the fact that neither the word "offering" nor the word "burnt" are found anywhere in the Hebrew text. It is true that the Israelites considered the word as meaning "burnt offering," but was that really God's original intent in setting up this ritual? Since nothing in this word implies offering or burning, the only clear conclusion that can be drawn from that was God was asking Abraham to dedicate, or bring Isaac "up high to the Most High." But Abraham's pagan background had scrambled his brain despite the clear assurances God had already given him that Isaac was the child of promise. The pagan mentality caused Abraham to doubt and misunderstand the call of the only true God. Since God does not tempt anyone (see Jas. 1:13), God could not have requested Abraham to kill his son.

It is not until Abraham was about to prove to the universe that his mind was still under strong pagan influence that God intervened. At the very last moment, when the life of Isaac was about to be snuffed out the angel of the LORD sounded the alarm: "Abraham! Abraham! Do not lay a hand on the boy," he said. We may not know all the details of the statement, but the angel might have said: "No! Don't lay a hand on your son! You must not kill your son; what you should do is to rid yourself of all pagan influences that are still having a negative impact on your thinking. Only pagan gods demand such disgraceful and meaningless offerings, not the only true God. Instead of killing your son you must kill from your own heart all the pagan influences responsible for bringing bloodshed and chaos upon the world. Kill the pagan ram god you see caught in the bush nearby, not your son!" Knowing that the ram was the main god of pagans, Abraham may have understood the message without an explanation. We might fail to perceive God's intended message because today rams are no longer regarded as gods, and also because we read the story with a false paradigm.

It is interesting to note that throughout his life Abraham had consistently been presenting burnt offerings before God. He perpetuated the type of offerings Noah presented before the Lord following the Great Flood. Though God had never requested offerings of appeasement or thanksgiving, Abraham still practiced them. What God had clearly requested of Noah was apparently forgotten by the time Abraham came along. God had told Noah: "But you must not eat meat that has its lifeblood still in it. And for your lifeblood I will surely demand an accounting. I will demand an accounting from every animal. And from each man too, I will demand an accounting for the life of his fellow man" (Gen. 9:4–5).

Clearly, taking the life of a human being was unacceptable to God; that would have included the life of Isaac. Abraham who was not shy to argue with God about sparing Sodom and Gomorrah for the sake of his nephew, Lot, had nothing to say when he misunderstood God who appeared to request the human sacrifice of his son. God did not ask for a human sacrificial offering any more than He asked Jesus to become one such offering two millennia later. God had to restate His position regarding human sacrifices during the Exodus: "When you come into the land that the Lord your God is giving you, you shall not learn to follow the abominable practices of those nations. There shall not be found among you anyone who burns his son or his daughter as an offering, anyone who practices divination or tells fortunes or interprets omens, or a sorcerer or a charmer or a medium or a necromancer or one who inquires

of the dead, for whoever does these things is an abomination to the Lord"
(Deut 18:9–12, ESV).[50]

It is simply amazing that God took charge of the situation to prevent
Abraham from carrying out the instructions of a misunderstood message.
Yet centuries later that same story is used to proclaim that God is
Himself guilty of actually carrying out the very atrocity of abomination
He prevented Abraham from committing. The sad irony is that God is
glorified in Christian churches for having committed the very act *Yahweh*
considers an abomination. It is an act that defies all logic. How could
anyone nurture the hope that such a message could bring salvation to a
lost world?

One can only wonder what would have happened if Abraham had
correctly understood God's request. He would not have been in the
awkward position of hiding from his wife the purpose of his journey with
Isaac—he might have taken her along. Abraham, Rebecca, and young
Isaac would have rejoiced over the fact that God's guidance was on track
and about to be confirmed toward His ultimate goal. Had the dedication
service taken place God might have revealed valuable information to both
father and son. A clearer picture of God's plan for humanity might have
spared Abraham's descendants from the bondage of Egypt. The history
of our planet might have been totally different. But Abraham's pagan
roots demonstrated to the universe that even the most faithful of humans
on the planet were not yet ready to receive the message of life from their
God. Their pagan mysticism was standing in the way of real progress.

It is true that the author of the book of Hebrews provides a list of the
pillars of faith. The list begins with Abel, Enoch, and Noah. God's call
to Abraham who *obeyed* not knowing where he would be led comes next.
The text reminds us that Abraham was "tested" (Heb. 11:17). Clearly,
the "test" was intended to show the universe and future generations of
humans that though Abraham had given up the worship of idols, the
mentality of idolatry was still much alive in his heart. It must be noted
that the passage recounting the "test" of Abraham in Genesis indicated
that "*Elohim*" tested Abraham not "*Yahweh*." According to our previous
assumption this implies that the family of God was united in the
administration and observation of the test (Gen. 22:2). It was not really

---

[50] The ESV is the English Standard Version of the Bible revised in 1971 from the
Revised Standard Version.

a test, but a demonstration for the universe to see. Abraham's pagan faith was indeed strong, but his faith founded on a persuasion founded on sound divine logic was weak. This story probably underlines for the entire universe to recognize that Abraham was still pagan at heart. Pagan thinking was still so deeply rooted in him that God could not yet carry out fully His purpose on Mount Moriah. A "Mount of Transfiguration" event might have taken place (see Mt. 17:1–13). Only God knows what would have happened if Abraham had been more receptive to a dedication service with God rather than a meaningless sacrificial burnt offering He never wanted in the first place.

Lamb of God? Or, Christ our Passover Lamb?

Another story from Scripture often purported to confirm substitution theology is that of the lamb the Israelites prepared to eat just before the Exodus, and following the Tenth Plague that befell Egypt. The Jews of today do not just commemorate this event yearly; they relive it personally every Passover, but without implying substitution. The nine previous plagues are generally recognized as God's way to denigrate some of Egypt's lesser gods. He was showcasing before them the utter lack of power of their idols. Not only did they lack the power to protect the people, but they also offered the demonstration that they could accomplish nothing positive in their favor. Through these plagues God demonstrated that Egyptian idols could only fail to prevent the chaos. When the waters of the Nile turned into blood God was showing the Egyptians that worshiping the life-giving Nile was an exercise in futility, because even the Great Nile is under the control of the "only true God." Later, the priests of Egypt showed themselves powerless to deal with the plagues of frogs, gnats, flies, cattle, and other nuisances, all of which were feared and worshiped.

Considering that John the Baptist is the one who proclaimed Jesus "the Lamb of God" (Jn. 1:29,36), and that John the Disciple is the only one who reported the statement, Christians have been trying ever since to identify which lamb of Scripture The Baptist was evoking. The search for answers became all the more complicated with Trinity theology in mind, especially considering that "the Lamb of God" is capitalized and is followed by the statement: "who takes away the sin of the world!" With a Trinitarian view the Lamb belongs to God and can only be the Son. All that becomes terribly complicated because the "Lamb" is portrayed as the servant of God, willing to accept death on the Cross to please the Father. If indeed Jesus is the servant of God, there is a pecking order within the divinity. If that is correct, then we have a bigger problem trying to explain that the Three Persons of the Trinity are indeed coequals. If one has to submit to another, they are not coequal and the discussion becomes endlessly confusing.

In an effort to avoid the vain discussions suggested when Trinity theology is given credence, let us consider the simple approach to the identity of the "Lamb of God." If there is no Trinity of Persons, the explanation as to whom Jesus served when He prayed to the Father is indeed the infinite, almighty, immortal God of the universe. The visible *Yahweh*, who is the mouthpiece portion of the immortal invisible God that chose to become mortal by becoming human was now called Jesus. Bear in mind that John calls "the Word" (Jn. 1:1) God's physical expression that *became* human and temporarily mortal. The purpose of God's expression was to convey to humans the correct meaning of love, how to love, and how much to love. Since all other avenues to accomplish this purpose had failed, this was the only option left for God to convey the message of Truth without violating the freedom of thought and belief He has unconditionally given to all His intelligent created beings of the universe.

Jesus, the mouthpiece of God, became the Lamb of God. The immortal God sent to our planet His own visible expression of which He had only One. But in His foreknowledge He also knew that "the Word," as John calls Jesus, would be butchered by the very people He came to save, and that, because He would share with them the key to everlasting life. It is important to note that the only lamb Isaiah mentions in his prophetic book is the one God sent, knowing He would be slaughtered in the process. If this was an offering, it was not an offering to God, but an offering to humans. The passage of Isaiah is not only translated with a paradigm of Trinity theology, but also with the false idea that God wanted Jesus to pay a death penalty for the sins of humanity. With the paradigm suggested in this book we would translate differently: "But He was pierced by (not, for) our transgressions, He was crushed by (not, for) our iniquities; the chastisement He suffered brought us the only way to have real peace, and thanks to the wounds He willingly suffered we received God's knowledge of the way to heal from sin" (Is. 53:5, paraphrased from NIV and KJV by author). The question that begs an answer is this: Was Jesus crushed for our iniquities or by our iniquities? If the translators' paradigm is that God wanted the death of Jesus, then He died for our sins. If we recognize that God did not want the death of Jesus but accepted the reality that it would happen, then it can be said that He was crushed by the iniquities of His fellow humans.

With a non-Trinitarian view of God who is not perceived as having suffered to pay off sin by way of a substitutionary sacrifice, the entire chapter of Isaiah's prophecy takes on a different meaning. Indeed, He suffered, but He accepted the ordeal for the sake of helping humans resolve their sin problem, not to pay for it. The reason I use the expression non-Trinitarian as opposed to the Unitarian approach is because Unitarians do not consider Jesus as fully divine. Jesus is decidedly *Yahweh*, the visible and approachable side of God that later became human as Jesus. Unlike Unitarian theology, Jesus is as fully God as was *Yahweh*, while at the same time He was also fully human during His stay on our planet. His identity as the "lamb" of Isaiah is clearly stated in that same chapter: "He was oppressed and afflicted," we are told, "yet he did not open his mouth; he was led like a lamb to the slaughter, and as a sheep before her shearers is silent, so he did not open his mouth" (Is. 53:7).

If we have any doubts about the identity of the "Lamb of God" John the Baptist was talking about, the answer to that question appears to be clearly established in the book of Acts. Here Philip, a deacon of the newly established Christian movement explains the passage of Isaiah to the eunuch Ethiopian. Luke, the author of Acts, reports: "The eunuch asked Philip, 'Tell me, please, who is the prophet talking about, himself or someone else?' Then Philip began with that very passage of Scripture and told him the good news of Jesus" (Acts 8:34, 35).

The "Lamb of God" was not the ram caught in a thicket. That ram was representative of the major pagan god of the time. God wanted Abraham to rid himself of the pagan mentality that would ultimately destroy the world—"the abomination that causes desolation." The "Lamb of God" was not the lamb the Israelites ate in haste before the Exodus; that lamb was also representative of a future ram all male lambs become as they mature. The "Lamb of God" was not the sacrificial lamb placed on the brazen altar of the Outer Court of the Tabernacle or Temple. Those burnt rituals were symbolic of the Children of Israel ridding themselves of idolatry prevalent among their neighbors. Their idols were to be burnt in the presence of the Lord before going further in the Sanctuary where they would eventually encounter God in the Most Holy Place. Burning the idols also meant burning the idolatrous mentality of which it can be said that they all focus religious practices and beliefs on self, as was the slaughter ritual Cain attempted to transform into an offering made to the Lord.

Indeed, the "Lamb of God" was *Yahweh* who came to this world knowing that He would be slaughtered like a lamb token to the butcher. But to Him the painful ordeal was worth the self-sacrifice. It was the only way the message of truth otherwise known as the Gospel could be proclaimed to the world. Salvation is not a substitution; it is a message that heals the sin disease, or the self-sacrifice of Jesus was meaningless.

By cutting and pasting unrelated portions of Scripture theologians can make it say whatever they want. Paul is translated as saying: "Get rid of the old yeast that you may be a new batch without yeast—as you really are. For Christ, our Passover lamb, has been sacrificed" (1 Cor. 5:7). Unfortunately the word "lamb" has been added in the NIV, and it is unfortunately implied in other versions though not in the Greek text. Christ is the Passover, not the Passover Lamb. *Yahweh* was the Passover of the Hebrews in Egypt; the male lamb was only the food God told them to prepare. God intentionally asked them to prepare a male lamb because it was a sacred animal in Egypt, but not for the Hebrews. This lamb represented the Egyptian god the Israelites were to kill and eat in haste before their departure. *Yahweh* protected those who executed His orders to the letter. The Hebrews were to manifest their disdain for the baby ram god of Egyptians by tying one of them to a post for four days before killing it and roasting it in fire, eating it, and painting its blood on their lintels. The ram was the god believed responsible for protecting and guiding all other gods, including the Pharaohs. The lamb eaten before the Passover was not the Passover. The only true God was the only One with the power to make Passing Over into the Promised Land possible. In this passage Paul is urging the followers of Jesus to symbolically rid their hearts of the element in the bread that slows down the preparation of the bread because it puffs it up. Get rid of the "old yeast," he says, because the former paganized sacrifices could only perpetuate both religious and personal pride in all its forms and slow down the preparation for heaven, and clearly, pride causes the evil-mindedness that produces sinful acts. Paul tells his people that Christ is our Passover because He made passing over into a new way of life possible at the price of being slaughtered like a lamb.

Another statement of Paul traditionally used to validate substitution theology is found in his Second Letter to the Corinthians: "God made him who had no sin to be sin for us, so that in him we might become the righteousness of God" (2 Cor. 5:21). If there is no Trinity of Godhead, substitution theology makes no sense. Indeed, why would Jesus have to pay a price to the Father and substitute His death for that of sinners? If Jesus is also the Father, how much sense does that make? Who in his right mind would sell his car to himself just to prove its value? And who would be persuaded of such a transaction to establish value? Here again Paul is misunderstood because penalty and substitution theology takes us down the wrong path. Contrary to penalty/substitution theology Paul is not saying that Jesus became sin because the sins of the world were transferred onto Him before He died on the Cross. Paul is saying that Jesus departed from His heavenly sinless nature to become a member of the family of God that sins, though "no sin was in Him." By so doing Jesus inherited all the consequences of sin including that of mortality, and He suffered these consequences all the way to the most painful way to die.

It is indeed for the sake of sinners that Jesus accepted the painful ordeal of life in a sinful world all the way to the Cross. He did it so that thanks to His ministry, we, like Him, would have the opportunity to "become the righteousness of God" in whose image we were created. This text does not imply that Jesus took our sins upon Himself in order to pronounce us righteous by substitution; it tells us that He accepted to dive into our cesspool of sin and suffer all of its pain and suffering in order to show us how to heal from the sin disease. The entire purpose was to help us take daily a step closer to God's righteousness. Such is the plan of salvation; it is all about the restoration of the image of God in us based on the free will we all have to accept His mind-set of unconditional love as our own. The alternative is to reject the mind-set of Jesus and remain as we have been since our birth. It comes down to accepting the new birth or rejecting it—accepting Jesus or rejecting Him. Accepting Jesus without accepting His mind-set is a rejection of Jesus.

Without splitting the Father and the Son into two separate Persons, both the theology of substitution and that of penalty as payment for sins become utterly illogical. Would the God who created logic and gave humans a mind able to process sound logic expect any of us to accept a religion devoid of logic? Either we fail to understand God and choose willfully to depart from His logic and way of life in the name of a pagan superstitious understanding of divinities, or we recognize that His religion for the universe harmonizes with perfect logic. Only pure logic can produce in us a persuasion worthy to be called faith. It is the persuasion of Jesus that produces the righteousness that was in Jesus all the way to the Cross. It is righteousness by the only faith that has the power to change human hearts.

A Person's spirit is not another person

It is a well-documented fact that as far back as human civilizations can be traced humans have widely believed that they have two natures, a mortal body and an immortal spirit. If there were such a dichotomy, we could say that humans are a duality of persons, a philosophy known as mind-body dualism. But this is not what the Bible teaches despite the fact that most Christians hold to the belief that when the body dies, the other, called the spirit, lives on. Without looking further, it becomes evident that Trinity theology has deep roots into pagan philosophy.

The reason the Pyramids of Egypt were erected was because of the dominant dualist belief of the time. It led the people to show the spirits of dead Pharaohs buried within the structure that they are loved and venerated beyond any living human being. It was believed that after the death of their bodies the Pharaohs still retained their knowledge, power, and divinity. In fact, because their spirit was no longer attached to a vile body, their influence over the affairs and well-being of Egypt was now greater than ever before. Throughout the world the spirits of deceased humans are believed to live on somewhere in a spiritual realm of the gods.

Most of our modern Christian churches and countless other religions share similar beliefs. Some non-Christian religions believe that the immortal spirits of dead humans find refuge in other forms of life. This is known as reincarnation, a common belief of Eastern religions. While some go so far as to say that reincarnation can be scientifically proven or that there is life after death, they cannot prove that these rather mind-boggling near-death, or out-of-body instances are not deceptions. Who could orchestrate such deceptions? And why? These questions are particularly compelling considering that Scripture condemns such views and calls them the work of the devil.

Some would argue that Scripture does teach the immediate passing from death of body to a new spirit life without a body—a ghost or phantom-like kind of life. A complete review of Scripture on the subject is not possible in the context of this book. However it is important to review just a few key statements traditionally perceived to imply passage from one kind of life to another upon death. This will make it possible to draw conclusions regarding the human spirit, Trinity theology, and the Spirit of God Scripture calls the Holy Spirit.

The problem is an age-old one. Is a human a single entity composed of a body, a mind, and a spirit? Or is a human a dual entity made up of a mortal body and an immortal spirit? Philosophers and religious leaders still debate the question. The problem is that the plan of salvation is impacted by the view we accept. If there is a better life after death religion would be nothing more than an attempt to manipulate people into being nice and kind while trapped in their mortal body. But why should God have given us flawed flesh and imperfect bodies in the first place? Did He not say, after creating Adam and Eve, that what He had created that day was "very good" (Gen. 1:31)? Is not that statement inclusive of their minds and their bodies? Or does God enjoy torturing us by giving us a malevolent physical body eager to do evil, only to release us from that body at death so that after all the pain and suffering we can live eternally in the form of a spirit or ghost? Why did He not create us as ghosts to begin with and save all the pain and suffering? Do we really have such a cruel and bizarre God? Is that kind of God really a divinity worth loving and trusting?

It gets worse, because the pain and suffering of those who have died continues as they observe their loved ones still suffering in a world of evil where things are going from bad to worse. What does the word "resurrection" mean with such a view of life? Why bother with teaching of Jesus about resurrection and the rest of the Bible? When we consider the religions of our world we have to wonder why they all try to make God sound loving and merciful, only to teach philosophies of religion that makes Him look everything but intelligent, caring, logical, or loving?

Reality is that the Bible teaches nothing of the sort. God is One, just as the human beings He created in His own image are one like Him—no dualism of humans is implied anywhere in Scripture despite arguments from theologians claiming otherwise. Like God, we have a visible component, our body and its actions. For God, His visible component is *Yahweh,* the Creator, who later accepted to come to this world in mortal human flesh, and whose name is Jesus. But like God, we also have an invisible component; it is our spirit. By the actions of our bodies we reveal the kind of spirit we have in us. Unlike God, who's Spirit is always Holy, the spirit of humans can be, mostly good, mostly bad, or somewhere in between but never either extreme. The reason for that is simple: the spirit of humans has been confused with the difficulty of determining the extent to which self-interests should be served first and the extent to which the interests of others should be served first. All ethical questions are debated and defined on the basis of this precarious balancing act. God has settled the question since the eternal past. In all that we think or do we should consider the best interests of others before our own; even when taking care of ourselves, we should do it to be in a position to better serve others. Today's airlines advise passengers to put on the oxygen mask on first, as soon as they drop from above. This is vital only because they might pass out before getting it on their children or helping the handicapped. Clearly, in such situations serving self is the proper action, but only because the purpose is to better serve others.

Like God, our invisible self is our spirit, and our visible self is our body. Almighty God whose name is ineffable, never to be uttered, is the invisible infinite entity of the universe whose visible physical representation is *Yahweh*, and whose Spirit is unconditionally loving. It is true that God made us all to be one in spirit, that is, one in the way we all think, one in the fact that we should become more loving and reach the ultimate goal of caring altruistically for one another in all that we do, as does God. This is how we become one with Him and with one another. Oneness with God and other created beings is the atonement. There is no atonement until that process takes place. Jesus made all the provision for this atonement to take place, but the atonement itself is still a future event. The oneness of fellow humans of all background with God will become more important to many than preserving their culture, their religion, their political party, and everything else that divides humans from God and one another. Dedication to the mentality of God will dissipate whatever culture they come from as they adopt and embrace the culture of God as revealed in Jesus. At that point in our spiritual development cultures, religions, and politics will cease to be divisive. The oneness God is leading His children to seek produces a unique culture unlike any this world has ever seen. Though we tolerate and even embrace diversities, we should understand that growing in Jesus implies letting go of whatever caused diversity in the first place, because unity in Christ will also bring perfect unity of religion and culture.

By claiming that humans have two different natures and that God is three different Persons, religious leaders of Christianity have created a theology capable of destroying both the image of God and the reality of who we are as humans. It denies the fact that the problem is not the flesh of which we are made that causes the problem of evil; it is the Spirit of God we refuse to accept. The restoration of His image in us cannot take place until we stop blaming the flesh and start adopting the mind of Christ as our own, because it is the Spirit of God, and it is the Holy Spirit that should fill our souls.

By destroying both images, that of humans by claiming that they have two natures and that of God by claiming that He is not One but three Persons, we are caught in such a complicated web of theological confusion and lies that we are left in utter ignorance about God. These pagan concepts have kept humanity in such darkness that our brains struggle to recognize a few strands of Truth contained in the message Jesus has come to reveal at great price. As He said: "the Truth shall set us free," nothing else. And since there is no such a thing as a half- or a three-quarter truth, we cannot expect to be set free until we have the Truth in its totality, as Jesus revealed it to the death. It is for the sake of sharing the saving Truth that Jesus died, because the Truth that comes from God is the only antidote to evil and sin, thus it is the only means by which true peace and freedom can become reality. The last time humans were free was in Eden. Salvation is all about the restoration of true freedom in the universe. Either we accept God's solution and live, or we reject it and accept the inevitable consequences.

When we read that Jesus came "for the sins of the world," we tend to assume that He came to pay for them, but this view is not biblical and frankly, as we have discussed the matter, it is a concept that lacks basic logic. Jesus came to provide free-willed sinners the key to overcoming their terminal sin disease. The problem is that as long as Christians will continue to believe that humans have two natures and that God is three Persons, the key to salvation will continue to elude them. Because translators are victims of dualist and Trinitarian prejudices their translations are tainted. Paul is translated to appear dualist, as though he might be in agreement with the pagan tradition. Some translators use the expression "carnal nature" (Rom. 7:18 Henry Hayman);[51] others call it the "sinful nature" (Rom. 7:18, NIV), or the "earthly nature" (Col. 3:5. NIV). All of these suggest that we have two natures despite the fact that there is no reference to a "spiritual nature" in Scripture. Let us consider a few examples to reconsider what Paul and other authors of Scripture were really saying:

When Paul writes: "Put to death, therefore, whatever belongs to your earthly nature: sexual immorality, impurity, lust, evil desires and greed, which is idolatry" (Col. 3:5), he seems to imply that we should have contempt against our earthly nature in order to benefit another more noble nature. In his Epistle to the Romans he talks extensively about "the sinful nature" (NIV) or "they that are after the flesh" (KJV), but is that because Paul believes in a dualistic view of humans involving a mortal body and an eternal spirit?

Here is a portion of his discourse: "Therefore, there is now no condemnation for those who are in Christ Jesus, because through Christ Jesus the law of the Spirit who gives life has set you free from the law of sin and death. For what the law was powerless to do because it was weakened by the flesh, God did by sending his own Son in the likeness of sinful flesh to be a sin offering. And so he condemned sin in the flesh, in order that the righteous requirement of the law might be fully met in us, who do not live according to the flesh but according to the Spirit. Those who live according to the flesh have their minds set on what the flesh desires; but those who live in accordance with the Spirit have their minds set on what the Spirit desires. The mind governed by the flesh is death, but the mind governed by the Spirit is life and peace. The mind governed by the flesh is hostile to God; it does not submit to God's law, nor can it do so. Those who are in the realm of the flesh cannot please God" (Rom. 8:1–8).

It is probably fair to say that there are only two ways to look at these passages from the pen of Paul. Either he is suggesting that we do indeed have two natures, one of which suffers bondage to the other. The body of sin may even appear to yearn for death in order to be released from the bondage. The other way to consider this text is with the idea that we have

---

51 Henry Hayman, D.D., *The Epistles of the New Testament*. Adam and Charles Black, London, 1900, p. 35.

one single nature of which the spirit is confused between two polarities. One polarity is inclined to serve the desires of the flesh while the other has the desire to serve the welfare and well-being of others before self.

The first text, from Colossian 3:5, gives us a couple of clues. When Paul advises the followers of Jesus to "put to death" whatever belongs to their earthly nature he is saying that they should rid themselves of the self-centeredness they are born with, not that they should kill their bodies. As previously said, we are all born with the self-centered rule of survival written in our DNA and psyche, but that does not mean that we are not intelligent enough to recognize that our flawed natural condition should be reversed. The animal world does not have the intellect to recognize such a flaw, much less the ability to change course on the basis of logic, but humans do.

Let us recall our previous discussion about Eve. She allowed herself to become self-serving before encountering the devil at the Tree. This understanding allows us to recognize that she made a mental choice at that moment. She was a single person with both a body and a mind, neither of which can function without the other. She deliberately chose to depart from "very good" pre-programed brain or Spirit she received from God. With the mind initially created in her she was in full possession of the Holy Spirit, or the way God thinks. She knew and understood perfectly well that eternal life is entirely dependent on considering the welfare and well-being of others *before* her own. It is only with such a perfectly unconditional dedication to others that God's system of government founded on everyone's free exercise of free will can last eternally. If humans were given the free will to depart from God's system, they are also given the free will to recognize that it is possible for them to return to the way God thinks. This is where there is a huge misunderstanding in most, if not all, Christian theological circles. By blaming the devil for the departure from God's system of life, the assumption is made that Jesus came to purchase sinners back from the devil, which was the position of the official Christian church until the latter part of the eleventh century.[52] The devil is not responsible for Eve's decision to depart from God's way of thinking; he merely pushed Eve down the precipice of desolation God had forewarned her not to get near. Self-centeredness was already present in Eve's mind before she met the

---

52   See our discussion in Chapter 3 of this book about Anselm of Canterbury.

devil at the Tree. She cannot blame the devil for her mental lapse; she had a perfect mind. Having chosen on her own volition to be self-serving, she merely proved that humans were created free and that they still are perfectly free.

Why should the freedom God gave our first parents be different from the freedom we still enjoy to this day? If humans could choose to break away from a perfectly altruist mind-set, they should also be fully capable of reversing the circuitry of their brain once again. The problem is not the brain; it is the polarity of the brain. But the change of polarity cannot fully take place as long as the problem is misunderstood. If we believe that humans have two natures and that God is three Persons, the material body can't help but sin, which implies that out of pity for such helpless beings God had to intervene by making sure that their sins were paid for. What a defeatist religion!

But what Paul is saying has nothing to do with a double nature of humans. He is clearly implying that humans are in a state of confusion and that the only way to remedy the situation is to behold Christ's life all the way to the Cross. It is the only way we can learn from Him the way to change the polarity of our minds. This is not a matter of believing that Jesus is mere example in whose footsteps we should learn to walk. Jesus is much more than an example. By recognizing and adopting His mind-set, sinners are led to accept a life unwilling to ever return evil for evil despite temptations to do so. What Paul is saying is that we are so mentally confused that we are always prone to rationalize the importance of self-defense and consider it perfectly acceptable in a world of evil. Until we realize that no compromise is acceptable in this regard and that unconditional true love must reign in the heart even when it is difficult to love, we will continue to accept the false notion that humans have two natures, one of which is hopelessly evil. With this view the "bad" nature is irreversible, unless God is willing to send the Holy Spirit Person to change the sinner or to pronounce a sinner righteous. The only thing a Christian can do with the "bad" nature is to wait for God to take action through the Holy Spirit Person of the divinity, but only if the sinner is willing to believe that Jesus died for his or her sins. All this appears to be so strange and far-fetched. Why should only those who believe in Jesus deserve the Holy Spirit, and what if there is no such a Person of the Godhead?

When Paul addresses "those who are in Christ Jesus," he is not talking about people who have the third Person of the Godhead in their hearts. He was talking about sinners who have accepted to learn from God how to think like Jesus in order to live and act as He did. What Jesus did by coming to this earth was not to pay for the sins of the world that we might ignore them or to hide them from the Father; it was to show sinners how to reduce and eventually eliminate the confusion of mind that causes sin. The spirit of God enters our minds and hearts only to the extent that the fog of confusion dissipates. As long as we are confused about the extent to which we should serve self versus others, we continue to mix good and evil in our hearts and fail to receive the fullness of God's Holy Spirit. As the confusion of mind and heart dissipates, the spirit becomes increasingly more like God's, thus increasingly more holy. As a result, a new persuasion takes over the heart. It is a new faith that changes sinners from a mind polarized toward self to a new mind polarized toward others. This is the new birth required for true spiritual growth to take place, the growth of true love in the heart.

Speaking of spiritual food for the soul, the author of Hebrews remarked: "Anyone who lives on milk, being still an infant, is not acquainted with the teaching about righteousness. But solid food is for the mature (spiritually speaking), who by constant use have trained themselves to distinguish good from evil" (Heb. 5:13–14, parenthesis mine). Here the author of Hebrews clearly implies that spiritual maturity is about the growth of a sinner's ability to "distinguish good from evil." It should be noted that the word translated "distinguish" is the Greek *diakrisis*. This word implies a logical assessment. But what should be assessed logically? The two Greek words translated "good and evil" are *kalos* and *kakos*, that which is harmless and beneficial from anything that might be injurious and destructive. If our life is totally focused on service and welfare of others it is harmless and beneficial. But if the focus of our life is in the least focused on self we cannot be fully trusted; therefore, we are injurious and destructive.

In our second text taken from Romans 8:1–8, notice that Paul does not say that there is no condemnation for those who have Christ or another Person of the deity in them, but that "there is now no condemnation for those who are in Christ Jesus." The word "in" here should really read, "into." Being into Christ means knowing Him with even more passion to know everything there is to know about Him than a person who is into Elvis Presley and wants to go so far as to eat and breath like Elvis, look like him, act like him, play the guitar and sing like him, drink and eat the same foods, and dress like him. These people can be passionately "into" Elvis. Then Paul adds a statement that confirms the views exposed in this book because he says, and I paraphrase: "Because when we are into Christ Jesus the law of the Spirit that gives life (others first) sets us free from the law of sin (me first) that leads to death. Therefore, what the law could not accomplish because it has been weakened by our focus on our own flesh, God did it by sending his own Son in the flesh of humans to condemn the power of sin by selflessly offering himself." He offered Himself to demonstrate that with the mind-set of God it is possible for a human to become selfless all the way to the death and even the death of the Cross (see Phil. 2:8).

Allow me to paraphrase the rest of Paul's statement with the paradigm of this book: Having shown that human flesh is not the problem, Jesus showed "that the righteous requirement of the law can be fully met in us if we do not live focused on our flesh but focused according with the Spirit of God (always focused on serving others before self). Those who live focused on their flesh have their minds set on what the flesh desires; but those who live focused in accordance with the Spirit of God have their minds set on what the Spirit desires (which is the well-being and welfare of others). The mind focused on the flesh leads to death, but the mind focused on the Spirit of God brings life and peace. The mind focused on one's own flesh is hostile to God; it does not recognize or accept God's law of unconditional love, nor can it do so. Those who live with a belief system focused on pleasing their own flesh cannot please God" (Rom. 8:4–8, my paraphrased version from the NIV)

Time has come to condemn the doctrine that should be called a dogma, according to which a person is sinful beyond repair—or should we say, to the point of being unrestorable to the image of God. If salvation is about restoring the image of God in humans it should never be said or implied that it cannot be done. Nor should it ever be said that it can be done without God's help, because Jesus came to set before us a table that includes milk for the newly born converts, but He has also placed on His table the bread that gives life. What God will not do is to spoon-feed us like babies. He expects us to choose from His table the foods we need to grow "into" Jesus, that we might know that His kind of love surpasses human knowledge—that we might be filled to the measure of all the fullness of God (see Eph. 3:19, my paraphrased version from the NIV).

God's definition of love and His method to acquire it clearly surpasses any knowledge about love humans could have ever conceived in this world. They have always recognized that the problem is lack of love. But they have failed to recognize what love is in truth, how to grow it in the heart, and how far love should be taken. Jesus has given us answers to all these questions. But let us not be mistaken, that knowledge does not come from the third Person of the Godhead; it comes from the "only true God," from *Yahweh* who became Jesus. It is not by waiting and praying for the third Person to influence our thinking and heart that we will gain the knowledge that surpasses that of our world; it is by knowing Jesus, who came all the way from His throne of infinite power to teach us all the fundamentals needed to acquire the Truth that gives life (see Jn. 14:6).

Some of Paul's statements appear to imply that humans are unable on their own to change the course of their lives or make any progress toward overcoming sin. In a way this is true; there is no way humans could have discovered the formula to overcome sin on their own. Without God's help, humanity would be well on its way to inevitable oblivion without hope of future existence. It is not only the future existence that is impossible without God, but He has also gone through the trouble of sharing with humans the mind-set required to live an eternal existence. It is an existence entirely founded on perfect love, and He has shared with us the formula to accomplish His purpose.

The religion of Jesus is all about living unconditional love to the fullest. Any expectations of rewards, fame, riches, supernatural powers, and mystical endowments can only destroy the most important prerequisite of love, humility.

It is for this reason that God avoids speaking to us directly. He only does so sparingly when a person is humble enough to receive information from Him without developing an attitude of superiority. Prophets are typically very humble people, who become increasingly humble as they begin to understand the messages from God. By contrast, false prophets and false spiritual leaders tend to become rather proud of their status as specialists of human enlightenment. God knows the spirit of humans. He knows that it is not their body that causes them to lack love and sin; He knows that the problem is the spirit that resides in their body.

It is no wonder that world leaders have always preferred the State to be the "god" of the people. Most leaders of ancient civilizations were considered divinities having supreme authority on both religion and government. The Romans were probably the first important social order that tolerated a multiplicity of religions, which makes it all the more surprising that they persecuted inoffensive Apostolic Christians. Their theocracy was not that of other religions, whereby God or the gods dictate their will for the people through their leaders. True theocracy implies that all humans receive individually from God the modus operandi He suggests but never imposes on anyone. That modus operandi is entirely founded on perfect love. In such a system, no one is superior or more important that anyone else, because all are seekers of love that cannot grow in proud arrogant hearts. With love in the heart it is indeed possible for everyone to become kings, because everyone has become priests of the "only true God."

It is a gross error to think that a human being cannot strive toward a lifestyle increasingly more in tune with God's definition of love. Those Christians who claim that improvements are not possible unless the third Person of the Godhead takes over their lives are in danger of expecting privileges that even prophets were not granted. They might wait indefinitely for the Holy Spirit because of their refusal to recognize simple Truth.

May the only true God help our lack of understanding: "Your statutes are forever right; give me understanding that I may live" (Ps. 119:14)

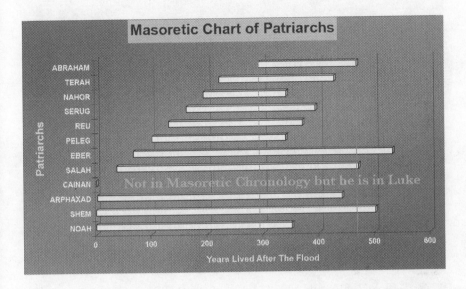

These charts show the time that elapsed since the Great Flood of Noah according to Masoretic Chronology and Septuagint Chronology.

According to Masoretic Chronology calculated on the basis of most common Bibles, Abraham would have been born about 300 years after the Flood, and at least three of the Patriarchs would have outlived him, including Shem, the son of Noah.

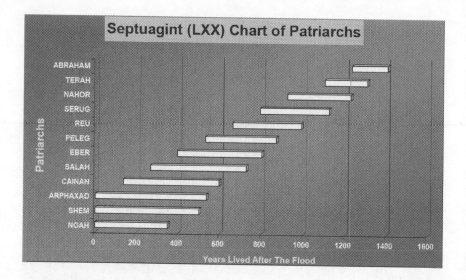

By the Chronology calculated on the basis of the Greek Septuagint, Abraham would have been born at least 1,200 years after the Flood and none of the Patriarchs would have outlived him. It should also be noted that Cainan, three generations after Noah, is mentioned in the Chronology of Luke in the New Testament, but is nowhere to be found in the Masoretic texts of common Bibles. On the other hand, Cainan is clearly named in the Greek Septuagint.